Wendy Hilton

A Life in Baroque Dance and Music

Wendy Hilton in sixteenth-century dress, from a promotional photo for the Domenico Dance Ensemble, early 1960s. Photo © Frederika Davis.

Wendy Hilton

A Life in Baroque Dance and Music

by Wendy Hilton
and Susan Bindig

Wendy Hilton Dance & Music Series No. 14

PENDRAGON PRESS
HILLSDALE, NY

Other Titles in the Wendy Hilton Dance & Music Series

Linda J. Tomko, General editor

No. 1 *French Court Dance and Dance Music: A Guide To Primary Source Writings 1643–1789* by Christena L. Schlundt and Judith L. Schwartz Karp

No. 2 *Dance and Instrumental Diferencias in Spain during the 17th and Early 18th Centuries* by Maurice Esses, Vol. I *History and Background, Music and Dance*; Vol. II *Musical Transcriptions*; Vol. III *The Notes in Spanish*

No. 3 *Rhythm and Life: The Work of Emile Jaques-Dalcroze* by Irwin Spector

No. 4 *Fifteenth-Century Dance and Music: Twelve Transcribed Italian Treatises and Collections in the Tradition of Domenico da Piacenza* translated by A. William Smith Vol. I, *Treatises, Theory, and Music*; Vol. 2, *Choreographic Descriptions with Concordances of Variants*

No. 5 *A New Most Excellent Dancing Master: The Journal of Joseph Lowe's Visits to Balmoral and Windsor (1852–1860) to Teach Dance to the Family of Queen Victori*a edited by Allan Thomas

No. 6 *A Work Book by Kellom Tomlinson: Commonplace Book of an 18th-Century English Dancing Master, A Facsimile Edition* edited by Jenifer Shennan

No. 7 *Philidor Manuscripts: Dance Music from the Ballets de Cour, 1575–1651, Historical Commentary, Source Study, and Transcriptions from the Philidor Manuscript*s, 2 Vols., by David A. Buch,

No. 8 *Nijinsky's Crime Against Grace: Reconstruction Score of the Original Choreography for* Le Sacre du Printemps by Millicent Hodson

No. 9 *New Song and Dance from the Central Pacific: Creating and Performing The Fatele of Tokelau in the Islands and in New Zealand* by Allan Thomas

No. 10 *Dance and Music of Court and Theater: Selected Writings of Wendy Hilton*

No. 11 *The Extraordinary Dance Book T. B. 1826: An Anonymous Manuscript in Facsimile,* commentaries and analyses by Sandra Noll Hammond, Elizabeth Aldrich, Jennifer Shennan, and Armand Russell

No. 12 *Nijinsky's Bloomsbury Ballet: Reconstruction of the Dance and Design for* Jeux by Millicent Hodson

No. 13 *The* Bals Publics *at the Paris Opera in the Eighteenth Century* by Richard Semmens

No. 15 Ballet de la Nuit*: Rothschild B1/16/6* edited by Michael Burden and Jennifer Thorp

To Molly Kenny and Eileen Cropley,

With my deepest love and gratitude as two of my oldest friends
and founder-dancers with the Domenico Dance Ensemble.

—Wendy Hilton

Cover design by Stuart Ross

Library of Congress Cataloging-in-Publication Data

Hilton, Wendy.
Wendy Hilton : a life in baroque dance and music / by Wendy Hilton and Susan Bindig.
p. cm. -- (Wendy Hilton dance & music series no. 14)
Includes bibliographical references and index.
ISBN-13: 978-1-57647-133-3 (alk. paper)
ISBN-10: 1-57647-133-0 (alk. paper)
1. Dancers--Great Britain--Biography. 2. Ballerinas--Great Britain--Biography. 3. Choreographers--Great Britain--Biography. 4. Dancers--United States--Biography. 5. Choreographers--United States--Biography. 6. Dance teachers--United States--Biography. 7. Dance--France--History--18th century. 8. Music--France--History--18th century. I. Bindig, Susan II. Title.
GV1785.H55A3 2010
792.028092--dc22
[B]

2010035410

Contents

Part III. In America

Illustrations

Part II.

Part III.

Preface

"Wendy Hilton. *She* was a force!" Stanford Professor Emeritus Leonard Ratner made this proclamation to Anne Witherell after hearing of Wendy's death in 2002, and I doubt that others who knew her as a dancer, teacher, colleague, or friend would argue. Wendy was ambitious, strong-minded, uncompromising, and completely dedicated to her work in baroque dance and music. Work, she once told me, was what was important in life.

This book is about Wendy's work. With barely a grammar school education, Wendy built a career as a distinguished artist and scholar in a highly specialized and previously little-explored field. Her dancing was unrivaled, precise in execution and exquisitely delicate in quality. We students marveled at her neat and firm *demi-coupés*, her softly arcing *pas tombé*s, her beautifully placed arms and hands, and attempted to copy them. As a scholar, Wendy established a place for herself in the academic world, teaching at universities internationally, advising doctoral dissertations and master's theses, and writing frequently cited articles for both dance and music journals. Her book, *Dance of Court and Theater: The French Noble Style, 1690–1725*, remains the definitive book on the elements of the baroque dance style.

Wendy's life however, was not all business, and neither is her memoir. Wendy was fun to be with and relished her leisure time. Attending music concerts brought her the greatest pleasure and is also part of her story. She loved going to the movies and enjoyed a wide range of films, from *Star Wars* to the Coen brothers ("You simply must see *Blood Simple*!") to westerns (*Butch Cassidy and the Sundance Kid* was a favorite). And Wendy enjoyed her friends, visiting with them—whether they were in Texas, Colorado, Michigan, or Florida—whenever she was able.

Writing this book played a significant role in the last years of Wendy's life. It nourished her, and many believe that it helped prolong her life when cancer threatened to shorten it prematurely. The story of the book's inception and how it ended up in my hands is told in the concluding chapter, so I will only say here that what began as an oral history of her life turned quickly into a more formal book project. With the increased complexity, she asked me to help her and to complete it after her death.

From the beginning of my involvement, Wendy saw the book as a joint effort. Initially, I was not to be a coauthor per se but an editor and contributor. She intended to write all but the chapter on her work at Stanford University. She asked me to take on that chapter since I had been part of the workshop she taught there for many years and knew much of its history and participants. I was to write it in my own voice, and it would stand apart from her text. Why she did not want to tackle the chapter herself is unclear, and she never offered an explanation.

As Wendy and I worked on the book, my role expanded. I began to write short segments on details I had gathered or transitions between sections based on her notes. All were written in her voice, and Wendy rewrote or added to them as she pleased. We discussed the overall shape of the book and spent hours poring over the text and the illustrations she wished to include. When she turned the book over to me, I had a good sense of how she intended the book to proceed. I also knew that she trusted my judgment to modify those intentions when necessary.

At Wendy's death, the first three chapters were fairly complete. The remainder of the manuscript, through Part II, consisted of a series of essays—some lengthy, some only three or four paragraphs long—arranged chronologically. The first task was to join these essays and create chapters, each of which traced a new phase of Wendy's growing career. Gaps in information quickly emerged. Interviews and correspondence with Wendy's colleagues from the early years of her career along with my own research filled most. Any remaining incomplete or vague information is documented in the footnotes. New information also surfaced. Wendy's personal papers, for example, contained no details of a few performances by the Domenico Dance Ensemble—in particular, of an important engagement in Rotterdam. Ensemble members offered memories of the performances as well as reviews and programs they had saved. In such cases, I augmented Wendy's text with their stories, as I would have in partnership with her, and annotated them as appropriate. Throughout Parts I and II, my footnotes are distinguished from Wendy's by my initials, SB, placed at the end of each citation.

In Part III, I followed Wendy's lead and continued with a chronological presentation of her work, which was based principally at the Juilliard School and at Stanford University. Chapters 16 and 17 on Stanford return to an earlier point in the chronological flow since they address activity that occurred in parallel with Wendy's work at Juilliard. The break in continuity should be clear and not pose a problem for readers. Wendy had begun to write segments on her work at Juilliard, and I have included the full text of those segments throughout Chapters 12 through 15. I crafted those chapters, however, mostly through materials in her personal papers and interviews with dozens of her colleagues, friends, and students. All esteemed Wendy highly and enjoyed and appreciated the opportunity to talk about her work and their relationship with her.

For the Stanford chapter, Anne Witherell did much research, interviewing, and preliminary writing. Other than a short review of one of the early workshops, which Anne herself wrote for *Current Musicology*, there was no organized written documentation of the workshop. Anne carefully gathered and sorted through notes, fliers, programs, syllabi, photographs, and other memorabilia donated by former workshop students and faculty from around the world. She conducted myriad interviews for information to complement those documents and helped develop a clear picture of a completely unique and invaluable artistic and educational experience.

A technical matter that arose in the writing of Part III was whether to address all individuals consistently by first or last names. Calling everyone by their last names after initial introductions might have been a reasonable and appropriate choice; for individuals whom I did not know at all or had met only casually, I adhered to that format. I, however, know a number of Wendy's colleagues and friends well, or at least well enough to use their first names. Others are friends of mine or fellow students of Wendy's. To address them, or Wendy for that matter, by their last names seemed fussy and at odds with Wendy's less formal approach in Parts I and II. I therefore opted for a mixture of the two—first names for those I know and last names for those I do not—and hope I have offended no one.

Another technical problem to solve was chapter titles. Wendy, I believe, intended to title each chapter but named only the first: "My Childhood Memories (Including What I Think I Was Told)." I pondered possible chapter titles for the rest, but in the end, opted for the years that each chapter spans. Subtitles were wisely suggested by Pendragon editor Linda Tomko. Together they anchor Wendy's widely varied career in time and provide a clear map of its progression.

The book does not address two areas in Wendy's life and work. The first is her intimate relationships. It was clear to me that she did not intend to introduce this topic, and I have honored those intentions. An intensely private subject for Wendy, only a few of her close friends knew the facts, and they were not shared with me. Second, the book does not examine the work of Wendy's contemporaries in historical dance, prominent figures such as Shirley Wynne, Ingrid Brainard, Julia Sutton, Francine Lancelot, and Catherine Turocy. Their work figures into Wendy's history as it both challenged and buoyed her artistry and scholarship. While it deserves critical attention and a comparative study would be welcome, this book did not seem to be the appropriate place for that discussion.

As with all books on dance, photographs play an important role in Wendy's memoir. All of the photos from her early career in London and many of the later photographs in America come from her personal papers. Despite careful searching, the copyright holders of some of the photos were impossible to contact or determine. I would welcome information on those individuals whom I have been unable to locate and on the provenance of the unattributed photos.

Wendy would have been delighted by all the individuals who so happily helped me bring her memoir to publication, and I'm sure she would join me in thanking them. Anne Witherell, as noted earlier was indispensable; without her, the Stanford chapter simply would not exist. I am also deeply indebted to Anne for her careful review and comments on the entire manuscript and for her tireless encouragement of interviews of Wendy's colleagues and friends. Paige Whitley-Bauguess was part of the process early on and also contributed valuable research, particularly on Wendy's work in southern California. Others who made valuable contributions include Patricia Rader, who began the project with Wendy and then helped me in numerous ways with research details; George Dorris, who read a very early draft of Wendy's writings, convinced me to complete the book, and published a segment in *Dance Chronicle*; Diane Winkleby, who volunteered her sharp proofreader's eye to the final pages; and Linda Tomko, who as the editor for Pendragon Press as well as a prominent dance scholar and baroque dancer, worked carefully through the various drafts, offered key advice, and provided steady encouragement throughout.

More than one hundred of Wendy's colleagues, students, and friends were interviewed for this book. Many also wrote letters and/or provided programs, photos, reviews and other memorabilia, all of which were invaluable to completing Wendy's story. A list of their names appears at the end of this preface. My sincere thanks go to them.

I am deeply indebted to my husband, Sandy Brainard, my strongest critic and most enthusiastic fan. An able writer, he read the entire manuscript—some parts, numerous times—and offered insightful comments and suggestions for revisions. Most of all, he always reminded me of the value of the project and, in every possible way, helped me meet the challenges I encountered along the way.

My final thought goes to Wendy—teacher, colleague, and friend for more than thirty years. Knowing and working with her in the very special world of baroque dance and music was one of the great privileges and inspirations of my life. With the completion of this memoir, I celebrate her life and work with the many others who also admired her, including: Linda Roberts Alexanderson, Julie Andrijeski, John Ashworth, Régine Astier, Julianne Baird, Thomas Baird, Geoffrey Bayfield, Joan Benson, Chrystelle Bond, William Burdick, Suzanne Burdon, Deanna Bush, Laura Carroll, Constantine Cassolas, Jill Chadroff, Albert and Betty Cohen, Kenneth Cooper, Eileen Cropley, Mary P. Crosten, Jeni Dahmus, Mark Dalrymple, Judith Davidoff, Janet Rawson Davis, Patricia DeCorsey, George Dorris, Ross Duffin, Dione Ewin, Margaret Fabrizio, Veerle Fack, Maria Fay, JoAnn Faletta, David Farrar, Ann Lydekker Fellows, Chris Francis, Molly Kenny Galvin, Charles Garth, Caroline Gaynor, Nina Gilbert, James Goldsworthy, Nicholas Gunn, Robert Gutman, Mark Haim, Patricia Halverson, Yasuko Hamanaka, Rebecca and Ronald Harris-Warrick, Baird Hastings, Timothy Hext, Harlan B. Hokin, Michael Holmes, George and Glenna Houle, Jan Irvine, Nicholas Isaacs, Natalie Jenne, Sterling Jones, Mark Kahrs, Elizabeth Keen, Yvonne Kendall, Judith Kennedy, Margaret Kimball, John Kobayashi, Leah Kreutzer, Carol Kutsch, Jennifer Lane, Frederick Lee, Jocelyne Lépine, Theodore Libbey, Judith Linsenberg, Ed Lipinsky, Meredith Little, Heather Mackler, William Mahrt, Judith Malafronte, Melinda McGee, Jody McGeen, Rebecca Menon, Mitzi Meyerson, Sonya Monosoff, Margaret Murata, Thea Musgrave, Herbert Myers, Lois Nisbet, Barbara Palfy, Scott Pauley, Paul Pentel, Louise Pescetta, Janis Pforsich, John Planting, Bronwen Pugh, Patricia Rader, Leonard and Inge Ratner, Elisabeth Rebman, Frederick Renz, Paula Robison, Sandor and Priscilla Salgo, Phil Schaap, Philip Schreur, Brenda Schuman-Post, Erich Schwandt, Judith Schwartz-Karp, Richard Semmens, Jennifer Shennan, Beverly Simmons, Joan Smiles, Marilyn Somville, Mary Springfels, Mark and Isabelle Starr, Geraldine Stephenson, David Sullivan, Yuko Tanaka,

Marcia Tanner, Carole Terry, Elizabeth Terzian, Emma Lewis Thomas, Linda J. Tomko, Lynne Toribara, Morag Cattanach Veljkovic, Marion Verbruggen, Philippa Waite, Donna Waks, Ruth Waterman, Janet Albisser Westenberg, Anne Witherell, Patricia White, Paige Whitley-Bauguess, Diane Winkleby, Marlene Wong, and John Zorn.

Susan Bindig

I.

My Childhood and Early Career

Figure 1. Maude Wall, Hong Kong, c. 1900.

Figure 2. Lewis Wall, Southsea, England, April 1900.

One: 1931–1946

Growing Up ~ My Family ~ Kingsley School ~ My First Dance Classes ~ To London

Within the joyful sound of ringing church bells, I was born soon after eight o'clock on Easter Sunday morning, April 5, 1931, to Dorothy and Frank Hilton at the Cedars, a cottage hospital in Cowley, Uxbridge, Middlesex. The hospital was very close to Cowley Church, the resting place of Hester Santlow, the famous dancer and actress of the early eighteenth century. Perhaps it was the pealing of bells from that nearby church that was the first musical sound I heard upon entering this world, as well as my first connection with Santlow, whose work would play a part in my as yet undreamed of career in baroque dance and music.

Like dozens of little girls at the time, I was named after Wendy Darling, the very, *very* good, obedient, yet adventurous heroine of J. M. Barrie's *Peter Pan.*[1] I suspect that the choice of name was my mother's and that my father merely acquiesced. More traditionally, my second name was Dorothy, after my mother.

Following the happiness my mother must have felt with my arrival, my early childhood was not easy for her. At eighteen months, I developed pneumonia and almost died. Just before my third birthday, I battled another almost fatal bout. At the same time, trouble was brewing in my parents' marriage. Perhaps they had always been incompatible, but now there were hints of serious domestic trouble, the details of which I would never learn. Dorothy, with me in tow, sought sanctuary with her parents who lived close by. I was too young to have known my father, and since he disappeared from our lives forever at this time, I have only a few brief memories of him today. Although I may have at first wondered where he was, such thoughts were short-lived.

For me, the separation of my parents meant living with my grandparents, Maude Agnes Wall and Engineer Captain Lewis Wall of the Royal Navy, two strong, generous, and loving people. They would be my anchors as I grew up, and the security of their wonderful marriage, I know, reflected well on me.

Maude in her youth was a beautiful and intelligent society girl—truly the belle of the ball. A gifted amateur pianist and a skilled dancer, excelling particularly in the waltz, she dazzled the young men in her circle. Maude received many proposals of marriage, but she waited for the right man: Lewis Wall, who was steadfast, kind, and honorable. As his abundant shelves of gold-tooled books proved, Lewis had been a diligent student. He won many academic prizes for his studies. In their marriage, Maude and Lewis were

[1]Wildly popular with London audiences, this Christmas pantomime-turned-play had seen almost continuous productions since the early 1900s. When I was born, two concurrent, very successful, and long-running productions were being performed on both the London and Broadway stages with British actresses Jean Forbes-Robertson and Eva La Gallienne, respectively, in the title role.

financially secure and enjoyed the many amenities of English upper-class society life. Sometime early in their marriage, by at least 1896 as some family photos show, Lewis's ship was based for a number of years in Hong Kong. It was in this exotic port that on July 8, c. 1900, Maude gave birth to my mother, Dorothy Maude Hilda. A second daughter, Lucy, came next, but she died very young, a crushing loss to Maude, who, for as long as I can remember, always wore a locket containing a photograph of the lovely child. After the family had returned to England several years later, Maude's third child, Gerald Lewis, was born on September 21, c. 1907.

In England, Lewis's ship was based in Portsmouth, and the family lived in nearby Southsea, as did most naval families. Lewis continued to serve in the Navy during World War I. But soon thereafter, he must have retired and moved the family to London (or to a nearby suburb, as I cannot imagine Maude without a garden). Dorothy, who had inherited her mother's musical talent, had won a scholarship to study the violin at one of London's most prestigious music schools, and the move would have accommodated her studies. I cannot remember—or maybe never knew—which school she attended, but I believe she entered the school at the age of eighteen, in the autumn of 1918. I remember her telling me about performing Mendelssohn's Violin Concerto in E Minor, op. 64—for her graduation recital, I think—and about the successful teashop trio she formed while still a student.

Dorothy was not as stunningly beautiful as her mother but was softly attractive. She took a keen interest in simple fashion, for which she had considerable flair. Like most young women, she enjoyed going to dances and meeting men and supposed that one day she would marry and have children. But Dorothy was in no hurry to settle down; she was busy with her violin.

Figure 3. The Walls. *Top*: Gerald and Dorothy; *bottom*: Maude and Lewis.

Gerald, rapidly growing up, did not know what work he wanted to do. He was a well-educated, upper-class young man, but he loathed business, towns, and cities. He wanted nothing more than to settle deep in the countryside.

But what profession was there for a man of his background in such country? In no hurry to make up his mind about such matters, Gerald indulged in a busy social life of dances and parties. Extremely popular (everyone liked Gerald) and very good-looking to boot, with a mischievous look that the girls loved, he never lacked invitations to social gatherings. With the most courteous manners, Gerald, as the saying goes, knew how to "charm the hind leg off a donkey." His agile and spirited dancing of the Charleston was also greatly admired.

Suddenly, though, the seemingly secure situation of the Walls changed radically and irretrievably. Lewis, never a good businessman, invested unwisely, and lost a sizable amount of his capital in the early 1920s. Fortunately for his family, he received a generous enough pension from the Navy to save them from desperate hardship, but serious adjustments to their way of living had to be made.

At about the same time, Maude became ill. Dorothy and Gerald now needed to become self-supporting. Dorothy unhappily was forced to give up the violin. Initially she stayed at home and nursed her mother but then trained as a typist. A dutiful daughter, Dorothy resigned herself to her new situation, seeing it as inevitable given the family's circumstances. Gerald, at eighteen, was offered an entry-level position by an uncle who had a very successful stock-exchange firm, Charles Feather, Ltd., in the City of London. Against all his instincts, Gerald accepted the position, taking the advice of those who urged him to "do the safe thing," and found himself in the type of work he hated most.

Lewis received the utmost support from his family, especially Maude. For him, the immediate problem was to find an affordable place for them all to live. The answer proved to be Willowbank, a new bungalow estate built on an island in Buckinghamshire, just west of Uxbridge, Middlesex, and about twenty-five miles west of London. The estate was built by an association that, I believe, had been formed by ex-servicemen from World War I. Thus it seems likely that Lewis heard of Willowbank through his Navy connections.

The surroundings at Willowbank were pleasant. On one side lay the Grand Union Canal, with horse-drawn barges, and on the other, the Colne River. A footpath encircled the island so that residents could walk the perimeter of the entire bungalow estate beside the water, a feature particularly appreciated by Gerald. He at least had a beautiful setting to return to each evening after his long workday in London and his grueling commute of one-and-a-half hours each way.

The bungalows, while comfortable, were small—much smaller than what the Walls were accustomed to. Their bungalow at 79 Willow Crescent West was just large enough for the family of four. The rooms were crowded with necessary but far too large pieces of furniture from their previous, more ample residence. Some of these pieces they simply couldn't bear to part with—Maude's piano, the tall bookcase with Lewis's gold-tooled prize books, and a beautiful carved black mahogany desk from Hong Kong. Depictions of Chinese mountains decorated the hallway.

The bungalow was truly jam-packed. Each room, however, had at least one window—even Gerald's very tiny bedroom—that provided plenty of light. In the winter, an open fire in the living room provided warmth and coziness. In true British fashion, the rest of the bungalow had no heat, but the family was used to freezing-cold English bedrooms and, even worse, a cold

Figure 4. The Walls' bungalow at 79 Willow Crescent West, Willowbank.

Figure 5. Lewis Wall and the swans at Willowbank.

bathroom. Electric fires did their best. Eventually, though, everyone made the best of things and established a new happy life.

To Maude's delight, each bungalow had its own generous gardens. Lewis tended ours lovingly, making them beautiful for her. Her favorite flowers, sweet peas, grew alongside the bungalow, ready to be picked and put into vases. In the front garden, clematis climbed the walls, and among other flowers there were always tiger lilies, Easter lilies, and gladiolas. A yellow privet hedge enclosed the garden. At the back, a big expanse of lawn was broken up by assorted trees—down the left side, a row of apple and cherry trees; in the center, a silver birch; nearby, a brown-leafed tree I could never and still can't name; and close to the bungalow, Maude's favorite, a lilac tree. An extra strip of land adjoining the back garden was concealed by a tall green hedge and cultivated for growing vegetables.

Lewis's back garden ended opposite the point of a small island within the river, where a pair of wild swans nested each year. The island was left to grow wild, except for some slow-growing trees whose wood was to be harvested to make cricket bats. No one seemed to go to the island, which, except for the trees, grew wild, and the swans lived there undisturbed. Lewis decided to try to win their trust. Over time they fearlessly made their way to him, visiting him regularly on the riverbank, even when they had newly hatched cygnets. My memories of my grandfather and his swans are some of my happiest of Willowbank.

Life at Willowbank was fairly serene. An unfortunate accident, though, disturbed the calm early on. Gerald, always up for a challenge, accepted a dare by friends to ride a horse that was too wild for him. The horse threw him, and in the fall, he broke his hip. Gerald was laid up at home for a long eighteen months, during which he was cared for by Dorothy, to whom the brunt of his recovery had fallen, a visiting district nurse, and a close neighbor, Muriel Wilson. The house had to be rearranged to accommodate Gerald's needs, with Dorothy even exchanging bedrooms with him as he now needed more space.

Fortunately, Gerald recovered completely except for a slight limp, which would barely hamper his activities.[2] But the happiest result of this misfortune was the strong and deep relationship he and Muriel forged during the long recuperation. Whether they had a special interest in each other before the accident, I can't say. But soon after he was up and about, Gerald and Muriel married.

Gerald's new family was highly influential in the Willowbank association. Muriel's brother, Donald Wilson, a man of swift intelligence with a great capacity for enjoying life, had trained as an engineer at Leeds University and then joined the RAF as a pilot during World War I. He survived active duty for two-and-a-half years, when the average lifespan of a pilot was three weeks! Later he had an influential position at Baker Perkins, a firm of food-processing engineers in Neasden. He moved his whole family to Willowbank in the late 1920s, where he, his wife, Elsie, and their son, Peter, lived a few bungalows down from the Walls at 14 Willow Avenue. His parents, Edward

[2]Sadly, it was believed that the deep X-ray therapy Gerald had required led to his untimely death from leukemia some forty years later at about the age of sixty-five.

("Ted") and Harriett Wilson, and his sisters, Mary and Muriel, lived close by at 57 Willow Crescent West.[3]

Once married, Muriel and Gerald left Willowbank and moved to Kilburn to be closer to their places of work in London—Gerald back at Charles Feather's, and Muriel for a producer at the BBC. They thus avoided the long commute to London from Uxbridge and the one-and-a-half mile walk between the station and Willowbank.

Dorothy, too, must have been looking for something, or perhaps someone, she could call her own. Soon she met Frank Hilton, who hailed from Yorkshire. He was a businessman, earning his living as an engineer's carding-machine maker. They married in 1929, and Frank too purchased a bungalow in Willowbank, at 69 Willow Crescent West, between the Walls and the Wilsons. About two years later, I was born.

The previous years had not, to say the least, been tranquil for Maude and Lewis. Now, with their children married and healthy and with a new granddaughter conveniently living just up the road, they could at last enjoy

Figure 6. The Wall and Hilton families, probably at Willowbank, mid-1930s. *Left to right*: Frank Hilton (?), Maude, Dorothy, Lewis, and an unidentified relative.

[3]An amusing anecdote from the Wilson family lore involved Muriel's sister, Mary. Not long after Muriel and Gerald wed, Mary married too—a local young man named Bill Alderson. The newlyweds bought yet another bungalow in Willowbank. Bill's original employment was as butler to the owners of Gilbey's Gin. At some point the Gilbeys decided to dispense with the services of a butler; but not wanting to fire Bill, they transferred him to the accounts department in their factory. A surprising benefit of his employment with the Gilbeys was that he was paid part of his pension in gin! How much, I wonder? And what did he do with it?

some peace alone in their bungalow. But as Dorothy's marriage deteriorated, they must have sensed that they would not be alone for long.

When the time came, a saddened Maude and Lewis welcomed us into their home. Our presence required some adjustments, and Lewis enlarged their bungalow by one room, which led out from Dorothy's old room into the back garden area, thus providing us with our own living quarters and some necessary privacy for everyone.

After Dorothy left him, Frank sold his bungalow and moved away. Dorothy obtained a legal separation on the grounds of cruelty, and Frank was ordered to pay alimony. But he never paid a penny despite several visits to court, which finally proved too much for Dorothy. I suspect that from Frank's point of view, he had made a disastrous marriage, had been deserted by his wife, and had his child wrested from him. Why, he may have thought, should I pay for this? But still, I was his daughter, and he certainly knew that Dorothy had no money and that Lewis was not in a position to take on the cost of raising a child.

My grandparents' financial situation was indeed not rosy. Fortunately, expenses in Willowbank were low. We lived comfortably, and there was money for necessary expenses like doctors' bills—especially important for me, a frail child. Like most people, we had no car. (There were probably only about six in all of Willowbank, one of which had belonged to my father.) Nor did we have a telephone. If necessary we could use the one public telephone in Willowbank, which, in view of the frequent visits from the doctor, luckily was located opposite Maude and Lewis's bungalow.

Dorothy now found herself more and more a caterer to family. Her outlets from the daily round were reading, visits to one of the three cinemas in Uxbridge, and teatime visits with a few close women friends. She was a great walker and so did not mind doing the daily grocery shopping in Uxbridge. Dorothy frequently took me along, wheeling me in a pram—while I sang constantly—until I was able to walk that far myself.

Occasionally there were opportunities for Dorothy to treat herself. Big but rare outings were our visits to Kensington to look at the dress shops—Pontings, Barkers, and Derry and Toms. Her interest in fashion was still strong. On a very small budget and therefore with very few but well-chosen clothes, she always managed to look smart and attractive.

I was happy in my new home. The only initial problem I can recall were the dolls given to me by Dorothy's friends, who felt sorry for me. Their remedy seemed to be that each should give me a new doll—one came with a pram and another even talked. The dolls inevitably were handed to me with gooey "oohs" and "aaahs" and an aside to Dorothy along the lines of "What a cute little girl!" I, however, loathed dolls, with their big blue eyes and fluttering eyelashes. Now I owned at least three. Poor Dorothy! I raged against them, hid them under my bed, and even tried to beat them up so that they would have to be thrown away. But what would Dorothy tell her friends? In the end, and in despair, Dorothy found a way to pass the dolls on to more appreciative little girls. I was happily left alone again with my cuddly teddy bear, whom I loved.

In the midst of all this doll-giving, however, I learned from another of Dorothy's friends the sugary origin of my name. The story goes that one day the very cute little daughter of a friend of J. M. Barrie's (just like me, of course) ran up to him, arms outstretched, and cried (unable to pronounce her r's) "You are my fwendy-wendy!" From her, Barrie coined the name "Wendy" for *Peter Pan*. More goo—and having no tolerance for it—I despised the name immediately and continued to do so for quite some time. Unfortunately, I wasn't able to discard it as easily as the dolls.

My mother and I had all our meals in our quarters, except Sunday lunch, which Maude cooked and which we ate at the large dining table in her living room. It was always the same but always a treat: roasted chicken, roasted potatoes, bread sauce, a vegetable, and, of course, a very tasty dessert, the only course that varied from week to week. Maude was a good cook. It remains a mystery to me where and when in her privileged upbringing she learned. Dorothy, on the other hand, picked up cooking with not very appetizing results.

I spent many other hours with my grandparents in their sitting room, where there was both the piano and that magic box, the radio. (Television had not yet arrived on our scene.) Here, at the age of three, I discovered the ruling passion of my life—music. Soon a second, smaller piano was bought for the house and installed in the Hilton sitting room. I began piano lessons immediately. Unlike Maude and Dorothy, though, my technical performing abilities at the keyboard were only passable. I had very strong musical instincts of both rhythm and phrasing, but they were soon to be reflected in a new, developing desire to move to music, to dance.

But how, in Willowbank, did I ever find out that there *was* such a thing as dance? My mother encouraged my new interest by taking me to all the dance-filled movies that came to town and were suitable for children. The first outstanding dancers I saw in the movies were Vera Zorina in *On Your Toes* and, of course, Ginger Rogers and Fred Astaire. Dorothy also collected postcards and had a few of Anna Pavlova, which she gave to me. But it was my mother's best friend, Mrs. Plumb, who had perhaps the biggest influence. I met up with Mrs. Plumb nearly every day when she walked her two little dogs up the riverbank. When I saw the dogs romping by our house, I would join them. She had traveled widely with her music-hall comedian husband, aptly known as Tubby, and had seen the Russian ballet and told me all about it—the costumes, the sets, the music, and especially the dancing. Her stories fueled my desire, my need, to study dance, particularly ballet.

My mother and Mrs. Plumb also encouraged and expanded my taste in music. On her old wind-up gramophone, Mrs. Plumb played records of Marian Anderson, whose rich, deep voice cast a spell on me. I made every excuse to visit Mrs. Plumb to hear those records over and over again. Later there would be other favorite artists, whom I first heard on the radio, with the voice range that would always have the greatest appeal for me—alto or mezzo-soprano. I was also passionate about the waltzes of Johann Strauss. At home one of my greatest treats was a brand-new record of Strauss waltzes. I became very particular about the performances, preferring the larger symphony orchestras to all others. I wanted to choose every record myself, and my mother soon learned not to shop on her own! Sometimes we spent a considerable amount of time in the record shop listening to different renderings before I made my final selection.

Another musical favorite in films and on records was the very popular North Country comedian George Formby, who sang funny and sweet songs, accompanying himself on the ukulele. He was a natural for children and made me roar with laughter. His records were placed alongside the Strauss waltzes and were equal favorites.

Given my passion for music and dancing, I obviously should have been given dancing lessons. I begged for them, but my mother was deaf to all pleas. Dancing lessons were out of the question. I would get overheated and then catch cold or pneumonia—and maybe even die. There was no moving her. (For the same reason, I was not allowed to enter the deliciously cool water of the river on even the hottest summer days. I was deeply pitied by all the swimming children and their parents. "Perhaps next year," Dorothy would say—every year.)

The issue of my education must have caused my family great concern, as the first day of school for me was fast approaching. There was no money to pay for it. The solution came from an unexpected source. The same Charles Feather who employed Gerald put a sum of money aside to be used for my education. Actually, I must say that I believe it was Charles Feather; I'm not really sure who my benefactor, whom I called Uncle Charlie, was. There was a second Uncle Charlie in my youth, but Charles Feather, because of his financial success, seems the more likely candidate. The details of that arrangement with Uncle Charlie were never clear to me. I have no idea where the money was put or who administered it. Gerald perhaps? I only knew that I had to be very grateful to Uncle Charlie. And I was and continue to be. I can also only assume that the money was meant to continue until I was eighteen, when most girls of my station in life would finish school.

And so, I went to kindergarten at the age of four, and at five to Fray's College, a coeducational school near Uxbridge. For me, the most exciting thing I learned at school was how to read, and I loved to curl up in a chair with a book. Maude guided my homework and kept me slightly ahead of my classes. Outside school, she taught me how to sew and knit, and we made needlepoint rugs together.

Lewis taught me other fun things. At the age of six, I learned from him the old sailors' gambling game of cribbage, and then later, spelling games. He taught me how to ride a bike, swing on a swing and jump off high, plant flowers and vegetables, play croquet, and do jigsaw puzzles. The latter was a much-needed pastime for those only too frequent winter days when I was ill and confined to bed. My mother's fears for my health, it turns out, were not all imaginary, and I'm afraid I missed many days of school.

Another favorite Willowbank memory is of an old salt, Captain Davis, who lived next door. Maude and Lewis made few friends at Willowbank, but he became a great buddy of the family. His wife, Ida, despite being very religious and attending church every Sunday, was ill-tempered and disliked children. Captain Davis, though, would haul me over the fence at the bottom of

Figure 7. Wendy, Margate, 1937.

the garden, as far away from Ida as possible, and there we would weed and plant together. One of the few car owners in Willowbank, Captain Davis would sometimes treat me to a ride.

When I was about seven, Maude's eyesight began to fail. The diagnosis was cataracts and glaucoma, both untreatable at the time, and Maude began a slow descent into complete blindness. Lewis became more devoted to her than ever. A great sadness fell over the entire family, but I was too young to fully understand what Maude must have dreaded.

But my family persevered and remained optimistic. My mother and grandparents saw a future for me in which I would finish school, earn a living, marry, and have children. There seemed to be no reason why my life should not turn out that way—except, of course, that I had other ideas. However, with the coming of World War II—a cataclysmic event for so very many—my prospects would slowly change for the better.

On the day England declared war on Germany, September 3, 1939, I was eight years old. My best friend, Joan Simon, and I were playing happily in the sun in Joan's family garden along the canal bank. Suddenly my mother appeared, clearly in a state of great anxiety, to tell us the news. She obviously expected bombs to drop at any moment and whisked me home, no argument about it. Lewis tried to calm her by explaining that the war was some distance away and that we had some time before Hitler would get around to us, if he ever did. Lewis was not successful for long because, in fact, there was no denying that the war everyone had dreaded but believed would not happen was now a reality.

Although there were no air raids near us during the first year of the war, almost the whole family moved for one reason or another. Donald, Elsie, and Peter Wilson moved to Peterborough, some ninety miles north of London, when Donald's firm relocated. Muriel's sister, Mary, and her husband, Bill, bought a house in Pinner to be closer to Bill's place of work, when commuting in wartime became more and more difficult. Ted and Harriett Wilson stayed behind at Willowbank, and Lewis, too, saw no need to move his family, at least at first.

Like many others, Lewis had felt certain that the war would come despite the efforts of Prime Minister Neville Chamberlain to prevent it. Over the few preceding months, he had stocked up the larder with durable provisions as well as he could, considering that everything had to be hand-carried from the shops in Uxbridge. An immediate priority with the declaration of war was blackout curtains, which were mandatory. I believe a large amount of the thick, heavy material was delivered to each bungalow so that the owners could custom fit the curtains to their windows. Most people, like Maude, had a sewing machine, or knew someone who did, and the Willowbank curtains went up in record time. The rules regarding their use were of necessity stringent. Lewis had to go outside every evening after dark to see that no chink of light showed, or a stern air-raid warden would soon be knocking on the door.

Life became bleaker, hungrier, and darker, and the wailing of air-raid sirens soon became a frequent and dreaded sound. Although there was an important air force base at the far end of Uxbridge, which the Germans might have considered a fairly significant target, Willowbank was far enough to the west of London for the initial German bombing attacks to cause only mild concern. But the Blitz of 1940–41 was a different matter. Bombs dropped closer and closer to Willowbank, and there was the threat of invasion. We could see that the night skies over London were becoming lighter and brighter from fires, bombs, and searchlights.

After some narrow escapes from bombs in Kilburn, Gerald, whose limp mercifully made him unfit for military service, returned to Willowbank with Muriel to live with his mother-in-law, Harriett, soon after Ted's death in 1940. With the situation looking bleaker and bleaker, Lewis decided to move, and he took the family to the safe distance of Cornwall for the summer of 1940. He rented the bungalow at Willowbank for the duration of the summer to two women schoolteachers and their housekeeper, who were likely to stay in the area despite the dangers, and we all set off.

Lewis had found an advertisement for rooms on a farm in Tintagel, Cornwall, that would accommodate Maude and him, my mother, and me. Meals would be provided. The farmer, Mr. Tremayne, lived with his wife and two sons, Ernie and Bill, who had not been called up for military service since farming was considered essential war work. The Tremaynes made us very comfortable, and the farm was a wonderful place of sanctuary. We all settled in. I was delighted and experienced so many new things on the farm. I liked the farm animals, except for the pigs, but most of all I loved to ride on the big cart horses with Farmer Tremayne.

When the summer was about over and the time to return home was fast approaching, the bombing in London was still intense. One bungalow in Willowbank had been destroyed and its owner killed by a bomb dropped by a German plane that had lost its way. Although it had been an isolated incident,

Lewis decided not to return home just yet. The tenants of our bungalow agreed to sign a lease for the duration of the war.

So in September 1940, Lewis, Maude, and Dorothy left the Tremayne farm and went to stay with Maude's sister, Hilda Hastings, and her husband, Arthur, who owned a vast house on a large estate in the Cotswold Hills, near Stroud, Gloucestershire. As for me, Hilda did not want a child in the house, so the family made a momentous decision to enroll me in the prestigious Kingsley School, currently evacuated from London to Tintagel. Although it was a great opportunity, my mother, I'm sure, did not agree to it easily. I wasn't very happy about it either. But despite our reservations, the change and new surroundings for me at Kingsley were, in the long run, definitely to be for the better.

The move to Hilda's was hard for everyone. For Lewis, it proved to be his undoing. Lewis was uncomfortable with his in-laws, so he often took the train to Stroud, where he snacked on unsuitable food and found cronies with whom to pass the time. He wrote constantly to me at school; he clearly missed me very much. And I certainly missed him. All that, combined with a selfish distribution of the rations by Hilda—who seemed to manage to keep most of the food for herself and Arthur—did him in. He died of a stomach disorder, so I was told, about two-and-a-half years after arriving at Hilda's. The family suffered great grief—Maude, of course, most especially.

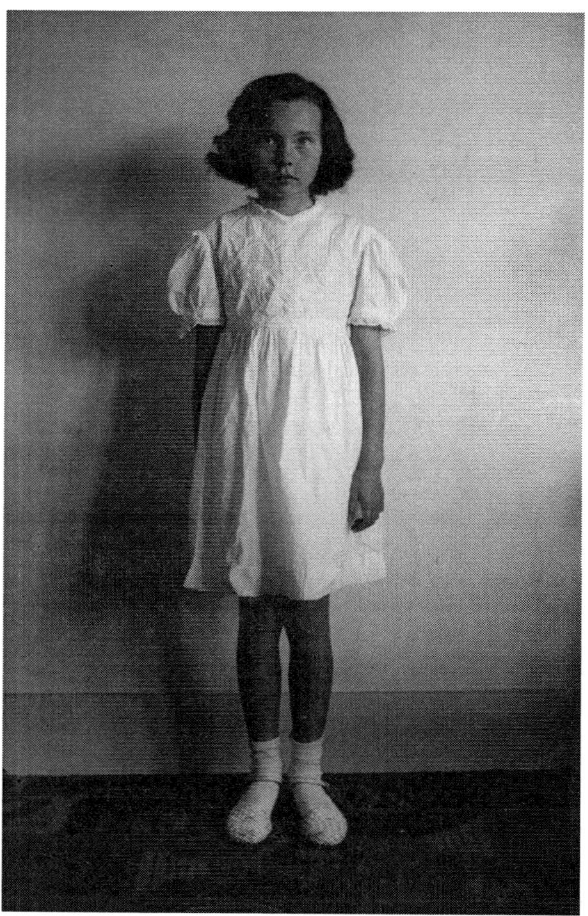

Figure 8. Wendy, Gloucestershire, 1940.

The hardships notwithstanding, my mother surprisingly enjoyed a period of fulfillment at Hilda's. Doing her part for the war effort, she became a postwoman, rising every morning at four o'clock to climb the Cotswold Hills and deliver the mail. In the winter she had to wear creepers on her shoes to prevent falling on the steep, icy slopes. Her only fear was of the dogs that guarded the houses, and she was, in fact, bitten once. She enjoyed the work, and her enthusiasm for walking now stood her in good stead. Her work helped her forget to some degree how much she missed me.

To say that I was at first lost and unhappy at Kingsley would be an understatement. But the school was the making of me. My health vastly improved in the fresh, sometimes freezing, Cornish air. Protected from my mother's anxiety about pneumonia and her fears that I would catch cold, I was seldom ill, except from the usual childhood diseases of measles and chicken pox when they ran rampant through the school. Most importantly, I received one of the best educations then available to girls, something I came to greatly appreciate later on.

Kingsley School was established in 1890 "for the daughters of gentlemen and doctors" at 46 Belsize Park, Hampstead, London. In 1915 it was bought by a group of college-educated women: Hilda Gavin, headmistress, who had previously lectured in education at Cardiff University; Vivian S. Shepherd; H. L. Stebbing; and L. Susan Stebbing, later Professor Stebbing, who was recognized as one of the most brilliant philosophers of her day.[4] The goal of these women—and achieving it was their life's work—was to establish a small independent school based on the English public-school model, which would provide a rigorous education for girls and allow them, should they so desire, to pursue higher education or enter a profession. They succeeded in developing the finest and most progressive school for girls in England. Kingsley became well-known for its high academic record and its small classes of twelve to fifteen pupils.[5] The teachers were excellent, and the undivided attention they could give to each student was quite remarkable

In 1919 the school expanded, acquiring the property at 27 Belsize Park and, in 1923, at 26 Belsize Park. The three houses were home to the school until the outbreak of war in 1939 when it was evacuated to Tintagel.[6] The war years inevitably saw a lowering of the school's high standards owing to the shortage of good teachers. But this was not an immediate effect.

The difficult evacuation process began on Friday, September 1, with about 100 of its 156 pupils (the others remaining with their parents in London) being sent to Tintagel, an area already known to the school through summer camps. The exile lasted for six-and-a-half years. The school was scattered over Tintagel and the adjoining Bossiney in at least thirteen different houses, with the largest, Tremorrab in Bossiney, as the central schoolhouse. Upon arriving in Bossiney, the staff and older girls, led by Miss Gavin, Miss Shepherd (who was soon to replace Miss Gavin as headmistress), Winifred Edwards (known as Teddy), and Dorothy Leech, set to work making Tremorrab suitable for a school. Three classrooms were constructed with outer walls and inner wooden partitions that could be removed to make one

[4]L. Susan Stebbing obtained a D.Lit. at the University of London and, in 1923, rose to become the University Professor of Philosophy, a chair never before held by a woman. A prolific author, she wrote numerous influential philosophical works, including *A Modern Introduction to Logic* (1930), *Philosophy and the Physicists* (1937), *Thinking to Some Purpose* (1939), and *Ideas and Illusions* (1941). Such time as she could spend at Kingsley was given to the most senior girls.

[5]Vivian S. Shepherd, opening letter, *Kingsley Magazine* 24 (1939–51), 1–2.

[6]After the war, the school was located in Harley, Surrey, until it closed in 1976.

large hall. An enclosed covered way, where each student had a peg for outer garments, joined those rooms to the main house.

The summer camps in Bossiney had been run in a field of Old Borough Farm, owned by Farmer Harvey Brown. Farmer Brown, his wife, Clwys, and a relative (yet another Uncle Charlie) were of enormous help to Kingsley. One of the rooms in their farmhouse was even used as a classroom. In return, the older girls learned to milk the cows, and the whole school helped in the fields on harvesting days.

I was left by Farmer Tremayne on the doorstep of Tremorrab, my family having already left for Gloucestershire the previous day. By this time, the school was established in its new home and the pupils firmly united by the evacuation and resettling troubles they had recently experienced and overcome. I was the only person, apart from very young local pupils, who had not participated in that communal experience. I was, in fact, the only quite new, lower senior girl. To boot, I arrived late, the term having already begun. For me, getting started and fitting in initially proved very difficult.

The comparatively harsh physical experiences of boarding school were not at all appreciated by me at the time. In fair or foul weather, pupils had to rise very early and walk to the main house for a breakfast of lumpy porridge and dry bread, always with blackberry jam. The rest of the meals were no better. The one cook at Kingsley, Mrs. Bennett, battling with the old range in the Tremorrab kitchen, certainly succeeded in making the worst of what meager food there was. One pupil later wrote, "The food at Kingsley, wartime or not, was dreadful. My worst memory is of boiled liver and rice—a disgusting, gluey mess."[7] I, too, loathed the liver, the tasteless dumplings, the eternal everyday boiled cabbage swimming in water, and the daily blackberries served in one form or another.

I was not suited to communal living and never saw the need to do what everyone else was doing. By nature, I did not run with the crowd. I was therefore regarded with some suspicion during the six months it took me to adjust. Preferring to go my own way, I often set off for a walk along the cliffs nearby as, surprisingly, my mother allowed me to do despite school rules. Once discovered, however, I was forbidden to go there again by the staff because of the danger—thwarted by fears of imagined dangers once more. Next I was urged to join the Brownies (junior Girl Guides) but had no wish to do so. The two arguments used to try to persuade me—"Everyone else is a Brownie," and "Your mother would like you to be one"—would obviously have no effect on me. But finally I gave in and became a reluctant Brownie and later a less-than-adequate Girl Guide. In Tintagel there simply weren't enough old ladies to help across the road.

I lived with my class and one or two younger pupils in Bossiney Court, a large, beautiful, early seventeenth-century residence close to Tremorrab. The experience of living in a Jacobean house, with the garden still in its original design, did not impress me then. All I was aware of was that the

[7]Pam Bauer Ansell, "The Kingsley School, 1936–1941: A Personal Account," unpublished essay, n.d., Wendy Hilton Personal Papers.

floor sloped and I slept with my head lower than my feet. Why weren't my neighboring roommate and I simply turned around?

The war seemed a long way away, despite the loathsome gas masks with which we were all fitted and the convoys of ships that slipped quietly by on the often gray Atlantic. The younger girls, in particular, were not really aware of Hitler's threat to England and of the possibility of German invasion. The war knocked on Kingsley's door one day when a very lost German plane dropped a bomb only a few miles away. (In alarm, or out of curiosity, some cycled over to see the crater.) But still, all around us, the staff managed to maintain a safe and secure feeling. We did not sense any danger.

A sense of security was particularly important for the many Jewish girls who were enrolled. Kingsley had always welcomed foreign students, an unusual attitude for an English school at that time. The principal teachers and others responsible for the school now opened the doors without hesitation to the flood of Jewish refugees coming from Germany to avoid Hitler's threats and as yet unknown worst atrocities. Not a great deal was made of this within the school. In fact, it was important for one to be discreet. Had the Germans invaded, about a third of the pupils at Kingsley would have been taken away.

The significance of the presence of the Jewish girls and how fortunate they were to have found such sanctuary were clear to me only after the war, when the Nazi concentration camps were opened. Of the eight girls in my class, six were Jewish refugees, most of whom had no idea where their parents were.[8]

Kingsley had an extensive sports program, which played a large part in school life. One-and-a-half hours each morning or afternoon were devoted to one sport or another. I had an excellent aim and enjoyed being the shooter in netball and playing tennis. I loathed hockey—unfortunately a school specialty—and the interminable game of cricket, which I persuaded my mother to let me drop to take riding instead. At first I rode the largest but most docile horse, Tom; there were times when the ground did seem a long way down. But later, when I had more experience, I rode a smaller more energetic horse, Blackie. I rode with a group of five or six girls led by the games mistress, Miss Fowler, and galloped along the Cornish cliffs, exhilarated and excited.

But where was music? On Tuesday afternoons, there was a sort of school band—in which my first task was to play the triangle—or a singing session. We sang the truly British patriotic staples: "I Vow to Thee, My Country," "Jerusalem," "Rule Britannia," and, of course, "Land of Hope and Glory." Piano lessons were available on a private basis with Miss Chesterman, who lived down a nearby lane. Here, though, there was a bit of an impediment to my music studies. Sheet music had to be collected from our

[8]Hilda Gavin wrote in the November 1938 *Kingsley Magazine* that an issue "of great interest at present is the establishment of the Jewish Refugees in surroundings where it is possible for them to live in peace and be happy. At present they are flocking into England and we have a number of them in our school and I am glad that the girls of Kingsley are helping to make life possible for them in any way they can. . . . The lesson it seems to me that we all have to learn in these days is toleration: to live and let live. No girls in the world have a better chance of learning this than the girls of Kingsley." *Kingsley Magazine* 23 (November 1938), 3.

classroom at Farmer Brown's farm, where in the yard there were six large white geese that loved to chase little girls. The availability of music for a lesson, therefore, depended largely on the presence or absence of the geese. Another source of music was a honky-tonk, out-of-tune piano in one of the classrooms, on which one of the senior girls sometimes played Strauss waltzes. There was no radio for understandable reasons; war news was kept from us, especially for the sake of the Jewish girls.

Thinking back to the many years during which I was sat down at the piano with various teachers, I cannot remember one piece of music that made me excited and therefore eager to play it. Every piece was a study for this, that, or the other difficulty, and every piece was boring. I remember that during one of the long summer holidays, Professor Stebbing gave to the senior girls who had to remain at school permission to play the beautiful piano in the room next to her living quarters, upstairs at Bossiney House. Of course, I at the age of thirteen considered myself a senior girl and was up there like a shot. I found a piece that took hold of me, Edvard Grieg's "Åse's Death" from *Peer Gynt*. It was mournful, and I loved sad pieces in minor keys. After I had played it over and over again, I was removed at Professor Stebbing's request.

My closest school friend, Renate Warburg, and I began to sing in the choir of the beautiful small church at Trevalgar, some distance away near the neighboring village of Boscastle. It was a stiff walk from the school, especially coming home, because the last haul was a long, very steep hill. We had to go so far afield to go to church because Miss Shepherd considered the church in Tintagel too high. Church was more or less unfamiliar to me, for my relatives were not churchgoers, although they professed the Christian faith.

Singing in the choir had its moments of joy and its moments of challenge. All the other girls in the choir were from the most senior girls at school. Younger and smaller, Renate and I did our best to sing louder than they, so as not to be outdone. Our great fear, however, was of getting the giggles in church. Miss Shepherd, who acted as church warden for three years and read the lessons, also seemed to feel that another of her responsibilities was leading the singing of the congregation. All of us were outdone by her strong soprano voice, which had been highly praised in her earlier days in the inevitable annual school production of a Gilbert and Sullivan piece. It now wobbled terribly. Her singing was a constant challenge for Renate and me, and we did our best to stifle our uncontrollable giggles. But two heaving masses could often be observed, heads buried in their white cassocks, during the prayer which usually followed. Added to that were the vicar's interminable sermons, a challenge to anyone, let alone two nine-year-olds. So, apart from the singing, Renate and I were relieved when the service was over. The long walk home would have made more food for lunch very welcome.

Then came a wonderful day. The Ginner-Mawer School of Revived Greek Dance was evacuated from London to Boscastle, and classes were offered to interested Kingsley girls. Ruby Ginner was a pioneer in the incorporation of freer movement—that is, much freer than ballet—in dance. In her work she collaborated with mime artist Irene Mawer, and their methods and teaching were highly revered by the larger dance community.[9]

I was the first Kingsley girl to enroll in the Ginner-Mawer dance classes. I was joined by another Kingsley day student about my age, Selena Uttley, who had dance aspirations similar to mine. The classes were given on Saturday afternoons. Later a ballet class was added. The excellent teacher of all the classes was Nancy Sherwood, who, like Mawer, was a close colleague of Ginner's and a collaborator in the development of the school's teaching methods. I was happy at last; I was dancing and even performing. We sometimes gave demonstrations on the big lawn in the vicarage garden.[10] Even my musical repertoire was expanded through my dance studies by the classical music used—albeit inappropriately—for the classes.

Other dance opportunities arose. There were dances, money-raising events, in the Village Hall. Nancy Sherwood was invited to start a ballroom-dance class to prepare the older girls for the dances, as well as for their future social lives. The younger seniors were allowed to take the classes but not to go to the dances. In addition, Miss Fowler taught longways English country dances. These sessions were held, I recall, one evening per week in the church hall of Bossiney Methodist Chapel, almost opposite the Jacobean house. Most of the girls despised dancing as soppy and me for liking it and, more than likely, for being the best at it. However, I had one admirer, Geoffrey Vayfield, a Tintagel resident who attended Kingsley as a day student and who later remembered me as "a nice little girl who agreed to be my ballroom [class] dancing partner without complaining!" That I had a male partner at all was amazing since males were, of course, a rarity at Kingsley. I recall only one other male pupil, Heinz, who was a boarding student and lived in the Jacobean house.

I had been at Kingsley for three years, was thoroughly settled in, and enjoying the dancing, when Aunt Hilda suddenly seemed to relent about me visiting her home. I was now allowed to go to Gloucester for the summer holidays. I was thrilled. But when my mother met me at the train, the reason for Hilda's change of heart became clear. Dorothy told me about my grandfather's recent death and how I must be a brave girl and help Grannie. I burst into tears. Lewis's death was a tremendous loss to me, but I didn't show my sadness to Maude. I did as I was told and hugged and talked to her but did not cry again until I was alone in bed. Surprisingly, Dorothy could not understand why I was so upset. Surely she knew how much I loved my grandfather.

Hilda's home was very large. It would have been very comfortable had she not owned three Pekingese dogs, the oldest of which, Sylvia, never got a

[9]In 1923 Ginner founded the Association of Teachers of the Revived Greek Dance. In 1951 the association became affiliated with the Imperial Society of Teachers of Dancing (ISTD), London, and the so-called revived Greek dance, based on the work of Ginner and Mawer, remains a part of the ISTD curriculum today. Mawer's work in mime was highly respected by the theater community as well. She published a number of books on the subject, the best known being *The Art of Mime: Its History and Technique in Education and the Theatre* (1949).

[10]The vicarage, at the far west end of Tintagel, was probably that of the parish church of St. Materiana, isolated on a high cliff west of the famous King Arthur's Castle.

bath. (Perhaps Aunt Hilda had a dog-pneumonia complex.) The house was infested with fleas, and about eight would float off each of us as we got into our daily baths. Hilda regarded my presence mostly as a nuisance but also as another ration book. Our one bond was that Hilda adored Beethoven and, seeing my love of music, she always let me listen to the radio with her when a Beethoven work was being aired. Surprisingly, she also let me practice the piano for about an hour each day, which must have been torture for her. But I did not play Beethoven again until we were back in Willowbank. So perhaps Hilda wasn't so bad in all ways, but I did notice that she usually walked the dogs during my practice time.

Shortly after arriving at Hilda's, I developed scabies, which, combined with the fleas, made for a very itchy time. My mother was sure that the cause was the undernourishing food at school—although it was probably the one five-inch bath per week that pupils were allowed—and she refused to let me return to Kingsley. This, of course, was a great pity in view of the exceptional education I received there. The scabies took several weeks to cure. When I was well, I attended a nearby Roman Catholic school, where once again hockey raised its ugly head. Here, we learned by heart not the Shakespeare that I had begun to enjoy at Kingsley but seemingly hundreds of verses of the Bible.

I had been at Hilda's for about eight months when the bombing finally eased and Maude and Dorothy decided to return to Willowbank. Poor Hilda, who had probably taken in her relatives only to avoid having any military personnel billeted with her, now had to take in three servicewomen. Their cotenants, the fleas, must have come as a great surprise to these women in Hilda's elegant, expensive home. How they dealt with them, I'd love to know.

In the spring of 1944, when I was thirteen, the family decided to return home. True, air raids were now less intense, but the V-2 rockets, those disembodied planes without pilots, were still a threat. Although I had no fear of air raids, those weapons really frightened me. When you heard the engine cut off, you knew that the weapon would immediately drop and explode on contact. The uncertainty was very scary. Aimed at London, the V-2s often overshot and flew toward but, luckily, always over and beyond Willowbank.

Before we could return to Willowbank, there was the issue of the three tenants to consider. They now had a duration-of-the-war lease on our bungalow. An agreement was reached for us to share the bungalow with the three women. So, until the war ended, Maude, my mother, and I slept side by side like sardines in my mother's old room. We also had use of the sitting room Lewis had added for us and the garden, while the three tenants occupied the rest of the bungalow.

We made the best of our once again cramped circumstances. Somehow the housekeeper and my mother shared the kitchen. Maude, most of all, must have found these circumstances the most difficult, and on returning home she probably missed Lewis even more. But she was always brave and had solid emotional foundations. Her devoted son Gerald now visited her every Sunday evening after supper, walking the short distance from Mrs. Wilson's bungalow with Muriel.

Returning home for me meant seeing old friends. I enjoyed visiting Mrs. Plumb again and resuming my friendship with Joan. Older than I, however, she was about to leave school and attend a secretarial college. Sadly, my old buddy Captain Davis had died.

I had to return to Fray's College of my earliest school days, which with its large classes and bad wartime teachers was very inferior to Kingsley. But when I reached the age of fourteen, I could legally leave school, which I did in May 1945 as the cessation of hostilities was announced and peace declared. I was no longer a child, but a teenager with my whole future at stake.

The tenants now moved out of the bungalow, giving us the space to resume more or less normal lives. Dorothy and I slept in what had been Lewis and Maude's room, while Maude had Gerald's old, tiny space. Since the only family income was Maude's naval widow's pension, money was, as usual, tight. So the two rooms we had just vacated were then rented to another schoolteacher, Miss Parfitt, who was a very nice woman and became a good friend of my mother's.

During the previous year, Maude's condition had deteriorated. Becoming increasingly blind from the glaucoma and cataracts, she had now developed dropsy and was almost completely dependent upon Dorothy. Maude's only diversion was the radio. Since I too loved the radio, I usually sat with her as she listened to her favorite programs. Like almost every man and woman in England, she greatly admired the great Austrian tenor Richard Tauber, who resided in England during the war. On Sunday evenings, she religiously tuned in to his half-hour series the *Richard Tauber Programme*, which first aired in the spring of 1945. Maude liked to listen to Tauber uninterrupted, and we all accommodated her. I noticed that even Gerald quietly adjusted the time of his weekly visits so that she could enjoy both of her favorite events of the week to the fullest.

For me, Tauber's program opened up new musical worlds, particularly those of the songs of Franz Schubert and of German lieder—although I didn't yet have the appreciation for them that I would in the future. I listened to Tauber whenever I had the chance. I vividly remember sitting with my family and listening to Tauber sing the role of Don Ottavio in *Don Giovanni* with the Vienna State Opera. He was considered unsurpassed in the role, and his performance that night reinforced that view. What I couldn't have possibly known that night was that that performance would be considered one of his greatest and his last. He would be dead in only a matter of months from lung cancer.

Only a few other singers' recordings were enjoyed in the bungalow—Marion Anderson being one of them. Dorothy loathed sopranos, referring to them as "those awful screaming women." If Maude really wanted to listen to one, Dorothy retreated noisily to the kitchen, closing the door tightly behind her.

But on the whole, music once again sounded through the day, especially piano music, Maude's preference. My best music and history instruction came from the excellent educational programs on BBC radio. I continued my piano lessons with a lady in Uxbridge, but the music she selected was as boring as ever, and she clearly hated teaching. It was Maude who led me to the Beethoven piano sonatas, encouraging me to try selected movements. I loved them. Then we tried other pieces that were also terrific challenges. At last I found music I really wanted to play. Dorothy and I also shared some enjoyable music-making playing piano duets after Maude went to bed.

Despite my mother's and Maude's careful attention to my music studies, it was Gerald and Muriel who realized that I had never seen live theater. My mother was not inclined to take me—she hated the trek up to London. So Muriel took the initiative. Knowing my love for Johann Strauss, she got tickets for *Gay Rosalinda*, the wartime title used for a production of *Die Fledermaus,* which had opened in February 1945 at the Palace Theatre in London. Richard Tauber conducted, and the noted choreographer Wendy Toye choreographed the ballet, which I loved. For the first time I heard the whole of *Die Fledermaus*, although sung of course in English.

I was as determined as ever to be a ballet dancer, but time was certainly of the essence. Perhaps it was seeing *Gay Rosalinda* that made me bring things to a head. After all, it *was* now or never. So began a battle royal with the family. My mother was still adamant: NO! Maude gave me a serious talking to about what a girl had to do for men to get on in the theater. (How little she, or anyone of us, knew about the world of ballet!) One night a very stern Gerald was brought down the road to knock some sense into me. I persisted.

It was Dorothy who finally gave in and agreed to dance lessons. Perhaps she remembered having to give up the violin and did not want me to suffer the same frustrations. My mother wanted me to be happy, and if the dancing didn't work out, at least I would have tried.

And so thanks to my mother and again to my benefactor Uncle Charlie, I began to take a daily private ballet class in nearby Rayners Lane in the method of the Royal Academy of Dance (RAD) until I was ready to audition for one of the famous London ballet schools. My mother's interest in ballet waxed with my enthusiasm for it. She soon got over her reluctance to take the train up to London, and we went to see companies like the International Ballet of the Marquis de Cuevas and the Royal Ballet at Covent Garden. Our favorite ballet was Michel Fokine's *Les Sylphides*, and we seldom saw a program without it.

After months of hard study, I was accepted into the Ballet Rambert School in Notting Hill Gate at the age of fifteen. It was time to move closer to London so that I could continue my studies more easily. With the help of a neighbor, Mrs. Mutters (a lady who never stopped talking!), the bungalow at Willowbank was exchanged for a house in Acton owned by friends of hers. The house was divided into two flats: Mr. and Mrs. Launder, longtime tenants, occupied the rent-controlled ground floor, and we prepared to move into the top flat.

The prospect of moving must have horrified Maude. The move also was an enormous sacrifice for her, although I did not realize it at the time. In Acton, Maude was confined indoors on the second floor, whereas in Willowbank she had spent several hours a day sitting outside breathing the fresh air. The Acton house did have a small garden, beautifully kept by the Launders. But it was for their use, not ours. Maude was very stoic, though, and held the philosophy that her time was almost over and that the old should not stand in the way of the young. I was very, very lucky to have such a wonderful grandmother.

Neither my mother nor I was particularly happy in Acton as well. It was noisy and unpleasant compared with our Willowbank home. But for me the move meant that I was at last going to do what I had always wanted to do. I would pursue my dream of becoming a dancer.

Finally, I was on my way!

Two: 1946–1949

The Rambert School ~ Maude's Death ~ My Best Friend Jean ~ Audrey Hepburn ~ Ballet Class with Marie Rambert ~ Rejected by the Ballet Rambert

I entered the school of the Ballet Rambert in the autumn of 1946, having been turned down by the schools of the Royal Ballet and the International Ballet because I was a late starter. While those ballet schools, like many others, had stringent age requirements for admittance, Marie Rambert was perhaps more concerned with having as many students as possible in her school as our fees would help support her company. So after only an interview with Rambert in her office, surrounded by her beautiful collection of nineteenth-century ballet lithographs, and a demonstration of an arabesque and a few simple exercises, I was accepted into the school. As with Kingsley, I entered after the term had begun and the other students were well settled in their classes. The difference, however, was that this time I arrived jubilant for my first day.

The school adjoined the Mercury Theatre in Notting Hill Gate in a building owned by Rambert's husband, Ashley Dukes. It had two studios, one bright and airy at street level, and another dark and gloomy in the basement. We students usually took class in the street-level studio but were unhappily relegated to the basement when the company was in town. Despite our delight in seeing the company members upon their return, classes in the airless underground studio were always a struggle to get through. I took my first class down there.

The school offered two levels of technique classes, each student taking two per day. In addition, there was a weekly repertoire class, usually of dances from the classics, and a weekly general-purpose character (national) dance class. On Saturday mornings, the students took one technique class. Each class had about fifteen students, and of course, most of them were female. The Rambert school taught the Cecchetti method, but that regimen was far from rigidly followed.

During the week there were two daily technique teachers: Anna Callas, who had danced with the International Ballet, and Marjorie Field, who had been in Rambert's company. Marjorie also taught the repertoire class. On Saturdays, three other teachers taught on a rotating basis, depending on their availability: Margaret Craske, a diehard advocate of the Cecchetti method; Mary Skeaping, who also taught the Cecchetti method; and Anna Ivanova (Nancy Hanley)—all buddies from their days of dancing with Pavlova. Anna Ivanova also taught the character class, which was later taken over by Brigitte Kelly-Espinosa. When she was available and felt inclined, Rambert herself would surprise us and teach the daily ballet classes—an event eagerly anticipated but also dreaded.

Although two levels of ballet technique were offered, all classes had students who were at different levels of technical proficiency. The teachers did their best to handle the inevitable problems that arose and were generally successful in achieving the necessary balance. But I sometimes felt frustrated or hindered by having to take class with less skilled colleagues.

As in any school, the teachers at Rambert's studio could make or break the classes for the students. Anna Callas and especially Marjorie were very popular. In the Saturday classes, though, problems arose, especially for the new students. Margaret Craske was an excellent teacher but to me lacked humor; Mary Skeaping was also excellent and had a very dry wit that, at our stage of maturity, we didn't always appreciate. The real problems for some, though, lay with Anna Ivanova. Anna was a pleasant teacher with a very round face and an absolutely beaming smile. She was very strong physically with enormously developed insteps, calves, and thighs. She believed that the harder you worked in terms of volume—that is, the number of repetitions of each step or sequence—the better you would get. Such an approach can indeed be beneficial, but the volume must be adjusted to the present level of each student. To benefit from Anna's classes, then, students had to have a certain amount of strength already. Very slow *développés en croix* twice round were sometimes followed by as many as 150 *grands battements en croix* at the end of an exhausting forty-five-minute barre. As Anna passed, legs would lower, the owners ready for a quick hoist should she turn in their direction. Two brave—or misguided—souls had a weekly private lesson with her. Luckily for them, their friends stood by, glucose in hand, to help revive the purple-faced, exhausted students who staggered into the dressing room.

The school had a wonderful accompanist, Miss White, affectionately known, I don't know why, as Goldie. She went to endless trouble to find unusual, beautiful music, perhaps for her own sake as much as ours. For instance, she would play the slow movement from John Ireland's Piano Concerto in E-flat, a piece very seldom heard, especially, I suspect, from a dance-class accompanist.

On my first day at the Rambert school, I made a close and lifelong friend, Jean Lanceman. Coincidentally, we shared the same birthday, although Jean was four years older. She had fought hard with her business-minded father to be allowed to study ballet, as had her sister Audrey who aspired to be a painter. Jean and I differed in our abilities. Jean was shorter and excelled as a humorous dancer, while I had long, simple, classical lines and excelled in lyrical, controlled work. There were a great many other friends at school, particularly Norman Dixon and Terence Bown (later Gilbert), a breath of fresh air if ever I saw one. His father was a miner and found Terry's desire to be a dancer rather surprising, but he agreed to it. Was there anyone who hadn't struggled to be allowed to dance? It seemed that on the whole only those with fashionable, well-off parents had come to it easily, as ballet was just becoming very au courant. From this well-heeled group came another good friend, Araminta Steer, "Minty," but in her case her rich parents also put up enormous opposition.

My first year ended gloriously with the company's season at the Sadler's Wells Theatre from May 19 to June 28, 1947, led by Sally Gilmour and Walter Gore. The dancers all seemed to be at their peak. Students at the Rambert school often had the enormous advantage of firsthand exposure to company rehearsals and many performances of its incomparable repertoire owing to the generosity of the business manager, Frederick Bromwich, who gave us free orchestra-seat tickets. At this time, the repertoire notably consisted of ballets by Antony Tudor, Frederick Ashton, Andrée Howard, Walter Gore, and Frank Staff, performed by such great artists as Gilmour, Gore himself, Joyce Graeme, Margaret Hill, and Paula Hinton, who would later become Gore's wife. They were supported by a wonderful company of individual artists, almost all of whom were equally at home in comic and serious roles. Nothing that summer, though, equaled Sally Gilmour's *Giselle*, still in my opinion the greatest I have seen next to Galina Ulanova's.[1] The more I came to know the Rambert repertoire during this season and the greater my opportunities to study it at close range, the more grateful I was that the schools of the Royal Ballet and International Ballet had rejected me!

After the excitement of the Sadler's Wells season, it was a sad day for the students when Rambert and the company left for an extensive tour of Australia on August 17, 1947. The tour, which began in Australia on October 17, proved enormously successful and was extended several times until January 13, 1949. In all, Rambert was to be away for sixteen-and-a-half months, a period that would span my second year and half of my last, precious, third year. Jean and I were quite depressed at the prospect of the company's and Rambert's absence. All our futures depended on Rambert. However, our spirits were immediately lifted and our excitement returned, when we found on our return to classes that autumn that we had been promoted to the advanced morning-technique class. We committed ourselves to working very hard pending Rambert's return.

But life outside the studio was not so inspired. During my time off that summer and winter, Dorothy and I sometimes went to see the Royal Ballet. Minty suggested that she and I go to some music concerts. When I realized that I had never been to one, I agreed eagerly, and thus began not just a new pastime for me but a vital part of my dance and music education. The first concert Minty and I attended had a particularly great appeal for me—Gustav Mahler's *Kindertotenlieder*. The ballet most loved and revered by everyone in the Ballet Rambert repertoire was Tudor's *Dark Elegies*, set to *Kindertotenlieder*. When the company was performing at the Mercury, students could absorb how deeply the dancers felt about this work. It was regarded as a ritual, and almost total silence was observed all day before a performance. So, deeply smitten by both the ballet and its music, I went with Minty to the Royal Albert Hall to hear the *Kindertotenlieder* sung by Kathleen Ferrier. The concert not only opened my lifelong love for Mahler's music but also introduced me to a singer whose artistry would inspire me for years to come. Her voice was quite familiar from the radio, but I had not realized that her presence and spirit matched it in nobility. Thereafter, unless I simply just couldn't make it, I never missed a concert in which Ferrier was singing. I heard her next, I believe, during Easter 1948, in a performance of J. S. Bach's *St. Matthew Passion*, a performance that both thoroughly convinced me that I had found my successor to Marian Anderson and inspired my love of baroque music. True, I had heard a lot of Bach's music on the radio, not to mention several interpretations of Handel's *Messiah*, but perhaps I only now was ready to truly appreciate it.

[1]In fact, I still consider these two artists, together with Margot Fonteyn and Evelyn Hart, the greatest female dancers I have ever seen.

Coincidentally, at about the same time, I had my first exposure to the fact that there was such a thing as baroque dance. Both Anna Ivanova and Mary Skeaping studied with Melusine Wood, a pioneer in the study of early dance (and about whom more will be said later). In Melusine's "Friday class," Anna and Mary worked with a group of dancers who, led by Melusine and reading from manuscripts, reconstructed dances from the fifteenth to the eighteenth centuries. One of my first public performances was in a lecture-demonstration in Worthing, Sussex, produced by Anna. She decided to begin her lecture with a few examples demonstrating the roots of ballet.[2] These included a pavane, some galliard passages, and part of Louis Pécour's "Chaconne pour une femme," published in 1704. This last piece was danced by the one among us who looked most like a lady from a Watteau painting, which wasn't me. The music by J. B. Lully, played on piano, did not impress me. In fact, baroque dance made little impression on me at the time, I regret to say. I can't clearly remember what I did dance that evening, although I may have demonstrated selections from Arbeau's *Orchesography*.

Life at home in Acton was becoming even more difficult as Maude's health deteriorated. What she missed most were Gerald's Sunday visits, although those would have in any case become infrequent as he also moved from Willowbank, having bought a beautiful country home with a large garden in Merstham, Surrey. But he was always on call (he had a telephone; we still did not) and very attentive when necessary. He handled all Maude's business affairs, and so she had no anxieties of this nature.

Over time, Maude became weaker and slept most of the time, finally passing away in early October 1947. Her death was a terrible loss, both emotionally and financially. The largest part of our income had been Maude's naval-widow's pension, and without it we were in serious trouble. The ongoing presence of the downstairs tenants in their rent-controlled apartment became more and more frustrating. Wouldn't they ever move out so that Dorothy could raise the rent? Dorothy would not hear of my taking a part-time job, and it was probably better for her sense of self-worth that she would work things out in her own way. She considered it her duty. So Dorothy rented out every other available room in the house. She also took up her second instrument, the piano, and played for a local dancing school. My friend Jean Lanceman, also feeling a financial squeeze, moved into our house. She and my mother got along absolutely famously, and Jean brought her good spirits and a little money into the home to help during a sad and especially precarious time. Since every possible penny that could be made from room rental was needed for expenses, my mother, Jean, and I crowded into one bedroom, sleeping on single beds, side by side.

At school, Jean and I were happy and totally absorbed in our studies. We would go home in the evenings to our waiting supper and regale my mother with the events of the day. After supper my mother would sometimes play the music for our repertoire class to help us remember what we

[2] Anna may have been the first person to incorporate historical work into ballet lectures. She continued her research in dance history throughout her career, which resulted in a number of publications, in particular, *The Dance in Spain* (1970).

had studied. She was so happy to be involved. We all had a lot of fun, and I think Jean's presence, combined with a Sunday visit to Muriel and Gerald's every six weeks or so, saved Dorothy's sanity.

Jean and I, now promoted to the ranks of the advanced dancers, took class with dancers who went on to have excellent careers. Among them was Yvonne Cartier from New Zealand, a wonderfully feisty dancer, who after much success as a ballet dancer studied mime in Paris. Beryl Goldwyn, who became a principal dancer with Rambert, was in the class as well. Also in the class were the few male students in the school: Ronald Hynd, Terry Gilbert, Ken Smalley, Colin Russell, and, I believe, Roger Tully. However, the student in our class who would become the most famous, although in another medium, was Audrey Hepburn.

Audrey came to England from Holland, where she along with her Dutch-baroness mother had been trapped by the Nazi occupation and endured great hardships. Oddly, however, she had managed to study ballet there, although probably without the consistency or level of instruction that we enjoyed. She chose specifically to study at the Rambert school, having heard of its reputation for developing choreographers, which is what she aspired to become if she were not good enough to be a dancer. She arrived at the school alone, having left her mother behind, and with almost no money. Rambert, Audrey has said, put her up in her own home.

My memory of Audrey, though, is of her with her mother and a friend who at some point clearly joined her from Holland. At school she and her friend were nice but quiet. They must have been far more mature, more aware of the problems of the world and of life than the rest of us. While all of us had lived through the war, Audrey, her mother, and her friend had suffered true deprivation and malnutrition. Audrey, I recall, seemed to feel very responsible for her mother, and she worked extremely hard, both inside and outside school. But her only passionate desire was to become a dancer. As has been reported elsewhere, her day of bitter disappointment was when Rambert told her she was too tall. (If this is the true reason, it surprises me because company member Joyce Graeme was *very* tall.) Audrey, therefore, had to find other goals, and she worked day and night to find her way. She became a successful model, and her photographs soon appeared in important advertisements.

I have thought a great deal about Audrey. She was a very attractive girl but not the beauty we see on the screen. She was, however, *extremely* photogenic, a fact that became apparent when she began to model for commercial advertisers. Soon her face was constantly seen on billboards and in expensive magazines. I believe it was her modeling that led to movie auditions, and the last time I saw her was on a train on her way to one. She was not at all optimistic about it though, feeling that she would be too tall for the leading man. The world knows that proved not to be the case; Audrey was on her way. Her disappointment at the Rambert school—for whatever reason—had proved to be for the best.

The absence of the company created a terrible gap for me, and so during the holiday of Christmas 1947 I decided to try my hand at choreography. I had no guidance and first attempted to create—as do so many beginners—far too long and overly ambitious pieces. I've always wondered why Rambert, despite her eagerness to find choreographers for her company, never made any real provision for students to try their hand at composing dances. (What would Audrey Hepburn, a once aspiring choreographer, have done if she had stayed at the school?) I did, however, at one point create one short and successful piece for the only performance we ever gave on the Mercury stage. It was for the twelve-or-so-year-old Vanessa Redgrave, also an aspiring dancer. Dressed in a white tunic, she danced it beautifully and with great pathos. Choreographed to Erik Satie's first *Gymnopédie*, it was, as I remember, about a little girl who was playing alone and had lost her ball. I wonder if Vanessa remembers. Like Audrey, she grew too tall to be a dancer, but I am sure she, too, has few regrets.

At home several changes were soon to be made. The downstairs tenants finally moved, and Dorothy was able to charge a good rent for that apartment. Jean moved to a more central location in London, perhaps to be closer to her sister Audrey, who also had moved to the city. Dorothy and I could finally spread out! A real treat for us, but we did miss Jean, especially Dorothy. I did, after all, still see Jean every day.

My second year at the Rambert school did not end with a thrill comparable to that of the Sadler's Wells season a year earlier. The company was very successful in Australia, and it seemed as though they would never come back. Also, I was diagnosed with scoliosis during the year, which meant medical treatments and an additional financial burden for Dorothy. My third year at the school found me (I hoped) much improved and longing for the return of Rambert and the company. The firm date for their return was January 13, 1949, in Liverpool. But when the company did return, it was without Sally Gilmour, who had married an Australian doctor. I missed her inspiration terribly, but we were to see her again later when she returned and danced with the company from 1950 to 1952.

Rambert's return was awaited by most students with a mixture of excited anticipation, fear, and dread. Would she like us? Had we improved enough? The tension when she walked into the studio was frightening. While she was away, however, I found in myself an astonishing change of attitude toward Rambert. The awe I had felt as a new student was now equaled by more censorious feelings. I came to realize that despite her brilliance as a producer and developer of performing talents, Rambert was a very poor teacher of ballet technique. It has often been written that Rambert dancers lacked good technique when compared to their counterparts in the Royal Ballet. Perhaps this gap could have been narrowed if a ballet master or mistress had been hired to teach technique classes for the Rambert company.

Rambert saw when a step, gesture, or sequence was performed well, but when they were executed poorly she seemed not to know how to correct the problem. She could even make things worse. For instance, one day in class, a dancer at the barre had very good hip placement, but to Rambert's eye her leg *à la seconde* in a *battement tendu* was insufficiently turned out. She bent down, grabbed the foot, and screwed the leg outward so that the student was forced to twist her hips way out of line. Rambert stood up in triumph seeing only the now well-turned foot and looked at the student with utter contempt.

Rambert screamed and shouted a lot during her teaching, creating enormous tension through her insults. "Stupid eeediot!" was probably her favorite, but there were many worse. Colin Russell recalls being told by Rambert that he "looked like a frog" but unfortunately "didn't jump like one."[3] Only occasionally was there any due praise or encouragement. Agnes de Mille in *Dance to the Piper* wrote with scathing humor of her own experiences of taking ballet classes from Rambert.

> In the center of the room darted Mim [Rambert], Madame Wasp, queen hornet, vixen mother, the lady boss of Notting Hill. Knobby, knotted with passion, her little legs in wrinkled black tights, her child's tough body in a shapeless baby-pink garment ruffled at the hips, a veil around her little dark head, she scrabbled from side to side in the room, pulling, pushing, poking, screaming and imploring. Now and then she would stamp her foot and literally howl with distaste. Her hands were not kind. "Long the arms," she would say, pulling an arm almost out of its shoulder socket, "Eggie" (that would be me). "Long the arms and the hands long to be in line," and she molded the fingers roughly into a pointed clump. "Now, relax!" And she sharply rapped the extended wrist bone. "Down the shoulders"—a blow on the collarbone. "Up the head!" A jerk behind the ears. "Frrrrreddie, pull in your great bottom. You flaunt your bottom like a banner. Schooling, how dare you be late. With your woolly legs? I give all my time and strength to making something we have not to be ashamed of and you bring your woolly legs to class late without a *plié*." Schooling's face goes like custard and she quietly walks out of the room. "Eggie! Relax!"[4]

The other ultimately tedious things in her classes were the "famous" cartwheels. Great fun at first, and a joy to every visitor—"What a character!" they'd say. De Mille describes these too: "[The class] ends at last. Mim does three cartwheels and stands on her head. She shouts, 'Frrrrreddie, catch me!' and jumps into the arms of the blushing Ashton. . . . Mim cackles like a banshee . . . and goes off to change."[5]

And then there were the jokes and puns with which she often held up the class—so funny to her and usually so unfunny to us. I remember a long, long story about an elephant during which she kept Joyce Graeme in full plié in second position, constantly stopping her from coming up until she had finished her story. Poor Joyce, by the end of it, couldn't come up out of plié, her thighs having turned to jelly. And she had to perform that night! I don't think any of us heard Rambert's story; our eyes were glued on Joyce because we felt so sorry for her.

But, as has been well said many times, the ballet world owes Marie Rambert a massive debt for her discovery and encouragement of so many creative talents and outstanding performing artists. She was tireless in all her endeavors and expected the same obsessive attitude toward work from everyone around her, especially her dancers. But here she often went too far, being absolutely blind to the understanding that an exhausted artist

[3]Colin Russell, interview by Susan Bindig, spring 2003.

[4]Agnes de Mille, *Dance to the Piper* (Boston: Little, Brown, 1952), 184–85.

[5]Ibid., 186.

cannot continue to give as much as a dancer whose life has at least some balance between work and play. The Ballet Rambert on tour worked six days a week—morning, afternoon, and most of the night—and on Sundays had the dubious "rest" of traveling on a weekend British Rail schedule to the next engagement. Company member Norman Dixon once came back with the tale of the dancers threatening to go on strike if they did not get some time off each week. After a tremendous fight, Rambert agreed that they should have Thursday afternoons off. No greater concession would she make.

Once established, many dancers left Rambert, and the reason usually given was that they could find more security and better salaries elsewhere. This was true, but many certainly left because they had a strong sense of self-preservation. Even after a superb performance, an artist was not safe. One evening I saw Paula Hinton excel as Silvia Tebrick in Andrée Howard's *Lady into Fox* during a season at the Mercury Theatre.[6] I happened to leave the auditorium and enter the adjoining studio by one door as a tired but elated Paula entered the studio by another door nearer the stage. Rambert suddenly rushed in by yet a third door, tore over to Paula, and screamed at her, berating her for the "disgusting" performance she had just seen. She went on and on at full voice. Paula disintegrated into a deflated, tear-ridden, exhausted creature draped over the barre. Rambert tore out as she had come in, never seeing me huddled in horror by my door.

Given my knowledge of the company's exhausting schedule and of Rambert's screaming, why didn't I look at things realistically and decide that even if I got into the company I might not fare too well? The reasons: the repertoire and the wonderful artists with whom I would work. And then there was the indisputable fact that if Rambert was working *with* you, she could get more out of you than you ever knew you had. I experienced this a couple of times in the studio when Rambert happened upon Norman Dixon and me working on a pas de deux and she took over. Our energy immediately soared.

In the spring of 1949, I realized I had to approach Rambert about the possibility of my joining the company since my funds were running out. When I first joined the school, Rambert had seemed well disposed toward me, often asking me to demonstrate by myself. Why? I had no technical finesse, so it must have been for reasons of musicality, quality, or phrasing. Since her return, however, our relationship was noticeably different. And now I even had some technique—not virtuosic, but lyrical and controlled. Perhaps I had not developed in some way that she had expected; perhaps she sensed that my awe at her antics had waned. In answer to my question, Rambert looked at me very coldly and spoke with a disdain and contempt quite out of place. She was obviously out to inflict as deep a wound as possible. It was not so much what she said to me but the arrogant and condescending tone in which she announced, "No, you have no stage personality. The best thing you can do is start a local dancing school in Acton." Ironically, she had never seen me on stage because students did not give performances. I was

[6]Howard's ballet premiered with the Ballet Rambert in 1939. The role of Silvia Tebrick was created by Sally Gilmour.

devastated by the cruelty of the delivery as well as by the disappointment. Most people had expected me to become a company member, and I think some had felt very confident about it.

Dorothy had to be told! It was a dreadful day.

The spring term had yet to run its course. I returned to classes feeling worse and worse as each day passed. A plan for the future had to be made, but this would take some time and advice. I was genuinely happy for Jean, who was taken into the company for large-scale works not usually in the touring repertoire, such as *Lac des cygnes, Act II*. But I would have so loved to have experienced some of the wonderful performances she told me about. During the summer of 1949, for example, the company performed at the Bath Festival from June 16 to 21. Jean remembers how thrilled Rambert was when Yehudi Menuhin, the festival director, came and played Ernest Chausson's Poème for Violin and Orchestra, op. 25, for a matinee performance of Tudor's *Jardin aux lilas*. To have been present for that would have been especially thrilling for me.

Jean stayed with the company during a three-week season at Harringay Arena, which ended on September 1, 1949. She then joined one of the many small, but not very good ballet companies that sprang up like mushrooms throughout England after World War II. Jean seemed content, but I had no desire to join such a company, whose artistic and technical skills were, to me, and in fact to many others, deplorable. I remember one casting decision that seems to sum up those groups. The director asked if any of his male dancers knew the mimed role of Hilarion in *Giselle*. None did, but one of them said he had seen the ballet performed once. "The part's yours," the director said. Such a situation definitely was not for me.

I, however, felt I must continue to study and set about deciding with whom. But in order to continue, for the first time, I now had to earn my own money.

Three: 1949–1952

Artist's Model ~ Audrey de Vos and Cleo Nordi ~ Ambassador Ballet ~ BBC's Ballet for Beginners *~ London Theatre Ballet ~ Movies ~ Kathleen Ferrier ~ Meeting Belinda Quirey*

The idea of making money to get rich had never occurred to me. It had always been the quality of the work that had and would continue to count. But now earning money to live and continue my studies was an urgent priority. Since I had no prospects of being employed in a full-time ballet company, was there another niche into which I might happily fit? The world of musical theater was not for me; I had neither the inclination nor the technique and style required for it. There were films, which of course paid well, but usually the engagements were short. Ballet for television was in its infancy, but developing. Then there was dancing in opera, an idea that greatly appealed to me, although joining an opera-ballet company was considered a last resort, if not failure, by most dancers.

I quickly realized that dancing jobs were going to be sporadic at best, and to get them, I first had to make contacts. A telephone now became a necessity, and one was installed at the Acton apartment. In the meantime, I needed something else to tide me over, but it had to be a job with flexibility, something that could be picked up and put down. Almost at once the perfect opportunity unexpectedly arose. An artist friend of mine asked me to make my feet available to him. He was sculpting a figure, and the feet simply were not coming out right. He needed a more beautiful pair than his current model provided. I quickly agreed to sit for him. When my feet were in place, my friend, upon hearing of my financial predicament, said, "You know, you could earn money doing this. Would you like me to pass your name on to some of my friends?" And so I was passed on.

I also made many of my own modeling contacts. I telephoned the Royal Academicians who were fashionable portrait painters. They were wealthy and could easily afford models. Many of their subjects were often very busy and only too glad to be replaced by a model for such details as hands and the draping of garment fabric. On one occasion, I was transformed by a famous and expensive artist into an authentic Spanish girl standing on a street in Spain. Well, the street was painted in Spain, but I was added in a studio off Kensington High Street.

I enjoyed working with artists. In so doing I entered a new world and learned a great deal about art and different techniques. The best painters were not, of course, always the successful, fashionable ones. Some were fun, some very serious, and some played recordings of classical music while we worked, further increasing my knowledge of the classical music repertoire.

As well as finding work, I had to find a ballet teacher with whom I could continue my studies in open classes. I discussed this issue with Marjorie Field and a great friend of hers, Michael Holmes, a dancer and choreographer who was later to become my colleague and friend. They concluded that I should try Audrey de Vos, who had gained a high reputation in recent years. I agreed, but rather nervously as de Vos had a reputation for being very unorthodox in her methods. My confidence after Rambert's destructive ways definitely needed a boost. I need not have worried.

Audrey de Vos (Audrey Mullins) had studied with Serafina Astafieva and Laurent Novikoff and had had some experience with Pavlova's company. She then began to teach dancing in Weymouth, working with her half-sister, Kathleen de Vos, at her de Vos School of Dance. De Vos later took over Kathleen's studio and ran it with her younger sister, Bettina, from 1916 to 1925. She then moved to London and, retaining the Weymouth school's name, opened her own in George Street on Manchester Square in 1930. During the early part of World War II, she moved the school to 42 Linden Gardens, Notting Hill Gate, where I studied and where she taught until she retired in 1966.

Audrey de Vos was a brilliant woman and a revolutionary and unorthodox teacher.[1] I entered her open classes not knowing what to expect except that her way of working would be very different from anything I had previously experienced. Her aim, of course, was the same as that of all great teachers—to produce fine dancers. To achieve this, she worked individually with every student, no matter how promising or unpromising they seemed, improvising her classes to suit the special needs of those present. She had a fertile and quick mind—to gain the most from what she had to offer, a student had to be able to think—and a spare, slightly tense body. Her piercing blue eyes were set in a beautifully structured face.

DeVos's teaching presence was compelling and intense because of her deep concentration on the problems of the students before her, whether they were comparative beginners like me or Royal Ballet ballerinas like Beryl Grey, a regular attendee whenever possible for a period of ten years. A great deal of de Vos's teaching was remedial. Here her primary aim was to reduce strain and overdeveloped muscles in dancers who had developed these faults through bad teaching. She offered special conditioning classes and was the first ballet teacher in London to also offer modern dance classes. In all her work, de Vos was assisted by a brilliant young teacher, Janet Albisser, who was always enthusiastic, uplifting, and encouraging. Her presence and work in the school were greatly appreciated by all the students.[2]

De Vos and Janet made me forever aware of two things vital to my dancing as a whole, but particularly later in my career as a baroque dancer. The first was to work always from the center of the body with evenly placed hips; the second was that between flat foot and three-quarter or full pointe

[1]Excellent, more detailed accounts of her work are available. See, for example, A. V. Coton and Piers Pollitzer, "Two Tributes to Audrey de Vos: The Critic; the Student," *Dancing Times* (October 1965), 20–21; and Anthony Cowper, "Teacher with a Difference," *Dance and Dancers* (October 1953), 19.

[2]Sincere thanks to Janet Albisser (Westenberg) for sharing her memories of Audrey de Vos.

there is a wonderful instep that can be used for technical and expressive purposes. The concept of regarding the floor as a friend, of standing on it and feeling downward through the legs and feet was totally new to me. It was wonderful, and many, many things became much easier.

To de Vos, the words "system" and "method" were anathema as they denoted ultimate stultifications. In turn, her work was frowned upon by orthodox teachers, especially those devoted to the claustrophobic, "from-the-waist-down" RAD method to which many young children in England and much farther afield had been and were being sacrificed. English dance teachers were exam-conscious to an almost fanatical degree.[3] To get pupils, you *had* to put letters after your name.

De Vos nevertheless attracted many open-minded students from companies and foreign countries. Indeed, a more diverse group could probably not be found anywhere else in London or even in the rest of England. In addition to Beryl Grey, there were Gillian Lynn, who much later would choreograph *Cats* in London, and other dancers from the Royal Ballet: Nadia Nerina from South Africa, Marilyn Burr and Robin Haig from Australia, and Lucette Aldous from New Zealand (although she had studied in Australia). Juliette Prowse, recently arrived from South Africa, and Margaret Black from the United States were also full-time students in de Vos's classes. Other personalities who dropped in at her studio from time to time were Sir Winston Churchill's daughter, Sarah; Sir Arthur Bliss's daughter, Karen; and Ronald Wilson, the costume designer. Kenneth (later Ken, the moviemaker) Russell, Walter Gore, Paula Hinton, and Joyce Graeme also took classes.

When Lucette Aldous came to the studio, she had until then been a student at the Royal Ballet school. She had hoped to join the company, but at only five feet she was considered too small. (The opposite problem from that of Vanessa and Audrey!) I choreographed what I remember being a good piece in the romantic style for Lucette. She danced very beautifully and was extremely responsive to the music (which, of course, helped me), which consisted of four of Robert Schumann's *Fantasiestücke*, op. 12. She later became Rambert's ballerina, sometimes dancing as many as six major classical roles per week on tour. Lucette eventually returned Down Under as a ballerina of the Australian Ballet.

There were those regular student attendees, like me, who became colleagues and friends over the next few years—Susan Richter, a Londoner and another strong-minded daughter whose parents were dead set against her being a dancer, even after she became a very successful, beautiful one; and most especially Pamela Lyon from New Zealand, as ardent a music lover as I was. Like so many of her compatriots, Pamela had longed for a European experience and had managed to obtain a sizable grant to study ballet in London. She was multitalented and could as easily have elected to become a writer as a dancer. Dance, as it turned out, proved an unfortunate choice for Pamela.

[3]The Imperial Society of Teachers of Dancing (ISTD) also favored exams. The society comprised different branches, each devoted to a particular style and technique of dance, such as Ruby Ginner's on Greek dance. Each branch had a committee, some members of which were also examiners of the numerous syllabi. There were usually three exams per branch: elementary, intermediate, and advanced.

During the six-week voyage to England, she developed pneumonia and suffered a considerable weight gain on her hips and thighs, her torso, though, remaining as beautiful as ever. Her doctor was convinced that this weight gain would reverse itself. It didn't. De Vos tried everything she could think of, but Pamela's weight seemed there to stay—a tragedy in so many ways, not the least being that she was a beautiful dancer. Pamela was terribly unhappy, humiliated, and frustrated. As I was still looking for seemingly unattainable work as a dancer and living with a terrible sense of failure, Pamela and I were quite a miserable pair, but we persevered. We shared a lot of valuable times, going to as many concerts, recitals, plays, and operas as we could afford—luckily gallery tickets were very cheap!—and we hoped one day to visit the Edinburgh International Festival.

Several times I almost decided to leave de Vos's studio because of the music. As she always improvised her sequences, her pianist had to improvise also. The results were intended to be functional, and they were, but very, very dull. Perhaps what enabled me to stay as long as I did were Janet's classes, designed to recordings of old friends like, yes, Johann Strauss. I continued with de Vos and Janet until about 1960, but after being at the studio for about one year, in 1950, I also began to study with another highly recommended teacher, Cleo Nordi, a student of the Russian style of ballet and a former member of Anna Pavlova's company. I believe I went to de Vos's and Janet's classes four times each week and to Nordi's twice a week.

Nordi's first studies were in Petrograd with Nicholas and Nadine Nicolaeva Legat, and Nordi was passionately devoted to the Legats' teaching. Later in Paris she studied with the Maryinsky ballerinas Olga Preobajenska, Lubov Egorova, Mathilde Kshessinska, and Vera Trefilova. After a time in her home country, Finland, she returned to Paris and joined the Paris Opera Ballet in 1924 as a *danseuse plastique*, a style she had studied with a pupil of Isadora Duncan. In 1925 Anna Pavlova invited her to join her company, where she remained until Pavlova's death early in 1931. She then taught as a guest in several schools but spent her final years in London teaching in her own studio. When I joined Nordi's class, her studio was in Philbeach Gardens in Kensington, but she later moved to a larger space at 48 Warrick Gardens, also in Kensington.

Cleo Nordi was a calm, beautiful, warm woman. She was an excellent teacher. Her classes were beautifully structured, and she worked equally on technique and style, often concentrating on *port de bras*. She had studied music and played the piano. She, therefore, employed very good accompanists. I deeply appreciate the work I did with Nordi. It was the first time I studied a purely Russian style. Nordi worshipped Pavlova and had little time for the performances of Galina Ulanova when the Bolshoi later came to London in 1956. As Ulanova was to become one of my favorite dancers, a supreme classical artist, I was sad about this. But, then, I had not worked with or seen Pavlova myself.

When I attended her classes in Warrick Gardens, Svetlana Beriosova, also trained in a Russian system by her father, Nicholas Beriosoff, was, not surprisingly, a regular attendee. She was wonderful to watch and her presence was an example and inspiration to everyone. It is a pity that when Svetlana joined the Royal Ballet as a ballerina, Dame Ninette de Valois with her fierce partisan feelings about the "English style" managed in many subtle ways not to give her quite the prominence she deserved.

In the summer of 1950, Pamela and I decided that we could just about afford one week at the Edinburgh International Festival. I had never traveled anywhere except to Tintagel and the southern seaside resorts in my early childhood. We were full of eager excitement. Having to do everything in the cheapest possible way, we took the night train from Kings Cross and crossed into Scotland just as the sun rose; it was beautiful. Leaving the train, we walked into Princes Street and had our first glimpse of the lovely city of Edinburgh.

A bus took us to our cheap lodgings. There we found "Jock," the owner, a man of some fifty years with an eye for young girls like us. He meant us no harm, though. In fact, he was very well-meaning and concerned for his guests. One day he let us know that he was worried about a young honeymoon couple who had failed to "make it." But in the middle of breakfast the next day, he rushed into the room shouting to all the guests, "It's okay, it's okay, they did it." We all cheered.

More than the events of the festival itself, I remember my growing love of the city and the stirring sound of the marching pipers at the Tattoo, perhaps above all the walk of the pipe major in his swaying kilt. I was determined to return to Edinburgh as soon as possible.

Soon after returning home, I was, much to my surprise, off to Scotland once again to dance my first professional engagement, which was with the Ambassador Ballet, a *good*, small company directed by Letty Littlewood (Letitia Browne).[4] My old friend and roommate Jean Lanceman was already rehearsing with the group and could vouch for its integrity. One afternoon I was walking in Notting Hill when Jean came rushing toward me waving frantically. One of Letty's dancers was injured, and she was in desperate need of a replacement, someone who already knew the "Mazurka" from *Les Sylphides*. There were other roles to learn, too, and the tour of Scotland (which unfortunately did not include Edinburgh) was starting in a week. Jean said that Letty was "okay," and, convinced, I hurried off with her to the studio. Proving that I could dance the "Mazurka," I was put to work immediately. Here, my ability for quick study of new roles was proved for the first time in a crisis situation.

Touring Scotland as the cold autumn set in had its good and bad sides. Traveling by coach provided a wonderfully scenic view of the beautiful countryside. But the rigors of the cold and intense winds, especially in Dunoon—which I will never forget—were horrible. More importantly, however, Letty

[4]Letty was previously the director of the Anglo-Russian Ballet. The success of that company led to the formation of the Metropolitan Ballet, a very successful company based in London. Despite its popularity, the Metropolitan Ballet had a short life, from 1947 to 1949, closing owing to lack of money.

was a person of great energy and enthusiasm, who always got the best from her dancers because she had high standards and they respected her. All in all, the three-week tour was very good for me. It provided my first stage experience and certainly whetted my appetite for more. It would have been easy to fall into deep depression again, but an invitation to Jean and me really lifted our spirits. Walter Gore intended to leave Rambert and begin his own company. He expected that a couple of years would pass before he had enough money, but when he did, would Jean and I be interested in joining him? We were thrilled and terribly flattered. Yes, we certainly would be interested in joining his company!

In the meantime, other dance opportunities came my way, and I was able to continue working in the field I loved. Now I was to discover the new worlds of ballet on television and in the movies, so different from ballet in the theater.

While I was still at the Rambert school, an idea was developing in the head of Cecil McGovern, controller of programming at BBC Television. McGovern was certain that there was a viewing audience ripe for a basic educational series entitled *Ballet for Beginners*. He approached producer Philip Bate, who had already produced successful ballet programs for television, to develop the series. Bate in turn approached Felicity Grey, a London-based dancer and choreographer, to join him in the endeavor. Together they gathered a small group of dancers and wrote the scripts for what was to become a highly successful and long-running BBC show. For me, *Ballet for Beginners* would be a great step in my career.

Felix, as Felicity was known familiarly, became a popular television personality, much to her surprise. Like me, she had been a late starter, beginning to train seriously for ballet at the age of fourteen. She studied at the Arts Educational School, a wealthy establishment owned by Grace Cone and Olive Ripman, and became, in due course, a gold medalist at the RAD. Early in her career, she danced in the theater and beginning in 1936 appeared occasionally on television, which is perhaps how Philip Bate became aware of her work.

In early 1951, after two successful seasons of *Ballet for Beginners*, Felix was invited to take part in the Festival of Britain. The festival was a five-month countrywide celebration comprising hundreds of exhibitions, concerts, and other events honoring British achievement in the arts, industry, and science of the previous one hundred years, since the Great Exhibition of 1851. The festival was also seen as a "tonic to the nation," intended to boost the morale of Great Britain, recently emerged from World War II and still suffering its aftereffects. The main festivities took place in London, but many cities and towns across Britain hosted events. Felix was engaged for the festival summer season at the fashionable and genteel seaside resort of Eastbourne—a prestigious invitation, proving the success of Felix's work.

At the same time, Felix was also asked to select the corps de ballet for a television production of *Les Sylphides*. She came to Miss de Vos's studio to select dancers. Since I had no television at home, I had not seen any of the *Ballet for Beginners* programs, although I was aware of the broadcasts. Nonetheless, I had no idea who Felix was or why she was watching de Vos's class. So you can imagine my excitement when she offered me both the Eastbourne and television engagements! Dorothy, of course, was overwhelmed with pride and delight and immediately planned a richly deserved holiday for herself in Eastbourne. First, I rehearsed and performed in *Les Sylphides*, which was broadcast live on Good Friday, March 23, 1951. The soloists were Violetta Elvin, Marjorie Tallchief, Svetlana Beriosova, and George Skibine; the producer, Christian Simpson; and the conductor, Eric Robinson. Cyril Beaumont was on hand as historical adviser and, joy of joys, the corps de ballet was rehearsed by the famous English soloist and star of Diaghilev's Ballets Russes, Lydia Sokolova, who had, of course, danced in *Les Sylphides* for Michel Fokine. This production was a rare and true experience, one in which I felt extremely fortunate to be included. Even the bright yellow dresses we had to wear because white glittered too brightly on black-and-white television failed to destroy the atmosphere so wonderfully created by Sokolova with her attention to style, nuance, and detail.

My trip to Eastbourne was to bring more than a valuable performing experience and a wonderful holiday. It brought me greater contact with Kathleen Ferrier and her great art. Soon after *Les Sylphides* on a perfect London spring day, I walked across Kensington Gardens, wearing for the first time a daffodil-yellow and white dress I had made, to buy tickets for Pamela and me for a performance of J. S. Bach's Mass in B Minor, BWV 232, scheduled for June 19 at the Royal Albert Hall. It had been a long time since I had felt that all was well with my world, but now I seemed to have good reason to be optimistic. On the way I met my artist friend. Hearing of my mission he said gently, "You know that Kathleen Ferrier just had an operation for breast cancer, don't you?" At this time, operation or no operation, cancer almost certainly meant death. I thought of Tauber, and a sense of doom came over me.

The performance on June 19 gave the audience great joy. The last performance by Ferrier had been Bach's *St. Matthew Passion*, BWV 244, in Lewes, Sussex, on March 23—Good Friday, the day of *Les Sylphides*, so I could not attend. The nature of her illness was a closely guarded secret, especially where the public was concerned. No one suspected a thing; she looked and sounded so well and strong. In those days, applause was not given before or after sacred works, it being deemed inappropriate. But enormous warmth radiated toward her from the silent audience. Pamela and I decided not to miss any of Ferrier's concerts given within a reasonable distance just in case the disease returned and proved fatal. I would see her next in Brighton.

The Festival of Britain season in Eastbourne ran from July 12 to September 15 in the Winter Garden Pavilion, with a week or two of stage rehearsals beforehand. For the festival, Felix created the London Theatre Ballet, which consisted of the six-or-so-member company of *Ballet for Beginners* supplemented by dancers like myself. Four weeks of rehearsals in a London studio in Notting Hill Gate preceded our move to the seaside. We were preparing twelve ballets for the season, including *Les Sylphides*; selections from

Figure 9. Wendy (center) with the London Theatre Ballet, Eastbourne, 1951. Photo courtesy of Ann Fellowes.

Coppélia, *Swan Lake*, and *Giselle*; and two new ballets, the delightful *Hoops* by Walter Gore and *Trio 1851* by John Hall, in which I was one of the three featured dancers. Felix was very fair and cast almost everyone in five or six roles. I also danced in the corps in *Les Sylphides*, was a washerwoman in *Le Marché* by Pirmin Trecu, one of the two leading swans in *Swan Lake*, a village girl in *Giselle*, and the Wolf (Red Riding Hood and the Wolf) in *Aurora's Wedding*. Looking back now, I'm amazed to see that I was cast as the wolf, clearly very unsuitably; I have no memory of doing the role at all. Shortage of men, I fear!

As essential as the season itself, however, was finding affordable, hopefully comfortable lodgings, which in a popular resort like Eastbourne would not be easy. As soon as the television production of *Les Sylphides* aired, another dancer in the troupe, Frances Pidgeon ("Pidge," who here danced under the name of Alleyne), and I decided to find a place to share and took a Sunday excursion from London to the seaside. Luck was with us. In a guest house close to the pavilion and the beach, we found a very large room with comfortable single beds. There was one problem, however. The room was already booked for the first two weeks of our stay. Seeing our disappointment, not to mention desperation, the proprietor, Mrs. Jones, said, "You can have this," gesturing to a covered space just big enough to hold a double bed. The ceiling was about eighteen inches above the sheets. The only way in and out was through a small square opening. The first one in was therefore trapped for the night, an arrangement that had little appeal. But since Mrs. Jones offered us the space free for two weeks, charging us only for our meals, and Pidge graciously offered to be the first one in every night, we quickly agreed to the arrangement. We paid our deposit for the larger room and returned to London feeling quite satisfied with ourselves.

Soon after, rehearsals with the London Theatre Ballet began at the Notting Hill Gate studios. The company consisted of Domini Callaghan (ballerina), Yvonne Cartier and Margarita Tate (soloists), with Pidge, me, Thalia Kallas, Ann Lydekka, Rosemary Syrett, Hazel Wiscombe, Marjorie Woodhams, and Selena Wylie Uttley (of Kingsley days) in the corps. Three men danced with us: Derek Rosen (premier danseur), Terry Gilbert, and Ken Russell. The ballet master, Michel de Lutry, directed rehearsals. Music was provided by two pianists, Marie Bingham and Kenneth Alwyn. Dancing to two pianos, at the most, was the fate of all small companies that lacked the money for even a small orchestra.

De Lutry was a very efficient ballet master, although in *Les Sylphides* he lacked the poetry that Sokolova had instilled in us. He was considerate and fair. The dancers were mature in their attitude with the exception of Ken Russell, who was still something of an angry young man eager to shock. The 1951 season with the London Theatre Ballet was about his third job as a dancer. He was not very skilled, having begun dancing only in his early twenties after serving in World War II. But his lack of technique was more than adequately compensated by his ability to act. Ken danced or acted: an artist in *Le Marché*, Hilarion in *Giselle*, Sir Plume in *Rape of the Lock*, and Puss-in-Boots and the Flame Fairy's Cavalier in *Aurora's Wedding*.

When we reached Eastbourne for the season, Pidge and I got settled in our temporary bedroom quarters. Mrs. Jones gave us a closet for our belongings. True to her word, Pidge was the first one in at night. Before the first day of intense rehearsal, a funny incident disturbed what should have

Figure 10. Wendy and Frances Pidgeon, Eastbourne, 1951.

been a good night's sleep. I awoke to what was to me a ghastly sight—a large furry spider poised on the ceiling just above my head. I have a terrible spider phobia, so I screamed and dove below the sheets. Pidge jerked awake but fortunately did not sit bolt upright and knock herself out on the ceiling. Instead she dealt calmly with the spider and got it out of our tiny space without hurting it or me. How, I don't know (and I really didn't care). At my insistence, it was removed to the safe distance (for me) of the garden.

The next morning, the first thing we did after breakfast was make our way to the pavilion. On the way, I caught sight of Selena with her mother trailing behind her as at Kingsley. For a moment, I was back in Tintagel. But soon I was laughing on the other side of my face. Dorothy came for her summer-long visit and worked in a hotel. She became, to my horror, one of the most doting, sentimental, proud ballet mothers I had ever seen. Fortunately, in Eastbourne she and a coworker, Henry, developed a romantic attachment, which occupied her spare time and made her happier than usual. But the relationship was not to last beyond the summer, and Dorothy was increasingly to become a problem for me.

I couldn't find any classical music concerts in Eastbourne, but in nearby Brighton a splendid Sunday series of star-studded festival concerts was being held in the Dome. Ferrier was scheduled to sing on Sunday, July 22, and I immediately sent for a ticket. But the final dress rehearsal for *Trio 1851* was also on July 22, the only Sunday I had to work during the entire season. Everything went wrong. The choreographer was late; my solo was the last of three to be rehearsed. My costume had to be altered and pinned while I was in it. Never can a person have so much wanted to be in two places at once. I stood through the pinning imagining all the trains leaving for Brighton. Finally I did get to the station, sprang onto an about-to-move train, and arrived at the Dome late for the concert but in time to sink into my seat just as Ferrier walked onto the platform for the second piece in the program, Brahms's *Alto Rhapsody*, op. 53. I did not stay for the second part of the concert—although it featured another excellent soloist, Johanna Martzy—in view of the tiring day, the rush to get there, the prospect of the trip home, and an opening night to come.

The *Alto Rhapsody* lasts only some twenty minutes, but the triumph of actually getting to Brighton and the beauty of the performance excited and inspired me. As a result, I danced especially well in *Trio 1851* at the premiere, and the audience loved it. The following review from the Eastbourne press—my first and a nice review for the whole company—appeared soon after the performance.

> The third programme in the repertoire of the London Theatre Ballet had its premiere at the Winter Garden on Monday evening.
>
> "Giselle," the classical story of a village girl, was the first ballet and served again to emphasize the artistry of the ballerina, Domini Callaghan, and of the principal male dancer, Michel de Lutry.
>
> "Le Marché," portraying incidents in a market place, was repeated from the first programme, followed by the delightful "Trio 1851," danced, in costumes of the period, by Wendy Hilton, Margarita Tate and Frances Alleyne.

> The final ballet was the colourful and altogether charming "Aurora's Wedding," which concludes with the Polonaise by the company.
>
> It is unfortunate that many people have seen, as their only experience of ballet, second and third rate companies. Not having enjoyed the experience, they are not anxious to be disappointed again.
>
> It cannot be stated too emphatically, that with the London Theatre Ballet, Eastbourne has an opportunity of seeing dancing of a really high standard, with first-class production, staging, costumes, and lighting.
>
> Those who love and appreciate good ballet will be regular visitors to the Winter Garden during the next two months. They who say they "do not like ballet" should pay one visit to see this company. They will probably change their minds.[5]

Gerald and Muriel came to see a performance, but they could muster only faint praise for my work, especially Muriel. Here would have been a chance to say something generous to Dorothy, but Muriel simply could never do it. (They had always been quite incompatible.) Gerald always followed Muriel's lead in his gentlemanly manner, and so, as usual, Dorothy was put down. To top it off, being thoroughly narrow-minded, they also disapproved of her relationship with Henry.

At some point later in the season, I slightly sprained my left Achilles tendon. I was heartbroken. Work at last, and I was grounded. A dancer familiar with the company's work had to be brought down from London to replace me. Miss de Vos was contacted, and I was very surprised—and pleased—to see a somewhat slimmer Pamela Lyon arrive at the pavilion to dance my corps de ballet roles in the classics. There was a good side to my misfortune, however, which surprised me and everyone else. In *Giselle*, I changed places with Margaret Tate, who was playing the mimed role of Giselle's mother. I learned the role in a day, but no one thought I would act well enough. I understood every emotion of the part, and my performance won me heartfelt and genuine congratulations, not only at the time but also later from many people in London who had heard of my success. I loved the role and wished I could have stayed in it. But alas, I was restored to the peasants when my foot healed, and Margaret resumed the role.

The entire season went smoothly and calmly. The company was well rehearsed, we liked the pavilion, and the audiences were warm and appreciative. And it was wonderful to be out of London for the summer. The weather at Eastbourne was unusually beautiful (by English standards), and Pidge and I, often with Ken and Terry and sometimes Selena, spent most of our free hours on the sandy beach. But on Sunday afternoons, when everyone was lying in the sun, I would instead lie on Mrs. Jones's sofa and listen to a broadcast opera. Ken loved music too, and he and I had a lot to talk about. He was full of ideas, one of which was a production of Alban Berg's *Wozzeck*, which he explained to me in great detail. Following the Eastbourne season, the London Theatre Ballet did a week's stint in nearby Bexhill, after which

[5]Wendy's papers contain numerous clippings that have no reference information; some lack even titles and authors. Those articles, therefore, were impossible to trace.

we went on to Canterbury for a week. I believe another projected week in Sheerness did not materialize. Those of us who had augmented the *Ballet for Beginners* group for the summer season now had the prospect of dancing in future episodes of the television series when a larger group was required. It had been a very good season, and I was now an experienced and, to some extent, recognized dancer.

Soon after our return to London, Michel de Lutry offered the female dancers of the London Theatre Ballet work in an MGM film, *Never Let Me Go*, starring Clark Gable and Gene Tierney as a ballerina. As glamorous as it may sound, I don't think any of us really enjoyed doing movies. Even though the engagements were typically short, only a few days to a week or so, getting to the usually far-flung studios, such as Shepperton and Elstree, meant a horribly early start. I remember setting out from Acton on a 4:00 a.m. train for this movie. Then there were long hot days under the lights. In the American studios, which were the lowest of the low and where this was filmed,[6] the extras were treated like cattle while we as dancers were only one step better off.[7] But this engagement, my first movie, was a significant step, even if, in the end, I didn't consider it a high point in my career. And my mother was particularly thrilled with this opportunity for me.

The obvious attractions of working in movies, especially where the dancing did not amount to much, were the money and the opportunities to see performers you admired in action. The London Festival Ballet performed the major dance sequences featured in the film, excerpts from *Swan Lake* with Gene Tierney (or her stand-in) as Odette. The London Theatre Ballet dancers did not dance but participated in what amounted to backstage crowd scenes as the corps de ballet. Very boring work, but I did get to be with the major actors up close. It is my back you see beside Clark Gable while he is talking to Gene Tierney after the ballet performance. Although Gable and Tierney were not among my favorite actors, through such close work I did come to admire Gable's very simple and relaxed camera technique.

As with any such engagement, new professional and personal connections were made. I believe that it was during the three-or-so days of work on this film that I struck up a friendship with another dancer, Shirley Slade. Shirley and I became very good friends, and for the next film that came our way through Michel later that year, *Knights of the Round Table*, she invited me to stay with her and her aunt who lived close to the studio. What a wonderful help that was! No early morning trains!

Knights of the Round Table was even worse than *Never Let Me Go*. Also released in 1953, it starred Ava Gardner and Robert Taylor. I have no specific memories of the movie or of my role. According to the reviewer for

[6]MGM's Boreham Wood Studios.

[7]David Niven gives hilarious accounts of his miserable experiences as a movie extra in his book *The Moon's a Balloon* (New York: Putnam, 1971).

Ballet Today, there was "a medieval court dance," for which Michel coached Gardner, Taylor, and Mel Ferrer. Michel also had "a novel solo—dancing blindfold on a banquet table strewn with eggs . . . without breaking a single shell."[8] Michel did his best, but in my opinion, the least said about this epic the better.

My third film, *Beau Brummel*, was the best. Time-wise, it comes a bit later in my story, 1953 (released in 1954), but it seems more appropriate to discuss it with the rest of my early career in movies. Michel again provided the choreography, and Stewart Granger, Peter Ustinov, Rosemary Harris, and Elizabeth Taylor starred. This was an elegant costume movie, and again, I have little memory of my role. I do recall, though, that Granger, Ustinov, and Harris enlivened the time during setups with brilliant, witty conversation, which I stood near enough to hear. Also, I was amazed to discover the lengths to which the extras would go to get close to the stars and therefore the cameras.

In all, I worked on five movies, four as a performer, one as a choreographer's assistant. (The remaining two are discussed farther on.) And in all, a good deal of the dancing that was filmed did not survive the cutting and editing process. When the movies were cut to allow the insertion of ads, it was usually the dancing that was removed. I don't think I can be seen in the final version of three of the four movies in which I danced. Only my brief moment with Clark Gable in *Never Let Me Go* remains.

Between these first movie engagements, I danced again on television. In late 1951 or early 1952, I danced in another program for the *Ballet for Beginners* series, the only one of the season that required extra dancers. It was a notable experience for one reason: Tamara Karsavina was brought in to coach Domini Callaghan in *Giselle*, Act I. I believe she came only once, but to hear what this great artist had to say and watch her expressive face with its deep soulful eyes was unforgettable.

In the spring of 1952 I was recruited by Mary Skeaping for a significant television production of *Swan Lake*. Since the television production of *Les Sylphides* in 1951, all my work—on television, on the stage, or in the movies—had been connected with Felix or Michel. It would be good to be working with Mary again, now as a professional. Her sense of humor and dry remarks that puzzled me in my days as a student at the Rambert school were no longer beyond my comprehension. And I really liked her. The producer was once again Christian Simpson, the conductor, Eric Robinson. Both the story and the Petipa/Ivanov choreography were adapted for television, the former by Cyril Beaumont, the latter by Mary. I danced the mazurka in "The Hall of Siegfried's Castle." I felt my usual excitement as the seconds ticked away before transmission, but otherwise for me, this production lacked magic. As Odette/Odile, Irène Skorik, prima ballerina of the Staatsoper Munich, left a great deal to be desired both in line and dramatic ability. Youly Algaroff, star of Les Ballets des Champs Elysées, was somewhat better as Prince Siegfried, but how much can a poor prince do?

[8] *Ballet Today* 6 (September 1953), 6.

Following *Swan Lake*, there was no work in sight for the summer. In fact, dance work would be sporadic into the winter. So, I renewed my work with artists, and Pamela and I continued going to the theater and concerts. We decided to splurge and go to the Edinburgh Festival in August and September; we booked the same cheap lodgings we had had before and ordered the tickets. Ken Russell moved into a spare room in Pamela's tiny London flat—an arrangement made while she was in Eastbourne—which livened things up considerably since Ken was so unpredictable. The roof over his room developed a leak, and on wet nights he slept on Pam's floor to avoid the incessant drips. If I were staying over, I did too—three sardines in a can again, a situation I was very used to by now. Ken was still trying to find his way, and life was not easy for him, especially as he sometimes seemed determined to shock and upset people. I think, though, that it delighted him to do so. Until the festival, I visited Shirley Slade and her mother, Helen, who lived in the beautiful Glastonbury area of Somerset. Then one of my artists suggested that I spend two weeks in the country with him and his family so that he could both work and be with them. Back in London, I worked in Chelsea with another artist. One day a friend of his dropped in—the Bloomsbury painter Duncan Grant. Not wishing to disturb his friend's work, Grant also drew me. I wonder if this undoubtedly excellent work of art exists somewhere. I was too shy to ask to see it.

All of this was very pleasant, but it was not dancing. As my trip to the Edinburgh Festival approached, however, I received a call from Michel offering me a part in a BBC production of *Coppélia*. The rehearsals and transmission coincided almost exactly with my festival plans. I could not believe it! Once again I was faced with the intense desire to be in two places at once. Of course I accepted Michel's offer and sat down with my calendar. As it turned out, it was possible for me to go to the last two days of the festival, and considering the program and the artists, I was profoundly grateful. My very tight schedule, then, was *Coppélia* on September 3; travel to Edinburgh on September 4; and attend the last two days of the festival on September 5 and 6 to hear Elgar's *The Dream of Gerontius*, op. 38, and Handel's *Messiah*, both performed by the Hallé Orchestra and Choir with Sir John Barbirolli and Kathleen Ferrier.

Barbirolli had persuaded the festival authorities to program *The Dream of Gerontius* with Richard Lewis as Gerontius and with Ferrier as the Angel, as well as Handel's *Messiah* with Irmgard Seefried, Ferrier, William Herbert, and Marian Nowakowski.[9] Barbirolli's main reason for wanting these works included in the festival was undoubtedly Ferrier's deteriorating health. When the time came, she was unwell and did not attend the *Messiah* rehearsal, undergoing radiation treatment instead.

[9]The other works Ferrier sang at the 1952 Edinburgh International Festival were the *Liebeslieder Walzer*, op. 52, of Johannes Brahms on August 2, and *Das Lied von der Erde* of Gustav Mahler, with tenor Julius Patzak and the Concertgebouw Orchestra conducted by Eduard van Beinum, on August 28. I am grateful to the festival's archivist, who sent me the program listings from 1947 to 1952.

Of the *Messiah* performance, Ferrier said, "It was so beautiful that it gave me one of the greatest experiences of my life."[10] I am sure this was true for all present, participants and audience alike. From my usual seat, high up at the center back of the Usher Hall, handkerchiefs began to appear like a flock of doves. There was a circle of them around the hall, so moving was the performance and somehow so significant the occasion. I had heard *Messiah* many times before, but I never again heard it after that night, August 5, 1952. I have tried to, but all I can do is leave. I feel that I truly heard it only once.

I was happy to have found the time to travel to Edinburgh, not only for the concerts but also to take my mind off what had been a very weak and disappointing production of *Coppélia*, despite fine performances by Domini Callaghan as Swanhilda and Michael Holmes as Dr. Coppelius. The following fall was also dull and provided few inspiring performing opportunities. Felix had come to an arrangement with Grace Cone and Olive Ripman that any extra dancers used in the *Ballet for Beginners* series would be seniors from their Arts Educational School, so that prospect was no longer open to me. There were no big television productions; these seemed to be reserved for the spring. And so, the only dance work I had until Christmas was a series of lecture-demonstrations for schools, arranged by Marie Bingham, who had been one of the pianists with London Theatre Ballet.

Again, I resumed my work with artists. I believe it was then that I met an American artist, Edward Hurst, who specialized in cultivating wealthy women and persuading them to have their portraits painted. He lived in a luxurious house in Eaton Square (remember *Upstairs, Downstairs*?) and gave frequent soirées to which those ladies, already enamored of him, brought more wide-eyed, adoring, prospective clientele. Eddie was actually a very genuine, nice man. He simply possessed the art of flattery, both in himself and in his painting style. Some of his clients wanted to learn the art of portrait painting—or did they just wish another evening with Eddie? Anyway, I sat for him, which meant good money and delicious food. Eddie did everything right. One day he decided he wanted to paint a serious picture for exhibition and asked me to sit for him as a Madonna. I was not very enthusiastic, but in retrospect the picture, both the sketch (inexplicably reproduced in *Ballet Today*) and the finished work are the few pictures ever painted of the full "me."[11] I don't know where the final version went, probably to the United States one day.

In November I got a ride to Manchester to see Jean, who was in the touring company of *Carousel*. She had some good reviews as the second lead dancer. One was Hannah, the other "the youngest Miss Snow" in the party dance. Jean was excellent. She displayed dramatic ability and a great sense of the comic. I felt very proud of her.

[10]Winifred Ferrier, *The Life of Kathleen Ferrier* (London: Hamilton, 1969), 168.

[11]"Madonna Dancer," *Ballet Today* 6 (September 1953), 7. Wendy's chaste picture of her modeling career appears not to be wholly accurate. According to Molly Kenny Galvin, who appears a bit later in this story, Wendy introduced her to working as an artist's model, and both modeled nude. Wendy preferred the jobs where she could lie down because they were less tiring. She passed the jobs that required standing to Molly. Molly Kenny Galvin, interview by Susan Bindig, October 22, 2005. — SB

And then, in late 1952, by chance, I met Belinda Quirey, an event that at the time did not seem to be of great significance, except that it provided some immediate work on television.[12]

It was the first day of ticket sales for upcoming performances of Gluck's *Orfeo* at Covent Garden, with Ferrier in the title role. Four were scheduled, the first on February 3, and I bought tickets for Pamela and me for all of them. That accomplished, I walked on to the Stoll Theatre (now gone) to see a friend at a *Ballet for Beginners* rehearsal. Belinda was there. From the first, she seemed a very unusual person.

Belinda was born in Northern Ireland into a family with four daughters, of which she was the second. She studied at University College, London, where she developed a deep interest in the ancient Greeks. Her real love and lifelong passion, though, was ballroom dancing, and she eventually gave up her studies of the Greeks in favor of dance. Belinda studied with Eve Tynegate Smith and landed her first dance job as a coach at the prestigious Gleneagle Hotel. She also explored the work of Rudolf von Laban, whom she greatly admired, and she studied ballet with Laura Wilson. Her introduction to what was to be her life's work came unexpectedly when she answered an advertisement in the *London Times* placed by Melusine Wood, who was looking for trained bodies to pursue reconstruction work on dances from the fifteenth to the eighteenth centuries.

In the Stoll Theatre rehearsal room, Felix introduced me to Belinda who, it seemed, was looking for two dancers to be "Elizabethan savages" in a television show starring Elton Hayes (well known to radio and television audiences of the 1950s as the man "who sang to a small guitar"). She explained about her work in early dance and regretted that this particular show could only be pseudo early dance and not in the noble style but rather the grotesque. "But you'll be paid," she said gleefully. The other savage turned out to be my friend from the movies, Shirley Slade. The show was a miserable experience. Shirley and I danced low to the ground around the star, sweating under full-face leather masks. Belinda did her best, but there was little to attract me to follow up on the field of early dance, and it was quite a long time before I saw Belinda again.

At least I had *Orfeo* and Ferrier to look forward to.

[12]I wrote in *Dance Research* that I met Belinda in January 1953, when in fact it was in late 1952. "Belinda Quirey MBE: A Tribute from Her Friends," *Dance Research* 16 (Winter 1998), 44–66.

Four: 1953–1954

Walter Gore Ballet ~ Grace Cone, Theatre Arts Ballet, and Early Choreography ~ Modeling for Portraits of Elizabeth II ~ Pauline Grant and the London Palladium

Four performances of Gluck's *Orfeo*, conducted by Sir John Barbirolli, with Kathleen Ferrier in the title role were scheduled to take place at Covent Garden during February 1953. Ferrier was losing her battle with cancer, however, and in the end, only two took place. Pamela and I attended both performances and also the dress rehearsal.

The first performance on February 3 was reviewed by Neville Cardus, the celebrated music critic for the *Manchester Guardian* and one of Ferrier's biographers. Enraptured by Ferrier's performance, he wrote, "Seldom has Covent Garden Opera House been so beautifully solemnised as when Kathleen Ferrier flooded the place with tone which seemed as though classic shapes in marble were changing to melody, warm, rich throated, but chaste."[1] Those qualities were also inherent in her every movement. Richard Buckle wrote in the *Observer*, "And none of the dancers moved with a more expressive simplicity than Kathleen Ferrier whose physical as well as vocal impersonation of Apollo's child is something I shall long remember." Buckle's review tickled Ferrier, who was inclined to think of herself as a klutz, never knowing what to do with her feet. Mary Clarke wrote similarly in the *Dancing Times*, a review that I don't think Ferrier ever saw, as the *Dancing Times* was a trade paper.

Oddly, Ferrier's performance reminded me of my brief work with Belinda. During the rehearsals, Belinda contrasted our work as savages with her passion: the baroque noble style of dance. In Ferrier's personal style surely was the essence of what Belinda wanted to convey to us—nobility of presence, mind, and spirit.

The first glorious performance of *Orfeo* went smoothly, but in the middle of the second, Ferrier suddenly began to limp slightly while crossing a ramp toward a staircase that she had to descend to complete Orfeo's return from the Elysian Fields. Her singing and bearing were totally unimpaired, the impression being that an ankle had merely been turned. It was not until a letter from Ferrier to a friend was published in 1955 that the public learned that she "broke the ligaments and a piece of bone of the hip in the middle of an Orpheus performance."[2] After the performance, which she finished, Ferrier was taken to the hospital. All her performances for the next two months were cancelled. In my heart of hearts I knew we had seen the last one, but hope dies hard. We and the others lucky enough to have been there, though, had indeed seen Ferrier's last performance in the role she seemed absolutely to have been born to sing.

[1]Neville Cardus, *Kathleen Ferrier: A Memoir* (London: Hamish Hamilton, 1954).
[2]Winifred Ferrier, *The Life of Kathleen Ferrier* (London: Hamilton, 1969), 176.

It must have been about the time of the performance of *Orfeo* that Jean and I received notice from Walter Gore saying that funding for his company had been promised. Were we still available and interested? We were! Jean and I had waited almost three years for this tantalizing dream to become a reality. Working with a great and highly respected artist like Gore was prestigious indeed and a big step forward in my career. As I recall, a plentiful eight weeks of rehearsal began in March for a tour to the Midland towns of Malvern and Cheltenham scheduled for May and June. Another rehearsal period would follow to expand the eight-ballet repertoire and make improvements for a London season beginning in September at the Prince's Theatre.

It was with enormous happiness and eager anticipation that Jean and I went to the first day of rehearsal. Wally, as he was affectionately known, was the first choreographer I had worked with in the creative process. As with many modern choreographers, he worked with the cast as it stood in front of him, creating section upon section. We dancers were required to stand absolutely still as he visualized the next steps and spatial moves. Once, I scratched my nose during a "quiet time" and Wally reprimanded me. Nonetheless, the process was exciting to me at first because it was so new and so interesting to see a work flower. Soon, though, my muscles began to react badly to the periods of stillness followed by periods of activity, and I expect everyone else's did too.

I think we were about two weeks into rehearsal when Jean and I celebrated our birthdays, my twenty-second, her twenty-sixth. We did so with a very spicy Indian lunch and wept throughout. We had not eaten spicy Indian food before. We looked quite tragic at the beginning of our afternoon rehearsal—inappropriately as the eight ballets for the tour were of a pleasant, funny, light, or tender nature.

The ballets we prepared for two programs were *Mr. Punch* (1946, Arthur Oldham), *Hoops* (1951, François Poulenc), *Street Games* (1952, Jacques Ibert), *Romantic Evening* (1952, Stephen Heller), *The Gentle Poltergeist* (1953, Gabriel Fauré), *Light Fantastic* (1953, Emmanuel Chabrier), *Classical Suite* (1953, Gioacchino Antonio Rossini), and an eighth, the name of which I cannot remember or document.[3] The complex score for *Mr. Punch* was composed for the ballet; music for the others was selected from existing pieces.

Wally had a very personal choreographic style. He was not naturally drawn to the romantic and especially classical idioms, but ballets such as *Romantic Evening* and *Classical Suite* would attract provincial audiences. For the latter, he hired Domini Callaghan as the star. Paula Hinton, the leading female dancer of the company and Wally's wife, was a brilliant dramatic dancer but by no means a strong classical one; this would be one of her ballets "off." I danced in *The Gentle Poltergeist*, *Romantic Evening*, *Classical Suite*, and with Jean

[3]Sources with comprehensive listings of Gore's ballets do not shed light on what the eighth ballet may have been. Clement Crisp, "Walter Gore's Choreographies," *Dance Research* 6, no. 1 (Spring 1988), 23–29; Katherine Sorley Walker, "Walter Gore," in *International Dictionary of Ballet*, ed. Martha Bremser (Detroit, MI: St. James Press, 1993), 1:590–93.

was one of the two scene-shifters in the hilarious *Mr. Punch*, in which Wally was brilliant in the title role.

The first weeks of rehearsals went smoothly and on schedule, but then we began to fall behind. No explanation was given. Wally was undoubtedly one of the greatest dramatic dancer-choreographers of his time, but he seemed to have trouble communicating. He was the most silent man I have ever met; sometimes even a simple "hello" seemed difficult. With growing apprehension, it began to dawn on us that although Wally was a brilliant creative artist and performer, he was not a good organizer. In that area he needed serious help.

Jean and I became really worried some weeks into rehearsal when we went to our first and, as it turned out, only *Mr. Punch* rehearsal. The entrances and exits of the two scene-shifters with a screen were vital to the plot because the efficient placements of the screen brought about scene changes or provided a hiding place for Mr. Punch. We had some eight entrances and exits with the screen. At this rehearsal none of the rest of the cast was present. Wally took us through the various entrances and exits but never with the music between each segment being played. We were left feeling very much in limbo. How would we know our cues? Just hearing them might have helped. After all, Arthur Oldham's score was not simple. Wally concluded the rehearsal with the remark, "It will be easier with the set."

Jean and I had seen *Mr. Punch* and did not see eye-to-eye with this expression of optimism. The set for *Mr. Punch* was a closed room. To see onto the stage and enter, one had to open a door. Entrance cues could not, therefore, be provided by glimpsing what was going on. If we had been given a chance to become totally familiar with the very modern score, there would have been some hope. "Well," said Jean, "there will be the dress rehearsal."

The other ballet that caused me problems in rehearsal was *Classical Suite*. To begin with, my partner, Norman Dixon, was a little too short for me, making for a tricky collaboration. The choreography had many supported pirouettes—to the right, of course, on my weak left foot. My old Achilles tendon injury started to play up, and I feared the worst. Domini said it was the most difficult classical choreography she had ever been asked to dance because it was so terribly awkward.

The choreography called for three or four supporting couples surrounding Domini and Michel de Lutry who danced only pas de deux; they had no solos as I recall. One day, late in the game, Paula came to rehearsal and danced a long solo in the middle of the ballet. It was carefully choreographed to show her classical strengths and none of her weaknesses. Domini was highly insulted. *Classical Suite* was her ballet! She disappeared from the studio, followed by Michel, and wept. After some discussion, they returned and behaved with great dignity. As a result of this episode, it was made clear to Wally that they would leave the company when the tour ended.

Jean and I were dismayed and beginning to be disillusioned about our adored Wally. We were also alarmed that the entire repertoire was not in better shape before we went on tour.

When we left for Malvern, about 130 miles northwest of London, we knew that there had been some delay in finishing the costumes. We were assured, however, that they would arrive on Monday afternoon on the one o'clock train, just in time for our evening performance. In the meantime, there was trouble with the size of the set of *Light Fantastic*, and so Monday morning was given over to organizing it to fit the stage. This meant that we would have an afternoon dress rehearsal—a rehearsal that we needed badly but in the end never had.

The costumes did arrive on schedule, but some were only cut out and others only partially sewn. Wally didn't say a word and shut himself in his dressing room until the performance. The wardrobe mistress, clearly distraught by the momentous task of finishing the costumes in such a short time, screamed and sat us down with needles and thread. The costumes for *Classical Suite* were of course tutus, far beyond our sewing skills, so she undertook to finish those. We tackled the others. We sewed and sewed. To this day I don't understand why the costumes were not properly finished. Perhaps Wally knew, but he didn't explain, just as he never expressed his appreciation for our help in getting them ready for our performance.

The performance that night was unbelievably dreadful. Early in *Classical Suite*, the crotch of my tutu split as Norman placed me in a lift to sit on his shoulder for a promenade for four couples around the stage. I slid to the ground, and we both walked "proudly" for what seemed an awfully long time. In the pirouettes, my unanchored tutu seemed to act like a sail, throwing me off balance, while the loose fabric around my waist gave Norman nothing secure to grip as I went around. My problem foot felt all of it.

Mr. Punch was next. Jean and I had still had only the one piecemeal rehearsal in the studio in London. With the entirely closed set, to see the stage, as I mentioned, you had to open a door. So, of course, we had no idea when our moves came. Wally, in the title role, spent the entire ballet calling us on to the stage, telling us in gesture where to put the screen and then when to take it off. It was worse than we ever dreamed it might be.

The third ballet, whichever it was, may have gone smoothly; I don't remember. But there was a half-hour intermission before the fourth ballet, *Light Fantastic*, owing to the unexpected complexity of the set change. Since the buses stop running early in the evening in the provinces, most of the audience, except those with cars, had left by the time *Light Fantastic* began. Or maybe they were just bored by what must have seemed an interminable wait.

Jean, Norman, and I left the theater and began to walk to our digs in gloomy silence. Gradually, though, as we remembered the events of the performance, we began to giggle and then to laugh loudly and somewhat hysterically because the future looked bleak.

We must have given better performances during the remaining one or two weeks in Malvern, but I have no memory of them. I think I struggled through one more *Classical Suite* before my foot could no longer take the strain. Wally never spoke to me about it, although he must have known how upset I was. The other dancers and I hoped for better things in Cheltenham, where we would have the luxury of an orchestra to play for us.

The week we arrived in Cheltenham was Coronation Week. Elizabeth II was to be crowned on June 2, and celebrations were planned throughout Britain. While our stint in Cheltenham was not part of any festivity surrounding the crowning of the new queen, the lively spirit that pervaded England at that time made this a particularly happy engagement.

We were booked at the Center for the Cotswold Hills. Working with an orchestra, even a pickup group, was to be such a treat for us—or so we thought. At rehearsal the conductor concentrated on the three most difficult scores first, which took the whole three hours allotted. He left unrehearsed the suite of keyboard pieces by Heller for *Romantic Evening*, which had been orchestrated. The conductor, however, was not worried. "Nothing to that," he said. In a way he was right because at several places in that evening's performance there literally *was* nothing; the orchestra simply did not play. The first instance was the most serious. Michel had a solo that began with a jump, and the orchestra was supposed to come in when he landed. After his third false start, Michel just kept going. Gradually a few instruments began to play, the first I remember was a lone cello. From there until the end of the ballet, parts of the orchestra came and went. Sometimes we had the top parts, sometimes the bass, and infrequently the whole orchestra played together. It seems that the conductor, in his overconfidence, had not even bothered to check through the score before the performance and upon turning the page to Michel's solo had found a note from the arranger: "So sorry old chap. Haven't had time to finish this bit."

Jean and I, and I presume the whole company, returned to London in low spirits. My dreams of a rewarding artistic future with Walter Gore were shattered. I am sure that Wally was not feeling too cheerful either. He had to regroup the company for the London season, due to start on August 22. Domini and Michel went their own way. Jean was retained by Wally, as was a beautiful Australian dancer, Mary Duschesne. I with my foot predictably was not.

The reviews of the London season indicate that the chaos continued. I neither attended any performances nor, at the time, saw the reviews as I felt I needed a change of scene. I visited Shirley and Helen to cry on their shoulders. Clive Barnes, reviewing the London performances, wrote one paragraph that, to me, summarized the whole sad state of affairs with Wally's company. I should love to have written it in Cheltenham.

> No man can run a ballet company single-handed. As a person who most devoutly wants to see the Gore Company establish itself firmly in the world of ballet, I do implore Gore to appoint an associate artistic director. I feel sure that such a person, if worth his salt, would not have let *Cyclasm* pass into performance in its present state. One sympathises with the sincerity and originality of the work but much of it remains tedious and obscure.[4]

[4]Clive Barnes, "New Ballets by Walter Gore," *Dance and Dancers* (November 1953), 15.

I resumed concert- and theater-going and, on October 8, remember attending the Sadler's Wells Opera with a music-critic friend of mine, Hugh S. Reed, who wrote for *Musical Opinion*. The opera was, I believe, Verdi's *Nabucco*. I had great difficulty concentrating. Perhaps I had some foreboding of the news to greet us the next day.

On the morning of October 8, Kathleen Ferrier died, and the newspapers the next day were flooded with the story, moving obituaries, and photographs. The musical population of the world was torn apart with shock and a desperate sense of loss. In my experience, only the death of Princess Diana compares in terms of the reaction of the populace.

Within the short space of only six years, two of the most beloved singers in the world had sung for the last time, both on the Covent Garden stage, each crippled by a form of cancer. Both finished their performances —Richard Tauber on July 27, 1947, and Kathleen Ferrier on February 6, 1953—against seemingly insuperable odds and showing incredible courage and determination. These two singers had special qualities that endeared them to a very wide audience and made them especially important to many—and to me, above all other singers of the day. Both had voices of exceptional beauty, and they possessed great musicianship and the ability to communicate the emotional content of music immediately and deeply to the listener.

That same morning, at about eleven o'clock, our phone rang. It was Grace Cone with much-needed uplifting news. She and her sister Lily, with Felicity Grey, were about to start a small group called the Theatre Arts Ballet. The group would consist of dancers from *Ballet for Beginners* and students of the Arts Educational School. The company would visit schools mainly in the London area with the purpose of creating further interest in ballet among young people. Felix had suggested me as a young choreographer who might be interested in creating a piece for the group.

I went to see Grace Cone that afternoon. For a rich woman, she was certainly not generous and offered me a ridiculously low fee for my proposed work. Felix was furious and made her raise the amount—even so, it was negligible, although today I couldn't tell you what the fee finally was.

Grace wanted a ten-minute piece for about three dancers. I remember very little about the concept of the piece I devised, but it was titled "You Had a Friend," to music by Alan Rawsthorne, his Four Bagatelles for Piano, with spoken text by A. V. Coton. The choreography was experimental for its day. I was fascinated by the idea of conveying a lot with very little, a kind of minimalistic approach to choreography. The story told of a young man and the two very different women he was drawn to. It was danced by Margarita Tate, Denys Palmer, and Susan Richter. The text was spoken by Leslie Crowether, who later became a well-known children's television presenter, comedian, and actor. Many found the piece full of potential, although the spoken text confused some. Susan Lester in *Ballet Today* found the story and emotion more than adequately conveyed by the choreography but was baffled by my use of Coton's text.[5]

The year 1954 was very black for me—and for Dorothy too, who had to endure the disapproval and we-told-you-so's of Gerald and Muriel, coupled with thoughts like, "Why doesn't Wendy find something practical to do? It's time she gave up this nonsense" and "Surely one day she will get married?" Well, the answer as far as I was concerned was no on all counts! After the fiascos of Dorothy's life and my total disinterest in things domestic, the idea of setting up house was not for me. In any case, I am not one to give up—although at this point, following the events of 1953, I felt emotionally more dead than alive.

I, of course, continued to take ballet classes, but I had no offers to perform. To add to my misery, my close friends were gone or married—Jean was on tour; Pamela had married an old friend, John Tomlinson, and I was definitely a crowd where they were concerned. My concert-going friend from our Rambert days, Araminta Steer, had married a television producer, Henry Caldwell. Tragically for Minty, Henry, who was somewhat older than she, died suddenly early in their marriage. Minty, then, seemed literally to drop off the face of the earth. I looked for her, hoping that she had overcome her grief, but I never found her.

One aspect of my work that flourished was modeling and the use of my hands by painters. Following the coronation, I was in great demand for the many portraits of Elizabeth II, which had been commissioned for public buildings and similar venues. My hands found their way into four paintings of the Queen. For one of the portraits, the artist surreptitiously had me wear the Queen's dress because of the fabric folds. When we were finished, we had to make sure that the dress gave off no sense of body warmth as someone was coming from Buckingham Palace shortly thereafter to collect it. I was not particularly thrilled by this arrangement, but Dorothy, as you might imagine, certainly was. I was not supposed to tell anyone about wearing the Queen's dress, but I did tell.

My reaction to seeing my hands attached to the Queen caused me to wonder about other hands in paintings. Why will someone else's hands do? They are such a singular feature of a person, their shape and size varying distinctively from person to person. Now I look at all portraits with the greatest suspicion.

One other development helped my spirits during 1954. The ballet critic A. V. Coton had the habit of liking to be seen at performances with young dancers whom he considered about to become known. For most of 1954, I was his companion at almost everything he saw, providing me with the rare and wonderful opportunity to see more dance than I ever could have on my own. But my star dimmed, and by the next year Coton was on the lookout

[5] A. V. Coton and Susan Lester, "Theatre Arts Ballet," *Ballet Today* (January 1954).

for the next up-and-coming dancer to escort to concerts, and I returned to fending for myself.

At the end of November of a very long and depressing year, I attended an audition for the very popular London Palladium Christmas pantomime and was accepted. A pantomime was not my idea of a desirable job, but I signed a three-month contract. Dorothy was so relieved, and even Gerald and Muriel were impressed. Christmas pantomimes are annual theater fare in most British cities and towns. The stories are traditional, such as "Mother Goose," "Dick Whittington and His Cat," "Jack and the Beanstalk," and the like. The tales are interspersed with popular songs, variety acts, and ballet sequences. Traditionally, the hero, the principal boy, is played by a woman.

The annual pantomime at England's premier variety theater, the London Palladium, was considered the cream of the crop. To be in the cast of one of these productions was very prestigious. For the dancers at least, prestige was the only benefit, as the pay was eleven pounds a week for two shows a day. Dancers in musicals, meanwhile, were earning about twenty-five pounds for eight shows a week.

In the early fifties, the established arranger of ballets for the Palladium pantomime was Pauline Grant. For the 1954 Christmas production of *Mother Goose*,[6] she needed thirty-six female dancers.[7] About two hundred turned up for the auditions. From de Vos's studio, several dancers were chosen—Juliet Prowse, Jennifer Trevelyan, Susan Richter, and me.

Additionally, three principal dancers, two men and one woman, were needed. The men who had already been engaged, Michael Bayston and David Davenport, former dancers with the Sadler's Wells Ballet, were acceptable to Pauline (oops! excuse me, Miss Grant). The woman, however, proved to be past her prime. (Her name I've mercifully forgotten.) She had to be replaced. One of the stars of the show, Max Bygraves, had noticed Juliet's technical ability as well as her beauty and suggested that she take over as principal dancer. Miss Grant agreed, and Juliet's foot was set upon the ladder to her future stardom.

The others stars in *Mother Goose* were Peter Sellers (of *Pink Panther* fame) as an Evil Squire, a riot on stage when he was supposed to be and also in his frequent sotto voce ad libbing, and Richard Hearne, a highly regarded comic actor and television star, in drag as Mother Goose. Well-known musical comedy actress and singer Margaret Burton played the principal boy. In the middle of one of her songs, Sellers suddenly murmured, "Oh, you underwater soprano, you." As usual he hit the nail on the head, as Margaret did indeed sound like a slightly submerged singer blowing bubbles. Margaret got the giggles and coughed through the rest of the song. Sellers always set

[6]The full title of the production was *Val Parnell's Seventh Magnificent Christmas Pantomime, "Mother Goose."* Parnell directed the show, written by Phil Park and Erik Sykes. Ed Sikov, *Mr. Strangelove: A Biography of Peter Sellers* (New York: Hyperion, 2002), 86. Mark Fox of the London Palladium provided Wendy with a copy of the program for *Mother Goose* from the theater's private collection. — SB

[7]Later in the chapter, Wendy indicates that a total of thirty dancers appeared in the production. As the program lists only the lead dancers, the exact number in the chorus, thirty or thirty-six, could not be determined. — SB

Figure 11. "Crystallized Fruits," *Mother Goose*, London Palladium, 1954. Photo by Matthews—News and Photoagency.

Figure 12. Detail of "Crystallized Fruits." Wendy *(far left)* and Susan Richter (*right*) as Green Grapes.

everyone off, even though the dancers were severely reprimanded if they laughed onstage.[8]

Dancers found Pauline Grant to be very efficient and organized in the handling of large groups but lacking in artistic sensibility and a sense of humor. Her creations, however, were certainly appropriate and successful fare for the pantomime family audiences.

Mother Goose contained two ballet scenes. The first was "Sammy's Dream," rather unsurprisingly for a Christmas ballet set to pieces from Tchaikovsky's *The Nutcracker*. One dance in which I performed, "Crystallised Fruits," was to the music for the "Chinese Dance" from Act II and was for seven pairs of dancers representing bright, differently colored fruit candies. At the opening of the dance, all the fruits were gathered in a Chinese-style pagoda and were raised to the stage from below. The front of the pagoda opened and then lowered to become a steep ramp to the stage, down which, couple by couple, the dancers plunged to run on full pointe to their designated places. There was a four-inch-wide, half-inch-high wooden block across the middle of the ramp, which had to be avoided during the precipitous descent. Susie and I were green grapes, who somehow became the downstage center couple. While all the other couples moved to places at the sides of the stage, thus breaking the impetus of their descent, Susie and I headed straight for the orchestra pit, where members of the orchestra who were not playing sat with outstretched arms and hopeful grins.

The first sequence of the dance was awkward and certainly did not easily follow a precipitous run. Loud shouts from Miss Grant helped us get through the sequence in rehearsals. Memories of her shouts lingered in performances. In one of the opening sequences, both dancers in each pair first made a whole turn to the right on both pointes ("STAY UP!" cried Miss Grant). They then raised the right leg and did a double rond de jambe ("STAY UP!") while standing on the left pointe and fell onto the right pointe with a bent knee. After the turn, Susie and I grabbed the backs of each other's dresses for support, so that we could be sure to obey Miss Grant's adamant "UP!" during the rond de jambe.

The next part of the dance that was filled with a potential for disaster was a tight, weaving figure for the fourteen fruits. When we were learning it, someone went the wrong way one time and everyone ended in a pile of interwoven limbs on the floor. I laughed. After all, it *was* funny. Miss Grant did not laugh. Instead, she threatened me with removal from the dance if I laughed again. As things were going, I would not have considered that a punishment.

Always in trouble, really through no fault of my own, I was doomed with Pauline Grant. In one of the scenes for all thirty dancers, a cut in the choreography had to be made, no easy task. The London Palladium has a

[8] In *Mr. Strangelove*, Sikov notes that Max Bygraves described Sellers's behavior in this production similarly, saying that "Sellers couldn't help but depart from the script and improvise throughout the show's run." Sikov, 86. Seller's shenanigans, however delightful for Wendy and the rest of the cast, almost cost him his job. Roger Lewis, *The Life and Death of Peter Sellers* (London: Century, 1994), 117–18. — SB

large stage, and to make a cut leaving everyone in the right place for the following sequence was a challenge. Finally it seemed done, but to make sure, Miss Grant asked any dancer who was in the wrong place to raise a hand. Mine was the only one to go up. I shuddered. I was on the opposite side of the stage to where I should have been. And surely if I were in the wrong place, my opposite must have been as well. Where was her hand? Miss Grant was terribly frustrated—understandably—but could not admit her error. "Oh, Wendy," she said in exasperation, "why do you always make difficulties?"

The pantomime ran its course. Susie and I managed to avoid the orchestra pit, enjoyed every minute of Peter Sellers, and found no challenges in the second, reasonably pleasant ballet set to music from Mendelssohn's *A Midsummer Night's Dream*. In that ballet, I remember only Jennifer Trevelyan and a lyrical solo, which she danced most beautifully.

The dancers participated in one more event at the Palladium that year, the Royal Command Performance, an annual event showcasing the finest of English variety and featuring favorite performers of the reigning monarch, then Elizabeth II. We dancers did it strictly for the money, which almost equaled a whole week's pay from the pantomime. We were engaged not to dance but to be screaming fans of one of the artists—whom, I don't recall. I think Gregory Peck was somehow involved in this event, but I cannot remember or imagine how. I just remember seeing his handsome face in the entrance to the theater. Perhaps we were his fans.

I don't recall most of the other acts. There was a very vulgar group of comedians, the Crazy Gang, high on the list of the Queen's favorites. There was also a really very good and very funny water act. (I seemed destined to be in shows with water acts.) The Nitwits, a group of ten men led by Sid Millward and Wally Stewart, mixed hilarious water complications with the music they played.[9] Like the "Crystallised Fruits" dancers, they were raised to the stage from below, and Susie and I used to laugh and talk with them about our entrance. After the Palladium engagement, I used to try to see them whenever they were close by on the variety circuit. Forever ingrained on my mind is the tune "Cool Water" to which they did their brilliant comedy routine.

[9] Wendy may have confused the two Palladium performances, as the Nitwits appeared on the bill of *Mother Goose*; see Chris Woodwards, *London Palladium: The Story of the Theatre and Its Stars* (Lindley, Huddersfield, UK: Jeremy Mills Publishing, 2009), 165. Their participation in the 1954 Royal Command Performance could not be determined. — SB

Five: 1955–1957

West Country Ballet and The Selchie ~ *Bolshoi Ballet at Covent Garden* ~ *Geraldine Stephenson,* The Tempest, *and* The Prince of Purpoole ~ *Maria Fay*

It was not long after the pantomime closed that I received a phone call from Shirley Slade telling me that she was planning to start a small ballet company, the West Country Ballet, with the backing and support of Helen Wingrave. Helen was an enthusiastic figure in the English world of national dance and was admired as a committee member and examiner of the National Dance Faculty of the Imperial Society of Teachers of Dancing (ISTD). Her support was very important for this undertaking. Although a regional company, all rehearsals would be in London. (For the new endeavor, Shirley decided to adopt a professional name, Frances Crossley, and I will henceforth refer to her by that name.)

The company was to have a rather unique mission—to combine classical ballet and folk dance in a new way. This mission was explained in the program for the company's premiere at a fringe event at the Edinburgh International Festival in the late summer of 1955:

> This Company has been formed with a definite and original policy, which is, to produce new works of wide and popular appeal, drawing for inspiration on British Tradition in music, literature, folklore, dancing and everyday life.
>
> We hope to provide a bridge between the folk dance enthusiast and the devotee of strictly Classical ballet, by blending the two dance forms and applying the result to show, in exciting and expressive dancing, various aspects, humorous or sad, of our national heritage.

The purpose of Frances's phone call was to tell me about the company, the repertoire of three ballets that was to be given in Edinburgh, and to ask me to dance in and choreograph one of them, *The Selchie*. The other two works on the program were to be *Black-Eyed Susan*, choreographed by Elizabeth West to music by Alec Rowley, and *Herne the Hunter*, choreographed by Michael Holmes to sixteenth-century music selections arranged by Edgar Hunt. If the company was successful in Edinburgh, plans would be made for a London season the following year.

The idea of *The Selchie* appealed to me and, of course, I was very happy at the idea of going to the Edinburgh Festival as a performer, even if only in a side event. Working on *The Selchie* proved very enjoyable. At last I was choreographing my own ballet and was dancing with an excellent dancer, Ronnie Curran, a former soloist with the Ballets Jooss. A synopsis of *The Selchie*, devised by Frances, was given in the Edinburgh program:

> It is an ancient belief on the western Coast that seals can take human form, but if anyone steals their skins they are unable to return to the sea. . . . This is the story of Angus and Jeannie, who on their betrothal day were nearly separated by one of the seal people.

Curran, himself a Scot, danced the role of Angus with Frances as Jeannie; I was the Selchie. But there were problems with the ballet. One was that I did not actually choreograph the whole ballet. It ended with a wedding celebration in which the only dancing was purely authentic Scottish and Highland dancing staged by Pipe Major P. T. Quinn to music that he played on the bagpipes. I think this also affected the inspiration of the composer of the rest of the ballet, Michael Hobson, whose score, although pleasant and very workable, was not inspiring to me. Nonetheless, *The Selchie* proved the most successful of the three ballets we presented—perhaps not surprisingly since it had a Scottish theme. My dancers and I received very favorable reviews in the Edinburgh press. One critic wrote, "The right atmosphere is created, Wendy Hilton's carefully stylised dancing and imaginative treatment of the theme contrasting well with the more traditional Scots dancing on [*sic*] the humans."

One of the many advantages of our run in Edinburgh was that we shared our theater, the very small Prince's Theatre, with the Edinburgh Play Club. When the Club was performing its three daily events, we had some free time to attend main festival presentations and some of the Usher Hall rehearsals. Outstanding for me was my first live encounter with the Berlin Philharmonic Orchestra. On June 20, their program included Beethoven's *Eroica.* The conductor was Joseph Keilberth. It dawned on me that I had never heard such a great orchestra, and I left the hall filled with wonder.[1]

The Edinburgh season proved successful enough, and we looked forward to further engagements, starting in London if something could be arranged. London, therefore, would be the real testing ground of the West Country Ballet.

Performances in London were finally scheduled for May 17–18, 1956, at the Rudolf Steiner Hall, under the auspices of the London Ballet Circle. The stage seemed enormous after our tiny space in Edinburgh.

Figure 13. Wendy in *The Selchie*, West Country Ballet, 1955. Photo by G. B. L. Wilson. Reproduced by permission from the Royal Academy of Dance, London.

[1]The Berlin Philharmonic remained my favorite orchestra.

Two ballets were added to the repertoire, one by me called *A Short Story* to music by New Zealand composer Edwin Carr. I tried to continue to work on my "minimalistic" technique begun in *You Had a Friend*, but this time the result was to me a dull failure. One critic, however, whose name I can't remember or track down, wrote that the piece was "unusual and extremely well designed." The other new ballet, *Arcadian Suite*, by company member Iain Montague, was a sad affair. Cyril Beaumont wrote in the Sunday *Times* that the ballet "should be promptly eliminated." He, however, spoke well of *The Selchie*, calling it the most novel on the program.[2] The critic who had enjoyed my *Short Story* also wrote favorably of *The Selchie* and of me, saying that the ballet "was both original and exciting and extremely well produced" and that I was "a fresh and intelligent choreographer . . . no carbon copy of [my] contemporaries." A. V. Coton was particularly supportive of my work, writing:

> The smartest choreographic talent here is that of Wendy Hilton, whose works, "Short Story" and "The Selchie," are distinguished because of their absolute difference from all other contemporary English offerings.[3]

Despite these and other favorable reviews of my work, I now abandoned minimalism. In the end, I think my search was really for simplicity, but I had been on a wrong path.

The London reviews of the West Country Ballet were certainly mixed but contained many complimentary remarks. So it is perhaps surprising that the company did not fare better. The London performances were its last because, I think, the company and the repertoire lacked theatrical excitement. In retrospect, the basic problem may have been that the stated aim of the company, that of "blending" the forms of ballet and folk dance, was, as seen by Frances and Helen, doomed from the start. *The Selchie* was a perfect example of a good idea gone wrong, if indeed it ever could succeed. In the piece, as Frances directed it, there was no blending. The story was told and then a huge chunk of authentic Scottish dancing, complete with bagpipes, was tacked onto the end. People were disturbed by the stylistic and aesthetic conflict.

Additionally, to promote a new company requires endless initiative and ceaseless drive, qualities that Frances did not fully possess. Elizabeth West, however, did have such qualities, and she and company member Peter Darrell established a new company, the Western Theatre Ballet, which possibly drew some benefits from the similarity of its title to that of West Country Ballet. Be that as it may, the Western Theatre Ballet thrived, and the West Country Ballet disbanded.

For Frances and Helen, the failure of the company was devastating. Frances as a result entered a secretarial course in search of financial security. For me, the experience and quite extensive press coverage had been advantageous. Ironically, however, the West Country Ballet would be the last ballet company with which I would actually dance, although I continued to work in ballet for several more years.

[2] Cyril Beaumont, "Ballet," *London Times*, May 20, 1956

[3] A. V. Coton, "Ballet with a Difference: Folklore Tales," *Daily Telegraph* (London), n.d.

As fate dictates, it was the demise of the West Country Ballet that led the way to my studying historical dance seriously with Belinda Quirey. But in the meantime, my next work was to be with a choreographer, primarily of theater and television, Geraldine Stephenson, whose choreography incorporated period dance styles.

A momentous dance event for me occurred in the summer of 1956—the Bolshoi Ballet came to Covent Garden. Galina Ulanova was still dancing. For the first and only time, I slept outside overnight to obtain tickets to a performance. My companions were Susie Richter and her fiancé, John Sandler. We took all kinds of things to keep us warm and created a sort of make-do shack alongside Bow Street Police Station opposite the Garden. The inmates complained bitterly at the noise made by those in the queue. They could not sleep, they said.

In the morning, it took several hours to reach the box office as many people before us had slept outside for three nights. Like everyone else, I was seeking to see the legendary Ulanova, who was to dance in *Giselle* and *Romeo and Juliet.* No casting schedule was available, and so no one knew which dancers they would see on any given nights. And by the time we reached the box office, tickets were available for those ballets only on two consecutive nights in the middle of the season. We took them.

Principal dancers in Russian companies usually danced only once a week at most. They were well looked after. At the *Giselle* performance, we were overjoyed that Ulanova danced, her Albrecht being the superb artist Nikolai Fadeyechev. The next night we returned to Covent Garden, very grateful for the good fortune of having seen Ulanova once. But when we opened our programs, we gasped with joy and amazement. Ulanova was to dance again as Juliet. It has always been unbelievable to me that she danced in the two performances for which I had been able to get tickets. They rank as the greatest dance experiences of my life. I remain eternally grateful that I saw them.

I again saw the Bolshoi later that season at, I believe, the Davis Theatre in Croydon. I saw *Swan Lake* with Raisa Struchkova and three performances of divertissements, two of which featured Ulanova dancing Fokine's *The Dying Swan.*

Particularly after the Covent Garden performances, I walked about in a daze for several days. Seeing the Bolshoi as they were then reminded me of Mrs. Plumb's descriptions of Russian dancers. This was ballet as I had always imagined it would be. I was so impressed by the excellence of the corps de ballet, with its precision, yet with every person an individual. I consider myself extremely lucky to have seen the Bolshoi while the company was at its peak.

In October 1956 I worked for the first time with Geraldine Stephenson, after being accepted at an audition for a television production of Shakespeare's

Figure 14. Wendy (*left*) and Susan Richter waiting to purchase tickets for the Bolshoi Ballet, Covent Garden, 1956. Photo by John Sandler.

The Tempest. Geraldine was gaining a strong reputation as the best choreographer for working with actors. She was wonderful with them. Her uplifting and cheerful personality worked miracles, and she always got the best out of her cast. She could also handle large groups of, say, two hundred in a pageant at the Royal Albert Hall, the mere thought of which makes me shudder.

The job of choreographing *The Tempest* came early in her career. Eventually, though, Geraldine would capture almost exclusively the BBC work in dramatic productions and was also working with the Old Vic (the National Theatre). To this day, she is not well known in America, but almost anyone who watched *Masterpiece Theater* saw her work in *The Six Wives of Henry VIII*, *War and Peace*, *The Pallisers*, and many others.

Geraldine studied modern dance with Rudolf Laban at Lisa Ullman's Art of Movement Studio in Manchester. Recognizing that she had a gift for working in dramatic productions, she began to study dance of all centuries. In doing so, she, in my opinion, essentially established the field of historical dance, which includes dance from the Middle Ages through the nineteenth century. She took classes from the historical dance specialists Melusine Wood and Belinda Quirey and studied the work of Mabel and Arnold Dolmetsch's performing group. She read Wood's and Dolmetsch's books on dance of the Middle Ages and Renaissance. Not all these teachers agreed on issues of style and technique, so Geraldine made dance selections from the available material depending upon their suitability for a particular production. Geraldine wrote to me of her work:

> In all the plays I worked on in the theater and television, when I choreographed an "historical dance," I had to adapt it to show the particular reason for the dance in the play. . . . There is no doubt that my major training in Laban's work has stood me in very good stead—the energy of each dance, the spatial orientation, the relationship of one character with another, etc. I doubt whether I have ever choreographed an historical dance for the dance itself. . . . [I] always had to find out why it was in the script.[4]

Geraldine's approach worked wonders for her and provided her with a very busy and fulfilling career. She truly found her niche.

For *The Tempest*, eleven dancers and I were attendants of Prospero and danced as nymphs in the masque toward the end of the play. The specifics of the dances elude me now. But I remember the performances of Robert Atkins as Caliban—one of his most famous roles—most vividly. Although critics were beginning to say that his style was flamboyant, overblown—an outdated style—I thought his Caliban was deeply felt and understood and full of poetry. Seeing such a masterly performance was a true inspiration for me. A particularly wonderful outcome of my involvement in this production was my friendship with Molly Kenny. We met at the audition and danced the same roles. We would remain close friends and colleagues over the years.

A month later, in November 1956, I danced in another production choreographed by Geraldine Stephenson, *The Prince of Purpoole*, which was given for Queen Elizabeth II at Gray's Inn Hall. It was a revival of very lavish Christmas/New Year's revels that were first played before her namesake, Queen Elizabeth I, in 1594–95, also at Gray's Inn Hall and at Greenwich Palace. Robert Atkins directed.

The revels centered on the reign of a mock prince, the Lord of Misrule, and his Privy Council and other officers of State. The first performances of the original, sixteenth-century production extended intermittently from December 20, 1594, until Shrove Tuesday 1595. The one-night, 1956 revival featured only small portions of the original. I was recruited by Geraldine for "The Masque of Proteus," which brought the original revels to a close. I was one of five nymphs, who along with three tritons and three porpoises made up the retinue of Amphitrite, danced by Geraldine. Molly danced with me here, too, as one of the porpoises.

The Prince of Purpoole was memorable for the text, which included verses by Sir Francis Bacon, and for the experience of dancing in Gray's Inn Hall in the historic Inns of Court. For the Queen, I think the event was totally uninteresting and a frightful chore. The day of the performance had been very cold and misty, during which she had launched a battleship, among other things I would imagine. In the evening, she arrived a little late for the masque accompanied by the Duke of Gloucester. She was immediately seated in an enormous red velvet chair in which she looked very small and trapped. I could not imagine anything worse for her obviously tired condition than a masque—especially since the leading actor, famous but past his prime, constantly forgot his lines.

[4] Geraldine Stephenson, letter to Wendy Hilton, July 24, 2000.

In the summer of 1956, the Hungarian uprising brought Maria Fai, dancer and ballet mistress at the Budapest State Theater, into my life. Through my association with her, which was to last for most of my remaining years in London, my work expanded into fresh areas.

Maria and her husband, Peter Fai, had to escape from Hungary, having been advised that the police were compiling a file on Peter, a botanist, as a person of possible risk to the country. Sensing life-threatening danger, the Fais decided to flee with a small group of persons similarly situated. Rudi Szigeti, a young dancer at the theater, decided to go with them possibly because he felt his future lay with Maria. As it would turn out, he would play a major role in my life, too.

The story of their escape goes that the trio and their associates walked and slept for three days before reaching the Drava River, on the other side of which lay sanctuary in Austria. The river was flooding, however, and the only bridge in sight was patrolled by armed guards. Fortuitously, Rudi was of strong, peasant stock with a broad muscular physique, a type of ballet dancer often seen then in East European companies but seldom in the West. It was said that on that third night of their journey, when it was dark, Rudi, with his strong arms and back accustomed to high Bolshoi lifts, carried quite a few members of the group across the ice-cold river. After the final crossing, freezing and exhausted, he was plied with strong apricot brandy by Maria, who with foresight for every possible emergency, carried a small flask of it in her pocket during this dangerous trip. No wonder that Rudi reached safety quite high spirited.

Figure 15. Class with Maria Fay, c. 1957. Wendy (*far right*), Eileen Cropley (*third from right*). Photo courtesy of Maria Fay.

Figure 16. Class with Maria Fay, c. 1957. Wendy is front left.
Photo courtesy of Maria Fay.

Figure 17. Class with Maria Fay, c. 1957. Wendy is second from the left.
Photo courtesy of Maria Fay.

Arriving in England, where Peter had relatives who had fled earlier from the Nazis, they anglicized their surname to Fay. The Fays and Rudi set about trying to build a new life, the first step of which was to learn English. Rudi had skills as a garage mechanic, which he used to tide himself over until he could find employment in dance. Maria learned English fast. She was very quick and loved to talk—to be able to converse was more than a professional necessity. But she was nevertheless fortunate to be in a profession that has a universal terminology and in which a great deal is achieved by physical example. She was thus able to begin working much sooner as a result. For Peter, several years older than Maria, learning a new language presented a great professional problem, and it was several hard years before he was qualified for a position of equal status to his work in Budapest. Maria, midcareer at the age of twenty-eight, did not immediately enter the classical ballet world in London. When directors of several vocational ballet schools in England became familiar with her résumé, they were mainly interested in one of Maria's special "hobbies," as she liked to call them. She had studied in-depth the national styles of several countries, especially, of course, those of her native Hungary, and also those of Romania, Georgia, Russia, and Poland. To teach these styles, she had developed preparatory barre exercises for each. Only one dance style was taught at a time, usually as a course. It was a very different experience from the old-style character classes, which contained step sequences from hither, thither, and yon, as in, for example, those I had taken at the Rambert school. All the exercises were beautifully designed to the best possible music. For the Hungarian peasant style, for instance, she used some of the simple folk tunes arranged by Béla Bartók.

Audrey de Vos offered Maria the use of her small studio free of charge for two classes a week. Maria took her chances, charging the going rate for open classes. De Vos energetically encouraged her students to attend, and about ten dancers, including myself, turned up for a class in a Hungarian peasant style. Maria was a wonderful teacher and a superb example of her own work. She was animated, encouraging, and delightful. Her struggles with the language did not throw her, and the class was fun. She was a brilliant and truly uplifting person.

To my amazement, I took to the Hungarian peasant style like a duck to water. Apparently I was the spitting image of a member of Maria's group in Hungary, both physically and in her dance style. So, this class saw the beginning of a new era for me in a variety of ways.

Maria was very anxious to help Rudi become established as a dancer. However, he was essentially a character dancer and not a very proficient ballet dancer, except for his expertise in the high Russian lifts. Maria asked me if I would be interested in working with him on a "Bolshoi lift" pas de deux and a Hungarian gypsy dance, which she would choreograph, with the object of obtaining employment in the commercial theater. I agreed readily. The preparation, though, took some time. We worked all through 1957 and did not get any jobs until 1958.

Maria had been established as a full-fledged choreographer in Hungary and had ambitions to continue this work in the West. But she had been sheltered. She had no idea of the developments in ballet in the West, and at first, much of the performances she saw was puzzling. When later I took her to see Tudor's *Jardin aux lilas*, thinking that it would be a revelation to her, it was only to discover that she found it totally incomprehensible and dull. I had not realized until that moment how wide the cultural gap between East and West was. Having lived just a few months in England was not sufficient time for her to break through the cultural barrier the Stalinist brainwashing had built around the artists working in the countries behind the Iron Curtain.

Maria's reputation spread quickly, and she was offered engagements at other studios: the Nesta Brooking School of Ballet in Oppidans Mews and the studio of Helen Wingrave in Warwick Square, Pimlico. At both, she taught classes in national dance styles. When she was sufficiently established, she rented a small studio in Scarsdale Villas, Kensington, and began to teach the Vaganova ballet system, as she had in Hungary. She built up a small but steady and devoted following very quickly. Later, as classes grew, she moved to a larger space in Earl's Court.

In 1957 I also worked with Maria on a movie, *The Inn of the Sixth Happiness*, which was released in 1958. Maria was the choreographer, and I, her assistant. The movie was memorable for me because of the spellbinding work of Ingrid Bergman and an actor I greatly loved, Robert Donat. I believe this was his last film. The asthma that had plagued him for many years was gaining hold, and he had to sit very quietly between takes in a quiet corner of the studio. It was so sad to see this wonderful artist in such trouble.

As with the other movies, none of the dancing reached the final version. One amusing anecdote comes from a candle dance that Maria choreographed for six women. In rehearsal, I noticed smoke rising from behind one of the dancers. On investigation, I saw that her very long pigtail was going up in smoke caused by the lighted candle she held behind her back. She was saved in the nick of time and took the incident very well.

I was one of Maria's devotees and took all of her classes, which opened new worlds for me. For the first time, I felt I was dancing ballet as I had seen it in the Bolshoi company. The fluid use of the whole body to build strength was a revelation. From the Hungarian classes, I developed a new ability to do fast, energetic footwork, something that had eluded me in previous years.

Six: 1958–1959

Gaiety Theatre on the Isle of Man ~ Margaret Dale, Giselle, *and* The Nutcracker *~ Mondial Dance Company ~ Welsh National Opera*

In the spring of 1958, Rudi and I auditioned Maria's dances for Sidney Myers, who produced and managed shows at the Gaiety Theatre in Douglas, a popular seaside resort on the Isle of Man. One of the big appeals of the engagement was, of course, the prospect of spending three months on a warm sunny island. The pay was good too. And there was only one show each evening because, during the day, the vacationers (and the entertainers) wished to enjoy the outdoors and the beautiful beaches.

Those unfamiliar with the tone of British seaside summer shows might have seen John Osbourne's movie *The Entertainer*; it depicts the typically seedy and second-rate variety entertainment that was generally presented. Several things about the plans for our engagement caused me to wonder just what we were in for. First, the name of the show, *On with the Modley*, was a play on titles due to the star of the show being the comedian Albert Modley. Second, Myers suggested that, for our performances, I change my name to match Rudi's, and overnight I became the exotic-sounding "Ilona Szigeti." As we were to find out, however, Sidney Myers had high aspirations for his productions, and my reservations about the show and our parts in it were unfounded.

My plans for a sun-drenched summer were quickly disappointed. The rain began as the boat left Liverpool and seemed to continue without pause throughout the summer. After alighting from the boat, we walked a long way to a taxi stand, getting soaked to the skin. The next day, under umbrellas, we made our way to the Gaiety, about one mile from our lodgings. The theater was being dried out—or so we hoped—after being closed for the winter. Upon entering my dressing room—which I was to share with soprano Pamela Moon and her dachshund, Heidi—I found a thick fog with a single bar of bright red light from an electric fire barely penetrating through it.

Then, from the stage came the sound of a Strauss waltz. Being curious, I made my way to the stage and found there—horror of horrors!—more water, fountains of it weaving different patterns over the stage. What on earth . . . ? I thought. *Of course*, the popular act "Currie's Waltzing Waters," in which the constantly changing cascades were lit by constantly changing colored lights. Under the rainy circumstances, though, it really seemed too much! Myers, a great kidder, saw me watching the waltzing waters, walked over, and said seriously, "Wendy, I want you to wear your bathing suit and pose amid those waters." Anger reared up in me, and I turned to him ready to give a sharp reply but was stopped by an amused twinkle in his eye. A few days later when the act was being rehearsed with the orchestra, he said, "You know, Wendy, the pipe carrying the water passes right in front of the conductor. I'm afraid that one day it will burst and he will get soaked." As though on cue, the pipe did just that. "What did I tell you?" he said nonchalantly and walked casually away to deal with the problem.

Figure 18. *On with the Modley*, Gaiety Theatre, Isle of Man, 1958. Wendy, in tutu, faces upstage.

Figure 19. *On with the Modley*, Gaiety Theatre, Isle of Man, 1958. Wendy (*sixth from right*), beside Albert Modley; Rudi Szigeti (*third from left*).

Figure 20. Ilona (Wendy) and Rudi Szigeti in a Russian lift, Gaiety Theatre, Isle of Man, 1958.

The acts in the show were first class—a great surprise and relief for me. There were acrobats from France, a trick cyclist, and a very elegant conjurer. The two singers, Pamela Moon, my soprano dressing-roommate, and Michael Ryan, a tenor, were certainly well above average for this type of show. Rudi and I did two numbers by Maria, a romantic piece featuring high Bolshoi lifts and a character dance in Hungarian gypsy style. The only weakness in the entire show was an introductory piece by a local choreographer, whose name now escapes me, for a rather pathetic group of chorus girls. It was embarrassing but quickly forgotten, as the acts that followed it more than compensated.

The wet summer was a great letdown, both to us and to the constantly visible, dejected groups of holiday-makers hopefully carrying buckets and spades to the beach. All summer, there was only one sunny day, which we relished. Despite a cool wind, we all put on our bathing suits and found large rocks behind which we could be warm enough to sunbathe. Believing this might be our only chance in the sun—and it was—we stayed out too long and got terribly sunburned.

To fill the gloomy wet days, I studied Ann Hutchinson's *Labanotation*, which I had wisely packed. I took a correspondence course and passed the elementary and intermediate exams by the end of the summer. Knowledge of this system was to prove invaluable when I worked in the United States. I also tried to learn the recorder, but my playing upset Heidi, the dachshund, so much that I gave up. Squeaks and howls do not mix well.

Myers was a generous and thoughtful man. Toward the end of the run, he learned that Rudi and I needed publicity photographs. He offered us a photographer and the use of the stage with full lighting for the purpose. All through the session, he kept saying, "Another hundred pounds." But, of course, we paid nothing. As I said, Sidney Myers was a generous man.

When the season ended, it was with a feeling of great relief that we left the cold, rainy island to head, first, for two equally freezing weeks in the Lancashire resort town of Morecambe and finally for London. Of course London might prove to be equally wet and cold, but there at least would be things to do. Returning to ballet class was essential. Rudi and I had given ourselves a ballet class every day in Douglas, but we needed Maria's eye for corrections. We also were ready for more work. As things turned out, however, Rudi and I were to have only one or two more performances together.

For me, 1958 closed with two television productions produced by Margaret Dale, *Giselle* on November 23 and *The Nutcracker* on December 21. Margaret had retired from the Royal Ballet only two years earlier and then trained for six months with the BBC to become a ballet producer. Her work was truly first-rate, and I was thrilled to be working on these productions.

When the contract for *Giselle* arrived, I was excited to see that Nikolai Fadeyechev, my hero of the Bolshoi season, was to dance Albrecht. I was somewhat less pleased by the presence of Nadia Nerina as Giselle but relieved that Margaret Hill was to be Queen of Wilis. Hill truly was beautiful in that role. Lydia Sokolova as Giselle's mother was also a great asset to the production. I was a member of the corps.

In *Giselle*, everything proceeded smoothly until the final rehearsal on the morning of the transmission. Margaret had not anticipated that, in Russia, no dancer rehearsed on the day of a performance. Fadeyechev refused to work. Nerina was furious with him but also refused to rehearse if Fadeyechev didn't, leaving Margaret in a terrible spot. The production was saved by a dancer who had watched Nerina closely and knew most of her positioning. She stood in for her, although I don't remember if anyone was able to do the same for Fadeyechev. Nonetheless, the rehearsal was saved.

The Nutcracker starred Margot Fonteyn as the Sugar Plum Fairy and Michael Somes as her Cavalier. I danced in Act I as one of the guests at the Christmas party. The production went smoothly. Fonteyn was beautiful and thrilling to watch; her dancing was perhaps just at its peak. Somes, however, was past his prime but revealed himself to be a most modest and open person. Margaret asked him if he could begin a double *tour en l'air* facing one diagonal and end facing the other. He was very uncertain about it but tried and succeeded. He gasped, "I did it?" and we all clapped.

I found live television very exciting indeed. Mounting a long ballet was a terrific challenge. But as I've suggested, the live television transmissions could become very tense. Union restrictions could result in the loss of precious rehearsal time. I remember one ghastly delay when a worker was needed to knock in a couple of nails before we could proceed. The appropriate union worker could not be found right away, but no one else was allowed to do the job. He finally appeared after about fifteen minutes, but even that small amount of lost time was vital to our performance.

Strict union rules also governed the music. Because of the high union fees of orchestras like the Royal Opera House Orchestra, who recorded the music for both *Giselle* and *The Nutcracker*, the BBC negotiated an arrangement that, while financially prudent, proved unsatisfactory for the dancers. The music for the transmission was recorded before rehearsals began, but the dancers were not allowed to hear one note until just before the transmission. Until then, the rehearsal pianist would wear headphones and play to the tape so that the tempi we rehearsed to were the same as those we would dance to during the transmission. A piano, however, does not approximate the subtleties of the orchestration of a full score. After the final camera run in the morning, we were allowed to *sit* and listen to the tape. Not one step could be danced. For *The Nutcracker* "sit-through," I found myself next to Margot Fonteyn, who expressed some sotto voce distress or surprise with the music from time to time.

Despite the many impediments, Margaret Dale did outstanding work. She never let her anxieties, caused by the pressures of time, show. I admired her tenacity very much and shared her obvious feelings of intense relief when yet one more difficult live transmission was over.

The last time I danced with Rudi for Maria Fay was with the Mondial Dance Company. An announcement in the *Evening News* on March 18, 1959, introduced Mondial as a new national-dance company, which was to be run by Helen Wingrave. Maria would serve as ballet mistress. Since Maria still taught most of her character dance classes at Wingrave's studio, this arrangement was both opportune and convenient.

Helen intended to share the responsibility of building the company's repertoire with Maria, whose work was a joy to her and whose arrival in England she had welcomed with open arms. She did everything she could to help Maria become established. With the development of the company, however, there was a problem. Maria was an experienced choreographer and teacher, used to working with professional dancers in the theater. The work of the ISTD National Dance Branch, whose work Helen still avidly supported, had a decidedly amateur flavor, and much of its work was based on somewhat shaky scholarship. Consequently, those of us recruited as dancers for the new company doubted that the work of the two choreographers would blend into an effective program. The two had such vastly different backgrounds; we couldn't see how they might combine to produce a well-blended program.

Figure 21. Wendy and Rudi Szigeti, Mondial Dance Company, 1959. Photo by John Vickers, © University of Bristol Theatre Collection.

Maria must have had some misgivings, too, because she discussed the matter with Molly Kenny, Rudi, and me before agreeing to Helen's arrangement. We told Maria that we would participate as long as we danced only in her works. She must have explained this to Helen tactfully because the three of us did indeed dance solely for Maria.

Rehearsals got under way in early 1959, and the Mondial Dance Company debuted on Sunday, March 21, at the Royal Festival Hall on London's South Bank.[1] A publicity photo of the new company, which appeared in the *Dancing Times* of May 1959, shows me, Molly, Rudi, Helen, and other dancers casually gathered around the studio piano during a rehearsal break.

[1] *London Musical Events*, May 1959. A letter from company member Timothy Hext confirms that the debut was at the Royal Festival Hall. He also recalled Wendy and Rudi at the premiere dancing the Bolshoi pas de deux, with a particularly "spectacular high lift" in which Wendy sailed "onto the stage sitting serenely on Rudi's hand—he with his arm at full stretch above his head." Hext, letter to Susan Bindig, July 5, 2004; "Remembering Wendy Hilton, 1931–2002: idem, A Program of Dance and Music Celebrating Her Life and Work," The Juilliard School, May 30, 2003. — SB

Figure 22. Wendy in *Chinese Ribbon Dance*, Mondial Dance Company, 1959. Photo by Jack Blake.

A few more performances followed. The first in Pimlico was reviewed by A. V. Coton in the *Daily Telegraph* on June 24, 1959. Maria choreographed many of the dances on the program, which Coton described as "dances of many nationalities, typical or stylised. . . . They were all in peasant, folk, or courtly modes." The court dances, however, were a sarabande and gigue taught to me by Belinda Quirey, who must have approved their inclusion on the program. Rudi and I also did our Bolshoi lifts number. So the company's program was not, after all, entirely composed of national dances. Coton also gave wonderful reviews to Rudi, Molly, and me, saying that we "stamped our dances with a vivacity and precision that inevitably overshadowed the other performers."[2]

A guest artist on the program was the great Indian dancer and actor Sesha Palihakkara. Sesha performed with Mondial through his teacher, Ram Gopal, the truly wondrous Indian dancer, who was also a good friend of Maria's. Sesha had come to London for the first time in 1956 with Ram and

[2] A. V. Coton, "Perfect Stage for Ballet," *Daily Telegraph* (London), June 24, 1959.

his troupe of dancers and musicians, having performed with them since the mid-fifties. Ram occasionally came to watch Maria's class, and one day he brought along Sesha, who struck up an immediate friendship with Maria. Sesha then took classes with us, and his dancing was an inspiration to all. He stayed in London for a few years, joining the Asian Music Society founded by Yehudi Menuhin and again coming into contact with Maria. Hence, his presence in our concert, in which he danced "Arjuna," described by Coton as "a splendid tour de force" that "showed its executant as a dancer of real quality."[3]

Ram must have been back in London around the time of rehearsals for the Pimlico performances and again stopped by Maria's studio on occasion. After class one day, Ram surprisingly said to me, "You are a beautiful dancer, but you simply don't belong in this century." I knew he was absolutely right, but the question was, where did I belong?

I didn't ponder the question for long, though, as I was working on a "Chinese Ribbon Dance" for an upcoming performance, which was a huge challenge for me. I had never enjoyed, indeed I dreaded, working with props and objects. So, the thought of the hazards presented by dancing with a very long ribbon were horrifying. Would I land on it? Would I get helplessly wrapped up in it? To my surprise—and relief—all went well.

The top of my costume for the ribbon dance was made from material given to me by the Chinese dancer in *The Inn of the Sixth Happiness* whom I had saved from severe burns when her pigtail caught fire. She was so grateful and gave me this beautiful gift, which I now put to very good use. It was a lovely costume.

The Mondial Dance Company gave no other performances after those in Pimlico for various practical reasons, mostly the unavailability of the dancers.[4] It was later re-formed by Helen with her star pupil, Robert Harrold. I also believe that the breakup of the company meant the end of Maria's classes at Helen's studio.

Soon after the demise of the Mondial, Rudi successfully auditioned for a touring company, whose name I can't recall. There he met his beautiful wife-to-be, Vyvienne Hetzel. After the tour, they married, and Rudi eventually gave up dancing for the security of garage work to support his three children.

Sometime in the mid-fifties, I did four, one- or two-week seasons with the Welsh National Opera (WNO), performing in Charles Gounod's *Faust* and Giuseppe Verdi's *La Traviata*. I have been unable to determine the exact

[3] Ibid.

[4] Molly Kenny Galvin noted that another probable reason for the dissolution of the company was that Helen Wingrave did not keep up with the research that was necessary to sustain the repertoire. Galvin, interview by Susan Bindig, October 22, 2005. — SB

year or years.[5] Both operas were choreographed by Norman Dixon, my partner from the Festival of Britain.[6]

I enjoyed working with the WNO immensely. Founded in 1944, it was very popular with singers, musicians, and dancers alike. The company set very high standards, which were almost always met. But because of the difficulties of scheduling rehearsals, there were often hilarious disasters along the way. The chorus members were, of course, amateurs, most of whom had daytime jobs. Almost all of the soloists were visiting professionals who often came from Covent Garden or some equally famous company to try out new roles that they were to perform in their home territory. True to tradition, a Wednesday matinee was always given, but the choice of opera did not always seem the wisest in view of the fact that very few of the chorus men could take the afternoon off from work. An "Entrance of Villagers," for example, might consist of all the women and perhaps three men, making the sound, to say the least, somewhat unbalanced.

When the season was in Cardiff, we also had the great pleasure of staying in some interesting theatrical digs, owned by a woman we simply called Ollie. Ollie loved her clients and loved to cook. With Ollie and her husband, we were one big happy family.

In 1959 Norman Dixon again asked me to dance in a WNO production, Rimsky-Korsakov's *May Night.* I accepted with delight, and it proved to be a very interesting job. *May Night* was a comic opera with a folk theme, first given in St. Petersburg on January 21, 1880. The libretto was by Rimsky-Korsakov after Gogol. This little known opera had been sung in Russian (*Mayskaya Noch*) at Drury Lane before World War I and had since been seen in Britain in an Oxford Opera Club presentation in 1931. The WNO production opened on September 28 at the New Theatre in Cardiff.

A crisis occurred during our first performance of this work, which gave me a small extra part for the rest of the run. I had danced in the second act as a water sprite. After dancing I was alone and settled in the wings to listen to the singing, as was my habit. Suddenly Heather Harper, who was singing the role of Pannochka, indicated to an attendant onstage that a letter was supposed to arrive. Heather, standing on the opposite side of the stage from me, stretched out her arm in my direction with an open, expectant hand, waiting for the letter delivery. I knew nothing about a letter and so naturally just stayed put. Gradually, however, Heather's hopeful expression and arm gesture turned to desperation. At the very last possible moment, someone grabbed my hand, thrust a piece of paper into it, and said, "Give it to her." I shot toward Heather like lightning, then past her to exit into a totally pitch-black space, where I could have been killed had a stage light been standing there. Afterward, an audience member said, "Wendy, what a wonderful

[5] Richard Fawkes, in the appendices to *Welsh National Opera* (London: Julia MacRae Books, 1986), listed only new productions and when singers first sang a role; he did not include actors or dancers. (So typical!) The WNO archives were unresponsive to my requests for information.

[6] Wendy may have been mistaken about Dixon's participation in these two operas, as he is credited as the choreographer only of *May Night* in 1959. Other choreographers at the WNO in the 1950s included Joyce Marriott and Philippe Perrottet. Fawkes, 279–86.—SB

entrance. It was almost as if you weren't there." Thereafter, I always delivered the letter—which, in fact, was a crucial moment in the opera—but I fear never again with quite the same effect.

Around the time rehearsals began for *May Night*, I had begun working in historical dance seriously. I realized that, to pursue it fully, I had to learn Beauchamps-Feuillet notation, the dance notation developed and used in Europe in the late seventeenth and early eighteenth centuries. By an amazing coincidence, John Broome, with whom I had been working in London in historical dance, had one day offered me a book—an authentic copy of John Weaver's *Orchesography*, his 1706 English translation of R. A. Feuillet's French textbook on notation, *Chorégraphie* (1700). I looked at him in wonderment. "Where on earth did you find this?" I asked. "By a college dust bin," he replied.[7] I was shocked but immensely grateful. The book accompanied me to Cardiff, and I studied it on my time off from *May Night*. Both my notation studies and the opera were very successful.[8]

To pass on momentarily in time, I danced with the WNO for the last time in 1965 in its new production of Johann Strauss II's *Die Fledermaus*, with choreography by Terry Gilbert.[9] This time we were not in Cardiff but in the Welsh resort town of Llandudno at the Odeon Theatre, where the WNO often gave a summer season. Dancing in this work brought back memories of my first visit to the theater and of Richard Tauber's conducting. For the 1965 *Die Fledermaus*, my memory is that the WNO conductor was Warwick Braithwaite, but per Richard Fawkes in his book *Welsh National Opera*, Bryan Balkwill conducted the orchestra.[10] Whoever it was, he was a large man with a good head of hair and, I believe, a beard. I also recall the role of Frosch, the jailer, was sung by Emyr Green, a Welsh amateur, who gave a superb and memorably funny performance—in my opinion, the best of the entire cast.

My most vivid memory is of my solo for which I entered and stood looking out at the audience, waiting for the orchestra to begin to play. I then began a complex series that included steps jumping on full pointe. At the last performance, I entered and no music sounded. After a while, I looked down. There, with an expression of terror and baton tensely raised, was a tiny man with no hair and rimless glasses shining in the light. He had no idea who should start, so I bowed to him and off he went—at a far too slow tempo for the dance, which made the hops on full pointe excruciating. So, I had to improvise a new dance for the evening. Since it was the end of the run, I never knew who that conductor was. I am sure the singers rehearsed with him; why not the dancers?

[7]Molly Kenny Galvin recalled that the college dust bin belonged to the Royal Academy of Dramatic Art. Galvin, interview. — SB

[8]Timothy Hext, who also danced with Wendy at the WNO, remembers that during the rehearsal period for *May Night*, Wendy rehearsed Norman Dixon in an eighteenth-century dance for a future recital of her own. As opera rehearsals had finished for the day, Wendy took advantage of the spare time, available space, and Norman's presence. Hext, letter. — SB

[9]Timothy Hext indicates that, prior to the 1965 *Die Fledermaus*, he and Wendy danced in the May 1961 WNO production of Arrigo Boito's *Mefistofele* at the Sadler's Wells Theatre in London. The program he provided also shows that Wendy's friend from Kingsley/Tintagel days, Selena Wylie, danced with them in the chorus. Hext, letter. — SB

[10]Fawkes, 88. Balkwill was the music director of the Welsh National Opera from 1963 to 1967. — SB

And so, in a way I had come full circle. *Die Fledermaus*, the overture to which had so thrilled me as a child, was the last opera in which I appeared before I began to work seriously in baroque dance and music. I was to have one more memorable experience dancing to Strauss, but this would be many years later, many miles away, and for an entirely different purpose. In the meantime, my concentration on historical dance had begun, with my work with Belinda Quirey and Maria Fay overlapping. To trace the beginning of my work in this field, we must return to late 1956 or early 1957.

II.

My Work in Historical Dance

Figure 23. Poster advertising Wendy and Michael Holmes in a lecture-demonstration by Belinda Quirey, sponsored by the Cambridge Ballet Club, May 4, 1958.

Figure 24. Poster advertising Wendy and Frances Crossley in a performance sponsored by the Cambridge Ballet Club, November 2, 1958

Seven: 1956–1959

Working with Belinda Quirey ~ Living on My Own ~ One Last Movie, Tunes of Glory *~Plans for a Historical Dance Company*

After I began studying with Maria Fay in 1956 and before my departure with Rudi to the Isle of Man in the spring of 1958, I also began studying historical dance fairly seriously with Belinda Quirey. Frances Crossley had started to take classes with Belinda and invited me to join her. Although I was far more excited by my work with Maria and Rudi, I decided to take advantage of what was clearly a unique opportunity.

Perhaps the first thing that Frances and I learned about working with Belinda was that we had a great deal to discover—both good and bad—about her as a teacher and as an individual. She was, without question, knowledgeable and dedicated to her work. But she was a woman of extremes and very unpredictable. For both Frances and me, working with her was as frustrating as it was fulfilling.

Our classes were held in Frances's flat in South Kensington, although Belinda lived quite a distance away at 22 Primrose Hill Road in the NW3 Hampstead area. For incomprehensible reasons, Belinda insisted on taking the interminable #31 bus ride to come to us. Surely shouldn't we, as the students, have endured the very long and tedious journey to *her* home? This generous willingness to travel, though, was offset by her inability to be on time. Belinda, we quickly discovered, was late for almost everything. Frances and I would get ready for class about a half hour *after* the scheduled starting time, which was when Belinda usually arrived, with the inevitable "So sorry to be late, dears!" When she was finally settled in a comfortable chair, class would begin. Frances and I would sit expectantly on the floor, pencils and paper at the ready. Our first instruction was, at her insistence and quite rightly too, survey history sessions covering the Middle Ages to the eighteenth century. Then we began to study early dance technique. Belinda addressed each of us quite differently. Frances she treated with the utmost respect, while she chose to view me as a moron practically incapable of even holding a pencil. I persevered.

I must have been studying with Belinda for about eighteen months (irregularly, of course; Belinda did nothing regularly) when it was time to leave for the Isle of Man. By that time, Frances and I had grown extremely enthusiastic about historical dance. We now sometimes demonstrated for Belinda at lecture-demonstrations. Frances, though, became interested in getting lecture-demonstration engagements that we could undertake on our own, and she planned to try to book a few while I was away.[1] We set about making plans.

[1] A poster from the Cambridge Ballet Club advertised Wendy and Michael Holmes in a lecture-demonstration on "Tradition in Ballet—The Fact and the Fiction" presented by Quirey on May 4, 1958, at Cambridge University's Downing College. The event was cosponsored by the Ballet Club and by Downing's undergraduate literary society, the Doughty Club. A Ballet (cont.)

For our new ventures, dresses in the baroque style became a necessity, and Frances and I decided that we must purchase our own. Money, of course, was always an issue for me, but with the long summer engagement forthcoming, I would be able—for the first time in my life—to put some money aside. I knew that when I returned to London in October, I would be in a position to look for a costumier to make my baroque dress. Frances ordered her own dress, from whom I don't recall.

During my summer absence, there were no classes with Belinda, but in the winter, they started up again. Frances and I were joined by two teachers, Anne Richards and Kate Newman. One day, Belinda talked seriously to the four of us. In her position as chair of the Historical Dance Branch of the ISTD, one of her responsibilities was to increase its membership. Here she had met with little success owing, she said, to lack of interest. More likely, however, her ability to insult people, often without realizing it, was the cause. Belinda was clearly in the doghouse with the ISTD; a crisis had been reached. She asked us to take the ISTD's elementary exam in historical dance. She would pay our dues and the studio expenses. Later would follow the intermediate and advanced exams. Kate and Anne were willing, being diehard ISTD members in other branches. Frances and I had no interest in exams, but we agreed for various reasons, one of which was that the speed of Belinda's teaching would no doubt increase with this goal in mind. Our chance to work independently would come more quickly.

The following encouraging letter from Belinda came just before we took the exam.

> Monday
>
> Wendy darling—
>
> I am sorry that this only reaches you now, but I have been penniless until this weekend and am so very anxious to pay for this silly old exam for you as a very small return for all your kindness and [illegible] over my lectures earlier this year and help with Edinburgh and everything. You are easily the best pupil I have ever had, and there is no need to worry—just go in and dance and you should come out on top
>
> Love—as always—
>
> Belinda
>
> P.S. I do not tell you [that] you are so good in front of the others because it would depress them so much, but I tell Michael [Holmes]. Do not worry about the forms being late. It is quite o.k. as long as they are in before Friday.

The forms she included with the letter were the application forms, and I believe they must have been submitted in typical Belinda fashion, *after* the exam. Nonetheless, we must have been allowed to take it. The letter shows a

---

Club poster from the following fall advertised Wendy and Frances Crossley in their own program on "18th Century Music and Dance" with the Cambridge Baroque Ensemble on November 2, 1958, also at Downing College. — SB

great change in Belinda's attitude toward me. Hitherto, I had been despised and, in her lectures, relegated to the dances of Middle Ages. But that was how it was, in one week and out the next. The exams being completed, Frances and I returned to our plans for branching out on our own.

As soon as I had returned from the Isle of Man, I set about having a costume made. Doreen Brown came highly recommended to me for the task. She had studied with the highly respected Norah Waugh[2] and now worked for BBC television and, in the summers, for Glyndebourne. I feared that she would be terribly expensive, but when she realized that I really wanted an authentic cut, that I was not just another singer who cared only about being able to breathe, she quoted me an extremely reasonable rate. And so I shopped for material and work began. Doreen's only fault was that she, too, was very unreliable about time. But she was brilliant, and a lot of her contacts benefited us. Expensive remnants of all kinds from the BBC and Glyndebourne wardrobes, which would otherwise have been thrown out, would find their place on future costumes made for me by Doreen.

When our dresses arrived, Frances and I thought Belinda would be pleased. But when we showed them to her, such was not the case. We began to realize that Belinda viewed historical dance as *hers* and that we were perhaps becoming a threat with our thoughts of finding our own engagements. Surely not—we were still such beginners.

Be that as it may, things now did not proceed smoothly between Frances and Belinda. Belinda was always so hypercritical of everyone else's work that, when she put on a show herself, one assumed it would be first class. We unhappily discovered that this was not always the case. The first big performance by Belinda in which Frances and I took part was at Horace Walpole's old house at Strawberry Hill in Twickenham. The cast included us, a number of mostly young students from, I believe, Nesta Brooking's school, and a few others.[3] The level of presentation was in some cases shockingly poor. Frances could not get over it. She was very upset and expressed her feelings to Belinda in a letter. Belinda's defensive response was twenty-five pages long! It was mainly a recitation of her old gripes and excuses, of her old problems with Melusine Wood[4]—the same stories over and over. We had heard them before and would hear them again. As time passed, I came to refer to such rants as "Belinda's tape." At our next Tuesday lesson, no dancing took place, only heated discussion. Belinda saw no fault with what she had presented,

[2]Norah Waugh was the author of three influential books on the construction of historical clothing: *Corsets and Crinolines* (London: Routledge, 1954); *The Cut of Men's Clothes, 1600–1900* (London: Faber & Faber, 1964); and *The Cut of Women's Clothes, 1600–1930* (London: Faber & Faber, 1968). All remain in print today.

[3]Michael Holmes, in an interview, noted that he and Wendy demonstrated baroque dance for a performance directed by Quirey at Strawberry Hill. Perhaps it was this performance. Holmes, interview by Susan Bindig, October 13, 2005. — SB

[4]Wendy never elaborated on the problems Quirey had with Wood. Molly Kenny Galvin explained that Quirey took material from Wood, as she never had been able to get access to the original sources herself. She also said that Quirey was far more interested in teaching than in theater. Both factors may help explain the deficiency Crossley and Wendy found in Quirey's theatrical work in this area. Galvin, interview by Susan Bindig, October 22, 2005. — SB

and if there were any problems, they were justified. I pitied our new accompanist, James Slater, this introduction to the world of historical dance. For one-and-a-half hours, he sat in amazement while we argued.[5]

More trying performances with Belinda followed, sealing our pact to branch out on our own. Sometimes James played and I danced for an out-of-town lecture by Belinda. Usually these were terribly embarrassing affairs where she patronized her audiences, which made them squirm. On one occasion, however—at a lecture-demonstration for a music society, somewhere just south of London—this did not happen. The inauspicious start of our trip to the performance, though, did not predict the success that would follow. The three of us were to catch a train from Waterloo Station, but Belinda was late, even for her. James and I began to cast anxious glances at the clock. We began to entertain thoughts of searching the very spacious station when we finally caught sight of a familiar figure dressed in pleated white. (Belinda frequently wore pastel-colored, permanently pleated skirts or pants and a matching top.) We noticed that she was weaving a little, and as she got closer we saw blood on her forehead. "Good god!" exclaimed James, and we ran to meet her. "Whatever . . .?" we said. Belinda replied nonchalantly, "It's nothing to worry about, dears. I was thinking and walked into a lamppost." "Where?" we asked. "Just by my house," she replied. James and I feared the worst for the lecture, but it was one of the best I had ever heard Belinda give. Not once did she patronize anyone. We congratulated her the next day, but she remembered very little about it. "Oh," I sometimes thought on really bad days, "for more lampposts!"

The really bad times were usually the lecture-demonstrations of the Historical Dance Branch at the two-week ISTD Summer Congress. The large audience of dance teachers made Belinda especially nervous and therefore defensive. At the 1958 meeting, a highly respected dancer in musical theater, Valerie Swinnard, had joined our group. The three of us—Valerie, Frances, and I, together—were to demonstrate the Minuet of Mr. Isaac (Pemberton, 1711), a very attractive solo dance. At the last moment, Frances was unable to attend, which left Valerie and me. We were standing, just ready to start, when Belinda turned to the audience and said, "I feel I must tell you that my really good demonstrator is not with us today." Truly professional, Valerie did the minuet, and that was the last Belinda ever saw of her. It is really not surprising that the Historical Dance Branch failed to grow under her leadership.

During this three-year period, life changed dramatically, mostly for the better, for me, my family, and many of my close friends. In very different ways, we all struck out on our own, developing new interests, finding spouses, and maybe even moving to new places.

[5]James later conducted the orchestra of the London Festival Ballet and was the music director of the Houston Ballet.

Besides our classes and demonstrations with Belinda, Frances passed her secretarial course and began to work for a real estate agent. Her connections in this area enabled us both to make an important change in our lives. An extremely small house in Philbeach Gardens, just off Kensington High Street, came up for rental. It consisted of three tiny rooms, one on top of the other, and a little courtyard. The rent was very reasonable, and Frances took it. She invited me to share it with her, and I leapt at the opportunity. It was time to leave Acton and be closer to town, as where to rest between appointments had become a real problem.

I had considered moving once before to share a flat with Jean. The problem, of course, was Dorothy. Without me, she would be alone in the Acton house, except for the tenants. But now I was twenty-seven years old and needed my own place for personal and professional reasons. Life was getting even busier and more tiring. It was with dread that I told Dorothy about the little house and explained that I felt I must move into town. She was terribly hurt at first, feeling that my leaving was in some way personal. But after a few hours of deep soul-searching, she saw the validity of my reasons and how much easier life would be for me.

I had a wonderful time living in Kensington with Frances. There was still a lot of traveling in London—to the artists in particular and to some classes. But many of my classes and other activities were in or close to Kensington. What a difference!

And Dorothy rallied. Always energetic and in excellent health, she soon became an usherette at the Lyric Theatre in Tottenham Court Road, the home of John Gielgud's Shakespeare productions. She worked in the dress circle, which meant climbing a lot of stairs, but she did not get tired, not even on the two weekly matinee days when patrons could be served trays of tea in their seats. She loved being at the theater. She had kept her figure and looked trim and very attractive. People really liked her, and she got excellent tips. I don't think she had been so fulfilled since she was a wartime postwoman. Her time was occupied, and she could still enjoy her afternoons at the movies. We had lunch together once a week, and Dorothy continued to visit Gerald and Muriel in Merstham every few Sundays.

But misfortune struck our family. Gerald's firm went bankrupt, and suddenly he was without work or income.[6] The shock was overwhelming, and he went into a deep depression, seldom speaking when we visited. For a year or so, he tried without success to find another position. Finally he had to sell his beloved house and move into a nice but quite ordinary flat at the bottom of the hill that he had loved to climb to reach home every evening. Eventually, he obtained a lowly, very poorly paid position, which was all he could get. For exercise and social intercourse, Muriel persuaded him to play golf; otherwise he would have sat at home at the weekends staring into space. It would be some years before he would reach age sixty-five and could retire, a day he longed for. Gerald's situation affected us all deeply, but in fact, there was little we could do for him besides provide the moral support he so desperately needed.

[6]I have no memory of what brought about the collapse, although I know I was told at the time.

I was happy, therefore, to be distracted by another film opportunity. Frances was asked to set Scottish dances for the film *Tunes of Glory*, starring Alec Guinness, John Mills, and Susannah York, and invited me to take part. Released in 1960, the film was probably shot in 1959. It was to be my last movie and was certainly the most interesting because it provided a wonderful opportunity to observe and appreciate the work of the great Alec Guinness at close range.

Guinness was wonderful, and it was interesting to compare his approach and technique with that of his costar, John Mills. Mills would busily prepare for a scene calling for extreme anger, looking around, it seemed, for an audience. Guinness on the other hand, merely walked quietly onto the set, awaited his cue, and then "turned on" the most ferocious anger seemingly most deeply felt. The take done, he relaxed and waited quietly for the next one, while Mills continued to prance about.

Another important benefit of working on the movie was that I got to know better Morag Cattanach, an acquaintance from my days at Rambert. Frances had recruited Morag along with Molly and me as dancers, and the four of us shared a ride to the studio each morning. (What a difference this made. No 4:00 a.m. trains!) Morag was six years younger than I and a feisty Scottish girl. She had a wonderful spirit and sense of humor.[7]

Even more changes were in store for me. My good friend Jean married Professor Albert Jordan on September 7, 1959. Although reluctant to give up her career, Jean had always wanted children and was thrilled by her new life. We were happy for her. They had a small wedding, and Frances and I were able to accommodate their reception in the tiny Kensington house.[8] This was one of the last happy times I had there, though, as Frances's mother, Helen, decided she needed to have a room available in London. I was asked to find another place as soon as possible.

The unexpected need to move was a terrible blow, but I was lucky enough to find a room in a big house nearby. The advertisement for it had mistakenly been placed in the "Jobs Wanted" column, and I just happened to catch sight of it! There were no other applicants. Not long afterward, Molly

[7] Years later, we discovered that Morag had followed me to Kingsley. We had both had a domestic science teacher named Dorothy Leach, and surely there could not have been more than one! But Morag had joined Kingsley only after the war and the school's return to London. Many years after the movie, we were to become close friends, but for now Morag was about to take off for Paris where she would be the only English girl in the can-can team at the Moulin Rouge. She entered that arduous schedule with a spot of tuberculosis on a lung, but nothing would deter her from her desire to be a dancer in musical theater. In Paris, she married a very handsome Yugoslavian, and they moved to Las Vegas, where they were very successful dancers.

[8] The marriage was not a happy one, but Jean had her longed-for family—two children, a girl and a boy. After moving to and from England and France, Albert accepted a position in the French department at Sir George William University (later Concordia University) in Montreal. After the marriage ended in divorce, when the children were grown, Jean returned to England for she had an ailing mother. Once her mother died and Jean suffered cancer surgery with good results, she returned to Canada, a grandmother, to live near her daughter. I saw Jean only twice after her first move to Canada—once in New York and once in Montreal—but we remained the same buddies.

decided to look for another place to live, and we teamed up and found a nice apartment in Notting Hill Gate in a small, quiet street close to the Underground. This location and situation was very advantageous during the next few years when I embarked on what proved to be an extreme endeavor.

I still spent many evenings with Frances and her mother, and our enthusiasm for historical dance was rapidly growing. Helen urged Frances to go into the field seriously, and we all agreed that more performances should be available to spread knowledge of the work that had been done and of which most people were unaware.

One night we decided to take the bull by the horns and approach Belinda to propose that Frances and I start a group of dancers and musicians. I was delegated to speak with Belinda and gain her approval and support as we needed a much larger repertoire, which only Belinda could provide. Frances and I were certainly not qualified to reconstruct dance from original sources, nor had we, at that time, any real desire to do so.

Why I was chosen adamantly by both Helen and Frances to be the one to put our proposal to Belinda, I shall never know. We all still believed that, in her heart, Frances was her favorite pupil. But I agreed reluctantly. Timing was important, and a good opportunity to broach the subject came one afternoon when Belinda and I were walking the short distance from her house on Primrose Hill Road to Nesta Brooking's school in Oppidans Mews. She was in an amiable mood, and I summoned up my courage and explained our plan to her. Belinda's response absolutely stunned me. It was to the effect that she would support and work with the group if I were to organize and direct the project myself. She would not work with Frances. I have no memory of my response. Nonetheless, this walk was certainly a time of great significance for me. I cannot remember Belinda's explanation against Frances—or even if she made one—or the defense I hope I put up on her behalf.

This was the news I had to take back to the little house. (I was very glad I wasn't still living there.) After anger and tears, it was agreed that I should form the group, which we three had already christened the Domenico Dance Ensemble, out of respect for the great fifteenth-century dancing master. After thinking things over, Frances generously and wisely withdrew so that the group could get under way.

My own feeling was still primarily one of amazement, but this was mixed with a strange sense of relief. I realized that I did not truly believe that Frances and I could work successfully together. In my experiences with her in the West Country Ballet, I had felt a lack of that extra inner drive that enables people to achieve the seemingly impossible by never giving up. I knew I possessed that quality in abundance, although at that time I don't believe that anyone saw it. But to use it fully, I would have to work alone.[9]

And thus, my work in historical dance became the focus of my career. It would be my contribution not only to the field of dance but equally to music. I was home at last. Early music was already a rapidly growing field, and it was initially largely through musicians that a wider interest in the dances

[9]Frances and I remained friends for at least several years, but then I lost track of her altogether. Numerous inquiries failed to produce any information about her.

was generated. But to form a group I had to start from scratch. There were no dancers, no musicians, no costumes, no money. Would we attract an audience? How should I begin? For answers, I turned to those who had worked so hard to encourage serious research in historical dance. They would become major figures in my new life.

Eight: 1960–1961

Cyril Beaumont and Melusine Wood ~ Forming the Domenico Dance Ensemble ~ Robert Atkins, Belinda Quirey, and The Tempest *~ First Performances of the Domenico Dance Ensemble*

While family and numerous friends and colleagues supported my new pursuit, three individuals were central to furthering my career in historical dance: Cyril Beaumont, as an unwavering advocate and sometimes patron; Melusine Wood, as a pioneer and tireless researcher in the field; and Belinda Quirey, as my teacher and, initially, adviser to the Domenico Dance Ensemble.

Everyone working in historical dance owes Cyril Beaumont an enormous debt. He translated into English several of the field's vital, primary sources, including Pierre Rameau's central work *Le Maître à danser* (1725). I first met Beaumont when I was a naive beginner in ballet. I had been given a copy of Arnold Haskell's *Ballet*, in which I read that all beginners should read Tamara Karsavina's *Theatre Street*. So I made my way to his bookshop, Under the Sign of Harlequin, at 75 Charing Cross Road, to purchase a copy. Beaumont was standing outside, as he so often did. He listened kindly to my stammered, most likely mispronounced request and told me that the book was out of print. Despite this initial lack of success at his shop, I was to return many times over the years to browse and buy. I would eventually become a welcome visitor in the inner sanctum at the back of the shop. It was an honor to be invited to join him there to discuss dance and my work in particular.

Beaumont always encouraged my enthusiasm for historical dance and my efforts to arouse a wider interest in the field by establishing the Domenico Dance Ensemble. He helped me in every possible way, even financially on one occasion. When he sent me a check in support of costumes for my new ensemble, I was surprised and humbled to receive it. When it came my turn to write a book, Beaumont was the first of the dedicatees.

Melusine Wood launched the careers of just about everyone who was working seriously in historical dance at the time. She began research into historical dance in the late 1940s. Central to her work was a group that gathered on Fridays at her large home in Kensington to assist her in reconstructing dances. Among the "Friday class" participants were Mary Skeaping, Anna Ivanova, Joan Wildeblood, Freda Burford, Belinda Quirey, Evelyn Fletcher, and William Milligan, Belinda's partner in baroque dance. They had all most likely joined the class in response to the same advertisement in the London *Times* that had caught Belinda's eye.

At Beaumont's invitation, Melusine formed the Historical Dance Branch of the ISTD in 1952. She devised the syllabi for the three levels of historical dance that were eventually taught there and wrote manuals to supplement the classes: *Historical Dances* (1952), *More Historical Dances* (1956), and *Advanced Historical Dances* (1960). Beaumont published the books to further the work of the branch and the ISTD. The Dance Research Committee, as the branch was renamed, has remained an active part of the society.

I participated in some of Melusine's classes and, with Beaumont's encouragement, in the ISTD. Belinda Quirey, however, would be my primary teacher and the repertoire adviser for my company until I left for America. Belinda rose to prominence in the field and at the ISTD, unfortunately at Melusine's expense. She was Melusine's demonstrator for lectures until they had a huge falling out over the level of a large performance Melusine put on. Perhaps there was even more to the argument, but the outcome was not only that their relationship was forever severed but also that Melusine resigned as chair of the Historical Dance Branch. Belinda took her place.[1] All of this made a continuing relationship between Melusine and me difficult to sustain, but I managed as I valued her guidance in my growing career.

It is a formidable task to establish a performing arts group of any kind. The group I decided to form offered, I think, particularly unusual challenges. I required dancers who were trained in historical dance styles and who would wear and be able to dance comfortably in elaborate and somewhat physically inhibiting costumes of various periods. I also needed musicians who were interested in performing what was, at the time, rather obscure music. Finally, all participants had to be prepared to do the initial performances gratis with the hope that the project would be successful and arouse enough interest to become financially viable. None of my requirements were easily met.

Because of my regular concert attendance, I was aware that only a few groups in London were playing early music. One group that had attracted my attention was the In Nomine Players, directed by Maxwell Ward. He also played in the Philomusica, as did his colleagues, and was a professor of violin at Eton College. I approached Max with a proposal that his group play for my yet-to-be-established dance ensemble's performances. He was interested, and his colleagues agreed to give it a try. So, a few days later, I took the dance music to Max to make sure that he understood the full nature of the project

[1]Michael Holmes, a longtime associate of both Melusine Wood and Wendy, shared the following synopsis of Wood's background. The daughter of an Australian sheep farmer, Wood came to live in England with a large inheritance that allowed her to pursue her passion, research on the seventeenth and eighteenth centuries. She lived in a seventeenth-century house, which she refurbished as authentically as possible; it had no gas or electricity. As part of her research, she produced period plays and performed with period musical groups.

Although not schooled in dance, Wood began to study period dance to complement her other work. The Royal Academy of Dance in Bond Street taught a class in period dance, but Wood was convinced that people of the seventeenth and eighteenth centuries, as she understood them, would never have danced in the RAD fashion. So, she began her own studies. As Wendy notes, Wood placed an ad in the press for dancers to work on reconstructions with her. Belinda Quirey responded, and what was to be a ten-day project turned into a ten-year collaboration.

Holmes met Wood when he was engaged to work on an eighteenth-century production. He called her for lessons, which she initially did not agree to give. She finally called him and invited him to her classes, where he then met Quirey. He noted that Wendy also met Wood in that class. He also recalled that one day Wood "threw Belinda out," which may have been the disagreement that Wendy refers to here. Holmes, interview by Susan Bindig, October 13, 2005. — SB

and that he was really willing to arrange all the dance music for which we had only the tenors. He was willing, bless his heart.

An unforeseen benefit of our ensemble's association with Max was his apartment, which had an enormous studio. He offered it to us for dance rehearsals on the days he taught at Eton. It was located just past the Mercury Theatre in Kensington Park Road, within easy walking distance of where Molly and I now lived. This was all too good to be true! We also were able to give our first performance, a private showing, in Max's studio.

With the music problem solved, the horrible expense of costumes had to be faced next. For our first showing, I needed three dancers—myself, another woman, and a man. We would perform two groups of dances: Italian fifteenth-century dances by Domenico da Ferrara and Guglielmo Ebreo and baroque dances. I needed three fifteenth-century costumes and two baroque costumes, since I already had one of my own. Fortunately, Doreen Brown agreed to make each costume at the same reasonable rate she had charged for mine. Even so, there was still the cost of the fabric, which I would choose myself. With no financial resources, this challenge seemed insurmountable at first.

I did not know where to turn for money. To get funds from recognized organizations, we first had to prove the value of our subject and the quality of our performance. One day I was sitting for one of my rich artists, and on the spur of the moment I asked him if he would consider donating a costume to my rather unusual project. To him the amount was so small that he laughed and said, "Of course I will." Thus encouraged, yet always with some embarrassment and trepidation, I approached others, and not one refused! Then the enjoyable, yet time-consuming, part of the project could begin—finding the fabrics and taking them to Doreen with pictures of the costumes I wanted copied.

Finally, the most important and most formidable problem had to be surmounted: finding dancers who would understand the subtle differences of style within early dance. Ballet dancers are too turned out by habit and too tense. A more relaxed dancer is necessary for period work. Fortunately there were by then in London a handful of modern dance teachers with whom dancers might study. Molly, for instance, was a student of Hettie Loman and Sally Archbutt. Hettie, an actress who had studied at the Laban Studio in Manchester, taught in London at Toynbee Hall and ran a small performing group. Molly danced with this group at its infrequent performances and was its outstanding performer. I already knew Molly, of course, and with her exceptional artistry, she was my first choice for the other female dancer in the ensemble.

There remained the question of whom to select for the man's role. Molly again helped out. She reminded me of John Broome. John had studied with, among others, Sigurd Leeder, perhaps the best known of the "modern ballet" teachers and who, for a time at least, taught in Regent Square, London. John was interested in working with actors and found the idea of learning period movement very attractive. John was a pleasantly relaxed dancer, and he and Molly were already experienced colleagues and good friends.

We were prepared to begin rehearsals, but it was not until 1960 that we were ready to give our private studio performance at Max's to good friends and supporters. The two years of preparation were a time of ferocious activity for me. There was so much to be done, and of course, money to be earned, classes to attend, and so on. We faced a continuing battle of getting Belinda to teach us our remaining repertoire in time. Molly swore that Belinda wanted to be in the group. "Surely not," I said. Her dancing days were really over, or so I thought. But Molly was right.

The problem with Belinda's dancing was not that she was about twenty years older than we—she was still a very beautiful mover. It was that she was very nearsighted. With her, this resulted in a constant motion of the eyes as she tried desperately to make contact with individual members of the audience. Several people who went to see Belinda, because I told them how beautiful her dancing was, remarked on this habit. I then realized how disturbing and ridiculous it was. No, apart from lecture-demonstrations, Belinda should have danced no longer. And she didn't—at least, not with us.

Before the debut of the Domenico Dance Ensemble, however, Molly and I danced for Belinda in *The Tempest*.[2] Despite our ongoing battles with her over the dance ensemble, we would have an enjoyable time working with her on the play. *The Tempest* provided the opportunity for me to work with Robert Atkins again. For several years, Atkins had been the director of the summer season at the Regent's Park Open Air Theatre. The 1960 season was to be his last, a situation that was rued by many. He was told—in the unkind way in which unpleasant news is so often delivered—that it was time for younger blood to be brought in. Fresh ideas were needed. Atkins's style, admired for so long, was now considered old hat.

Figure 25. *The Tempest*, Regent's Park Open Air Theatre, 1960. *Left to right:* Molly Kenny, Priscilla Pritchard, Sara Kestelman, Penelope Bartlett, and Wendy.

Atkins attempted to bring period authenticity to his production of The Tempest. The music consisted of Elizabethan pieces played on three recorders and a lute. The dances, choreographed by Belinda, for five female and five male dancers who represented nymphs and reapers, respectively, were based on sixteenth-century choreographies from Fabritio

[2]The program for *The Tempest* does not list the performance dates. . — SB

Caroso, Cesare Negri, and Thoinot Arbeau. The costumes, designed by Cedric White, to some extent, it was said, followed original designs by Inigo Jones from some of his masques, which were contemporary with *The Tempest.* I believe this must have been true since no modern designer would have dressed the reapers in short, pinkish tunics with straw hats on their backs. Most of the matinee audiences consisted of school children, and the reapers' appearance brought howls of laughter from the children, especially the boys. In this case, Atkins's call for authenticity was, it seems, unwise.[3]

The main hazard of putting on any outdoor production in England is, of course, the weather. As boldly stated on the program, the performance would be "undercover if wet." And it often was. "Undercover" meant that we performed on a platform in a large tent, and I could not help noticing that these performances took about one half-hour less than those given in the open. They were indeed damp and miserable, often with the sound of heavy rain pounding on the tent.

During the rehearsals for *The Tempest,* Molly's fears of Belinda's expectations to dance with the Domenico Dance Ensemble were realized. We were discussing my thoughts on fifteenth-century costume colors while leaving the park one day. Just as we were about to go our separate ways, Belinda said, "And I think mine should be red. Good night, dear." My heart sank. I asked Molly, "What should I say?" It was what we had both dreaded. But Belinda never mentioned the subject again, and we were still speaking when the run of *The Tempest* ended.

After *The Tempest,* preparations for the launch of the Domenico Dance Ensemble continued. To get through this period financially, however, I also had to get a job with regular hours. I found well-paid work at the BBC radio news center in the Strand. Here all the news was typed, copied, and delivered to a box for every newscaster in the building, the foreign news as well. We worked from 7:00 a.m. to 3:00 p.m. for three days and then from 3:00 p.m. to 11:00 p.m. for three days. It was a long, tedious day, but we sat waiting for news for quite a bit of the time—unless there was a crisis in the news, and then we rushed about so as not to keep the announcers waiting.

With my job and rehearsals, fitted around everyone else's freelance-work schedules, I got very tired but was also very excited that, somehow or other, things seemed to be working out. What a joy to be working with fine musicians, beautiful costumes, and wonderful dancers! It was a time of incredibly hard work for me, but we did it!

[3]Dione Ewin, the production's stage manager and, subsequently, a good friend of Wendy's, tells another amusing costume story from this production. "One of Belinda's criteria for selecting the dancers for the roles of nymphs was long, flowing hair. But then, to Belinda's dismay, the costume designer covered their hair with large hats. On the last night of rehearsal, Belinda and Wendy contrived to lose Wendy's hat so that none of the others could wear theirs either, and their hair flowed free." Ewin, letter to Susan Bindig, April 2005. — SB

Figure 26. Wendy in a promotional photo for the Domenico Dance Ensemble, c. 1959.

DOMENICO

DANCE ENSEMBLE

The Domenico Ensemble has been formed to present in concert form the Court Dances of Western Europe. These range over a period from the Twelfth to the Eighteenth Century, and their reconstruction is the fruit of over thirty years research.

This work has been taught to the Ensemble by Miss Belinda Quirey. Chairman of the Historical Research Committee of the Imperial Society of Teachers of Dancing.

"Dancing is the result of sweet harmony created within us by music which can only issue forth as beautiful movement"

DOMENICO of FERRARA. *15 cent.*

MOLLY KENNY	JOHN BROOME
EILEEN CROPLEY	MICHAEL HOLMES
SUZANNE BURDON	TIMOTHY HEXT

WENDY HILTON, *Director of the Domenico Ensemble*

Figure 27. Promotional flier for the Domenico Dance Ensemble, early 1960s.

At a late hour on a Monday night in 1960—toward the end of October, I believe—the Domenico Dance Ensemble and the In Nomine Players gave a private preview performance in Max's studio to an invited audience of twenty.[4] This trial performance was not for the press, but we did invite the eminent ballet critic A. V. Coton and a critic from the Kensington local paper. Coton had been very supportive during the formation of the ensemble, especially when it all seemed hopeless, as it often did. He, I believe, wrote our one unsigned review, noting encouragingly that we "provided a unique occasion of dance pleasure considerably sustained by the skilled performances of Wendy Hilton, Molly Kenny and John Broome." When the Kensington review appeared, my heart sank initially. I was not aware that the paper was having technical troubles, and when I read the headline, "Dancing Back into Histo," I thought the review would poke fun at us. Happily, that was far from the case! The "ry" missing mistakenly from the end of "history" in no way foretold the delightful review that followed. It was clear that the Domenico Dance Ensemble was on its way!

> "Dancing Back Into Histo[ry]: Unique Recital"
>
> A unique event took place in a drawing room in Kensington Park Road late last Monday evening. The In Nomine Players (Maxwell Ward) and the Domenico Dance Ensemble (director, Wendy Hilton) offered a selection of Historic Court Dances to the public for the first time. It was held before an invited audience of 20 in Mr. Ward's candlelit studio. . . .
>
> The dancing took place amongst the audience and was spritely, impressive and happy. All the costumes worn had been designed with special attention to exact reproduction in each period represented and most were strikingly colorful. . . .
>
> A minor part of musical and dancing history was created that evening. It was so well-presented and performed that it should become a small, but established part of the contemporary musical scene.

We performed only fifteenth- and eighteenth-century dances. As I pointed out earlier, much work had yet to be done to build a comprehensibly wide repertoire. I think, however, that the reason for the gap in this program was that I had failed to raise the money for sixteenth-century costumes.

Belinda was, of course, present that night. The next morning she telephoned to express her horror at Max's realization of the fifteenth-century dance music, which was quite different from what she was used to, the nineteenth-century keyboard arrangements made by Elsie Palmer for Melusine's classes. Belinda quite definitely preferred those. I think that she was totally unaware of the extent, even then, of the explorations by musicians into the sources for early music and performance practice, dismissing them as dull musicological studies. She did not go to concerts, or to my knowledge turn on the radio, and so had scant knowledge of how the field of early music was beginning to grow with such illuminating results at this time. To her, what Max had done was simply not danceable. I felt sorry that here her vision

[4] No program remains of the studio performance, and the reviews in Wendy's papers neither have publication details nor provide the performance date. — SB

Figure 28. Domenico Dance Ensemble, Raphael Cartoon Court, Victoria and Albert Museum, London, early 1960s. *Left to right*: John Broome, Molly Kenny, and Wendy. Photo by Edward Brown.

Figure 29. Domenico Dance Ensemble, Raphael Cartoon Court, Victoria and Albert Museum, London, early 1960s. *Left to right*: Molly Kenny and John Broome. Photo by Edward Brown.

Figure 30. Domenico Dance Ensemble. Molly Kenny, Michael Holmes, and Wendy in a fifteenth-century dance, early 1960s. Photo © Frederika Davis.

Figure 31. Molly Kenny in the costume funded by Cyril Beaumont through the ISTD, 1961. Photo © Frederika Davis.

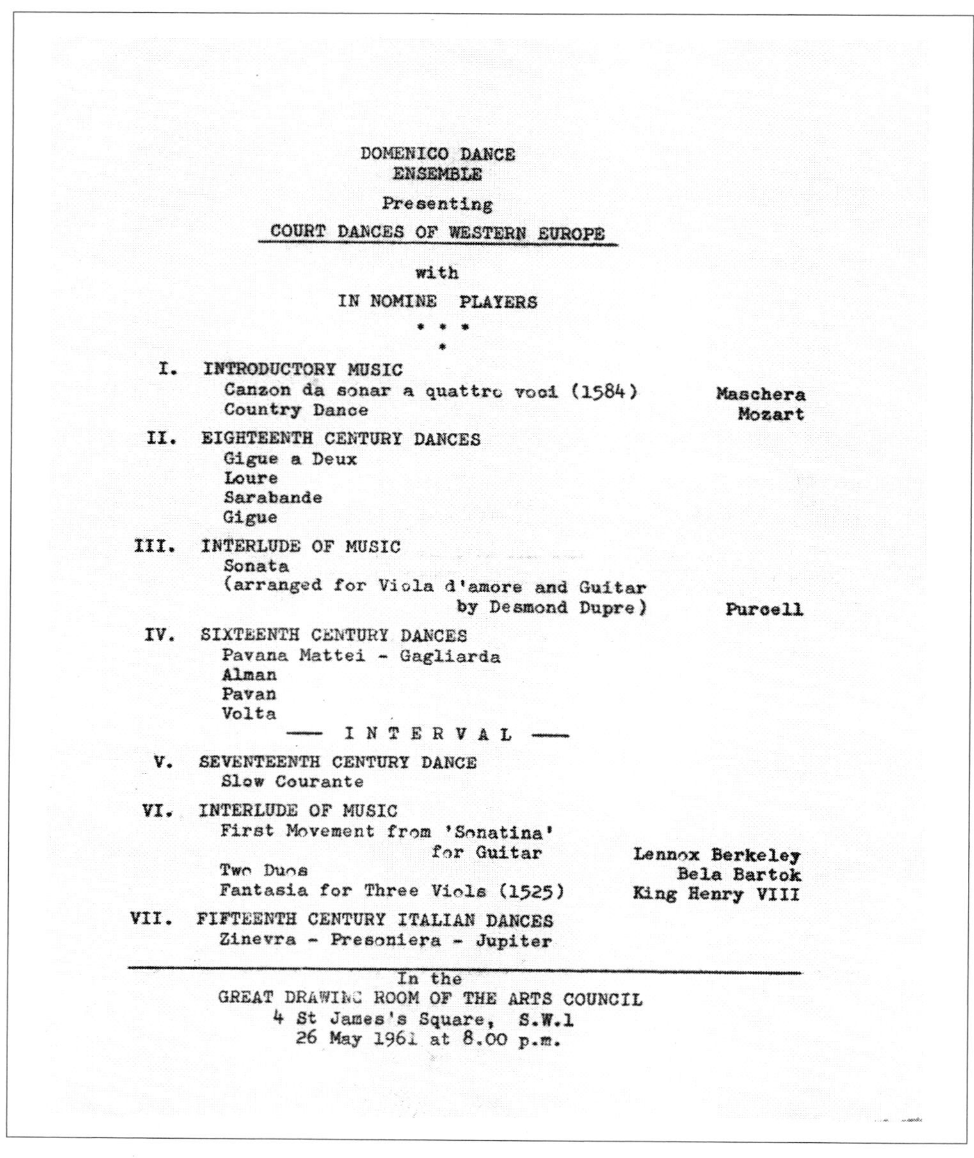

DOMENICO DANCE
ENSEMBLE

Presenting

COURT DANCES OF WESTERN EUROPE

with

IN NOMINE PLAYERS

* * *
*

I.	INTRODUCTORY MUSIC	
	Canzon da sonar a quattro voci (1584)	Maschera
	Country Dance	Mozart
II.	EIGHTEENTH CENTURY DANCES	
	Gigue a Deux	
	Loure	
	Sarabande	
	Gigue	
III.	INTERLUDE OF MUSIC	
	Sonata (arranged for Viola d'amore and Guitar by Desmond Dupre)	Purcell
IV.	SIXTEENTH CENTURY DANCES	
	Pavana Mattei - Gagliarda	
	Alman	
	Pavan	
	Volta	
	— INTERVAL —	
V.	SEVENTEENTH CENTURY DANCE	
	Slow Courante	
VI.	INTERLUDE OF MUSIC	
	First Movement from 'Sonatina' for Guitar	Lennox Berkeley
	Two Duos	Bela Bartok
	Fantasia for Three Viols (1525)	King Henry VIII
VII.	FIFTEENTH CENTURY ITALIAN DANCES	
	Zinevra - Presoniera - Jupiter	

In the
GREAT DRAWING ROOM OF THE ARTS COUNCIL
4 St James's Square, S.W.1
26 May 1961 at 8.00 p.m.

Figure 32. Program from the first public performance of the Domenico Dance Ensemble at the Arts Council of Great Britain, London, May 26, 1961.

was so limited. However, the main thing at this point was to keep the peace and move on. I said, perhaps unwisely, that, yes, Max's realizations certainly required more musical understanding on the part of the dancers than Elsie Palmer's earlier renditions, which had served their purpose and were a genuine product of their time.

The Domenico Dance Ensemble and the In Nomine Players gave their first public performance on May 26, 1961, in the Great Drawing Room of the Arts Council of Great Britain in St. James's Square. Molly, John, and I danced; Max, Rosemary Green, and Ian White, all on viola d'amore, and Desmond Dupre on viola da gamba and guitar, played both the dance music and instrumental interludes. Since October, we had rehearsed new repertoire and now presented dances from the fifteenth to the eighteenth centuries.

The additional repertoire required additional costumes. In all, I had somehow managed to add five costumes, one of which owed to the support of Cyril Beaumont. There is a nice story attached to this. I was close to his bookstore one day and noticed a shop that specialized in fabrics copied from various periods. I went in and browsed. The fabrics were beautiful but very expensive. Sadly I said no to the salesman and walked away, on to see Mr. Beaumont, who had recently written a note asking me to stop by. His purpose was to offer me some financial support through the ISTD to help the Domenico Dance Ensemble! Very soon I was back in the fabric store with the astonished salesman, buying what I had wanted for the sixteenth-century dress for Molly. It was some time before the check came, but it did![5]

Belinda suggested that she write a commentary for the performance so that the audience could perceive more. Reluctantly I agreed. A great mistake! Belinda also recommended that Dione Ewin, with whom she had worked on *The Tempest*, should read it. True to form, the day before the performance, Belinda had not yet begun to write it. At ten o'clock that evening, she phoned Dione and dictated it to her. Dione stayed up all night shaping the text and becoming familiar with it.

Now we did invite critics. Everything would depend upon the reviews, which turned out to be incredibly good. We were reviewed very favorably by critics from the *Daily Telegraph* and *Musical Opinion*, but the most perceptive review came from Geraldine Stephenson writing in *The Stage*:

> A rare opportunity was provided on May 26 of seeing a programme of authentic Historical Court Dances of Western Europe, presented by the Domenico Dance Ensemble, directed by Wendy Hilton, in the appropriate setting of the Great Drawing Room of the Arts Council. Years of research originated by Melusine Wood and continued by Belinda Quirey, tutor to the group, have gone into the preparation of this highly accomplished recital. Technical perfection is needed to perform such dances as the 18th century Sarabande and Gigue with their intricate step patterns, rhythms and hand gestures. The extravagant Italian Pavana was clearly contrasted with the simple English Pavan and the capricious Volta, authoritatively danced by John Broome and Wendy Hilton, demonstrated the possible truth of a contemporary writer's comment that when performing this dance "honour and health are threatened.". . . Most striking of all was the grandeur of the 15th century Italian dances. Their deceptive simplicity requires a dancer like Molly Kenny, who instinctively transformed herself into each character, and in "Zinerva" was like a Botticelli painting come to life.

On October 4, 1961, the Domenico Dance Ensemble gave its next performance in Forest Hill, South London, at the Horniman Museum, well-

[5]The letter from the offices of the ISTD, dated March 29, 1961, notes that the donation was for £15 "as a help towards the cost of costumes for the Domenico Dance Ensemble in which, due to its association with the Historical Dance Branch, this Society feels most closely interested." — SB

known for its collection of musical instruments. It also had a vibrant, weekly concert series. A quarter-page ad in the October 1961 *Musical Times* is the only record that remains of our performance, and I recall nothing about it. It appears, though, that we danced the same, or a very similar, program as in May—"Court Dances of Western Europe: 15th to 18th Centuries"—but only two musicians played with us, Max on viola d'amore and Desmond on guitar.

A week later, on October 11, we performed for a second time in the Arts Council's Great Drawing Room, with a slightly expanded program. Perhaps the program at the Horniman had served as a rehearsal for this more highly visible performance. We again had a full music ensemble; Max, Desmond, and Rosemary were joined by Michael Mitchell on viola and Anita Lasker on violoncello. The dance ensemble still numbered three—Molly, John, and me. I was a little bowled over by the excellent reviews we again received because, after all, we were just starting.[6] I concluded that we arrived on the scene at just the right moment; enough people were really interested in early music at this time to form an equally enthusiastic audience for early dance. And apart from the music and dance, they loved to see Doreen's beautiful costumes. There is no doubt in my mind that the excellent reviews put early dance on the map, and word began to spread.

[6]Wendy's personal papers do not have reviews of this performance. — SB

Nine: 1962–1965

Choreography for Television ~ Domenico Dance Ensemble Abroad ~ Choreography for the Handel Opera Society and the Barber Institute of Fine Arts ~ The Wizard of Oz *and the Century Theatre ~* Rigoletto *and Franco Zefferelli ~ My Teaching Career Begins*

Shortly after our successful premiere at the Arts Council, the Domenico Dance Ensemble gave another performance with the In Nomine Players at a music club in the far north of England.[1] But it would be another two years before the ensemble would perform again, in March 1963. Things take time, I thought.

I was grateful, therefore, for the chance to choreograph for and appear in a number of television productions in the early 1960s. Unfortunately, I no longer have any materials on them—or hardly any memory of most of them—so I can describe those productions in only the most general way.

For the BBC, I choreographed *The Man Shakespeare*, which of course required Renaissance dances,[2] and a Christmas production of *The Princess and the Pea*, for which I based my choreography on the style of Domenico da Piacenza. I danced a pavane and galliard with John Broome for a program devised by Ronald Smedley, and I danced in *Amahl and the Night Visitors* for Maria Fay.[3] I wish I were able to say more about all of these.

[1] No records of this performance can be found among Wendy's papers. But an undated program provided by dance ensemble member Suzanne Burdon documents a performance given in North Yorkshire for the Northallerton Music Group. It seems likely that the performance Wendy mentions and that program go together. Like the three previous London performances, the North Yorkshire performance was funded by the Arts Council of Great Britain; no subsequent performances of the group had its backing. Per extant documents and the memories of the ensemble members, the group never again performed in Great Britain that far outside the immediate London area. That the Northallerton program lists the Capriccio String Quartet (Marion Hillier and Noel Broome, violins; Roger Best, viola; and Ruth Bennett, violoncello) and not the In Nomine Players as the musicians might seem to refute this conclusion. But given that Wendy was working strictly from her memory here, a mixup of the accompanying musical ensemble cannot be ruled out. Additionally, a note on the program indicates that "the dance music has been arranged from original sources by Maxwell Ward," showing Ward's involvement, even from a distance, with this performance. — SB

[2] Produced by Hal Burton and written by Ivor Brown, this 1964 production for BBC2 examined Shakespeare's life and marked the four-hundredth anniversary of his birth. Memorabletv.com, http://www.memorabletv.com/bfm1.htm (accessed March 22, 2009). — SB

[3] Ronald Smedley was a well-known folk-dance specialist who worked closely with the English Folk Dance and Song Society and directed many of their festivals at Royal Albert Hall. He later became deputy head of BBC Schools TV. He contributed an essay to Belinda Quirey's *May I Have the Pleasure? The Story of Popular Dancing* (London: BBC, 1976) and produced the BBC two-part television production that accompanied the book.

Amahl and the Night Visitors was broadcast on Christmas Eve 1959 and featured the Royal Philharmonic Orchestra conducted by Bryan Balkwill. Other dancers from Wendy's circle of friends were Molly Kenny, Terry Gilbert, and Norman Dixon. A Rudi Saigeti is also listed as a dancer; given Maria Fay's participation and the date of the telecast, it seems highly possible that this dancer was Wendy's partner, Rudi Szigeti. "*Amahl and the Night Visitors* (1959)," *EOFF: The Encyclopedia of Fantastic Film and Television*, http://www.eofftv.com/a/ama/amahl_and_the_night_visitors_1959_main.htm (accessed May 18, 2010). — SB

A truly unusual opportunity came my way to choreograph for a series featuring Acker Bilk and his Paramount Jazz Band.[4] I told the producer, Kevin Sheldon, that I knew nothing about jazz, but one of the male dancers who worked with me in *The Princess and the Pea,* Roy Staites, took me aside and said that he was a jazz dancer and needed the work. He offered to show me all the material that I would need to choreograph in the style. I couldn't believe I was doing it, but I was. I had three dancers, Roy, Eileen Cropley, and Rudi Szigeti's wife, Vyvienne Hetzel. The band played wonderfully, and the tune was a beautiful spiritual—something about a mountain. Actually, in a way, I had four dancers because all the camera moves were part of the choreography; that is, sometimes the dancers stood still while only the cameras moved. I also included the musicians in a final triumphant procession. I was very pleased and believe that this piece in a totally foreign idiom is one of the best things I have ever done.

Although not as interesting, I did two more Acker Bilk programs for Kevin. One dance was to "Mr. Ghost Goes to Town," which could not be shown at the last minute because of an ultraviolet light problem. The other used two dancers, but I cannot recall the music and therefore the theme. I enjoyed my work with Kevin very much indeed, surprising as the latter part of it was.

While the long wait for another performance possibility for the Domenico Dance Ensemble was disappointing, it proved beneficial for our repertoire. In the gap between the 1961 and 1963 performances, I tried to persuade Belinda to put the ensemble members and me through the ISTD intermediate historical-dance exam, but she was far from interested. We had already studied most of the material in the ISTD syllabi for Belinda's lecture-demonstrations, so we were well prepared. However, on December 17, 1962, I received a letter from the ISTD inviting me to serve on the Historical Dance Branch Committee. As a committee member, I would bypass the need to take the two remaining exams. Was this deliberate, I wondered?

Gradually it dawned on me that Belinda had no more dances to add to our repertoire. She did not have a reader's card for the British Library and therefore no access to the valuable dance materials and notations found there. Although with her experience she could help others to reconstruct dances, she had no inclination to do so. She gave me one lesson in Beauchamps-Feuillet notation, explaining some of the pitfalls, and then I was on my own.

[4] Acker Bilk, the well-known clarinetist and his band rose to fame in 1962 with "Stranger on the Shore." Over the course of his long career, he recorded many spirituals. His recording of "Go Tell It on the Mountain" appeared at least as early as 1961(see *Mr. Acker Bilk's Lansdowne Folio*, Columbia Records, 1961) and may be the song Wendy refers to here. Sincere thanks to Phil Schaap, curator of Jazz at Lincoln Center, who told me of his conversations with Wendy about Acker Bilk and discussed Bilk's recording history. Schaap, interview by Susan Bindig, June 30, 2006. — SB

Determined, I obtained a reader's card to the British Library and spent every spare hour looking at the possible repertoire in the dance materials housed there. I studied the notation system at home from the copy of Weaver's *Orchesograpy* John Broome had given to me. When I reached the more complex theater dances, I asked Belinda some questions on the notation, but she had never gotten that far herself and could be of no further help. I pressed on.

Then, another disappointment. The In Nomine Players would no longer be able to play for us. Max had begun to look unwell, and it turned out that he had a degenerative nervous condition, which necessitated cutting down his workload. But disappointment soon turned to delight. Wonderful man that he was, Max passed us on to another group of fine musicians, the Jaye Consort of Viols, directed by Francis Baines, who would join us for performances beginning in 1963. A double bassist and composer, Francis played in the London Philomusica. He was also a collector of early instruments and sometimes featured a hurdy-gurdy in our performances, which added much texture and color. The other consort members were Elizabeth Baines, Jennifer Ryan, and Peter Vel.

Our first performance with the Jaye Consort was on March 18, 1963, for the Maidenhead Music Society. The dance ensemble now numbered six, with Eileen Cropley, Suzanne Burdon, and Timothy Hext joining Molly,

Figure 33. Domenico Dance Ensemble, 1963. *Left to right:* Wendy, Michael Holmes, Eileen Cropley, and Timothy Hext. Photo © Frederika Davis.

John, and me. Occasionally, Michael Holmes also performed with us. Our repertoire now reached back to the thirteenth century for a selection of estampies, and country dances were now included in the seventeenth- and eighteenth-century segments.

Figure 34. Molly Kenny, Desmond Smith, and Eileen Cropley, dancing at the Banqueting Hall, Whitehall, in a program devised and directed by Belinda Quirey for the Friends of Covent Garden. Photo by Reg Wilson, © Reg Wilson/Rex Features.

Four more performances in London followed that year: one on May 13 at the Emma Cons Hall at Morley College; two in mid-May at the Arts Council; and one on July 22 at Mahatma Gandhi Hall.[5] All were with the Jaye Consort and featured dances from the Middle Ages through the eighteenth century. At Mahatma Gandhi Hall, we were thrilled to have the wonderful countertenor Willard Cobb join us. A lovely review of our performance at Morley College appeared in the *Dancing Times*:

> The Domenico Dance Ensemble, which is directed by Wendy Hilton and owes much to the guidance and advice of Belinda Quirey, gave a performance of Court Dances of Western Europe at Morley College on May 13th.
>
> The group now consists of Wendy Hilton, Molly Kenny, Eileen Cropley, Suzanne Burdon, John Broome and Timothy Hext. They have a wardrobe of authentic and very beautiful costumes (made by Doreen Brown) and were fortunate to be accompanied by the Jaye Consort of Viols, a group as dedicated to historical music as the Domenico people are to historical dance.
>
> The programme ranged from the Estampie Double and Simple of the thirteenth century, to the celebrated "La Volta," and to the Minuet danse a deux, the standard ballroom version from Rameau's *The Dancing Master* (1725). For sheer period charm, Suzanne Burdon's Minuet—to illustrate the standard expected of young ladies leaving school at the beginning of the eighteenth century—stole all honors.
>
> The Historical Branch of the Imperial Society has done magnificent work in this field which will now, one hopes, reach a wider public. It was good to see Peter Clegg of the Covent Garden Ballet in the audience. It would be better if historical dance could be taught at the Royal Ballet School.[6]

No programs from the Arts Council performances survive; the only evidence of them is a brief note, dated May 18, 1963, from Cyril Beaumont sending his best wishes to me and my dancers:

> Dear Wendy,
>
> Just a few flowers to wish you and your Ensemble every possible success. The Arts Council Room is the right setting for you, and I am sure you will do full justice to it.
>
> Sincerely,
> Cyril Beaumont

[5]Ensemble member Timothy Hext provided the program from the performance at Mahatma Gandhi Hall and shared the following anecdote:

"In 1963 I was dancing with the Walter Gore Ballet Group at the London Palladium, and during this period Domenico was rehearsing a program to be shown at the Mahatma Gandhi Hall. The ballet group made one appearance in the variety show, then we waited to take a bow with the rest of the company in the finale. Seamus Gordon was the ballet master for the show in general, so Wendy, who had worked with Seamus previously, got permission for me to miss the final curtain call of the first house (this was a twice-nightly show), take part in the Domenico recital at the Gandhi Hall, and get back to the Palladium in time for the ballet group's appearance at the second house. If Wendy was determined something should happen—then it did!" Hext, letter to Susan Bindig, July 5, 2004. — SB

[6]M. C., "Court Dances," *Dancing Times* (June 1963).

Our next significant engagements would not be until 1965, but they would take us out of England for the first time, to Rotterdam in April and Munich in June. Michael Holmes was now teaching ballet in Rotterdam and would join us for the April 13 performance as a dancer and narrator. Our engagement at the Atrium Building was sponsored by the Werkgroep Danskunst Rotterdam, a group that was dedicated to encouraging "interest in dance and to shedding light on its form, content, style and historical context."[7] No program from the performance remains, but as the reviews make clear, we presented the same type of program as in the past, with dances from the fourteenth through the eighteenth centuries. Michael's narration provided the audience with an overview of the origins and development of the dances we performed. I have no recollection of the musical group who must have performed with us.

We were delighted that the press came, and we received encouraging, though puzzling, reviews—puzzling in that the reviewers didn't seem to quite know what to make of us, and encouraging in that they nonetheless enjoyed what they saw and heard. The *Algemeen Dagblad* called the concert "extremely enlightening" and noted that it was "much applauded."[8]

Then, on to Munich and a performance with the Studio der frühen Musik, an already significant early music group whose influence in the early music world would only increase over the next few decades. The four central members of the group were Thomas Binkley, Andrea von Ramm, Willard Cobb, and Sterling Jones. For this performance, they were joined by Don Smithers, Caroline Butcher, and Johannes Fink. Our group had a few new members. Besides Molly, Suzanne, and me were Birte Lav, Desmond Smith, and John Joyce. Michael's name appears on the program, but he in fact did not go to Munich with us.

Performing with a dance group was a new venture for the Studio der frühen Musik. Given the focus of the quartet's repertoire, the program differed from others we had given in that it did not include baroque dances, only dances from the fourteenth through the late sixteenth centuries. These were interspersed with vocal and instrumental music from the same time periods. The June 10 performance at the Theater in der Leopoldstrasse was magical, as Suzanne recalled. Molly remembered that the audience was particularly appreciative (despite someone falling asleep in the first row), giving us a standing ovation and showering us with flowers at the end of the program.

The reviews were wonderful. Th. Koebner writing in the *AZ-Feuilleton* wrote, "The Domenico Ensemble (Wendy Hilton, director) performed with tasteful understatement, charm and beautiful costumes of the time. Great applause."[9] The Studio der frühen Musik had tried to interest Bavarian television in the project but without success. Not only would it have helped all of

[7]"From Pleasure to Art," unattributed review of the concert from the Rotterdam press. Company member Suzanne Burdon provided and translated the review from the original Dutch. — SB

[8]"The Origins of Ballet," *Algemeen Dagblad*, April 14, 1965. Company member Suzanne Burdon provided and translated the review from the original Dutch. — SB

[9]Th. Koebner, *AZ-Feuilleton*, June 17, 1965. Anne Witherell translated the review from the original German. — SB

us professionally, but also, more practically, it would have helped pay the bills of a costly project, which was financed at a loss by the quartet.[10]

The Domenico Dance Ensemble would give only one more performance, a year later on May 23, 1966, at Morley College with the Morley College Consort.[11] This was not because of waning interest in us or our work, but of what I was hoping would be my departure for America. But I'm getting ahead of myself.

Interwoven with these performances by my company were other wonderful opportunities to perform, choreograph, and teach. With all the work that goes into developing a new performing group, my schedule was quite full. These new opportunities, however, particularly in opera, were too exciting, and I certainly couldn't pass them up. The paychecks that went with them—no matter how small—were also helpful!

The first of these opportunities had come in early 1961, just a few weeks before the premiere of the Domenico Ensemble. I danced in my first Handel opera, *Rinaldo*, presented by the Handel Opera Society at the Sadler's Wells Theatre on May 16; at the Händelfestspiele in Halle, Germany, on June 21; and, in between, in two performances at the Komische Oper in East Berlin, the dates for which I cannot document. Charles Farncombe was the conductor, and Shelah Wells, the choreographer. I was one of twelve dancers who portrayed Furies.

Rinaldo provided two firsts for me: it was the first complete Handel opera I had experienced, and it provided my first trip to the continent. The traveling was exciting, although I found East Berlin very depressing. Next, though, was Leipzig, where we were to stay and travel to and from Halle by bus. I had not expected to be in Leipzig and was overjoyed. The arrangement provided a wonderful opportunity to spend time in and savor the atmosphere of Bach's church, the Thomaskirche.

Rinaldo had, for the most part, an excellent cast. Helen Wells sang the lead role of Rinaldo, giving a beautiful performance, both vocally and dramatically, while Jennifer Vyvyan was her usual wonderful self as Armida. All of the performances were very successful, and in general, *Rinaldo* was my best performing experience to date.

A wonderful result of my performance in *Rinaldo* was my friendship with Eileen Cropley. An aspiring modern dancer who had studied with Sigurd Leeder, Eileen, like me, danced as one of the twelve Furies. She was the first of two dancers I invited to join the Domenico Dance Ensemble when it expanded in 1963.

I was again engaged by the Handel Opera Society, this time as choreographer, for its 1962 production of Handel's *Jephtha*. Like *Rinaldo*, it premiered

[10]For a detailed discussion of the Studio der frühen Musik, see Sterling Jones, "The Story of an Early Music Quartet" (unpublished ms., n.d.), Sterling Jones's Personal Papers. Jones refers briefly to this performance on pages 55 to 56 and gives the full program on page 172. — SB

[11]Per an undated program, the Domenico Dance Ensemble also gave the closing performance of the 1965–66 season of the Apollo Society of Rugby, a group that brought professional performers and lecturers to Rugby. — SB

in London at the Sadler's Wells Theatre and then traveled to Europe, to Liège, Belgium. My memory of my work on this production is cloudy, but I recall that from the outset it promised to be an odd assignment since *Jephtha* is a sacred drama and hence has no dance music! But the society's producer, Anthony Besch, had decided that dancing should be added wherever the music allowed for it, which, not surprisingly, was still very scarce.

The London production employed six female professional dancers. Eileen, happily, was one of them. When the production went to Liège, however, the "dancing" was done by five girls from the Wimbledon High School, with a sixth dancer who presumably was in charge of them. Since there really is so little opportunity for dancing in *Jephtha*, it was decided that simple moves given by the producer, rather than my choreography, would suffice for the Liège performances. The society, then, would not have the expense of dancers' fees for the trip abroad. I understood, I think.

On a brighter note, *Jephtha* was the first of three productions in which I rubbed shoulders with the young Janet Baker, who, on the threshold of her wonderful career, sang the role of Jephtha's wife. Ronald Dowd was very moving as Jephtha, as was Elizabeth Harwood as Iphis, his daughter. While *Jephtha* was not, indeed, could not be, a great choreographic experience, for a listener it was an extremely rewarding one.

Late in the autumn of 1963, I received an offer to participate in an unusual (for me, at least) production at a highly unusual theater. I was engaged to choreograph the 1963 Christmas production, *The Wizard of Oz*, for the Century Theatre, England's famous "Playhouse on Wheels," which was in residence in Guildford, Surrey. The following note on this unique and very remarkable theater appeared in *The Wizard* program:

> Theatre on Wheels . . .
>
> The Century Theatre was founded in order to take good plays to people normally without opportunities for seeing them, and the unique "theatre-on-wheels" was built specially for that purpose.
>
> Designed by John Ridley, the theatre was built by him and a small group of craftsmen during the years 1948–52. The capital was raised by public subscription: donations were made by individuals, clubs, charitable trusts, firms, trade unions; by celebrities of the theatrical profession, and uncelebrated but none the less significant members of audiences. Many gifts were "in kind": for example, aluminum, rivets, timber, paint, tools, lighting equipment—the list is as varied as the construction of the theatre and its accompanying living-quarters is complex. A total of £22,000 was involved, of which approximately £4,000 came from H.M. Treasury.
>
> For the first few years the theatre stayed in each town for as little as one or two weeks, and many hundreds of miles were travelled. The theatre has the unique distinction of having housed audiences in the counties of Cheshire, Cumberland, Flintshire, Gloucestershire, Lancashire, Leicestershire, Middlesex, Oxfordshire, Staffordshire, Warwickshire and Worcestershire. Recently "stands" have been of longer duration, and have frequently been associated with some special event—such as standing-in for a theatre closed for alterations (as at Oxford recently), or testing the local reaction to

the proposed creation of a permanent theatre (as at Harrow). We are here in Guildford to help bridge the gap to the opening of the Yvonne Arnaud Theatre.[12]

Two colleagues from *The Tempest* at Regent's Park were now with the Century Theatre: Wilfred Harrison, who had played Gonzago, was the director, and Dione Ewin, *The Tempest*'s stage manager, was most deservedly a leading actress.[13] I suspect that it was Dione who suggested me to Wilfred as a possible choreographer for *The Wizard.* Anyway, Wilfred offered me the job, and I was pleased to accept.

I think in many people's minds the title *The Wizard of Oz* calls to mind only the 1939 movie starring Judy Garland. The Century Theatre provided

Figure 35. Advertisement for *The Wizard of Oz*, produced by the Century Theatre, December 23, 1963–January 18, 1964. Courtesy of Dione Ewin.

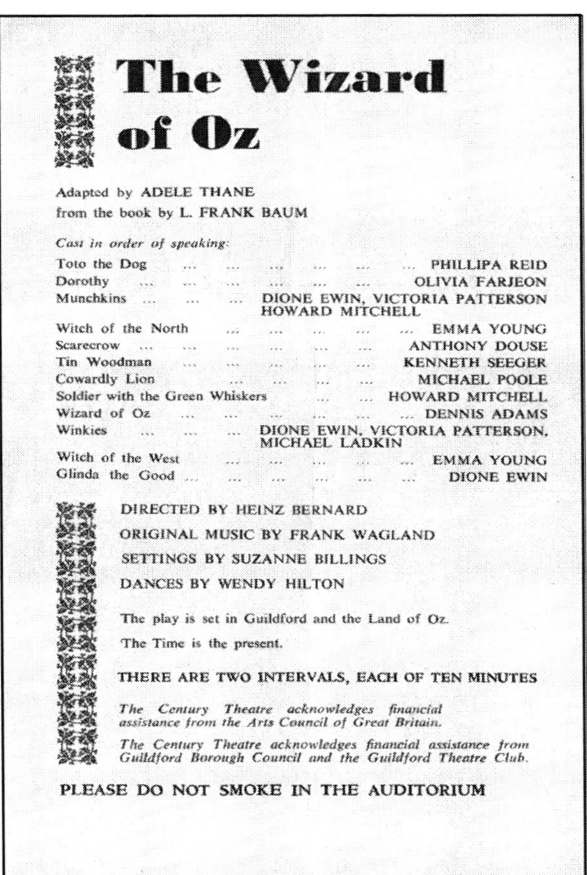

The Wizard of Oz

Adapted by ADELE THANE
from the book by L. FRANK BAUM

Cast in order of speaking:

Toto the Dog	PHILLIPA REID
Dorothy	OLIVIA FARJEON
Munchkins	DIONE EWIN, VICTORIA PATTERSON HOWARD MITCHELL
Witch of the North	EMMA YOUNG
Scarecrow	ANTHONY DOUSE
Tin Woodman	KENNETH SEEGER
Cowardly Lion	MICHAEL POOLE
Soldier with the Green Whiskers	HOWARD MITCHELL
Wizard of Oz	DENNIS ADAMS
Winkies	DIONE EWIN, VICTORIA PATTERSON, MICHAEL LADKIN
Witch of the West	EMMA YOUNG
Glinda the Good	DIONE EWIN

DIRECTED BY HEINZ BERNARD
ORIGINAL MUSIC BY FRANK WAGLAND
SETTINGS BY SUZANNE BILLINGS
DANCES BY WENDY HILTON

The play is set in Guildford and the Land of Oz.
The Time is the present.

THERE ARE TWO INTERVALS, EACH OF TEN MINUTES

The Century Theatre acknowledges financial assistance from the Arts Council of Great Britain.

The Century Theatre acknowledges financial assistance from Guildford Borough Council and the Guildford Theatre Club.

PLEASE DO NOT SMOKE IN THE AUDITORIUM

Figure 36. Program for *The Wizard of Oz*, produced by the Century Theatre, December 23, 1963–January 18, 1964. Courtesy of Dione Ewin.

[12]The local repertory theater burned earlier that year, and the Arnaud Theatre would not open until 1965. — SB

[13]Dione's work was highly praised by a friend of Wilfred's, Alec Guinness, when he visited the theater one day.

its audience with a broader view to lead up to its own modern production set in Guildford as the Land of Oz:

> The Story Behind the Wizard
>
> In the autumn of 1900, when "The Wizard of Oz" first appeared on American bookstalls, its author, Lyman Frank Baum, was 44. His life had been a restless one: newspaper reporter in New York, manager of a chain of theatres, playwriter and actor, owner of a general store in Aberdeen, South Dakota; editor and publisher of Aberdeen's weekly paper, traveller in china and glass, founder in Chicago of a window dresser's trade union, and editor of their journal, "The Show Window."
>
> It was in Chicago that he began writing books for children with some success, but when "The Wizard of Oz" appeared it was an instant hit; it became America's best-loved fairy-tale, and was translated into most known languages.
>
> In 1902, it was turned into a play with music for the first time, but although Baum himself wrote the book, this version departed considerably from the original—it even included a love-story between Dorothy and a boy poet!
>
> It has been filmed three times; twice as a silent film, in one of which Oliver Hardy, fat man of the Laurel and Hardy team, played the Tin Woodman. The last and best known version was in 1939, with the young Judy Garland as a singing Dorothy.
>
> All these versions in one way or another have taken considerable liberties with the book; this dramatization by Adele Thane of the Boston Children's Theatre, is probably closer to the spirit of the story.
>
> The changes which The Century Theatre has made for this production have been designed to keep "The Wizard of Oz" as its author intended—a modern fairy-tale.

The Century Theatre's modern production required the dance then the absolute rage, the Twist. I had never done the Twist since I did not like dancing socially, and it did not come at all naturally to me! In fact, I had to work very, very hard before approaching the company! I think they took to the dance more readily than I. Anyway, everyone seemed to have great fun, and I did too.[14] The production ran from December 23, 1963, to January 18, 1964. I remained in Guildford to enjoy Christmas with the company and the enthusiastic holiday audiences.

My foray into modern productions was brief, and I returned to opera in February 1964, when I was engaged to provide some choreography for a Covent Garden production of Verdi's *Rigoletto* directed by Franco Zeffirelli. I'd like to say that Zeffirelli hired me, but actually I never met him. The dances for Zeffirelli's productions were the responsibility of the resident opera-house choreographer (whose name I can't recall), but for this production, nothing he did for the *tempo di menuetto* in Act I, Scene 2, pleased

[14] Sincere thanks to Dione Ewin for providing much information and lending photos and other materials on the Century Theatre. On a program from *The Wizard of Oz*, Ewin indicated that it was the main characters—Dorothy, Toto, the Scarecrow, the Tin Woodman, and the Cowardly Lion—who Twisted down the Yellow Brick Road. — SB

Zeffirelli. After several of his efforts had been rejected, the choreographer expressed his despair to the rehearsal pianist, the much sought-after Lily Barker (Ames), who also played for some of my classes. At Lily's suggestion, the choreographer arranged for me to be contracted by Covent Garden to do this one dance, in return for which I was to receive a fee but no credit in the program. I agreed but not really wholeheartedly.

I arrived at Covent Garden for my first rehearsal to see the entire company on stage in full dress and learned that the *tempo di menuetto* was to be danced in this production by six dancers dressed in white representing virgins. So much for anything resembling any kind of period minuet! Mercifully, the *tempo di menuetto* is brief. In Zeffirelli's inimitable style, the stage was crowded to the point of suffocation, the women's dresses complicating things by having enormous shaped skirts. The six dancers simply had no room to move at all. So, I reduced the number of virgins to five and gave them simple weaving patterns, which kept them within their own tiny piece of territory. They were suitably unobtrusive, and this pleased Zeffirelli. The resident choreographer took full credit for the dance and carefully kept me out of view. Zeffirelli, it seems, never knew that two choreographers contributed to his production.

My next opera was *Ariodante* for the Barber Institute of Fine Arts of the University of Birmingham. Musically, it was one of the best experiences of my life, as *Ariodante* is one of Handel's greatest works and Janet Baker sang the title role. It was glorious and extremely moving. The conductor was Anthony Lewis, the producer/director was Brian Trowell, and the set and costume designer was Mark Haddon—a wonderful team.

The opera was set to be performed on May 7 and 9, 1964. Brian Trowell had written to me some months before to engage my services as choreographer, having heard of my work with the Domenico Dance Ensemble. He wanted choreography in authentic style for his production. I accepted his exciting offer with delight since this would be the first time since the eighteenth century that authentic-style dancing would appear in a Handel opera. The initial excitement over, however, reality set in. With a small budget and a small stage, only four dancers could be used, hardly enough to provide the spectacle expected by Handel. But we did our best. There was me, Molly Kenny, Suzanne Burdon, and Desmond Smith.

One of the prize opportunities and challenges for a choreographer in *Ariodante* comes at the end of Act II. It is a dream sequence originally danced by Marie Sallé. Somehow, Belinda, rather than I, became the choreographer for a dance beautifully performed by Molly. I do not know now how this came about. What I do remember most clearly is Belinda staking her claim by making it clear that any really worthwhile work that I found was hers by right. In the future I should automatically lay the "best bones" at her feet. Belinda considered Brian Trowell one of the best bones that had ever come along—which he most certainly was—and proceeded to take him over.[15] For

[15]Brian Trowell, in a eulogy of Belinda Quirey, mentioned meeting Wendy, the Domenico Dance Ensemble, and Quirey through this production of *Ariodante*. He wrote, "I asked around, trying to find a group of dancers with ideals like our own [at the Barber Institute], and (cont.)

me, the result was that I never told Belinda of my future plans again. I did everything I possibly could without her, but sometimes it had to be in spite of her, and, unfortunately, occasionally still with her, as in a 1965 opera production of *Hippolyte et Aricie.*

Following *Ariodante*, Brian Trowell engaged Belinda to choreograph Jean-Philippe Rameau's *Hippolyte et Aricie* at the Barber Institute. She wanted me to dance in it; the other dancers were Jill Gomez, a singer who could also dance, and Desmond Smith. I, of course, had reservations. Janet Baker, however, was to sing Phèdre and John Shirley-Quirk, Thésée. That and the fact that I had never experienced a full-length Rameau opera won the day. My heart sank, though, when I found out that Belinda herself intended to dance, and my fears were well founded.[16]

There were many dances in *Hippolyte et Aricie*, but those in Act II proved the most compelling for me. Working on them also revealed a new aspect of Belinda's curious method of handling a difficult choreographic challenge. Desmond and I danced as two Furies. On the first day of rehearsal, Desmond arrived at the studio before me, and by the time I got there, Belinda had taught his parts to him. My part was handed to me on a piece of paper which read: measures 1–3, Desmond; measures 8–12, Wendy; etc. This was fine, I thought; it provided a preliminary map. But I waited for Belinda to give me some steps. To my surprise, she said, "You work it out, dear." With some sarcasm, I asked, "Do you happen to have the music?" Belinda said, "Sorry dear, later," and walked away. Some days afterward, Belinda was finally forced to set my part, and the problem seemed to have been that she really did not know the music. One specific aspect of Act II that I recall is Desmond and me kneeling at Pluto's feet. Brian Trowell did not direct us at first, and so we set about creating our own movement. It turned out that Desmond and I had very different ideas. Desmond waved his arms about

---

came across the Domenico Dance Ensemble, run by Wendy Hilton. They proved willing, and admirable to work with. One day at rehearsal, Wendy asked if her teacher might come along, and so I first met Belinda Quirey." Trowell did not say why he asked Quirey to choreograph the dream sequence, but what seems to have been an innocent and polite introduction on Wendy's part reaped a choreographic coup for Quirey. Trowell, "Some Memories of Belinda Quirey," in *Belinda Quirey and Historical Dance* (London: Early Dance Circle, 1997), 45. Interestingly, though, Quirey was not directly credited in the program with the choreography of the dream sequence; Wendy received full credit as the choreographer of all the dances. In the program notes, Trowell acknowledged Quirey's services as more of a consultant to the production and to the Domenico Dance Ensemble. In her program notes on the dances, Quirey implied the same and did not mention her role as choreographer of the dream sequence. — SB

16 Wendy did not explain her dissatisfaction with Quirey's dancing in *Hippolyte*, but Trowell found it more than satisfying despite some initial reservations of his own. He wrote:

"When we mounted *Hippolyte*, she had not quite decided to give up dancing herself, and proclaimed that she would perform the long Chaconne, the crown of the fifth-act sequence of dances. I had not expected this, and she said, even before I had responded, 'Of course, you're anxious not to have an old hag dancing in your opera with a lop-sided face' (she had endured some kind of infection that had distorted the muscles)—'but it'll be all right, you'll see.' And so it was all right, for she advanced downstage with such majesty and elegance that we thought of nothing except how the magnificent music was seeming to dance itself. Belinda had a unique way, so unerring was her artistic instinct, of making musical phrases lift themselves out of the orchestra-pit and move about the stage like dramatic characters, or lines in a living painting." Ibid., 46. — SB

trying to look like Von Rothbart in *Swan Lake*, while I stayed absolutely still, like a cat ready to pounce. I think my costume, all black with a tight hood topped with an enormously long, thin orange feather made me feel like a cat, albeit one at the Folies-Bergère. Brian Trowell finally came out in my favor, and Desmond had to keep still. I was so grateful for this, because the scene is so frightening and the music sent chills down my still, erect spine every time.

Despite my problems with Belinda, both *Ariodante* and *Hippolyte et Aricie* proved to be unforgettable musical experiences, so much so that I never was able to see another performance of either opera. The thrill of these productions was later almost matched, however, by a recording of *Hippolyte et Aricie* by Lorraine Hunt Lieberson, whom I found to be a wonderful successor to Janet Baker.

In addition to these wonderful performing opportunities, my teaching career also began in the early 1960s. I had never before considered teaching—to do so had just not appealed to me. But to my great surprise, Maria Fay, with whom I was still studying, turned her studio, in part, over to me in early 1962 when she accepted the position of ballet mistress with the Grand Ballet du Marquis de Cuevas for an indefinite period. Everyone who knew Maria was amazed at her choice. With her studio well established and dancers from the Royal Ballet such as Merle Park attending regularly, this seemed the height of madness. Her work at her studio was surely more significant!

Soon after Maria's departure, I was teaching two classes a day, either ballet at her studio or character dance at one of the various studios around London where she also taught. After some initial nerves, I found that I had a distinct talent for teaching and, another surprise, even enjoyed it. I also discovered that I had a sharp eye for corrections. Among my students, I would eventually gain the title "Wendy, the All-Seeing."

In the end, Maria was away at the most for six months, as the De Cuevas company disbanded in June 1962. Perhaps, because De Cuevas had died a year earlier, the company lacked the necessary leadership and direction. Upon her return, Maria, of course, resumed her classes. I missed the teaching, but another opportunity soon arose. Belinda received a phone call from a friend explaining that the teacher of the two ballet classes at Morley College had been taken ill. Could she suggest someone who could take over the following week? Belinda suggested me, and I was accepted at Morley without question. My teaching career had firmly begun.

A little later at Morley, I suggested that I might also offer a beginning historical dance class. It was agreed that I should give it a try. To my delight—and relief—a sizeable group enrolled, including Peggy Dixon and Madeleine Inglehearn, who later were also to do significant work in early dance.[17] The classes covered basic work on fifteenth- to eighteenth-century

[17] Peggy Dixon was the artistic director of the London-based Nonsuch Dance Company, dedicated to the research and performance of early dance, and directed the Nonsuch Summer Schools in early dance. Madeleine Inglehearn is the artistic director of the early dance (cont.)

dances. With the success of those classes, I was later able to devote a full semester to one period. These teaching engagements also led to the performances at Morley by the Domenico Dance Ensemble.

Between 1963 and 1968, I taught early dance and/or ballet for various periods of time at the following schools or studios around London:

1963–68	Morley College, dance department
1963–68	Marylebone Institute for Further Education, open classes
1964, 1966, 1968	Guildhall School of Music and Drama, drama department
1964–66	Royal Academy of Dance, teachers' training course
1965–68	ISTD, special courses for teachers
1965–68	Nesta Brooking School of Ballet, children's classes
1966–67	British Drama League, special courses for actors
1966–68	Institute of Choreology[18]

I also went to Germany for several brief visits as a guest teacher to Brigitte Garski, an extremely talented and intelligent modern dancer, who wished to add historical dance to her teaching credentials. She, too, went on to make important contributions to historical dance.[19]

I grew to really love teaching and was thrilled to see an increasing interest in historical dance. Teaching would also lead me, around 1965–66, to one of the most influential collaborations of my entire dance career.

group Companie of Dansers, also based in London. Inglehearn has also published on early dance, including a translation with Peggy Forsythe of Antonio Cornazano's *The Book on the Art of Dancing* (London: Dance Books Ltd., 1981). — SB

[18]This last school is most likely the Benesh Institute of Choreology, now known just as the Benesh Institute, founded in 1962. Both Wendy and Quirey are listed on the institute's website (http://www.benesh.org/ext_whoswhoRJB.html [accessed May 30, 2009]) as teachers. — SB

[19]Brigitte Garski studied dance at the Folkwang Hochschule, Essen, and the Wigman-Schule, Berlin, among other places. She directed the historical dance group Corona di Danza, based in Cologne, which performed throughout Europe. Garski's publications on historical dance include a translation into German of Cesare Negri's *Le Gratie d'Amore* (Hildesheim: Georg Olms, 2003). — SB

Ten: 1966–1968

Meeting Rosalyn Tureck ~ My First Trip to the United States ~ International Bach Society and the Dance Collegium ~ Research Grant from the Arts Council of Great Britain

Of the classes I taught in London, the most significant were those in diverse dance styles at Morley College. But for me personally, the most significant class was to be at the Marylebone Institute for Further Education in St. John's Wood, a baroque dance class begun because of an enthusiastic recommendation to the dean from one of the artists who had painted me, Eric Rodwell. He also taught at the institute. Thank you, Eric! This class started me on my path to America.

One of the students at Marylebone was a pianist, Maureen Longman, who was then studying with Rosalyn Tureck. I had long thought that Rosalyn, more than any other musician, felt the dance rhythms and tempi in Bach's keyboard music, being sympathetic to both the music and its roots in dance. Maureen told Rosalyn about my classes and how appropriate and insightful I found her interpretations of Bach. When, around 1965, I attended one of Rosalyn's recitals at the Royal Festival Hall and Maureen took me backstage to meet her, I repeated my admiration for her playing. Rosalyn then asked if I would consider coming to her studio in Knightsbridge to show her some baroque dances.

I believe three of us went: Desmond Smith, Suzanne Burdon, and I. Molly was in America and missed the opportunity. Maureen was there too, as was George Downs, whom Rosalyn was soon to marry. We showed a considerable number of dance types to Rosalyn, who became more and more excited. When we had finished, she went to the piano and said, "Is this suitable for your dance?" She began to play through the Bach keyboard pieces that she felt were the closest to actual dance music. For one-and-a-half hours, I danced a succession of bourrées, gavottes, minuets, and gigues with Rosalyn playing. We seemed made for each other.

As we were leaving, Rosalyn said she would contact me to discuss future possibilities of working together when she returned from the tour she was beginning in a day or two. I drove Desmond, Suzanne, and Maureen to the station. On parting, Maureen said, "Wendy, I think your life has been changed forever." In more than one way, she was right.

I left Rosalyn's house feeling completely transformed. The experience of dancing to Bach's music played by such a great artist whose interpretations I felt were completely compatible with mine was awe-inspiring. Afterward, my whole way of being was completely changed in baroque dance. Someone asked me what I had learned by the experience, and I replied, "How to stand." And that was the essence of it; I had an entirely new feeling of my physical center from which everything flowed outward. And so, by following my dream, despite every struggle and frustration, I had reached an experience that had far exceeded any of my expectations. And the experience seemed to be leading to a future where there would be others. This was indeed one of those great life moments.

But I had to be patient. Rosalyn told me that she would contact me in about a year, and she did. In May 1966, I received the following letter, which brought joy to my heart. Dance and music together at last! And Bach above all!

> Dear Miss Hilton,
>
> Thank you for your kind letter and your willingness to help me with packing up my scores. I shall be writing to Maureen within the next day or so to give her full instructions.
>
> Meanwhile I should like to tell you what I have in mind concerning yourself. I am on the verge of starting an Institute for Bach Studies in the United States. It may actually begin first with an International Bach Society, but the Institute will follow closely after, probably within a year or two.
>
> I have planned eleven divisions of study and activities for this Institute, one of them being a dance division. For this latter, I have you in mind to head it and develop through research, teaching and performance a department devoted to the dances of Bach's music.
>
> I am writing to ask whether you would be interested to come to this country to try this out for a while and perhaps, if it succeeds, eventually live here. You would have free scope to work on all aspects of research, developing a dance group and of course, dancing yourself. We would work together at various times of the year, when I would be present and I would hope that we could develop the first major school of the Bach dance in the world. There is no money for this Institute but I have received a number of invitations both on the West Coast and on the East Coast and the next year or two will be taken up in organizing and making plans for going into operation.
>
> I should be most interested to hear what new material you have. Please feel free to write me any new ideas you may have had or the results of any research or work that you have done since I saw you last. If you have any questions, I would be happy to be of help, if I can. I shall look forward with pleasure to hearing from you.
>
> With kindest regards,
> Rosalyn Tureck[1]

Of course, I accepted this wonderful offer and then waited again. Just after I had received Rosalyn's letter, the Domenico Dance Ensemble gave what I believe was its last performance, at Morley College on May 23. Then I devoted my time to preparing for my new venture with Rosalyn. I worked with Maureen on relating specific eighteenth-century choreographies to specific pieces by Bach, and I did a lot of research at the British Museum. Otherwise, life continued as usual.

But I did not hear from Rosalyn Tureck for a long time. Was nothing to come of our meeting after all? I began to get nervous and feel terribly suspended. I finally saw her when she returned to play at the Royal

[1] Wendy Hilton Personal Papers.

Festival Hall, and she apologized for the delay. Some funding that she had expected had not come through. But I was not about to let the opportunity of working with her go by. So I said that if she herself would play for me, I would visit America at my own expense to take part in the Second Annual International Congress of the International Bach Society (IBS) in New York in the summer of 1968. If the idea of dance related to Bach's music was not greeted favorably there, then we would know to abandon the idea. Rosalyn agreed. She would play for me in two sessions and provide hospitality.

In 1968 three of the collegia Rosalyn had in mind for the future Institute for Bach Studies would already be functioning: the Clavier Collegium, the Cantata Collegium, and, with my presence, the Dance Collegium. The others would begin in the course of time. The three-week IBS Congress at Lincoln Center would feature early evening presentations by Rosalyn and the collegia from Monday through Thursday in the auditorium in the Library for the Performing Arts. Rosalyn would give three presentations on the *Well-Tempered Clavier*, BWV 846–893; the Cantata Collegium and the Dance Collegium would have two evenings each for their own sessions; and the remaining five evenings would be devoted to the Advanced Bach Study Group. At the first meeting of the latter group, Pina Carmirelli would play Bach's Sonata in E Major for Violin and Clavier, BWV 1016, with Rosalyn; at the four others, there would be lectures by distinguished musicologists. All in all, it was a very exciting prospect, and I set about trying to make my trip a reality—not an easy task.

Money was, as always, a problem. The British government did not help by imposing a restriction on the amount of currency that could be taken out of the country—a measly sum of £50. I would be in America on a visitor's visa and therefore unable to work. However, things have strange ways of working out. Generous supporters of baroque dance raised most of my airfare—I couldn't believe it but was thrilled! Even so, I still needed to find the cheapest airfare. Molly had been to the United States and had flown Icelandic Airlines. Two things put them above the rest of the airlines for me—the fare was the cheapest by some £200, and they served free wine throughout the flight. I think it might have been the latter that was the deciding factor! Although extremely excited at the upcoming prospects, I was a little nervous at the idea of my first long journey to a foreign environment. Also, Rosalyn Tureck was a person of moods, not always reassuring. But at this point in time, she was as excited as I and was desperately anxious that her idea should succeed.

Then another unexpected but wonderful thing happened. Régine Astier (then Kunzle), who had visited my classes in London from California and wanted to study baroque dance seriously, invited me to come to the United States as early as January 1968 and stay with her as a "guest teacher," as it were, until I went to New York in May.[2] She would unofficially also reimburse my airfare, which would nicely supplement the £50 allowance and the other contributions I had already received. I would have no expenses while I stayed with her. I was on my way to America! So, I booked the London–New York–London leg of my trip on Icelandic and the New York–Los Angeles–New York leg on TWA. I departed London in early January 1968.

The trip was a disaster from the start. I arrived at Heathrow in plenty of time for my flight, but Icelandic had "lost" the plane. After three hours, they put passengers on an old prop plane—"Sort of old crock we flew during the war, held together with bits of string," my neighbor said encouragingly—and we set off for Glasgow. In Glasgow, Icelandic "found" a plane, and we were soon on our way to Iceland. A good meal was served along with the free wine. We got to Iceland without a hitch. After a couple of hours, we reboarded for the flight to New York. I took a sleeping pill to get me through it. However, we didn't leave the ground as promptly as planned because the air supply failed, and we had to get off the plane again. I wandered about in the ice and snow trying to stave off the effects of the sleeping pill and the wine and stay awake for two hours or so.

I made it to Los Angeles after what seemed like several days. I was so happy to have finally arrived. But no one was there to meet me! I called Régine; her husband David answered. Régine was on her way home. TWA had not told her of my plight. David said that he would come for me and suggested I go to a nearby hotel and wait. It would take about two hours, he said. I waited and waited. Two hours passed, then three, four—five hours later he arrived, having been stopped at random by the police for a routine car check.

My disastrous trip, though, quickly became nothing more than an irritating memory when I was finally able to relax and enjoy the glories of California. Régine lived on a hillside in Santa Barbara. When we first got to her home, I slept and slept. But I awoke to a wonderful view of the Pacific Ocean and a hillside with orange trees—bearing oranges! And the sun! To a sun-starved Englishwoman, this was heaven indeed. And I was to know it for three months! I had a wonderful time with Régine and David, needless to say.

Just after I arrived in Santa Barbara, I received a letter from the Arts Council of Great Britain telling me that I had been awarded a grant to visit European libraries for six months and conduct research on historical dance. Three meetings with people in the worlds of books, dance, and music would be arranged while I was in America. My prospects in my newfound career were becoming more and more exciting.

But a wonderful dance-book collection awaited me in California as well. On hearing of my upcoming visit to America, Cyril Beaumont had given me a letter of introduction to friends of his living in Los Angeles, Doris Niles and Serge Leslie, who owned an extensive library of dance books. Régine joined me on a trip to Los Angeles where we combed through Doris and Serge's lovely books. Among the books we viewed were original editions of Raoul Auger Feuillet's *Chorégraphie* (1700 and 1701), John Essex's *For the Further Improvement of Dancing* (1710), Pierre Rameau's *Le Maître à danser*

[2] Astier was pursuing her own work in baroque dance and preparing for a concert at the Santa Barbara Museum of Art on March 31, 1968. She recalls a visit from Rosalyn Tureck, also in California at the time, to discuss with Wendy details of their upcoming performances at the IBS. Astier, letter to Anne Witherell, April 18, 2005. — SB

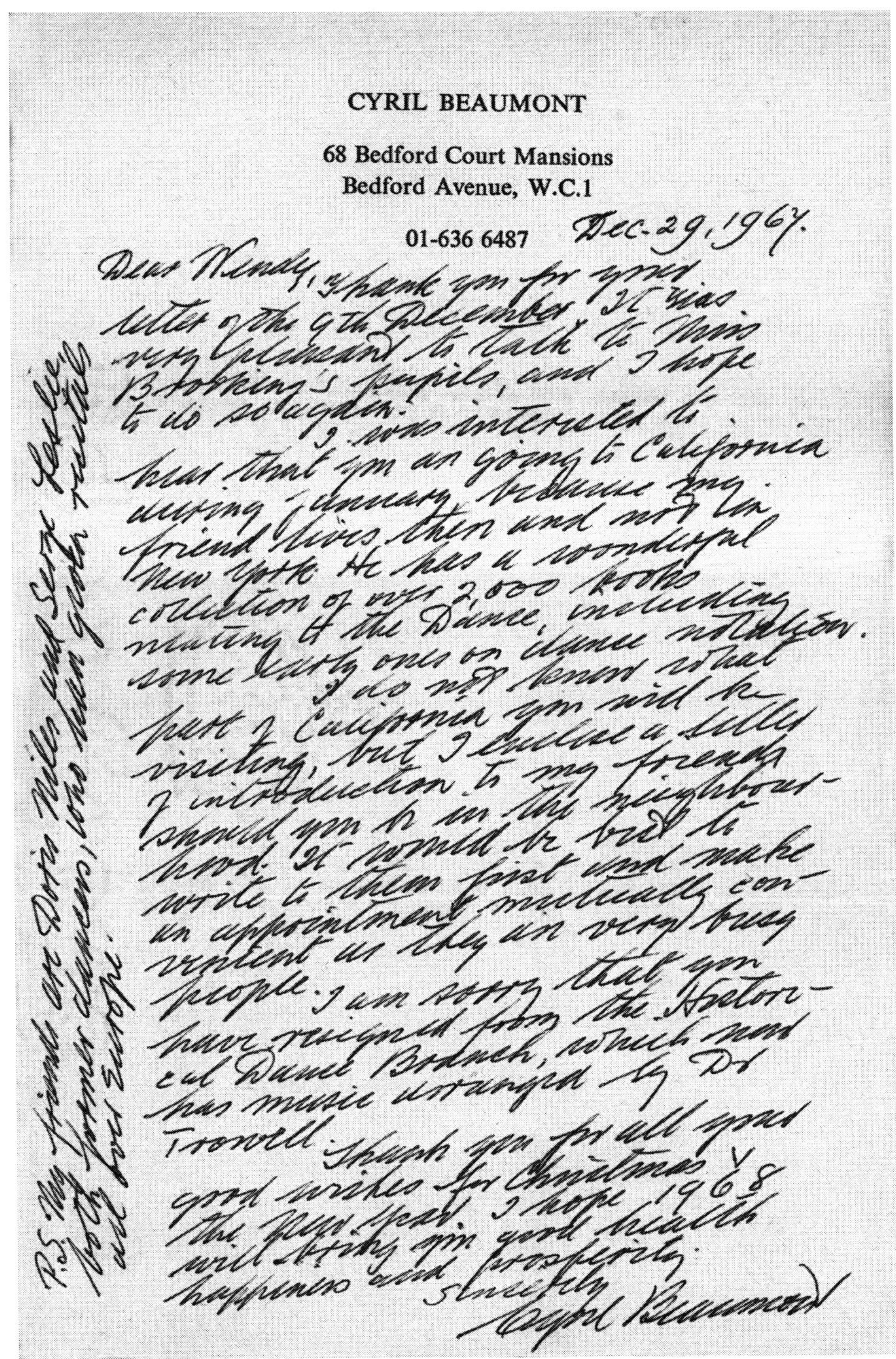

CYRIL BEAUMONT

68 Bedford Court Mansions
Bedford Avenue, W.C.1

01-636 6487 Dec. 29, 1967.

Dear Wendy, Thank you for your letter of the 9th December. It was very pleasant to talk to Miss Brooking's pupils, and I hope to do so again.

I was interested to hear that you are going to California during January, because my friend lives there and not in New York. He has a wonderful collection of over 2,000 books relating to the Dance, including some early ones on dance notation.

I do not know what part of California you will be visiting, but I enclose a letter of introduction to my friends should you be in the neighbourhood. It would be best to write to them first and make an appointment mutually convenient as they are very busy people. I am sorry that you have resigned from the Historical Dance Branch, which now has music arranged by Dr Trowell.

Thank you for all your good wishes for Christmas & the New Year. I hope 1968 will bring you good health happiness and prosperity.

Sincerely
Cyril Beaumont

P.S. My friends are Doris Niles and Serge Leslie, both former dancers, who have given recitals all over Europe.

Figure 37. Letter to Wendy from Cyril Beaumont, December 29, 1967. Beaumont suggests to Wendy that she visit Doris Niles and Serge Leslie to consult their dance library during her 1968 visit to the United States.

(1725), and Kellom Tomlinson's *The Art of Dancing* (1735). Régine and I had a delightful time.

We combined our library exploration with seeing a performance by the modern dancer Sybil Shearer, about whom I had heard so much. She proved to be everything I had been led to expect. The day after her concert, Régine and I had tea and a long and rewarding chat with her.

My third meeting was to prove extremely significant. Régine drove us to Stanford University to introduce me to George Houle, a professor in the early music department and director of the Stanford Baroque Orchestra.[3] Following the research of one of George's professors, Putnam Aldrich, studies in early dance had become an essential part of the early music curriculum at Stanford. George was very eager to work with me further and expressed the desire to bring me to Stanford when I was safely settled in the United States.

While I was in northern California, I was further introduced to the splendors of California's seemingly endless summer. George's future wife, Glenna, worked at Big Sur. As a treat, she arranged for all of us to sit in a warm pool and watch the sunset—a first for me. Oh, how I loved California! Another day trip, with David navigating, took us up a long steep hillside until we reached snow, in which we walked and then we sat. Looking far down on one side was hot yellow desert, on the other, the blue Pacific. I was awe-struck. Such contrasts, such beauty, and such sun!

But work beckoned. I also had a teaching engagement at the University of California, San Diego, with Rosalyn while I was in California, although I don't remember how it had been arranged. She was a guest professor for the quarter, presumably having accepted the position to be with her husband, who lived there.

Rosalyn and I did not have much preparation, but the class was informal, which lessened the pressure. At one point in the class, Rosalyn made a false entry, and, as I always do when something goes awry, I made a joke of it so that we could all laugh together. But Rosalyn was furious. "Don't you ever make people laugh at me again," she demanded later. She simply could not see that it was all right to join in and make light of the matter. The students would have loved her for it. While it seemed a minor incident, it did worry me for the future of our work together.

I was well paid for the class, a very positive outcome of the engagement. As I was in America on a visitor's visa, however, I could not be paid directly. Therefore, it was arranged for my fee to be sent to England, where it would be waiting for me when I got home. Well, with this and the Arts Council grant, I was going to be quite rich for a time!

My next stop was New York, where I was due, I believe, sometime in early June. From the airport, I made my way to the Port Authority Bus Terminal, where I was met by a friend of Rosalyn's, Alice Bonnell. We got into a yellow cab (just like the movies!) and drove to 113th Street and Riverside Drive, where Alice, a librarian at Columbia University, resided. I was to

[3] Ibid. Astier had met Houle at a meeting of the American Recorder Society. She recalled that during her visit with Wendy to Stanford, Wendy gave a class and a demonstration for Houle's students. — SB

stay one half of each week with Alice, and the other half with Rosalyn at her house in Ridgefield, Connecticut. Actually, Rosalyn had not quite moved into the house and was living in a rented house nearby. For about three weeks, until she did move, I found myself staying alone in a small-ish, old-ish house about two miles off the nearest road at the end of a dirt-track driveway. I could have been very nervous in these circumstances, but I did not feel frightened. I was happy, though, to move into Rosalyn's more spacious, better located new home.

My first impression of New York was that it was very old and run down. But I had a wonderful guide in Eileen Cropley, who was now dancing with Paul Taylor. We spent as much time as possible together, which, in the end, was not really so much, as we were both very occupied elsewhere.

Finally, the first performance at the IBS Congress approached, on Thursday, July 11. With my whole future depending on the outcome, a true New York heat wave engulfed the city, and Alice had no air-conditioning. There would be no much-needed rest for me. I thought of a story Tim Hext once told of a similar, stiflingly hot night when he lay in a full bathtub all night with only his nose showing. I moved to another IBS member's house that was air-conditioned until the weather cooled down.

There had been plenty of time to prepare the lecture-demonstrations, but Rosalyn turned out to be a procrastinator. She was enjoying leisure and relaxation. I began to get a little worried as time passed and feared I had met another Belinda. A large part of the lecture-demonstration would depend on my cuing Rosalyn, and the San Diego mishap was still fresh in my mind. But once she started working, Rosalyn never stopped, and we were ready in time. The work sessions were an absolute joy to me, as were the rehearsals when we were alone in the auditorium and completely free of tension. With no audience, the music absorbs the artists; there is this wonderful feeling of working on it—the artist existing only for the music. The bond between Rosalyn and me in our work was the greatest for me at these times. There were other absorbing times working at her Ridgefield home, usually after dark on warm summer nights when Rosalyn would feel like playing a particular piece. Her love of Bach's music simply overflowed. "Look what he does here," she would say, "and here . . . and now *this*." Those evenings and rehearsals certainly rank among the greatest experiences of my life.

The day of the performance arrived. First, I went to a hairdresser at 57th Street and 7th Avenue. I then tried to get a taxi to Lincoln Center. The first driver who stopped spoke only Spanish and didn't know where Lincoln Center was—a mere five or six blocks away. I hailed another cab. The second driver went shopping en route. He would stop, go into a store, and come out with a package. When he stopped for the third time, I quickly hopped into yet another cab. The shopping driver, whom I had just abandoned, ran out of the store shouting after me furiously.

I did get to Lincoln Center finally. Even after the nerve-shattering ride, the performance went very well, as did the second one, a week later on Thursday, July 18. Both performances were lecture-demonstrations with Rosalyn at the keyboard, Ruth Waterman on violin, and me. On July 11, our presentation was titled "Dance Forms Employed by Bach in His Music," and

Figure 38. International Bach Society, New York Public Library for the Performing Arts, 1968. *Left to right*: Rosalyn Tureck, Ruth Waterman, and Wendy.

Figure 39. Wendy lecturing at the International Bach Society, New York Public Library for the Performing Arts, 1968.

on July 18, "The Influence of Dance Forms upon Musical Performance." I no longer have the programs from these performances, but a transcript[4] of the accompanying lectures shows that, despite its title, the first lecture explored primarily the loure and the relationship of its dance steps to its accompanying music. To illustrate, I performed the woman's part from the danse à deux "Aimable Vainqueur" (Pécour/Campra, 1701) and the solo loure to music from *Scylla*, "Entrée pour une femme seul dancée par Mlle. Guiot" (Pécour/Gatti, 1712). Per the transcript, I clearly performed a third dance, which we never named in our talk and which I cannot now recall. But based on the surrounding discussion, it may have been the gigue lente "Entrée à deux Dancée par Mr. Dumirail and Mlle. Victoire à l'Opéra *Hésionne*" (Pécour/Campra, 1704), another danse à deux for which I again would have danced the woman's role. Our second performance continued the discussion of the first, exploring the courante, allemande, passepied, and bourrée. According to the transcript, I danced the courante from "La Bourgogne" (Pécour/Anonymous, 1700), "L'Allemande" (Pécour/Campra, 1702), an unnamed passepied perhaps also from "La Bourgogne," and "La Mariée" (Pécour/Lully, 1700) to illustrate a bourrée. This last was a curious choice since "La Mariée" is not strictly identified as a bourrée. In both performances, I also danced these entire choreographies or parts of them to selections from Bach's partitas and suites to show how Bach's music was informed by the dances.

The big excitement was that *New York Times* dance critic Don McDonagh was in the audience for the second performance, the only session to which the press was invited. That night was spent wondering if he would in fact review us, and if so, what he would say. The next morning, there it was! The idea was a success! Don wrote:

> The rich loam that nourished ballet's development was European court dancing, an almost forgotten genre now totally shadowed by its buoyant offspring. The form was partially restored from its undeserved obscurity last evening at the Lincoln Center Library Auditorium by Wendy Hilton and Rosalyn Tureck in a program of scrupulously reconstructed 18th-century court dances.
>
> Working from original manuscripts, Miss Hilton, in period costume, performed a selection of the proto-ballet dances that had engaged the wide-ranging musical interests of J. S. Bach.
>
> Miss Hilton's fluid grace and carefully modulated movements distinguished the pieces, which had a muted though broad range of expressiveness. Without a trace of theatrical extravagance, which would have been jarringly out of place in chamber dances, she interpreted them with tasteful, stylistic aptness.
>
> For one nurtured on ballet it was fascinating to see the ancestral family tree of steps and positions as they were actively employed before being modified for the theater.

[4]Wendy Hilton and Rosalyn Tureck, "Dance Forms Employed by Bach in His Music," July 11, 1968, audiocassette; Rosayn Tureck Collection, New York Public Library for the Performing Arts; and Hilton and Tureck, "Dance Forms Performed by Bach in His Music," July 18, 1968, audiocassette, Rosalyn Tureck Collection. The titles of the tapes are not consistent with the titles of the lecture-demonstrations themselves, but the tapes are, in fact, recordings of these particular events. — SB

> The comments of Miss Hilton and Miss Tureck, the noted Bach interpreter, on the relationship of the dances and the music were pointed, informative and devoid of any pedantry in the best traditions of scholarship.[5]

We were sure that, on the strength of that review, it should now be possible to obtain some funding so that the Dance Collegium could expand and continue.

First, though, I had to return to England, use my Arts Council Grant, and get a visa for permanent residency in the United States. Unfortunately, the United States had just very drastically cut the number of immigrants per country that were to be allowed to enter each year. For once, money was not the obstacle. But the visa problem would prove to be difficult to solve. I left the problem with Rosalyn and her attorneys, providing her with the necessary letters of recommendation from such people as Clive Barnes of the *New York Times* and Martha Hill of the Juilliard School.

Before I left, I thought, too, to ask Genevieve Oswald, curator of the Dance Collection at the New York Public Library of the Performing Arts, if she would like me to obtain copies of research materials for the library. She was extremely enthusiastic and not one to let a golden opportunity go by. Within a few days, a sizable amount of dollars was put into my hands. I suppose I signed for it, but I do not remember. I, however, remember thinking of the incredible amount of time such arrangements would have taken in England.

Finally, it was time to return home. The return trip on Icelandic was without incident! From the moment I had arrived at Régine's until I left New York, I had had a wonderfully exciting and rewarding time. I felt very confident about the future.

The grant from the Arts Council of Great Britain took me to Europe and some of its great libraries. Régine decided to come too, which was a tremendous help, particularly in Paris, as she knew the ropes and how to deal with French civil servants. She also found us a cheap apartment.

We were aware that there were important manuscript collections of notated dances, which were not yet generally known, in the Bibliothèque Nationale and the Bibliothèque de l'Opéra. These we found and others besides. We had everything microfilmed and got quadruple copies—one each for me, Régine, the proposed IBS library, and the Library for the Performing Arts. A laborious but very important task was identifying the tunes of the dances so that we could obtain their music in full score. Weeks were spent carefully turning pages of *partitions générales* at the Opéra. We located many tunes, and at the end of our time there, each of those had to be microfilmed.

I shall never cease to be amazed at the different procedures involved in gaining access to and then using the libraries. At the Bibliothèque Nationale, because I did not have a doctorate, I had the greatest trouble in obtaining a

[5] Don McDonagh, "Wendy Hilton Gives Bach Court Dances," *New York Times*, July 19, 1968.

pass to do the research. Even with the pass, I felt like a prisoner in the printed rare book area; they watched me so suspiciously. But in the manuscript room, it was all so casual. I felt I could have walked out with anything, and no one would have noticed. Especially tempting would have been Lorin's *Livre de la contredance du Roy*.[6] The Bibliothèque de l'Opéra was even more amazing. I needed various pages of music from about thirty rare scores by Lully, Campra, and others. To get these microfilmed, I was allowed to go with the photographer, a Monsieur Hawkins, to his studio in a taxi. We carried the precious scores between us.

Régine and I also went to Versailles for about a week. She then had to return to California, and I went on alone to Salzburg to visit Derra de Moroda and her wonderful library.[7] There I stayed in a small hotel close by Derra's home and visited her every day of my two-week stay. We worked in the mornings. Afternoons were spent sightseeing, including scenic rides in ski lifts, as it was still warm autumn weather. Derra was very generous, both with her time and knowledge. I copied everything I needed that was in notation.

One day Derra received a phone call from Munich. The caller, who represented Insel Films, was searching for someone to teach two dancers, I believe from the opera, the minuet for an educational film. Well . . . there I was. Soon I was on my way to Munich. The dancers did very well; the costumes and settings were fine. Unfortunately the film, *Das Menuett*, was edited after I had left, and only in the very final minuet step were dance and music correctly synchronized.

In Munich I saw Thomas Binkley (of the Studio der Frühen Musik), and he looked at me with sorrowful brown eyes and said how he regretted that I was going to sell my soul to capitalist America. On parting, he shook my hand solemnly in sadness. I was amazed when he turned up several years later to enjoy a lucrative life in his old capitalist country and a position at Indiana University.

I believe my next port of call was Berlin. I visited a few libraries, but although the staffs were very courteous and helpful, I failed to unearth anything of particular interest there. A Herr Dr. Wagner was especially helpful to me. The most significant part of my visit to Berlin was my time spent with the early dance specialist Karl Heinz Taubert, author of one of the first contemporary books on early dance, *Höfische Tänze*.[8] Derra had told me that Karl had initially been a pianist, but his hands were injured in World War II. At a loss as to what to do with his life, he was responsive to Derra's suggestion that he explore the relationship of early dance and music. Karl presented

[6] André Lorin, *Livre de la contredance du Roy* (Paris, 1698). — SB

[7] Friderica Derra de Moroda's extensive library was acquired by the University of Salzburg. For the complete descriptive catalogue, see Derra de Moroda, *The Dance Library: A Catalogue*, eds. Sibylle Dahms and Lotte Roth-Wölfle (Munich: Robert Wölfle, 1982). Highlights of the rich baroque dance materials in the Derra de Moroda Dance Archives can be found in Sibylle Dahms, "Derra de Moroda's Collection of Baroque Dance Sources," *Dance Research* (Winter 1997), 142–49. — SB

[8] Karl Heinz Taubert, *Höfische Tänze: Ihre Geschichte und Choreographie* (Mainz: B. Schott's Söhne, 1968). — SB

me with a copy of his recently issued book, which covers Renaissance and baroque dances and is handsomely illustrated. The music for the dances is arranged for keyboard and comes separate from the text in a size that can be slipped into a pocket on the back cover—a very good idea. I enjoyed meeting Karl very much. He was a sweet man and a wonderful host—I was well cared-for. Besides sharing insights on early dance, he took me to outstanding performances of Alban Berg's *Lulu* and Wagner's *Der fliegende Holländer* at the opera.

My next destinations were Lüneburg and the court in Celle, where Bach was exposed to so much French culture. Here, though, I developed an infection and, so, decided to return to England, deposit what I had acquired, regroup, and set forth again.

My remaining priority was to visit the theater in Drottningholm, the best-preserved eighteenth-century theater in the world. Built in 1766 on the remains of the original theater that was destroyed by fire in 1762, it fell into disuse after about 1792 for well over one hundred years. In the early 1920s it was restored to its eighteenth-century glory by literary and theater historian Agne Beijer, opening again in 1922. Today the Drottningholm Court Theatre still offers performances in the summer months of historical theater and opera productions.

Mary Skeaping was lucky enough to work at Drottningholm beginning in the 1960s, in addition to her duties as ballet mistress of the Royal Swedish Ballet. She had invited me to stay with her, which provided us with a chance to catch up and also helped me to save some money. Mary provided a performance schedule, and I saw two of her works at Drottningholm, the names of which unfortunately now escape me—one to music by Purcell, the other a late eighteenth-century piece in which Ivo Cramér participated with wonderful mime. I saw one performance from the seat behind that for the Présence, right in front, and one from far back and so got a wonderful perspective on the workings of this beautiful theater. Mary saw to it that I was given the most comprehensive tour. I am very grateful to that fine, witty, and fun-filled lady.

There was plenty to do and see in Stockholm, and I left with regret and with great appreciation of Mary. I took an SAS flight home. The food was wonderful, and the landing so smooth that everyone applauded. It was a perfect homecoming. But I came home to a period of great frustration because if the new visa rules could not be circumvented, it would be two years before I could return to the United States—and that would be two years too late. I made many futile visits to the American Embassy over that cold winter to try to resolve my dilemma.

One bright spot during this seemingly endless waiting period was taking part in the production of the first BBC color television presentation of *Vanity Fair*, with Susan Hampshire as Becky and with choreography by Geraldine Stephenson. Other than this one interlude, I had little to do; I had no work, having given it all up in hopes of my next trip to America. I again contacted the artists for some modeling jobs and waited in a state of extreme frustration and anxiety.

Figure 40. Wendy called this photo "Contemplation—Shall I Go to the U.S. or Not?" late 1960s.

Eleven: 1969–1971

Emigrating to America ~ Congress of the International Bach Society ~ Tureck and the Metropolitan Museum of Art ~ End of the Dance Collegium

The United States immigration officials who were unable to give me a visa because of the new quota restrictions had not reckoned with Rosalyn Tureck. If she wanted something, she seldom gave up trying to get it. On March 6, 1969, Becker and London, the IBS attorneys, wrote a firm letter to the United States Immigration Office in London. The letter outlined how many important persons had written asking for me to be granted a United States resident visa without delay. Rosalyn later told me that even Senator Jacob Javits, a friend of hers, had been involved.

The letter did the trick. On April 24, 1969, I had a medical examination, followed by an interview under oath. The interviewer told me that they would be quite pleased to be rid of me because they had never been so constantly badgered about anyone. He also advised me not to become an American citizen. I was surprised and asked why. "Well," he said, "it's good to have a foot in two countries." I thought it very kind of him to so advise me. A short time later I received an IMPORTANT NOTICE, a form communication with the date "Apr. 69" added at the bottom. My visa was enclosed.

Now, after the months of waiting and frustration, I was in a rush. I found passage on the *S.S. Rotterdam*, which was leaving for New York in late May. Rosalyn asked me to take along some of her things from her Knightsbridge house because my taking them as an immigrant would save her money. I said that I would be happy to do so as long as they were professionally packed and transported to dockside. They were—in ten large crates! I had only three smaller ones.

Even in my departure, Belinda was true to form. On the one hand, she genuinely wanted me to succeed in America. On the other, she was obviously immensely relieved that I was going to be so far away, removing any threat of competition with her. It is true that from then on her career progressed in leaps and bounds: Covent Garden, Versailles, and an M.B.E. The last communication I ever received from Belinda was a postcard from France on which was the ecstatic exclamation, "Versailles at last!" But I doubt that she was ever truly happy, except in her usual pattern of ups and downs.

I boarded the *S.S. Rotterdam* with expectations of five beautiful days of sunbathing on deck and of learning dances. In reality, I had yet another uncomfortable trip to the United States. The problem this time was a three-day storm, with winds averaging seventy-four miles per hour. I love storms, or so I thought, and sat on a leeward deck for the whole first morning while the waves pounded on all sides. When I got up to go for lunch, disaster struck. My sea legs—and sea stomach—were not quite as strong as I thought. Somehow I made it to my cabin at the far lower end of the ship, where I remained prone for the next three days. Even the captain was ill. Once recovered, I was able to go to the exercise room, where I learned some new dances for the

IBS sessions. It was a bit rocky, but I managed to read the notation and not fall over as the ship swayed from side to side.

I arrived in the United States as a resident alien at 8:00 a.m. on Friday, May 30, 1969, Memorial Day. At noon, exhausted, I was still on the pier with Rosalyn's secretary and about thirteen angry customs officials. One of the boxes containing, not mine, but Rosalyn's possessions could not be found. When it finally turned up after what seemed like hours of searching, it was given a cursory search, and we were then on our way in a removal van hired for the purpose. I don't know where the secretary and the boxes went, but I made my way to Rosalyn's Connecticut home with one very small suitcase. Alice Bonnell was there with Rosalyn and her sister, Margaret Tureck. They were planning to serve the Thanksgiving dinner they had left in the freezer since November. Rosalyn cooked most of the meal, and everyone was nice enough to give thanks for my eventual arrival. It was a beautiful evening, and we ate our Thanksgiving meal outside under the trees.

I stayed with Alice, pending the time I could find my own apartment. Eventually I moved to Riverside Drive at 82nd Street, into an apartment owned by Lillian (Lil) Levine, a great music lover and IBS supporter. Her family had grown and moved to other parts of New York, leaving her with this lovely apartment. I had a room with a river view and the use of almost the whole apartment. Lil was wonderfully generous and helpful. She adored cooking, which was a blessing for me, as I am a disaster in any kitchen.

And so, once again, I spent half the week in New York and the other half in the country. Rosalyn let it be known, though, that she was not happy in her Ridgefield house. She wanted water on her land, and so at some point she bought another house in Pound Ridge, New York, situated beside a small lake. I, however, found Ridgefield very comfortable and a great break from the city.

Rosalyn and I had a little more than a month to prepare for the IBS's third Advanced Study Group, which was scheduled to meet from July 7 to 24, 1969; I was to participate on July 7, 9, and 21. Our first session on Monday, July 7, which opened the meeting, was "Performance Style According to Bach's Indications, Forms, and Structures," in which I danced two choreographies: "Aimable Vainqueur" (Pécour/Campra,1701) and the "Gigue à deux" ("Gigue de Roland") (Feuillet/Lully, 1701) with Rosalyn playing. Rosalyn related "Aimable Vainqueur" to the Loure from Bach's French Suite No. 5 in G Major, BWV 816, and the "Gigue de Roland" to the Gigue from his Partita No. 1 in B-flat Major, BWV 825. That this latter gigue by Bach is perfectly danceable in the French style was as much a surprise to me as to anyone. In this session, Rosalyn also played selections from the *Goldberg Variations*, BWV 988; Cantatas BWV 51 and 169; the Prelude and Fugue in G Minor, BWV 861, from Book I of the *Well-Tempered Clavier*; and Passepieds I and II from the French Overture in B Minor, BWV 831.

The July 9 and 21 sessions were specifically intended for members of the Dance Collegium, although anyone could attend. In the first session, Rosalyn and I discussed "The Step Vocabulary of Baroque Dance Forms," specifically the gavotte, bourrée, sarabande, minuet, passepied, and courante. We continued our examination of "The Step Vocabulary of Dance" in the July

21 session, adding the gigue and gigue lente. I again danced the "Gigue de Roland" and a gigue lente from Campra's *Ballet des Fragments de Lully* (1702).[1] As with the previous year, these sessions were well received by the attendees.

Soon afterward, Lydia Joel, the editor of *Dance Magazine*, surprised Rosalyn and me by asking us to write complementary articles for the October issue. Rosalyn was very excited. "So soon!" she said. Our brief work together in the United States had already begun to establish our reputation. In "A Celebrated Pianist and a Dance-Scholar Discuss the Interrelationships of Baroque Music and Dance Forms,"[2] Rosalyn and I each discussed our work in our respective fields and our collaboration. Rosalyn wrote about the Dance Collegium and how essential she found the knowledge of baroque dance to the performance of baroque music.

> I recognized that dance might help one achieve a better understanding of historical performance practices, and a musical reading closer to the composer's intentions.
>
> Essential as music is to the dance, indeed, dependent as this art is upon music, I have always believed that a large segment of music is equally dependent upon the dance. The linking role which each art demands from the other produces an evolving series of meaningful levels, ranging from the most literal plane of recognition to the most subtle allusions and nuances.[3]

This article and another by Rosalyn published earlier that year in *Music Clubs Magazine*[4] were perfectly timed for our next performance together at the Metropolitan Museum of Art, on October 23. The performance was highlighted in the *Dance Magazine* article.

At the museum, Rosalyn presented a three-part series on "The Interpretation of Bach." The first two lecture-demonstrations in the series, on October 9 and 16, were on the "History and Development of Performance Style" and "The Range of His Music," respectively. I joined her for the third presentation, "The Role of the Dance," in which we concentrated on the French Overture and on the Loure from the G Major French Suite. Here my role was to assist only by dancing, not by lecturing. A review in *Dance Magazine*, which I believe was the only one for this event and which I had really been looking forward to, was complimentary.

> Rosalyn Tureck, the highly-esteemed concert pianist, presented three programs on The Interpretation of Bach. The third, "The Role of [the] Dance," included Wendy Hilton who has reconstructed 18th-century dances from notation. Miss Tureck gave relevant historical background, understandably from the musical standpoint, and then played while Miss Hilton danced. Drawing from the French

[1] I have not been able to document the gigue lente to which Wendy refers and is noted in the IBS program. — SB

[2] Rosalyn Tureck and Wendy Hilton, "The Dancing Bach: A Celebrated Pianist and a Dance-Scholar Discuss the Interrelationships of Baroque Music and Dance Forms," *Dance Magazine* (October 1969), 47–50, 82.

[3] Ibid., 49.

[4] Rosalyn Tureck, "Bach and the Dance: A New Dance School of the Institute for Bach Studies," *Music Clubs Magazine* (April 1969), 28–29.

> Overture, the courante, gigue, bourrée, and passe-pied [*sic*] were performed. Miss Tureck isolated a few sections to illustrate a point, such as the rise in dance movement on the beat in the courante.
>
> Miss Hilton—with her slender figure, delicate wrists, articulate feet, and pleasant intelligent expression—might have stepped quietly from an 18th-century engraving. Her full-skirted, white gown was above her ankles, allowing her soft-slippered feet to be seen. The bodice, low and tightly bound, limited the torso to a quietly erect position. And the mild-length [*sic*] sleeves permitted freedom for the low, graceful arm movement.
>
> It was interesting to notice carry-overs to classic ballet; arms sloping gently from the shoulders, pliés and relevés, and turn-out. Miss Hilton was decidedly in command of what she did and brought to life what Miss Tureck called a dancer's ability "to feel a phrase."[5]

Earlier that fall, the IBS Dance Collegium classes had already gotten under way. They were held initially at a studio at the Ansonia Hotel. There were both adult and children's classes, but enrollment was small, owing, I think, to inadequate publicity. Even the *Dance Magazine* articles did little to increase the number of pupils. Given the unimpressive enrollment, I was surprised when Rosalyn turned up with her dog to watch the adult class on the first evening, as though to celebrate some grand opening. It would have seemed more discreet to stay away and leave things to me. She remained throughout, however.

The two children's classes were held on Saturdays. In the first, four girls of about twelve years of age took part. Ann and Catherine Mayberry and their friend Edna Calabrese came together from New Jersey. Ann and Catherine's mother, who had high theatrical ambitions for all three, brought them. Edna, I think, hated the class and came only grudgingly. All she seemed to long for—even at this age—was a husband, a home, and several children. Rebecca Gutman, was the fourth student, and she too was brought by her mother, Madeleine, who wanted the best of everything for her daughter. Two younger children came to the second class: David Castro, age seven, and Victoria Brown, who was slightly older.[6] All the children were to participate in the 1970 IBS summer sessions.

It must have been about this time that I met, by the greatest good fortune, another great musician, the pianist Virginia Hutchings. Realizing that I would soon need a musician for classes and lecture-demonstrations (Rosalyn, after all, would not be available), I called the Juilliard School and was put in touch with five alumnae. The first one I called was out, and the second was Virginia. She agreed to come to one of my classes.

I had moved the dance classes from the hotel to the studio of the Dance Notation Bureau, which had a small, rather seedy, upright piano. Virginia joined us there. After the opening sarabande, I gazed dumbfounded

[5]Jocklyn Armstrong, "The Interpretation of Bach: The Role of Dance, The Metropolitan Museum of Art, October 23, 1969," *Dance Magazine* (December 1969), 78.

[6]Victoria Brown Geduld, in a memorial tribute to Wendy, recalled a third student in their class, Nan Rosengarten. She is not, however, listed in the program for the 1970 IBS Congress. Geduld, "Remembering Wendy Hilton: A Program of Dance and Music Celebrating Her Life and Work," The Juilliard School, May 30, 2003. — SB

at her and said in awe, "You play beautifully." Thus began a long and highly valued collaboration and friendship. Because of the quality of Virginia's playing, I did not really miss Rosalyn. Virginia had studied with Rosalyn in London and had worked with George Balanchine and toured, I believe, with Melissa Hayden. She had also given numerous recitals in Europe, which had received outstanding reviews. Virginia's experience with ballet made her curious about baroque dance, which was very lucky for me. I have always been so grateful that the first pianist I called was out.

For my own part, I needed a partner badly for future performances and was able to interest Jonathan Watts, a well-known former soloist with New York City Ballet and the Joffrey Ballet, at this time associated with the Joffrey school, American Ballet Center. Another male dancer who turned up from time to time in New York to make guest appearances or to teach was Jürg Burth, whom I had met in Cologne.[7] In the spring of 1970 it became clear that both Jürg and Jonathan would be available to participate in the next summer's IBS sessions.

As Rosalyn had indicated to me in her letter of May 1967, in forming the International Bach Society, her goal was to establish an Institute for Bach Studies with large premises and eleven colloquia devoted to in-depth studies of different aspects of Bach's music. Such an ambitious enterprise would, of course, require considerable funding. The first step to obtaining funding was the launching of the IBS's summer sessions, from which the institute would grow. Everyone who contributed their time and energy to the enterprise did so with enormous faith. Certainly no greater efforts at fundraising could have been made than those of Rosalyn Tureck. But despite the success of the IBS and the great interest and praise aroused by the summer sessions and the concerts by Rosalyn and the IBS orchestra at Carnegie Hall, financial support was not forthcoming.

By 1970 the Dance Collegium had grown as far as it could without funding. The most urgent need if the group were to expand was costumes. In a modest attempt to raise some money, I organized a concert by the Dance Collegium with an excellent group of performers. The concert was on Sunday, April 19, at the Dance Center at 2080 Broadway. Eileen Cropley was available and contributed her performance to the IBS, as did Jürg, over from Cologne, and Max Dooyes, a choreographer from Holland who had been studying with me. Jonathan Watts and Ellen Holmes,[8] a lovely dancer whose mother was a keen IBS member, also danced. Virginia Hutchings was at the keyboard. The dances on the program were:

[7]Jürg Burth studied and performed historical dance with Brigitte Garski. He joined the ballet of the Opera Cologne in 1968, cofounded the Dance-Forum of Cologne in 1971, and was codirector, with Hans Meister, of the Zurich Opera Ballet Company for a few seasons in the early 1970s. His choreography has been performed by the Finnish Dance Theatre Raatikko and the Brooklyn Dance Theatre and at Berlin's Theater des Westens. — SB

[8]Per the program notes, Ellen Holmes was a dancer in the Interborough Civic Ballet at Manhattan's Clark Center for the Performing Arts. At that time, she was also the company's acting director. — SB

INSTITUTE FOR BACH STUDIES IBS INTERNATIONAL BACH SOCIETY, INC.

ROSALYN TURECK, DIRECTOR

PRESENTS

a demonstration of BAROQUE DANCES by the members of the professional dance classes of the IBS Dance Collegium, director, Wendy Hilton.

****

GIGUE POUR UNE FEMME. Seul non dancee a l'Opera. Music anonymous
Contained in: Nouveau Recueil de Dance de Bal et celle de Ballet de la Composition de Mr Pecour. Par Mr. Gaudrau 1712

WENDY HILTON

L'ALLEMANDE. 1702 Music probably by Campra
Dance by Pecour

The Allemande was danced by M. Ballon and Mlle. Soubligny in the ballet Fragments de M. de Lully. The tune appears in a manuscript score in the Bibliotheque Nationale in Paris which contains other music by Campra. It became one of the most popular ballroom dances, and appears in dance collections throughout the 18th century.

WENDY HILTON *JURG BORTH*

LE MENUET A QUATRE. A ball dance by Pecour.
Published in 1706, this became one of the new dances for 1707.

EILEEN CROPLEY *ELLEN HOLMES*
MAX DOOVES *JURG BORTH*

LE MENUET. According to Pierre Rameau in Le Maitre a Danser, 1725

ELLEN HOLMES *MAX DOOVES*

AIMABLE VAINQUEUR. Loure Music by Campra, Dance by Pecour
Aimable Vainqueur, a new ball dance for the year 1701, is composed to the air for the violins which precedes the song of that name in the opera Hesionne.

WENDY HILTON *JONATHAN WATTS*

GIGUE DE ROLAND Music by Lully, dance by Feuillet
Contained in: Recueil de Dances de Mr Feuillet. 1700

EILEEN CROPLEY *JURG BORTH*

VIRGINIA HUTCHINGS - keyboard

SUNDAY, APRIL 19, 1970 THE DANCE CENTER
3:00 P.M. and 6:00 P.M. 2080 Broadway, New York

140 WEST 57TH STREET, NEW YORK, NEW YORK 10019/TELEPHONE (212) 247-4788

Figure 41. Program for a fundraiser for the Dance Collegium, International Bach Society, April 19, 1970.

Gigue pour une femme, seul non dancée à l'Opéra (Pécour/Louis de Lully-Marais, 1712)—Hilton

L'Allemande (Pécour/Campra, 1702)—Hilton and Burth

Le Menuet à quatre (Anon./Anon., 1706)—Cropley, Holmes, Dooyes, and Burth

Le Menuet, according to Pierre Rameau (1725)[9]—Holmes and Dooyes

Aimable Vainqueur (Pécour/ Campra, 1701)—Hilton and Watts

Gigue de Roland (Feuillet/Lully, 1700)—Cropley and Burth

While the concert was well received by the audience, there were two unhappy outcomes to this venture: the money we raised was a drop in the bucket toward our needs, and Rosalyn was furious that I had not secured her direct, personal permission to sponsor such a concert. I had gotten the approval of her lawyer, as, before money could come in, a little had to go out. He had given me the go-ahead, and so the recital was done. This episode made me realize that even if we got funding, I could never continue with this venture if I had to get permission for everything.

The 1970 IBS Advanced Study Group was the last to include the Dance Collegium, although this was not immediately clear. Dance classes had already been advertised for the fall, despite our increasingly questionable financial situation. At the Study Group, which ran from July 6 to 23, Rosalyn and I presented two lecture-demonstrations. In the first on Thursday, July 9, Jonathan Watts and I opened the program with "Aimable Vainqueur," but one of the main interests of the afternoon was the work of my young students. My four older students—Edna Calabrese, Rebecca Gutman, and Ann and Catherine Mayberry—danced Pécour's "Le Menuet à quatre." Rebecca and Ann then danced together the solo Minuet by Mr. Isaac. The girls were lovely, but the absolute hit of the evening was Le Menuet, according to Pierre Rameau, in *Le Maître à danser*, danced by the seven-year-old David Castro and the nine-year-old Victoria Brown. David was a beautiful little boy; he could easily have been a young prince. The minuet is not easy, and he was determined to perform without mistakes. The beautiful concentration on his young face and his success won the audience. The applause was rapturous.

Following the minuet, I joined Rosalyn for a discussion of the sarabande and its step vocabulary and closed the dance portion of the program with "Gigue pour une femme, seul non dancée à l'Opéra." Music selections for the session were the Minuet and Gigue from Bach's Cello Suite No. 1 in G Major, BWV 1007, and the Gavotte and Loure from the Partita in E Major, BWV 1006, played variously by Ruth Waterman, violin; Eve Dickens, flute; Judith Davidoff, cello; and Virginia Hutchings, keyboard.

The Tuesday, July 14, program featured "L'Allemande" and the "Gigue de Roland," danced by Jürg Burth and me; a "Sarabande pour Deux Hommes" (Pécour/Louis de Lully-Marais, 1704), danced by Jürg and Jonathan Watts (which Jonathan said equaled in difficulty anything he had done with Balanchine); and two "Sarabande(s) pour une Femme" (Pécour/Lully, 1704),

[9]The program does not include the music for the minuet. — SB

danced by me. The featured musical selection again was the G Major Cello Suite, played by Peter Snyder. Oboist Brenda Schuman also played for this performance. Byron Belt of the Newhouse Newspapers wrote a particularly enthusiastic review:

> One of the most imaginative aspects of the work being done by the Bach Society has been the study of the pianist [Rosalyn Tureck] with English dancer Wendy Hilton. Miss Hilton, one of the most enthralling performers we have ever seen, has worked with Miss Tureck and original sources to reconstruct the patterns, tempi and other aspects of 18th century dance. This study has led to some astonishing approaches to the interpretation of the dance movements that are such an integral part of Bach's instrumental writing.[10]

Despite its success at the summer sessions and the clearly positive direction in which we were heading, the final decision that the Dance Collegium would be discontinued was announced a month or so later. I was devastated. It had been such a promising and prominent appointment. On the bright side, because of its prestige, through the IBS, I had made some significant contacts that would provide a number of opportunities for me. I now began to forge my own career in America.

[10]Byron Belt, *Newhouse Newspapers*, n.d. — SB

III.

In America

Twelve: 1971–1973

An Independent Career ~ Beginning Dance of Court and Theater *~ Dorothy's Death ~ Juilliard School, Rutgers University, and SUNY Purchase ~ Torticollis ~ First Ventures in California*

Wendy's career in America took off quickly. Despite her great disappointment at the demise of the Dance Collegium, her reputation in the New York dance and music worlds had been made, and numerous opportunities soon opened up for her through the many contacts she had developed with Rosalyn Tureck and the IBS. At times, these opportunities did not result in actual jobs as speedily as she may have preferred, and it would take a few years for her professional life to have any semblance of stability. But Wendy knew what she wanted, and her doggedness at pursuing every tantalizing prospect almost always secured her a position. The most significant of these appointments was at the Juilliard School, which provided her with opportunities to mount gloriously costumed and musically sophisticated performances in the baroque dance style, and at Stanford University, where, most importantly, she directed a highly respected annual workshop in baroque dance and music. These two appointments continued for more than twenty years and were professional anchors around which she negotiated other significant appointments in teaching, choreographing, and performing.

In her new ventures, Wendy hoped to retain at least a cordial professional relationship with Tureck. When the Fifth International Congress of the IBS was about to convene in the summer of 1971 without her or the Dance Collegium, Wendy wrote to Tureck to try "to heal a wound I know we both felt."[1] Wendy, however, received only a brief and curious reply from Tureck's assistant.

> July 5, 1971
>
> Dear Miss Hilton,
>
> Thank you for your letter of the 26th June, but right now Miss Tureck is in the midst of her work with the International Congress of the IBS.
>
> She has requested that I write to you and say that she does not object to your saying any good things about her either verbally or in writing. She also wishes to convey to you that by no stretch of the imagination can it be construed that you left IBS. It was IBS which severed connections with you.
>
> She sends you every good wish.[2]

Whatever the wound was between them, either it was too deep for repair or Tureck simply no longer cared. I believe that Wendy felt it was the latter. This was one of the last times they corresponded.

[1] Wendy did not keep a copy of her letter to Tureck, so we can only speculate about "the wound" between them.

[2] Wendy Hilton Personal Papers.

Even before the final decision to discontinue the Dance Collegium was made at the close of the 1970 Congress, other opportunities had begun to develop for Wendy. Her first invitation came from the Dance Notation Bureau (DNB) to teach at a one-week Institute of Court Dances of the Renaissance and Baroque Periods. Held at Lake Fairlee Camp in Ely, Vermont, from August 29 to September 7, 1970, it was the first institute on early dance offered in the United States. The idea for such an institute grew out of the 1969 meeting of the Congress on Research in Dance (CORD), where the three most prominent early dance scholars in America at the time—Renaissance specialists Ingrid Brainard and Julia Sutton and baroque specialist Shirley Wynne[3]—had presented significant, detailed papers on reconstructing dances from the fifteenth through the eighteenth centuries. Their papers and the great interest they sparked pointed up the pressing need for such an institute.[4]

The invitation to teach at the institute came from DNB vice president Mireille Backer, a highly respected dance notator and one of the institute's three organizers (Herbert Kummel, director of the DNB, and Julia Sutton being the other two). Backer and Wendy had met at the 1968 IBS Congress and quickly become good friends as well as colleagues. Backer also had taken it upon herself to introduce Wendy to the work in early dance being done in the United States.

> Mireille was an ardent supporter of those engaged in reconstructing early dance, passionate about Labanotation, and a beautiful Playford dancer. That same year [1968] she took me to the DNB to observe a class taught by Julia Sutton on the dances she had reconstructed from Thoinot Arbeau's *Orchesography*.[5]

The class highlighted for Wendy the significantly "different style [in Renaissance dance] that had emerged from Julia's work as opposed to that

[3] Ingrid Brainard, a musicologist and specialist in Renaissance dance, wrote frequently on early dance, including an unpublished manuscript "The Art of Courtly Dancing in the Early Renaissance" (West Newton, Mass., 1981), and directed the Cambridge [Massachusetts] Court Dancers. Julia Sutton, also a musicologist and Renaissance dance specialist, has numerous publications to her credit, including an annotated reprint of Mary Stewart Evans's translation of Thoinot Arbeau's 1596 treatise *Orchesography* (New York: Dover Books, 1967); an edited translation of Fabritio Caroso's 1600 dance manual *Nobiltà di Dame* (New York: Oxford University Press, 1986); and, with Rachelle Palnick Tsachor, an edited volume, *Dances for the Sun King: Andre Lorin's* Livre de contredance (Annapolis, Md.: Colonial Music Institute, c. 2008). She also directed "An Entertainment for Elizabeth" (1968) with the New York Pro Musica Antiqua. Shirley Wynne, a dancer with a specialization in baroque dance, is the author of "The Charms of Complaisance: The Dance in England in the Early 18th Century," (PhD diss., Ohio State University, 1967), and "Complaisance: An Eighteenth Century Cool," *Dance Scope* 5, no. 1 (1970), among other publications. She collaborated frequently with her husband, the musicologist and harpsichordist Alan Curtis.

[4] Joann W. Kealiinohomoku, ed., *Dance History Research: Perspectives from Related Arts and Disciplines* (New York: Congress on Research in Dance, 1970).

[5] Wendy had begun to make notes for this part of the book. That text is included whenever possible. I have, however, exercised some editorial freedom and rearranged her original order of the text or shortened some overly long passages.

being practiced in England." She therefore approached teaching at the Vermont institute—where she, Julia, Ingrid, and Shirley would be the lead faculty—with some reticence. As Wendy would teach only the baroque style, she didn't foresee conflicts with Ingrid and Julia, but a clear inconsistency between her style and Shirley's could cause problems. She decided to tackle the problem head-on.

> Before I agreed to teach at the institute, I thought it wise to meet with Shirley in case our ideas were so different that beginning students might be confused. We met one day at Lincoln Center and compared our performances of the basic eighteenth-century steps. We decided that we could work safely side by side.

If difficulties ultimately arose, Wendy never discussed them.

Wendy found her participation at the institute to be both personally gratifying and professionally significant.

> Three things were emphasized at the workshop: dance, music, and notation. In the case of the earlier periods when no systems of notation were in use, the primary sources that provided verbal descriptions of the dances along with the dances' accompanying music were explored. The dances taught were put into Labanotation and published in a report of the institute.[6] Here my long ago studies of Labanotation on the Isle of Man were, for the first time, put to good use. Although Mireille notated most of the dances, she and I collaborated on the Labanotation of "La Bourgogne," the dance I was teaching in my classes. In class, though, I taught Beauchamps-Feuillet notation, and from it the students learned the dance's step patterns.
>
> Evenings were dedicated to special presentations and concerts. I gave a lecture-demonstration in which I showed three dances: the loure from *Scylla*, the gavotte from *Atys*, and a canary from *Alcide*.
>
> The workshop was extremely important for the future of historical dance and early music. For me personally, as with the IBS, it opened many doors. I made many friends and contacts—among them, Ingrid, Julia, and Shirley, of course; the musicologist Daniel Pinkham and the early musicians Michael and Kay Jaffe, who were part of the institute's music faculty; the Renaissance dancer Charles Garth; and Christena Schlundt of the dance department at the University of California, Riverside.

Wendy left Vermont with a fresh perspective and great hopes for her future. Back in New York, considerable interest remained in the dance classes she would have offered that fall under the auspices of the IBS Dance Collegium, as they had been advertised earlier in the year. So she decided to offer the classes on her own: one for children on Saturday mornings at the Ansonia Hotel and another for adults during the week at the DNB. She also began a weekly class for musicians. This class, which also met at the DNB, was to have far-reaching effects as it was attended by members of three of the most prominent early music groups at that time: Judith Davidoff's New York Consort

[6] See Juana de Laban, ed., *Institute of Court Dances of the Renaissance and Baroque* (New York: Congress on Research in Dance, 1972).

of Viols, Sally Logeman's Calliope, and Michael and Kay Jaffee's Waverly Consort. Other students in the class included the musicologists Judith Schwartz Karp and Carol Marsh (Rowan), whose future research would contribute significantly to baroque dance literature. Wendy would talk about this class years later, referring not only to the seriousness and hard work of all involved but also of the sheer pleasure of sharing this learning experience—for it was a learning experience for her too—with this wonderful group.

Figure 42. Wendy preparing for a performance in the United States, early 1970s.

In early November 1970, Wendy traveled to Canada for the first time to participate in the annual meeting of the American Musicological Society (AMS) at the University of Toronto. Meredith Ellis Little, a Stanford University Ph.D. in musicology and a specialist in the music of Jean-Baptiste Lully, particularly as it related to dance, invited Wendy to dance to illustrate her paper "The Contribution of Dance Steps to Musical Analysis: The Early Eighteenth-Century Sarabande." For the November 8 lecture-demonstration, Wendy showed some basic steps of the baroque style and danced the woman's roles in the sarabandes from the danses à deux "La Royalle" (Pécour/Lully, c. 1713) and the "Sarabande à deux" (Pécour/Campra, 1704) from *Tancrède.* She closed the program with the solo "Sarabande pour une femme" (Pécour/Lully, 1704). George Houle, from the Stanford University early music faculty, whom Wendy had met two years earlier during her first trip to the United States, accompanied the dancing on baroque oboe with Meredith at the harpsichord. For the many musicologists and musicians present, Wendy's performance was a revelation. Although they had been playing the music for years, for many this was the first time they had seen the dancing they would have been accompanying; they were eager to see and learn more. For her own part, Wendy made more influential contacts: Leonard Ratner and Joan Benson from the Stanford music faculty, Erich Schwandt from the Eastman School of Music, and Anne Witherell, a student of Schwandt's at Eastman with a keen interest in baroque dance. All would have a significant impact on Wendy's career, particularly in California.

Wendy's and Meredith's collaboration at the AMS meeting marked the beginning of a long and important relationship. They had met in 1968 in Connecticut during Wendy's first collaboration in America with Tureck. Wendy also had read and commented on Meredith's doctoral dissertation, "The Dances of J. B. Lully," and shared with her copies of many of the baroque dance sources she had gathered in Europe.[7] Their presentation in Toronto inspired new ideas for future collaborations. Meredith hoped to review the different dance types with Wendy to better determine their relationship to the music.[8] She also wished to inventory the hundreds of eighteenth-century dances that were available in Beauchamps-Feuillet notation so that anyone interested in baroque dance could learn of the available repertoire or be able to locate a needed notation score.[9] Wendy welcomed the collaboration—and a chance to get out of the city, always a plus in Wendy's estimation.

> Meredith and her husband John lived in the country in Maryland, and I visited them there frequently. I took all my microfilms from my research in Paris, and we made copies of everything for her, including all the music Régine and I found through all that diligent page-turning. You could say that *La Danse Noble*[10] began here in a way.
>
> Meredith and I had many wonderful working weekends going over one dance type, such as the bourrée, each time. She ranks among my lifelong friends.

In January 1971 Wendy resumed her various classes in Manhattan and received an invitation to teach a weekend workshop, another Institute of Court Dances of the Renaissance and Baroque Periods, in late March at the DNB. This workshop was an offshoot of the previous summer's institute in Vermont. Because interest in these programs was so high, plans were well under way for another summer institute, for two weeks this time, at Mount Holyoke College in South Hadley, Massachusetts, to which Wendy also would soon be invited.

The weekend workshop in Manhattan offered a concentrated version of the material presented at the longer institutes. The students studied technique and attempted to reconstruct part of a dance from Beauchamps-Feuillet notation. But the workshop was especially important because Anna Kisselgoff, the dance critic for the *New York Times*, observed one of Wendy's sessions and published a highly favorable article, "Baroque Dances Stir Interest Anew," complete with a photo of Wendy teaching in full costume.[11] The article was well timed, not only because it appeared in the *Times* on April 5, 1971, Wendy's fortieth birthday (she couldn't have received a better gift),

[7] Meredith Ellis Little, interview by Anne Witherell, August 17–18, 2004. Helen Meredith Ellis, "The Dances of J. B. Lully (1632–1687)," (PhD diss., Stanford University, 1968).

[8] Little, letter to Wendy Hilton, November 10, 1970.

[9] Little, letter to Wendy Hilton, January 17, 1971.

[10] Little and Carol G. Marsh, *La Danse Noble: An Inventory of Dances and Sources* (New York: Broude Brothers, 1992).

[11] Anna Kisselgoff, "Baroque Dances Stir Interest Anew," *New York Times*, April 5, 1971.

but more importantly because it provided Wendy with much needed publicity. Kisselgoff pointed out the wide range of students in the classes, from a convention assistant looking for a new dance experience to New York Consort of Viols director Judith Davidoff to the well-known modern dancers Eileen Cropley and Elizabeth Keen. She quoted Davidoff on how her "ideas about playing baroque music had changed after doing some of the dances upon which it was based. . . . 'We never land on the strong beat. That's when your weight is up. In Bach's cello suites, I have now felt that the articulation should be much lighter and clearer. I have been playing much too legato'." Many musicians would flock to Wendy's classes over the years for the possibility of gaining just such insights for their playing. Dancers would come to learn about an important facet of the history of their art or, like Keen, to find new material for their own work in other dance styles. As Kisselgoff pointed out, Keen had "incorporated a minuet into her most recent [modern dance] work, *Quilt*."[12]

Woven within all Wendy's teaching and performances were two publication projects. The first was a video, "French Dances of the 17th and 18th Centuries."[13] Exactly how Wendy came up with the idea for the project and when she began it are not clear, but in a letter dated January 17, 1971, Meredith Little wrote, "Good luck on your film-TV project, and I hope the next attempt works." How many attempts it took is also not clear, but the video was finally published and available from Wendy ($25/rental) by the following year. If Wendy in fact had hoped for it to be televised, she was never able to make those arrangements.

Given that serious dance video and film production, particularly as a teaching tool, was in its infancy, Wendy was a pioneer in exploring this medium to bring her work to a wider audience. The video examines the basics of baroque dance technique and its historical background through Beauchamps-Feuillet notation and the ballroom and theater dances of Louis Pécour. It is also one of the few recordings of Wendy dancing, showing her full technical range, from the slow, exquisitely fluid "Sarabande pour une femme" (Pécour/Lully, 1704) to the technically demanding canary from *Alcide*, "Gigue pour une femme seul, non dancée à l'Opéra" (Pécour/Louis de Lully-Marais, 1712).

In the video, Wendy demonstrates some atypical and idiosyncratic ideas about costuming for baroque dance. As would be expected, she dances

[12] Keen's *Quilt* premiered at Judson Memorial Church, New York, in January 1971. According to Keen, the dance was "a quilt of people of all ages, black and white." One segment featured Wendy's young student Anne Mayberry with David Briggs in a minuet danced at the same time as an African dance, one on each side of the stage. The entire piece ended with a country dance. Elizabeth Keen, interview by Susan Bindig, November 2004.

[13] The title of the video is sometimes listed as "The Art of Dancing: French Dances of the 17th and 18th Centuries." The only readily available copy is in the Dance Division of the New York Public Library for the Performing Arts (DD-NYPLPA). A few years later, Wendy lengthened the video by adding a selection of dances she choreographed to the music of Michel L'Affilard from his *Principes très-faciles* (Paris, 1705). Only a preliminary version of this later composite tape remains in a few private collections. A video of only the L'Affilard dances is also in the DD-NYPLPA: Wendy Hilton, Erich Schwandt, and Julianne Baird, *Music and dance from the court of Louis XIV: 14 dances and airs from Michel L'Affilard's* Principes très-faciles *(Paris 1705)*, 1975, videocassette. The L'Affilard dances are discussed briefly later in this chapter and in chapter 16.

complete choreographies—"Gigue pour une femme Dancée par Mlle. Subligny en Angleterre" (Pécour/Gatti, 1704) and "L'Allemande" (Pécour/Campra, 1702) as well as the sarabande and the canary—in full period costume. However, in a short costume that reveals her feet and lower legs and allows her movements to be seen more clearly, she demonstrates individual steps of the technique and their accompanying arm movements. To close the program, she dances the 1704 sarabande barefoot and dressed in a modern, short shift to demonstrate how the dancing can be successfully performed freed from all its usual accoutrements.

Wendy was only moderately satisfied with the video. A few years later, she wrote to Meredith with regret, "I am not too pleased with my own performance apart from technique. Probably the best part is the step demonstration. These I could keep back in the well lit area of the studio. However, I guess it's better than nothing."[14]

Wendy also entertained the notion of writing a book on baroque dance. She admitted that, although the thought "appalled" her, "it was becoming increasingly clear that there was a great need for a basic text for the small, but growing number of students worldwide who were expressing an interest in baroque dance." Her preliminary outline for the book included a general history of the period and of the dancing, a full explanation of Beauchamps-Feuillet notation, and an analysis of the verbal descriptions of the style found in Pierre Rameau's *Le Maître à danser* (1725) and *Abbrégé de la nouvelle méthode* (1725) and in Kellom Tomlinson's *The Art of Dancing* (1735). With these basic tools, Wendy hoped her readers would be able to teach themselves the style.

Like most books, the road to the publication of *Dance of Court and Theater, 1690–1725* was long and difficult. The writing, fit in among Wendy's many engagements, would take almost ten years to complete. Attracting a publisher, although not as difficult as Wendy expected, provided a tale with unique and challenging twists, and, fortunately, a happy ending.

> The first step was to interest a publisher. The chance of success seemed small, but surprisingly I had no difficulty. I approached Robert M. MacGregor, who had seen my work in 1969 at the American Society for Theatre Research Conference at Lincoln Center. I had been invited to participate in the conference at the recommendation of Selma Jeanne Cohen. Robert was a charming, relaxed, very well-educated Canadian. I liked him and respected him and his publishing company, Theater Arts Books, enormously. He was very enthusiastic and helpful and gave me a contract straight away as well as a very welcome and much needed advance.
>
> Disaster, though, loomed on the horizon. Robert developed lung cancer and died in 1974. He continued working at home almost until the end. With my agreement with Theater Arts Books then dissolved, I offered my book to Al Pischl at Dance Horizons Press, and he sent me a contract. But this arrangement, too, would be brief—due to a flood! I spent many weekends in Connecticut at the home of Mireille Backer, working on the analysis of my material

[14] Wendy Hilton, letter to Meredith Ellis Little, January 17, 1975.

> for Labanotation. Mireille insisted that Labanotation be included and offered to contribute her work to the book. Luckily, I remembered enough of the system from my studies on the Isle of Man to participate in Mireille's work. One late September weekend in 1975, a friend of Mireille's called with devastating news. It seemed that hurricane Eloise, which battered the East Coast that week, had destroyed almost all of Al Pischl's stock, which had been stored in a warehouse in Pennsylvania.
>
> I was terribly upset for Al and for the dance world, because of the loss of so many of his reprints, which I was afraid he would not be able to afford to replace. Such proved to be the case. Amazingly enough, yet another publisher was interested in my book: Charles Woodford, who was just setting up his business, Princeton Book Company. I soon received a contract, dated November 12, 1975.

As meticulous with her writing as she was with her dancing, Wendy oversaw all aspects of the book's production. She had a clear vision not only for what the book should say, but also of how the material should be presented and paid close attention to the layout. Always money-savvy, Wendy sought and received generous funding that helped her fulfill that vision.

> As well as writing the book, I also designed the pages with eighteenth-century notation examples. I feel that cluttered pages are a deterrent to the learning process. Although the book turned out to be far larger than I had ever imagined it would need to be, it had a spacious appearance. I remember that someone said it looked choreographed.
>
> I received two generous grants from the Ingram Merrill Foundation to help with the pre-publication costs. Without this help, the book could not have been published. That it was ever finished was largely due to the help and encouragement of Mireille, my wonderful editor Caroline Gaynor, who also tested the practical sections of the text as a student, and Anne Witherell, who drew by hand all the Beauchamps-Feuillet notation examples.

Wendy's very full schedule and her many plans for her book and for future engagements were cut short when she learned of her mother's very serious illness. She received a letter in the late spring of 1971 from her uncle, Gerald, saying that her mother had been diagnosed with ovarian cancer and was in the final stages of the disease with only a few months to live. He advised her to travel to London right away while her mother could still enjoy her visit.

Wendy immediately set about booking her flight and settling a few other matters that required her attention before she could leave. She was house-sitting in Maryland for Meredith and her husband, John, who were in California for part of the summer. They had asked Wendy if she "would like to look after their house and their two goats, Gofer and Rofer," and use Meredith's extensive library for her book. After a few productive weeks of research and preliminary writing, the letter from Gerald arrived.

> Well, besides the crisis with my mother, I had no money for the airfare. I was in remote countryside, without transportation, and I was responsible for a house and two goats. I reached for the phone.
>
> Alice Bonnell lent me the airfare; Eileen found the cheapest ticket, while I dealt with the house. The kind neighbors who had been taking me shopping offered to take my place and watch the house and Gofer and Rofer. The problem of getting to the train was solved by the police, who, upon hearing the nature of my emergency, drove me to the station in a police car.
>
> I stayed one night in New York, then Eileen saw me off from Kennedy [Airport]. Mireille Backer was on holiday in London, and I stayed the next night with her, which enabled me to regroup before going to Acton to see Dorothy in the hospital. Gerald and Muriel were there too. The doctors had not told Dorothy the truth of her condition since no treatment was possible. Because she had no pain, she never suspected cancer. Her body was very thin apart from an enormous abdomen. Her face looked just the same, and when under the covers she appeared to be her old self.
>
> She was very excited to see me, and we had a good visit. After two weeks the doctor said she could go home. They had drained the fluid from her abdomen, but it would come back, so the problem was to find her something suitable to wear. Someone suggested a maternity outfit, and I went to a very expensive shop in Bond Street to find her a really nice one. The very superior saleslady inquired, "Is it for you, madam?" looking disapprovingly at my ringless wedding finger. "No," I said, "it's for my mother"—which equally flustered the poor woman. Dorothy laughed heartily with us about this.
>
> Dorothy was weak but delighted and encouraged to be going home. I was scheduled to teach at an early dance workshop sponsored by the Dance Notation Bureau from August 22 to September 4 in Massachusetts. Gerald and I decided that I should go because, if I stayed in England too long, Dorothy might begin to wonder why. I also needed the money and the contacts I would make. I remained until Dorothy was settled at home, promised to return at Christmas, and then left for the United States. The kind young tenants in the house promised to watch over Dorothy.

Back in the States, Wendy resumed her teaching, rehearsing, and various publication projects. She remained attentive, however, to her mother's declining health.

> It seemed like fate that in the fall of 1971 I was not busy, apart from some private teaching. I could have left for England at the drop of a hat. I wrote to Dorothy every day. Her letters became fewer and her handwriting weaker. Soon she went back into the hospital at her own request. Gerald asked her if she would like me to come. "No," she said, "Wendy will be coming at Christmas." In the mid-fall, she died, with Gerald and Muriel present. I did not go to England for the funeral. I just sat quietly for the day and thought about Dorothy and wished her life had been a happier one.

The workshop to which Wendy returned from England was the second Institute of Court Dances of the Renaissance and Baroque at Mount Holyoke College. Much of the faculty at Lake Fairlee Camp of the previous summer gathered again for the two-week institute. Wendy's teaching and performances were highlighted in a CORD monograph that detailed the classes, research, and performances of both the Lake Fairlee and Mount Holyoke institutes.

> One of the most memorable events of the [Mount Holyoke] Institute was a lecture-recital by Wendy Hilton, one of the few researchers in Baroque dance who is a dancer and performer as well. In her recital Miss Hilton picked the most typical and best solos and parts of several dances in order to demonstrate the range and different rhythmic types of dances. Among those included were the following: *La Royalle*, *Sarabande* and *Bourrée* by Pécour with music by Lully, first published in 1712; *L'Allemande* (1702) by Pécour with music probably by André Campra; the *Gigue de Roland* by Feuillet (1700) to music by Lully. In addition to performing the dances she informally presented a demonstration of many of the individual steps (*coupé*, *pas de bourrée*, *contretemps*, *glissade*, etc.) of which the dances are composed, and which she had been teaching.
>
> Hilton feels strongly that in conjunction with the importance of study and research the added dimension of performance can demonstrate the style and deportment of the period in a manner that gives life to the pictures, books and notation we have inherited.
>
> In the actual class situation Miss Hilton feels that the style is most important of all to teach correctly. Despite a short learning time the *way* in which a dance should be done—the deportment, the bearing of the body in general and use of dynamics—is of primary concern. Trained dancers must become used to eliminating a lot of the effort they are used to using; non-dancers must learn where effort should be concentrated. The steps must be learned accurately, and the correct use of the foot is of paramount importance. For example, the pliability of the instep is hard for ballet dancers used to a rigid foot; it is much easier for modern dancers to learn. The eighteenth-century turnout, the deep bending of the knees, the stylized use of the arms are all important too.
>
> For her classes at Mt. Holyoke Miss Hilton devoted the time to teaching steps rather than a complete dance, giving different combinations of them to *sarabandes*, *bourrées*, and *gavottes*, etc. Knowledge of these steps is also essential to the study of Feuillet notation for which one must know the steps to be able to interpret the score. Her class in Feuillet dealt primarily with the basic principles in the notation as well as helping to clear up details not clearly discernable in the Feuillet text.[15]

Wendy closed 1971 with what may have been her first independent concert in the United States, "Baroque Court and Theatrical Dances of the 18th Century," sponsored by the Westchester [New York] Dance Council and performed on December 12 at the Washington Irving Junior High School in Tarrytown. Jonathan Watts joined Wendy as a soloist and as her partner; Sonya Monosoff on baroque violin and Virginia Hutchings on harpsichord

[15] Katherine S. Cunningham, "Baroque Dance and the Teaching of Wendy Hilton," in de Laban, *Court Dances*, 74–75. Cunningham must not have observed Wendy's sessions with students in which she coached them in the choreography "La Bourgogne" (Pécour/Anon., 1700). Those sessions are highlighted in "'La Bourgogne' and Feuillet Notation," in de Laban, *Court Dances*, 58–73.

played both the dance music and baroque instrumental works.[16] The program included danses à deux and theatrical solos that had been seen variously in the performances at the IBS and the early dance institutes. Perhaps for the first time, Wendy included an example of the men's solo repertoire, the virtuosic solo "Aimable Vainqueur" (Pécour/Campra, 1704), which was danced by Watts. At first blush, this mid-Sunday afternoon performance at a junior high school may not seem particularly significant, regardless of the high caliber of all the performers. The Westchester arts community, however, was active and influential, and had as one of its leaders Madeleine Gutman, the mother of Wendy's student Rebecca and a truly tireless arts advocate.[17] Gutman arranged this engagement, which, if it did not lead directly to other opportunities for Wendy, introduced her to a prominent and well-connected audience. As Rebecca Gutman Menon noted in a 2005 interview, her mother had cultivated many important associations in the New York arts community and, at this time, was also the president of the American Dance Guild. "She sat at a desk and connected people, adopted people, and made sure things got done."[18] Gutman was definitely Wendy's kind of person. Over the years, the two collaborated on other projects and developed a great friendship along the way.

In her notes on this period, Wendy referred to the "lull that surrounded Dorothy's illness and death." Given her numerous teaching and performing engagements and the projects she was developing, this seemed hardly a quiet time. With the new year, however, work in baroque dance opened up appreciably for Wendy, and any lack she may have been feeling was quickly forgotten. Juilliard was the first to call.

> One morning I received a phone call from Margot Harley, assistant administrator to John Houseman at the Drama Division at the Juilliard School.[19] Their period movement teacher, William Burdick, had been taken ill, and a replacement—perhaps temporary, perhaps permanent—was needed. Could I take over his twice-weekly classes starting on the following Monday? Virginia Hutchings, who accompanied the class, had recommended me. I gladly accepted the offer, and within a week I was teaching at Juilliard.

[16] Per performance programs in Wendy's papers, Virginia occasionally played harpsichord in their performances.

[17] For an overview of Gutman's work, see, for example, Roberta Hershenson, "Westchester Q&A: Madeleine Gutman; Making Arts and Culture Work in Greenburgh," *New York Times*, October 9, 1988.

[18] Rebecca Gutman Menon, interview by Susan Bindig, July 26, 2005.

[19] Wendy, in her notes, was not clear about exactly when she began to teach in the Drama Division, indicating both 1971 and 1972 as the possible years when she first replaced Burdick. Her biographical file at the Juilliard School places her in the Drama Division beginning in the 1972–73 academic year. It seems, though, that she initially replaced Burdick sometime during the spring semester of 1972 and then, when it was clear that he would not return, officially took over his position the following September.

This was not the first attempt to hire Wendy at Juilliard. Martha Hill, director of the Dance Division, had first approached her about teaching at the school in 1969. That year, Hill had been one of Wendy's many supporters in her battle to obtain a resident visa to work in the United States. In a letter to Hill, dated June 9, 1969, Wendy thanked her for her help and invited her to the IBS Dance Collegium performances on July 9 and 23.[20] Hill did attend, along with William Bales, then head of the dance department at the State University of New York (SUNY) at Purchase. Wendy wrote of these initial contacts with Hill:

> The Juilliard School had moved [from 120 Claremont Avenue] to its new premises at Lincoln Center in 1969. Martha Hill attended the IBS Summer Sessions that year and was very gracious and invited me to see the Juilliard School's new premises. She also expressed her wish to invite me to join the faculty. At this time, however, the prospect seemed extremely remote. Peter Mennin [president of the Juilliard School] had tried to eliminate the Dance Division and yet, to be true to the school's charter that it must incorporate music, drama, and dance, had invited George Balanchine's School of American Ballet to move into Juilliard's dance facilities. The dance community was in an uproar because the Juilliard Dance Division at Claremont Avenue was set up primarily as a modern dance school (ballet and other dance forms included, of course). Public opinion forced Mennin's hand, and Martha Hill and the Dance Division remained at Juilliard but with the use of only two of the large dance studios. The School of American Ballet remained firmly ensconced in the other four with a private door separating them from Juilliard proper.[21]
>
> Martha Hill told me of her constant battles with Mennin, whose one desire seemed to be to make life so difficult for her that she would resign. But he certainly underestimated Martha. At the time, however, there was no chance of a salary for me to join the dance faculty. My way to Juilliard was unexpectedly through the Drama Division.

While very happy with her new appointment, even if it proved to be only temporary, Wendy was distressed by Burdick's predicament. She had met him through the IBS, where "Bill had been an enthusiastic member of the audience, especially at question time." He then began to study with Wendy

[20] Wendy Hilton Biographical File, Juilliard School.

[21] Janet Soares provides a few more details on the precarious position of the Dance Division in 1969 in "In Music's Domain: 50 Years of Dance at Juilliard," *The Juilliard Journal Online*, vol. 17, no. 8 (May 2002), http://www.juilliard.edu/update/journal/438journal_story_0205.asp (accessed July 4, 2007):

"Yet another setback came when [Lincoln] Kirstein wanted to acquire Juilliard's planned dance facility for his company's School of American Ballet, and Martha Hill found her beloved division in a precarious position. President Mennin, faced with the projection of sixfold costs to maintain the new Juilliard building, informed the dance faculty that the School of American Ballet, having received a 10-year grant from the Ford Foundation in 1963, would be given a lease as an autonomous unit for three-quarters of what had originally been intended as the facility for the Dance Division. Mennin warned of the possible elimination of the division altogether if funding for its support was not found. At the very least, ballet would be removed from the curriculum, in deference to the Balanchine contingent. Only Martha Hill's determination—behind which rallied outraged colleagues and dance alumni, as well as an outspoken press—preserved dance at Juilliard. . . . (cont.)

from time to time, finding her "very accurate in her work."[22] Wendy, in turn, admired his work, as he was "one of the first pioneers of early dance in America." In the early 1960s, around the time Wendy formed the Domenico Dance Ensemble in London, Burdick led a comparable performing group in the United States, Dances and Music of Court and Theater. His class was the first in historical dance offered at Juilliard.[23] By the fall of 1972, however, it was clear that Burdick would not return to Juilliard, and Wendy accepted the invitation to take over his class long term.[24]

Wendy received two other significant teaching invitations: from Douglass College, then the women's college of Rutgers University in New Brunswick, New Jersey, and from SUNY Purchase. Both appointments were to start in the fall of 1972, like Juilliard. At Douglass, Wendy was offered a one-year position as Associate Alumnae Visiting Lecturer through the efforts of Miriam Cooper of the dance department, another of Wendy's contacts through Mireille Backer. Cooper had seen Wendy perform in New York and attended the 1970 DNB institute in Vermont. Keen to build interest in baroque dance within the Douglass community, she invited Wendy and Virginia Hutchings to the college in the spring of 1972 to present a lecture-demonstration. The audience included many faculty of the performing arts departments, who received Wendy's and Virginia's work enthusiastically. All agreed that baroque dance would be a valuable addition to the curriculum. So, the stage was set for Wendy to be offered the position when it opened up at the last minute.

> The position was intended for an expert in an "unusual subject," and I clearly filled that requirement. I didn't mind that I was a last-minute substitute for someone who had been engaged but then could not fulfill their commitment. I was happy to be widening my teaching opportunities and contacts.

Wendy was hired to teach three classes at Douglass in both the fall and spring semesters, one each in the dance, music, and theater departments. Her only

---

Martha Hill's last recourse was to point to an earlier board ruling, which stated that the school chosen for the complex must teach all of the art forms. The study of ballet alone did not encompass all aspects of dance. Therefore, the solitary presence of the School of American Ballet would violate Lincoln Center's mandate to the people, she argued (successfully).The Juilliard School (the new name reflecting the inclusion of its Dance Division, then 75 dance majors strong, as well as a newly created Drama Division) moved into its new home at Lincoln Center Plaza in 1969. The dancers' new training ground consisted of two pristine studios, with glass doors separating it from the School of American Ballet's large complex with four studios next door."

[22]William Burdick, interview by Susan Bindig, August 4, 2005.

[23]Ibid. Burdick's work with the Metropolitan Opera took him to London in the early 1960s to study with Melusine Wood at the recommendation of Antony Tudor, who had himself studied with Wood in preparation for his ballet *Romeo and Juliet.* Returning to London, in the summers, Burdick had private classes with Wood until 1967. Wood also took him to the British Museum to examine original dance sources.

[24]Ibid. Burdick went on to teach at Adelphi University, the State University of New York at Purchase, the Yale Drama School, and at New York University's Tisch School of the Arts. Among many other credits, he choreographed for Broadway, the Metropolitan and New York City Operas, and American Ballet Theatre.

other commitment was a lecture-demonstration to be given sometime over the course of the year.

At about the same time, William Bales, the chair of the dance department at the newly opened SUNY Purchase, offered Wendy a two-year contract to teach one class per week for one semester each year. Wendy's dance-teaching card was now filled for the 1972–73 academic year. She would teach every day of the week—Mondays and Wednesdays at Juilliard, Tuesdays at Purchase, and Thursdays and Fridays at Douglass. Wendy had myriad other projects and engagements to balance. This was nothing new, however, and she would manage it all with the same determination that she brought to the work itself.

> With my classes for musicians to maintain and lecture-demonstrations and other performances, I had the happy prospect of being very busy and financially stable—at last! My only regret was that my book would have to be shelved for a while.

Another challenge arose, however, that did not respond so easily to her iron will. She began to show the early symptoms of what would be diagnosed a few years later as torticollis, a neurological movement disorder that affects the neck and head. In Wendy's case, it would eventually rotate her head a full ninety degrees to the left. At this early stage, however, the affliction manifested as tremors, similar to symptoms of Parkinson's disease. Over the years, many came to believe that she did in fact suffer from Parkinson's. When I began to take her classes at Douglass College in the spring of 1973, not knowing of her condition, I frequently thought that she was shaking her head in disapproval at our performance. I recall stopping dead in my tracks midway through a step sequence one day because she looked straight at me but was unable to control the tremors that I was sure signaled bad news about my dancing. I waited for her correction, but she just waved me on. Wendy would never overcome the torticollis, although she tried desperately through a variety of treatments, including acupuncture and massage. Despite the disfigurement, pain, and physical limitations that eventually resulted, she faced her affliction with grace and did what she could to minimize its effects on her life and on others.

Around 1972–73, though, it began to seriously affect her performing life. I attended the lecture-demonstration she and Virginia Hutchings presented at Douglass on May 29, 1973,[25] and have clear memories of Wendy's dancing. She told me some years later that by that spring she prepared for performances by being absolutely still, maybe even lying down, for at least half an hour immediately before a concert to quiet the tremors. Eventually, even that would not help. For a while longer, though, she was able to accept the numerous performing opportunities that opened up for her.

In the spring of 1972, Wendy traveled to Los Angeles to participate in the third annual meeting of the American Society for Eighteenth-Century Studies, held at the University of California, Los Angeles (UCLA) from March 23

[25] Wendy presented another lecture-demonstration at Douglass College the following fall, on November 30, 1973. This appears to be the last required by her contract. "New Jersey Calendar of Events," *New York Times*, November 25, 1973.

Figure 43. Wendy at Douglass College, Rutgers University, early 1970s.

to 25. The invitation to the meeting was finessed by Judith Schwartz Karp, who as a graduate student in musicology at New York University had attended many of Wendy's Manhattan classes. She had also seen Wendy perform with Rosalyn Tureck in 1968, most likely at their IBS concerts at the New York Public Library for the Performing Arts. As a new music faculty member at the University of California, Riverside (UCR), and a member of the society, Judy saw the meeting as a perfect way to get Wendy to southern California, not only for the meeting but also for a residency at UCR.

For the conference, Wendy agreed to present a concert, "A Program of Baroque Court and Theatrical Dances of the Eighteenth Century," on Friday evening, March 24, and to share a panel the next morning on "The Dance in Early Eighteenth-Century Europe," in which she would speak on "A Personal Discovery of Baroque Dance," and Shirley Wynne would discuss "Images of Early Eighteenth-Century Dance."[26] In her notes on the meeting, Wendy mentions nothing about the panel, perhaps because it was overshadowed by the events leading up to the March 24 concert.

[26]Grateful thanks to Judith Schwarz Karp for sharing personal correspondence on the arrangements for Wendy's participation in both the concert and the meeting as well as for providing the programs for both.

Although lauded by those who attended, the concert was fraught with problems from the outset. Wendy arrived in Los Angeles to find that the music for the concert had not been prepared as promised, and the small ensemble that was to play with Virginia Hutchings for dancing was inadequate. In her own account of the crisis, Wendy wrote that she had been

> asked to send the music three months before the performance so that it could be fully prepared for the rehearsal when I arrived. Instead, it was handed back to me, the envelope unopened, with the words, "Here's your music." The union musicians hired for the occasion were unfamiliar with baroque music; one of them asked, "What are these squiggles above the notes for?" Here was a crisis, and no help could be found. Virginia Hutchings, trouper that she was, rehearsed the musicians all day. Without her, there could have been no performance.

Virginia, though, apparently had only limited success. John Rockwell's review of the concert in the *Los Angeles Times* on March 27 was mixed ("puzzled," according to Wendy), praising Wendy's dancing and Virginia's playing but calling the string trio "close to inept."[27] He placed the responsibility for the musical problems squarely on Wendy, and she was compelled to reply in "A Discordant Note" to the *Times*:

> John Rockwell, in his review of my baroque dance program at UCLA (March 27), has assumed that the inadequate and unprepared musicians who took part were chosen by myself. While Miss Hutchings came with me from New York, the other players were provided by the music department of UCLA. It was my understanding with Dr. George Rousseau, chairman of the American Society for 18th-Century Studies, that professional musicians, fully experienced in baroque music, would be provided for the concert. Such was not the case, and yet it was only on this basis that I agreed to give the performance.[28]

To make matters worse, Wendy and Virginia had been promised luxury accommodations at the beach. For Wendy in particular, private and quiet rooms away from the center of things were paramount, and it was a boon if they also happened to be sumptuous. Their congenial hosts, however, felt that they were housing two celebrities and wanted to show them off, subjecting Wendy and Virginia to parties neither wanted to attend.[29] This arrangement only fueled Wendy's anger with the entire engagement.

After such a disappointing experience, Wendy and Virginia needed to escape and recuperate. They rented a car and drove up the Pacific Coast Highway, visiting Carmel and Monterey and forgetting about Los Angeles. Wendy wrote that on this trip her "love for California grew and grew." The trip was of necessity brief because they had to return to southern California and their engagement at UCR.

[27]John Rockwell, "Miss Hilton in Baroque Dance Program at UCLA," *Los Angeles Times*, March 27, 1972.

[28]Wendy Hilton, "A Discordant Note," *Los Angeles Times*, April 2, 1972.

[29]Judith Schwartz Karp, interview by Anne Witherell, June 26, 2005.

The two-week teaching residency from April 3 to 14 was arranged by Judy in conjunction with Christena Schlundt of the Department of Theatre.[30] Christena had met Wendy in Vermont at the court dance institute and had discussed with her the possibility of visiting UCR to teach. Christena, though, was not able to follow up owing to lack of adequate funds. Now that Judy had managed to bring Wendy to the Los Angeles area via the conference, she was eager to help raise the additional funds needed to hire Wendy for a residency. They waged an ambitious campaign and, with money donated by the Departments of French, Music, and Theatre, were able to organize a seminar and an opening concert on April 3. They tried to secure additional engagements for Wendy and Virginia at the other University of California campuses through the Intercampus Cultural Exchange Committee but were unsuccessful. Stanford University, however, engaged them to teach a few classes over a long weekend.

Per Judy and Christena's funding proposal, the course Wendy was to teach, Seminar in 18th-Century French Music and Dance,

> would concern itself with the study of the interrelationships between music and dance during the 18th century: historical background of Western European Court Dance; styles and forms associated with 18th-century dance and dance music; performance and practice of dance and dance music.[31]

It was designed for both dancers and nondancers, and UCR even opened it to the local community through its Extension Program. Students studied not only baroque dance technique but also Beauchamps-Feuillet notation, through which they reconstructed a dance to be presented at the end of the term. Bibliography classes taught by Judy and Christena introduced the students to the dance and music literature associated with baroque dance.

After UCR, Wendy headed north to Stanford University and then east to Cornell University, where she gave a lecture-demonstration.[32] A week or so later, Wendy was back in New York with great hopes for two significant concerts with pianist, conductor, and founder of the Jupiter Symphony, Jens Nygaard, another IBS contact:

> Jens was eager to do two performances with me, and I was certainly eager to work with Jens. Everyone loved working with Jens because of his deep love of and total commitment to music combined with the respect he had for his colleagues.
>
> The first concert was on April 23, 1972, at the YM & YMHA of Washington Heights for the Inwood Sunday Evening Concert Series, which Jens directed. There were four participants: Robert Mann, violin; Lucy Rowan, narrator; Jens; and I. The widely varied program consisted of selections from Bach, Schumann, and Mozart. I danced eight baroque-style dances to Jens's playing of Bach,

[30] The dance program at UCR was part of the theater department at this time.

[31] Sincere thanks to Judith Schwartz Karp for providing the course proposal for Seminar in 18th-Century French Music and Dance,

[32] Judith Schwartz Karp, letter to Wendy Hilton, April 24, 1972. "Your photograph left here [UCR] on the 17th [of April], hopefully in time to be of use there [Cornell University]. . . . Hope all went well at Stanford and Cornell."

> Handel, and Rameau. At the last moment, and so it is not listed in the program, Jens suggested that Robert Mann play the loure from Bach's Partita No. 3 in E Major, BWV 1006, for me to dance to. Robert agreed, and so we did it with me dancing the choreography of the loure from *Scylla*. It went beautifully.
>
> A month later, on May 16, I repeated the dances with Jens in "One Hour of Chamber Music" at Carnegie Recital Hall. This was again a varied program directed by Jens and featuring the music of Gounod, Chopin, Richard Strauss, and Spohr. The other musicians this time were the tenor Paul Sperry and the clarinetist Stanley Drucker. Lucy Rowan again was the narrator.

The concert at Carnegie Recital Hall was particularly significant for Wendy as Anna Kisselgoff attended and gave her another favorable review in the *New York Times*:

> Miss Hilton, in period court costume, gave her series of dances the assurance and refinement that have always characterized her presentations. Because this field is so specialized, the fine points of these court and theatrical dances may be lost to the viewer. Yet their variety and the differences among them are brought sharply into relief by Miss Hilton's excellent execution of the steps and general bearing.
>
> The first five dances—allemande, courante, sarabande, minuet and gigue—to music by Bach and Handel, were performed in the usual suite sequence of the 18th-century court ballroom. A more stately loure and a gavotte, both to Bach, and a rigaudon, to Rameau, completed the segment.[33]

Other engagements around this time included a concert for the American Society for Theatre Research (Manhattan) and a lecture-demonstration at Smith College (Northampton, Massachusetts), sometime between March and June.[34] In early summer, Wendy and Virginia traveled to Wichita, Kansas, for a lecture-demonstration on June 17 sponsored by the American Dance Symposium and to Norfolk, Virginia, for a weeklong residency in mid-July arranged by Madeleine Gutman at Old Dominion University. These two engagements brought Wendy additional positive press, a welcome relief after what she viewed as the fiasco in Los Angeles.[35]

That same summer, Wendy also attempted to establish her own workshop at Lake Fairlee Camp in Vermont, the site of the first DNB court dance institute. Scheduled for July 1 through July 9, 1972, it was only recommended for students with previous dance experience. The workshop flier advertised:

[33] Anna Kisselgoff, "Miss Hilton Excels in 8 Baroque Dances," *New York Times*, May 18, 1972.

[34] See "Dancer to Perform Concert of Baroque Court Dances at UCR," *The [Riverside] Press*, March 29, 1972, in which the engagements at both Smith College and American Society for Theatre Research are mentioned. Wendy's résumé lists an engagement as a dancer and lecturer at Smith in 1972. My efforts to unearth other information on these engagements were not successful.

[35] Marilyn Gump, "Lecture-Recital Offers Step Back in History," *Wichita Eagle and Beacon*, June 17, 1972; Linda Waller, "She Dances in Courtly Fashion," *Virginian-Pilot*, July 19, 1972.

> The exclusion of beginners will enable students not only to consolidate their work, but greatly enhance it. Daily activities will include two dance classes—one technique and steps, the other "repertoire"—and a Feuillet notation class. Many musicians will be attending and the evening activities will be concerned with dance and music, discussions, performances, etc. . . . Janis Pforsich, who attended the first Institute and has been studying with me ever since, will be my assistant during the course.

Unfortunately, the workshop was not sufficiently enrolled—perhaps because of the barring of beginners—and was canceled.

The 1972–73 academic year got under way with Wendy juggling the demands of her three teaching positions. At SUNY Purchase, where she would teach only in the fall, she was challenged by both the space and the students.

> As Bill [Bales] warned me, very little of the facilities at Purchase was finished. My class was held in the gymnasium,[36] which lacked glass in the windows through which noise of the planes going to Westchester airport roared loudly. Not all the walls were yet equipped with mirrors, and my class was occasionally interrupted by workers with loud drills and sometimes spark-producing tools. Behind a half-height wall, a drama class was held concurrently with mine, and for part of the semester, its students seemed to be learning to clap rhythms. To teach baroque dance, you need peace and surrounding silence. I had neither.
>
> My class was large, consisting of forty-five students, most of whom were big fish from small ponds devoted only to ballet. By far, the best students were a group from the High School of Performing Arts. They all did extremely well. I was not sorry to see the course come to a close. The pianist and I had to endure twenty-four couples dance "La Bourrée d'Achille" for their practical exam—the pianist nearly went crazy. I also gave the students a short written exam containing forty very simple questions. One student gave forty very wrong answers. She had also failed the practical test. When the full exam results were posted, she stormed up to me shouting, "You can't fail ME. I know I haven't learned anything, but I've been to all your classes." She complained to Bill, but he backed me up. I sighed with relief on the last trip home. Next year would surely be more congenial.

Wendy left no notes about the classes she taught at Douglass College. As a sophomore dance major there, I began to take her dance department class in the 1972 spring semester, enrolling purely out of a sense of duty to my adviser and my major, not out of any particular interest in baroque dance. I also had no notion of Wendy's rapidly growing professional reputation, and even if I had, I doubt it would have mattered much to me then. I recall that, despite its highly specialized subject matter, the class was well enrolled—there must have been about a dozen students. We followed the same syllabus as Wendy's students at Purchase—and nearly all her beginning

[36]Per Leah Kreutzer, a freshman dancer at SUNY Purchase in 1972–73, dance classes were held in the museum, with temporary floors laid over brick. Kreutzer, e-mail message to Susan Bindig, June 23, 2004.

students thereafter—learning the elements of baroque dance technique and notation and reconstructing "La Bourrée d'Achille" for the practical final exam. We also took a written exam, which, I recall, focused at least in part on basic aspects of the notation.

I did not like the class at all. I was studying modern dance at the time and envisioned myself a teacher, choreographer, and performer in that style. Baroque dance with its small, nuanced movement held little appeal for me, and although I did very well, I was hopelessly bored by it. So, like Wendy with her Purchase class, I was relieved when the semester ended. I vowed not to return to her classes or to any baroque dance class for that matter. And I didn't for another year.

My dislike of baroque dance was not shared by very many others. There was, in fact, great interest in Wendy's classes, and ours received quite a bit of publicity that semester. In mid-May, two Philadelphia newspapers, the *Inquirer* and the *Evening Bulletin*, and the local New Brunswick *Courier News* sent reporters to observe classes and interview Wendy.[37] The *Courier News* also sent a photographer, who captured our mostly jeans-clad group (we must have been photographed outside regular class time) poised confidently to begin a dance, our poorly placed arms with drooping elbows notwithstanding.

Wendy enjoyed her classes at Douglass and eventually at SUNY Purchase, but that Juilliard was her prized appointment will surprise no one. She would have preferred and still hoped for a chance to work in the Dance Division, but teaching for the Drama Division provided an excellent starting point. Wendy wrote of those first classes that

> the problem with teaching drama classes is that most of the women have had some dance and movement experience, while the men have not. I think this is why I find working with such groups a strain and rather unsatisfactory. The students, particularly the men, feel awkward, and even foolish. Interestingly, vocal arts students do not seem to have those problems.
>
> Nonetheless, the drama class, while personally unsatisfactory, was a success for me professionally. Despite any misgivings I had about teaching drama students, my group progressed and seemed to find the class beneficial to their study. I was to find the same with other drama students in my future teaching.
>
> At a school like Juilliard, as one might imagine, many of the students are destined for great success in the arts. The student in that first drama class whom I remember most was Christopher Reeve. He was lovely to have in class but to me seemed nervous at Juilliard. Away from school, he blossomed, revealing a sense of comedy that, from my class, I should never have dreamed was in him. I last saw him on a #11 bus, seeming depressed and feeling sure that he wouldn't make it as an actor. But he certainly did, as we well know.

[37] "On Learning the Minuet, Courante, Passe-pied and Gavotte," *Courier News*, May 12, 1973; Ann Curley, "Rutgers Students Getting Lessons in Court Dances of the 18th Century," *Evening Standard*, May 14, 1973; and Curley, "Students in Levis Do Stately Dance," *Philadelphia Inquirer*, May 17, 1973.

Wendy would teach in the Drama Division for the next two years, but the opportunity to also teach in the Dance Division arose sooner than she expected. After that first semester, she braved the type of social gathering she hated most, a faculty party. Attending and enduring this one, however, proved to be an excellent professional move.

> I was now an officially recognized member of the Juilliard faculty and continued working in the Drama Division. At the Christmas party of 1972, the door was opened for my future appointment on the dance faculty. I do not enjoy such parties but felt that as a fairly new faculty member I should go. It was one of the most fortunate decisions I have ever made.
>
> I was talking to Martha Hill when Albert Fuller [harpsichordist, conductor, and Juilliard music faculty member][38] came over. He told Martha that he was planning to put on a baroque concert in Alice Tully Hall on March 16, 1973, and would like to include some baroque-style dances to music from the prologue of Jean-Philippe Rameau's *Les Indes Gallantes*. Albert's fine battle over many years to establish baroque performance-practice studies at Juilliard had finally paid off in a small way. Martha said quickly, "Well, Albert, now we have Wendy here in the school, I should be able to get a fee for her to do this. After all, a performance in Alice Tully Hall would be good exposure for the school."
>
> And so it was. After the holidays, I auditioned dance students and invited one of the drama students who had noble carriage, Stephen Schnetzer, to join us. Of the women in the group, Elizabeth Haberer stood out as being ideal for the baroque style. It was hard to work up a sufficiently stylish performance with dancers untried in the style, but perhaps we pulled it off.

Wendy and Fuller did far more than pull it off. Their collaboration for this "Concert of Baroque Music" was "the revelation of the evening," according to music critic Andrew Porter in the *New Yorker*. Porter reviewed the entire concert, which also featured instrumental works by Telemann, J. S. Bach, Scarlatti, and Rameau, very favorably. He wrote that Fuller "fired his small band of instrumentalists with his enthusiasm for the period, and guided them toward the kinds of attack, phrasing, dynamic levels, rhythms, and ornaments that are required. They played with spirit and devotion." About the dancing, he continued:

> The difficulty of staging Rameau's theatre pieces lies largely in the dances, which are integral to the score, not detachable divertissements; one happy solution . . . is to re-create the dance style of Rameau's day. For this Juilliard performance, Wendy Hilton had set four of the Prologue [to *Les Indes Galantes*] dances—the entrée, a musette, a polonaise, and a menuet—to eighteenth-century sequences. Student players and student dancers had worked together on their execution, and Rameau's dance music made a new sense as

[38]Albert Fuller joined the Juilliard music faculty in 1964. In 1972 he founded the Aston Magna Foundation for Music and the Humanities, which spawned an annual summer festival and institute in Great Barrington, Massachusetts, as well as an ensemble for which he was the harpsichordist and conductor. In 1985 he established the Helicon Foundation. For information on both foundations, see http://www.astonmagna.org and http://www.helicon.org.

> we discovered how musical and choreographic images fit so fascinatingly together. There was nothing merely quaint or self-consciously archaic in the enterprise; the dancers' Ailey-inspired grace flowed through the heavier, formal movements notated by Feuillet in the early eighteenth century. . . .
>
> With Mr. Fuller and Miss Hilton as guides, the Juilliard's music, dance, and drama departments must combine to stage in their theatre a complete Rameau opera. And after that they may as well show the City Opera how Monteverdi, and the Metropolitan Opera how Gluck, and the "Piccolo Met" how Purcell should be performed.[39]

High praise for Wendy from a highly influential critic. This was only the first of a number of positive reviews of Wendy's work by Porter, reviews that she would revere for their astute understanding of the dancing and the music and of the larger context in which they were developed.

With Juilliard and critics like Porter now firmly backing her, Wendy's career was quickly gathering momentum.

[39]Andrew Porter, "Musical Events: Branching Out," *New Yorker* (March 24, 1973), 137. The "Piccolo Met" was a small, two-hundred-seat hall within the Vivian Beaumont Theater at Lincoln Center for performances of operas, like those of Purcell, that might benefit from a smaller setting than the spacious Metropolitan Opera House.

Thirteen: 1973–1975

La Dafne ~ *Wendy Hilton Baroque Dance Company* ~ Masque of a Midsummer Night ~ Dardanus

Wendy's growing success and increasing opportunities at Juilliard did not curtail a varied, independent performing schedule. The demand for her as both a dancer and lecturer grew, and new, more challenging choreographic ventures developed.

A more intimate performance at the Hebrew Arts School for Music and Dance followed her enthusiastically received Juilliard premiere.[1] She wrote briefly about this concert:

> On Sunday, March 25, [1973], just ten days later, a group of my students, if we can call Eileen Cropley a student, danced with a group of five musicians at the Hebrew Arts School for Music and Dance. I have no idea how this performance came about, but I suspect it had Juilliard faculty connections.

For this afternoon "Family Concert," as the program was called, Wendy gathered some of her young students—Victoria Brown, David Castro, and Rebecca Gutman—along with Eileen, on loan from the Paul Taylor Dance Company, as well as Joseph Taylor and Stephen Schnetzer, students from SUNY Purchase and Juilliard respectively. The Musical Consort, comprising musicians mainly from the Hebrew Arts School, accompanied the dancing and also played instrumental works by Corelli, Telemann, Isaac, Vierdanck, and Vivaldi. The printed program contained extensive notes on the music and the dance with recommendations for further listening to dance-inspired music, all written in a tone suggesting that the concert was primarily intended for a young audience. Wendy selected dances with a simple structure and a light quality that would have great appeal to children, particularly when performed by dancers close to their own age: the Minuet by Mr. Isaac, "La Bourrée d'Achille," the "Gigue de Roland," and Le Menuet, according to Pierre Rameau.

For her next engagement, at the College of New Rochelle for the Music Educators' League of Westchester, Wendy returned to the lecture-demonstration format she refined with Tureck and found suitable for this type of audience. The first half of the April 2 program was a lecture with slides, in which she explained the baroque dance forms and steps and danced numerous examples. Following intermission, Virginia Hutchings, who now worked with Wendy on a regular basis, performed Bach's Partita No. 2 in C Minor, BWV 826, and the two collaborated on what they called "Dances Related to Pieces in Dance Forms by J. S. Bach," in which Wendy danced to the allemande from the French Suite in E Major, BWV 817; the second courante

[1]Now the Lucy Moses School, part of the Kaufman Center, which also comprises Merkin Concert Hall and a Special Music School.

from the English Suite in A Minor, BWV 807; the minuet from the *Notebook for Wilhelm Friedemann Bach*; and the loure from the French Suite in G Major, BWV 816.

In the spring of 1972, Wendy had been approached by George Houle to choreograph Marco da Gagliano's 1608 opera, *La Dafne*, which he planned to mount as part of his new post as director of the New York Pro Musica Antiqua. Four major performances were scheduled from June 1973 through March 1974: in Spoleto, Italy, at the 16th Festival dei Due Mondi; in Greece at the first Corfu International Festival; and in New York at the 28th Caramoor Festival and at the Hunter College Playhouse.[2] Although the project appealed to her, Wendy hesitated to take it on at first. *La Dafne* has no actual dance music, so her task was to choreograph the choruses, which George felt strongly should be danced. Wendy countered, though, with her firm belief that early dance should be presented as it would have been in its time—meaning, in this case, that the composer did not intend for dancing to be a part of the opera, and it therefore should not be inserted arbitrarily. As George put it, Wendy "did not want to make things up."[3] Nonetheless, she finally agreed to the assignment, although it's not clear who or what finally persuaded her, and may have insisted on the following program note to clarify her position on the choreography:

> The inclusion of dances during the choral songs is implied in Marco da Gagliano's introduction but clearly indicated only by the dance rhythms of the music. The dances composed by Wendy Hilton are based upon the steps described in *Le Gratie d'amore* by Ceasre Negri and are not exact reproductions of specific choreographies.

Wendy wrote an overview of her work on *La Dafne*, giving an insightful look at how the whole thing came together successfully despite some artistic differences. Through her account of the troupe's sometimes comical adventures on the road, particularly in Corfu, Wendy also reveals her great capacity for fun, a trait that was not always obvious to those who came in professional contact with her.

> In 1972, George Houle was offered the position of director of the New York Pro Musica Antiqua. George was extremely flattered and excited. It was a risky assignment to take on, though, because the group faced many problems, particularly financial problems, and its future was uncertain. George, therefore, took a two-year leave of absence from Stanford to ensure that his position would remain

[2]The performance dates for *La Dafne* were June 30–July 8, 1973, at the Teatro Caio Melisso, 16th Festival dei Due Mondi, Spoleto; July 21–22, 1973 (originally scheduled for July 20–21), at the Venetian Theater, 28th Annual Caramoor Festival, New York; and March 12–17, 1974, at the Hunter College Playhouse New York. I was unable to locate a program for the Corfu International Festival, but those performances fell between the close of the Spoleto festival on July 8, and the opening at Caramoor on July 20, 1973.

[3]George Houle, interview by Anne Witherell, August 30, 2004.

open in case things did not work out in New York. He also knew that his wife, Glenna, hated the idea of leaving her beloved California for the horrors of Manhattan.

Even though George knew of the many challenges he would face, he had not anticipated the hard fact that a large part of his time with the Pro Musica would be spent trying to raise money to pay the next month's office rent and salaries. Music, it sometimes seemed, just had to be fitted in. Another problem was that George had had no experience in working with hard-boiled New York musicians. Much of his life had been spent in the San Francisco area teaching early music students at Stanford or performing with equally easy-going colleagues.

During his first year in New York, George directed concerts that had been scheduled before he took the reins as the Pro Musica's director. One was "An Entertainment for Elizabeth," for which the dances were staged by the Renaissance dance specialist Julia Sutton. The director was William Woodman, then on the drama faculty of Juilliard. George wanted to follow "Elizabeth" with a fully staged production of Marco da Gagliano's *La Dafne*. He asked me to choreograph the dances for the five or six choruses in this work because there was no actual dance music. The production was to open at the Spoleto Festival, go on to Corfu where the first-ever summer festival there was being planned, and then return to New York and the Caramoor Festival. A year later, it would be given at Hunter College.

This was a very attractive engagement. I had four dancers and some of the singers danced as well. George was careful that the latter artists we designated as both singers and dancers on the program.[4] The choruses were not ideal for choreographic purposes and achieving sufficient variety in the dances difficult. Santo Loquasto's costumes for the nymphs were too Watteau-esque for the period, but the production as a whole was very attractive.[5]

We had a month to rehearse, which was wonderful, and we all enjoyed every minute. I do remember, though, some terrible disagreements about musical proportions. For me, I suffered with the extremely cold air-conditioning, which always seemed to be blowing on the back of my neck. It was after these rehearsals that I became aware that my neck problem had developed a new symptom; I was developing a slight tremor. I gave it little thought at the time, believing that it would heal in the warmth of the Mediterranean.

[4]The four dancers were Juilliard students Elizabeth Haberer and Stephen Schnetzer; the Renaissance dancer Charles Garth, whom Wendy had met in Ely, Vermont; and Susan Crapanzano, perhaps a student from SUNY Purchase. (Wendy mentioned in her notes that she wanted "to be fair" and include a student from SUNY Purchase as well as from Juilliard. I've been unable to locate any information on Susan Crapanzano, but it seems likely that she was the Purchase student.) The two singer-dancers were David Britton and Susanne Delery. For the spring 1974 Hunter College performances, former Joffrey ballet dancer Haynes Owens replaced Schnetzer, Anne Tedards assumed Delery's dancing and singing role, and SUNY Purchase student Deborah Green replaced Crapanzano.

[5]Santo Loquasto's very long list of major costume and set design credits includes ballets for American Ballet Theatre (*Sephardic Song, Don Quixote, Raymonda*) and Twyla Tharp (*Baker's Dozen, Short Stories*), Paul Taylor (*Arabesque, Cascade*), and many New York and regional theaters and festivals. He also served as production designer for many movies, including some of Woody Allen's (*Zelig, Radio Days, Mighty Aphrodite*).

William Woodman, who was also directing this production, suggested that the production staff fly ahead one day earlier so as to be rested and full of vigor when the company arrived. We all agreed, and the flights were duly booked. Alas, everything went wrong, and I endured another terrible flight.

About five hours out from New York, the plane developed engine trouble, and we had to turn back. New York, however, was fogged in, so we went instead to Washington and sat in the plane all night because all hotels were full—or so TWA said—with delegates to a political rally. I was lucky enough to have two seats and could spread out somewhat.

It was our air hostess's first long flight, and she went to pieces. We took over the kitchen, made coffee and mustered such food as we could find. After a very long night, we were transferred to another plane, which had breakfast but no other food for the long flight to Rome. There we collapsed overnight. The next day, we went on by train to Spoleto. (I was not too tired to enjoy the train ride past the small Italian towns and resolved more than ever to visit Assisi.) When we arrived, it was the cast that was rested and ready to go.

The Spoleto performances went well. We were entertained by Giancarlo Menotti in his palatial residence and heard a closing performance of Britten's *War Requiem* in the square. I fulfilled my desire to see Assisi and spent one night in a hotel room overlooking the long views of flat countryside so familiar from paintings.

Before heading to Corfu, we had one weekend free, and most people opted to take the long train trip to Venice, spend eight hours there, and return. I can't bear rush trips, so I went to a small hotel high on a hillside overlooking Spoleto. Here I was in true Italian countryside. I walked all day and did not see anyone. The only living creatures were a distant white cow, complete with bell, and myriad unfamiliar butterflies and what I think were bees with bodies the color of honey, flying from blossom to blossom in a field covered in wildflowers. I sat in the sun in that field for a couple of hours and have seldom felt in so much harmony with nature. On walking further, there were views of lush green foliage for miles and miles and miles.

Then we went on to Corfu. My job was actually done, but I decided to pay my way and have a holiday. Corfu turned out to be a very different experience. I was really glad that I was not responsible for anything, unless I chose to be.

The Corfu festival was, I believe, the idea of a group of English living there. They were rich and the worst kind of snobs England can produce. And, of course, they were amateurs as far as music and opera were concerned and had no idea of how to do anything for the performance. With opening night one week away, we were taken out to see the site of the theater. Situated about one-and-a-half miles from the town, it consisted, at that time, of a large hole in the ground at the end of a long, as yet unpaved, pebble-ridden road. There was no actual theater in sight!

We were to stay in a European-style hotel, right by the airport. Perhaps our hosts meant well, but the accommodations did not suit us and were inconvenient to boot. Danny Collins [the countertenor who sang the role of Apollo] investigated places in the town and found a real Greek place with white-washed walls and a courtyard for $3.50 a night. It was, ironically, called the New York Hotel. We all moved there. We were close to the water, surrounded with delicious little restaurants serving coffee and retsina. The real thing—a true Corfu experience! Thank you, Danny.

Much to my surprise and pleasure, one of the first persons I saw was Brigitte Garski. She had come to meet Putnam Aldrich and look around for a cottage for her future retirement. It was wonderful to see her. We rented a car and explored Corfu. On searches for "the cottage," we encountered many locals. They were so courteous and hospitable—especially the women, who seemed to find us funny. Well, why not?

One incident that has stayed with me was watching a lady try to persuade a three-week-old duckling to swim. Somehow it had been hatched on land and was terrified of water. It was too late. The woman would wade into the sea and put the duck down, only to have it squawk in terror and flap its way to land again. By contrast, a tiny lamb she happened to have with her just walked into the water and swam about happily. We left her still trying to persuade the duckling that water was its natural habitat.

Working day and night, a theater was gradually raised out of the hole. Then came opening night, which was planned as a grand affair in the true Glyndebourne tradition. All the ladies were in full evening dress and high-heeled shoes. But while the hole had been transformed into a theater, the road leading to it was still as pebble-ridden as before. So, they had to pick up their long skirts and hobble for about a mile. I don't know why their cars could not travel that road; Brigitte and I drove all the way.

The rest of the opening reminds me of a Jacques Tati movie. Brigitte and I followed behind the Corfu peasant band, which was playing its way up the road to the theater to greet the bishop, who was to open the festival. But alas, once they got there, a great shouting arose, and they were halted and waved back. Confusion reigned. The bishop was late. The whole process had to be repeated. Brigitte and I backed up and were in the midst of the spectacle as they regained ranks and set forth again. The bishop made it this time, and the festival began.

With all the excitement of the lead-up, I have no recollection of the performance, but I guess it went well. Afterward, we all joined a celebration in a nearby field. At one point, the local ladies began a dance and opened up their line to let us join. They laughed loudly at the trouble we had picking up the steps. It was a great day!

The "Jacques Tati movie" continued a week or so later at the Caramoor Festival in New York, where a delay in the arrival of the sets and costumes from Corfu forced "the first cancellation of a concert in the 28-season history" of the festival. The opening, scheduled for Friday, July 20, was moved to Saturday, July 21, and a second performance was added for Sunday evening.[6] The high quality of the performances seems to have more than made up for the inconvenience of the delay.

[6]Robert Sherman, "Music: 'Dafne' Premiere: After 365 Years, the Work Arrives at Caramoor a Day Late," *New York Times*, July 24, 1973. The program lists the performance dates as July 20–21, 1973.

THE NEW YORK PRO MUSICA ANTIQUA
fondatore Noah Greenberg

presenta

LA DAFNE

libretto di Ottavio Rinucciani

musica di
MARCO DA GAGLIANO

Personaggi	*Interpreti*
Ovidio	Ray Devoll
Apollo	Daniel Collins
Tirsi	Ray Devoll
Cupido	Judy Hubbell
Venere	Christine Whittlesey
Dafne	Judy Hubbell
Pastori	Rodney Godshall, *basso*
	Ben Bagby, *tenore*
	David Britton, *tenore e ballerino*
	Charles Garth, *ballerino*
	Steven Schnetzer, *ballerino*
Ninfe	Lucy Shelton, *soprano*
	Susanne Delery, *soprano e ballerina*
	Susan Crapanzano, *ballerina*
	Beth Haberer, *ballerina*

Strumentisti

Stan Charkey, *liuto* – Wendy Gillespie, *viola da gamba* – Shelley Gruskin, *flauto, flauto a becco,* – George Houle, *flauto a becco, dulciana* – Catherine Liddell, *liuto, viola* – Frederick Renz, *clavicembalo, organo.*

Direzione della musica
GEORGE HOULE

Direzione scenica
William Woodman

Direzione delle danze
Wendy Hilton

Scena e costumi
Santo Loquasto

Luci
Martin Kapell

LA PRODUZIONE DELL'OPERA È STATA POSSIBILE GRAZIE A UN CONTRIBUTO DELLA FONDATION FORD

Figure 44. *La Dafne,* program, Teatro Caio Melisso, 16th Festival dei Due Mondi, Spoleto, June 30–July 8, 1973.

The mishaps along the way did not dim the enthusiasm of the press for *La Dafne*, which received high praise from critics abroad and in New York. In Spoleto, the opera had opened to highly positive reviews:

> Though a lesser work than the Monteverdi masterpiece [*Orfeo*], the *Dafne* has considerable charm, when performed with intelligence. And intelligence marked every aspect of this production. The small group of first-rate players—visible in the center of the stage—offered a convenient focus for the audience's attention, since the action of the opera is static. It is a narrative, not a drama. The staging of William Woodman therefore was appropriately limited to a few, essential, telling movements, just as Wendy Hilton's choreography was never obtrusive, of pastoral simplicity.

The *New York Post* called the Hunter College performances of the following spring (which appear to have gone smoothly) "elegant" and noted that "a volume of imagination has brought *Dafne* from the shelf to an exciting life on stage." The *New York Times* enthused that *La Dafne* was a "near-perfection swan-song" for the Pro Musica, which would disband shortly thereafter:

> It was hard to know what to admire most about the New York Pro Musica Antiqua's production of *La Dafne* at Hunter Playhouse on Tuesday night, the scrupulous scholarship and care with which the 366-year-old opera by Marco da Gagliano had been prepared, or the charm and gaiety with which the troupe brought the piece to life.

Figure 45. *La Dafne,* Hunter College Playhouse, New York, 1974. Photo courtesy of George Houle.

Of Wendy's choreography, the *Times* wrote that: "the nymphs not only carry off their florid vocal lines accurately, but also show astonishing grace and agility in Wendy Hilton's historically credible dances."[7]

After the close of *La Dafne* at Caramoor, Wendy enjoyed a brief hiatus and some much needed rest, but the arrival of fall brought another very busy teaching and rehearsal schedule. She resumed her classes at Juilliard, Douglass, and SUNY Purchase, and prepared for upcoming collaborations with Albert Fuller on a concert at Alice Tully Hall and with the New York Consort of Viols for a performance at the Cubiculo Theatre.[8] Rehearsals for the spring performance of *La Dafne* at Hunter also had to be planned.

Her schedule well booked, Wendy was surprised—and not a little disturbed—when a couple of friends remarked enthusiastically about her upcoming performance at Carnegie Hall. She protested that they were mistaken; there was no such performance. They insisted, however, that there was a large advertisement outside the hall announcing her dance-company's performances with the Buffalo Philharmonic Orchestra and Michael Tilson Thomas the following April. Wendy went immediately to see for herself. Wendy had met Thomas (it's not clear how), but she certainly had not agreed to this or any other performance with him. When she finally tracked him down, she recalled that he said to her, "Oh, there you are. I've been looking for you all winter." And he not only wanted her to perform with him in Manhattan, but also in Boston with the Boston Symphony Orchestra and in Buffalo, again with the Buffalo orchestra, all within three weeks.

With the advertising out, particularly in Manhattan, Wendy had to go forward with the performances. She also, of course, recognized them as plum opportunities and set about making plans immediately. That she did not actually have a dance company might have been a complication, but by the first performance in Boston, she had officially registered a business certificate for the Wendy Hilton Baroque Dance Company with the State of New York and had engaged Elizabeth Haberer, Eileen Cropley, Haynes Owens, Jürg Burth, and Paul Taylor dancer Nicholas Gunn as company members. Eileen had recruited Nicholas for the new company, and it was pure coincidence—and very good luck—that the Taylor company was off during the two weeks of performances in Boston and New York, allowing them to perform. The new company rehearsed sporadically throughout the winter, when a few of them happened to be free, but they were never able to put the whole program together until three weeks before the opening performance in Boston.

The inaugural performance of the Wendy Hilton Baroque Dance Company on April 11, 1974, was part of the Boston Symphony Orchestra's

[7]William Weaver, "A Vintage Year for the Spoleto Festival," *International Herald Tribune*, July 3, 1973; Harriett Johnson, "Words and Music: Pro Musica Closes with *Dafne*," *New York Post*, March 13, 1974; Donal Henahan, "Music: Delightful *Dafne*," *New York Times*, March 14, 1974.

[8]The Cubiculo Theatre was located at 414 West 51st Street in Manhattan from 1969 to the mid-1990s.

1973–74 season, for which Thomas and Colin Davis were serving as principal guest conductors. The concert as a whole was called "Three Centuries of Drama in Music" and featured Wendy's company dancing to J. S. Bach's Suite No. 1 in C Major for Woodwinds and Strings, BWV 1066, and the premieres of two contemporary works, "Recital I (For Cathy)" by Luciano Berio, and "Melodramas for Speaker and Piano," which included works by C. P. E. Bach, Schumann, and Liszt, and accompanying spoken text.

The company danced to all movements of the Bach suite except for the overture. The gavotte and bourrée were choreographed by Wendy, and the other four dances were based on extant choreographies from the eighteenth century. The courante, which followed the overture, was based on "La Bocannes"[9]; the forlana and passepied on "La Forlana" (Pécour/Campra, 1700) and "Le Passepied à quatre" (Feuillet/Anon., 1711); and the minuet on Le Menuet, according to Pierre Rameau. The program did not indicate who danced each piece, but Eileen recalled that she and Nicholas performed the minuet.[10]

A week later, on April 18, the company was back in New York to repeat the program with the Buffalo Philharmonic Orchestra at Carnegie Hall with Thomas again on the podium. This time, the program was called "Spectrum Concert: Music Theater." The reviews were enthusiastic, even rapturous. Byron Belt, critic-at-large for the Newhouse Newspapers and a fan of Wendy's, was swept away by the entire evening, but particularly the dancing. He wrote in "A Brilliant 'Happening'":

> The second portion of the Spectrum trilogy was an utterly beguiling performance of Father Bach's First Suite for Winds and Strings, with Wendy Hilton and five excellent dancers performing the dance movements in authentic baroque manner. Some of the movements were historic reconstructions and some were in the style by Miss Hilton.
>
> Miss Hilton is real—I know she is, for we sometimes shop in the same west side stores. But when she is on stage, she breathes and visionates (it's a night for making up words!) the 18th century as though she just stepped out of a Fragonard painting. The regal poetry of her movement is one of the dance world's current great delights and she and her unhappily unnamed associates were perfection.[11]

Baroque dancer, dance scholar, and Laban movement analyst Janis Pforsich, then a student of Wendy's, attended the concert. She found the company's performance "flawless" and each dance "elegant and well-differentiated." Janis described Wendy in her off-white satin gown as looking "like a porcelain doll. Her technique was magnificent: precise, clear, rhythmically beautiful. She glided around the space. Everyone loved it."[12]

[9]For a discussion of the provenance of "La Bocannes" and its accompanying music, see Wendy Hilton, "A Dance for Kings: The 17th-Century French Courante," *Early Music* (April 1977), 163–64.

[10]Eileen also recalled being terribly nervous for this performance because the entire Paul Taylor Dance Company attended. Eileen Cropley, interview by Susan Bindig, August 2005.

[11]Byron Belt, "A Brilliant 'Happening,'" *Newhouse Newspapers*, April 19, 1974.

[12]Janis Pforsich, interview by Susan Bindig, December 9, 2004.

The Buffalo *Courier-Express* sent a reviewer to Manhattan to preview the concert for the hometown audience who would see it a few days later. This reviewer described the dramatic aspects that Thomas incorporated throughout the concert, giving a sense of the evening's overall theatricality, maybe even eccentricity, and justifying its title. It is worth quoting this review at length if only to ponder how Wendy and her company fit into this program.

> What was impressive about this "Music Theater" concert was not the effect made by the orchestra—which literally never held center stage—but its demonstration of Thomas' bent for uninhibited program-making.
>
> But although the audience here could not have left the hall with a good understanding of the Buffalo orchestra it certainly got a taste of what Thomas does in Buffalo. . . .
>
> The major attraction was mezzo-soprano Cathy Berberian, who appeared in the mad scene which Lucian Berio composed for her, titled "Recital I (for Cathy)." . . .
>
> Miss Berberian begins by singing Monteverdi accompanied by an off-stage harpsichord; but soon her real accompanist, Sahan Arzruni, shows up, tiptoeing to his place at the piano. There is also a wardrobe mistress, who adds costume parts to the singer during the recital, and finally traps Miss Berberian in a kind of haute couture headnet. . . .
>
> Thomas conducted 19 musicians from behind a screen. Five of them had dramatic roles. They entered wearing masks, and their identities were further confused when they played games of sharing instruments.
>
> For example, the normal clarinetist, in this game of changing roles, blew into a trombone, while the violist took a turn on the clarinet. This ensemble was a big hit. . . .
>
> The program began in the 19th Century, with three melodramas performed by Thomas at the piano with narrator Michael Wager, who was dressed in blue velvet circa 1870.
>
> Wager delivered "Hamlet's Soliloquy" in the original Shakespeare until he reached the part about sleeping and perchancing to dream, at which point Thomas began playing C.P.E. Bach's "C Minor Fantasy." Wager again asked the question about being, this time in the German version of Heinrich Wilhelm Von Gertenberg (who used the same music to accompany the last words of Socrates).
>
> Thomas displayed his considerable piano skills during the melodramas, which included Schumann's "Schoen Hedwig" and Liszt's "The Blind Singer."
>
> Translations were provided in the program book, but the hall was too dark to allow reading during the performance; instead English subtitles were projected on a screen (which was too small to hold all the words), a visual aid which, along with the potted palms that framed the scene, increased the sense of campy humor.

Sandwiched between all this drama and camp was Wendy and her company. The review did not address the dancing specifically but described the bit of drama Thomas brought to this segment and the high quality of the music that the audience enjoyed all evening.

> For Bach's "Suite No. 1," the Philharmonic was off to one side of the stage while the Wendy Hilton [Baroque] Dance Company performed baroque period steps in beautiful costumes, the men wearing wigs and three-cornered hats.
>
> Thomas, in one of his theatrical moods, used a long pole to beat the introductory pulse for those movements which did not start on the downbeat, and to reinforce the beat if necessary. He meant to recall the practice of the French baroque composer Lully, who died from a foot wound inflicted by his time-beater.
>
> The Philharmonic strings (reduced) and winds (oboes and bassoon) with harpsicord [*sic*] played the Bach very cleanly, and the tone was lean but beautiful. One Philharmonic player remarked that it is impossible to sound bad in Carnegie Hall: yet it is another thing to sound beautiful.[13]

For the two performances in Buffalo on April 21 and 23 at the Philharmonic's home venue, Kleinhans Music Hall, there were only four dancers, as Nicholas and Eileen were back with the Taylor company. The program was altered slightly and now included David Bedford's audience-participation composition "With 100 Kazoos for Ensemble and Orchestra" in place of the "Melodramas." The Bach suite with the dancing was again oddly placed on the program, between the kazoos and intermission; the Berio piece remained in the second half. I can only imagine what the musically uncompromising Wendy I knew thought of the Bach suite following a composition with kazoos. It might have appealed to her great sense of fun, but fun was never a factor in her serious concertizing. She must have had great trust in Thomas, or for the sake of the opportunity, was willing to ignore the musical clash.

Amid the preparations for these concerts with Thomas, Wendy was also organizing another production, "A Concert by the Baroque Ensemble," to be performed on March 15 at Alice Tully Hall in New York with Albert Fuller. It featured, as a year earlier, a piece danced by Juilliard students to close the evening. Wendy's participation was again finessed by Martha Hill. The first half of the concert was devoted to J. S. Bach and featured the Trio Sonata from the "Musical Offering," BWV 1079, and Cantata BWV 56, "Ich will den Kreuzstab gerne tragen." After intermission, the focus switched to Rameau, with this half opening with the Overture to *Zaïs*. Wendy choreographed a "Nouvelle Entrée: 'Les Sauvages,' from *Les Indes galantes* (1735–36)" for eleven dancers, six women and five men. Through these concerts with Fuller, Wendy was quickly establishing herself as a valued choreographer at Juilliard, although not yet with the Dance Division.

Wendy also began to collaborate with some of the most respected New York early music ensembles in performances for herself and for her company. On March 31, 1974, just two weeks after the baroque concert with Fuller and before her Carnegie Hall debut with Thomas, Wendy appeared with the New York Consort of Viols (Fortunato Arico, Lucy Bardo, Judith Davidoff, Grace Feldman, Alison Fowle, and John Gibbons) in the second of three concerts the ensemble presented that spring at the Cubiculo

[13] "Buffalo at Carnegie Hall," *Buffalo Courier-Express*, April 20, 1974.

Theatre. In "Viol Music of the Continent," Wendy danced a suite of her own choreographies to the music of Charles Dieupart and three of the theatrical solos that had by now become staples of her repertoire: the Minuet by Mr. Isaac, the loure from *Scylla*, and the canary from *Alcide*. The *New York Times* and *Dance Magazine* covered the concert, although both reviews were more descriptive than analytic.[14] Many reviewers, it seems, were still trying to come to terms with the movement vocabulary and quality of this unfamiliar style. All, though, were struck by the grace, nobility, and elegance of Wendy's dancing.

That September, Wendy would embark on a series of performances with the newly formed Ensemble for Early Music. Four members of the now defunct New York Pro Musica Antiqua—Frederick Renz, Wendy Gillespie, David Hart, and Jean Lamon—formed the new ensemble. Wendy and her company danced in one of their first concerts, a tribute to Noah Greenberg, the founder of the Pro Musica, on September 29, at the Cathedral of St. John the Divine. Because the scope of the concert was so broad, featuring music from the entire seventeenth century, Wendy was asked to include Renaissance dances in the program, an unusual request for her at this time. She added dances from the manuals of Fabritio Caroso, Thoinot Arbeau, and John Playford to the more familiar baroque pieces in the company's repertoire. The concert was repeated on October 5 at Sullivan County Community College, just outside Manhattan in Westchester County, New York. Wendy would join the ensemble for three more concerts: in Manhattan on October 20; in the ensemble's first out-of-state performance, in St. Louis, Missouri, on November 1; and in Croton-on-Hudson, New York, the following spring on April 26, 1975.[15]

Wendy's life during this period was more than one dance engagement after another. In the early 1970s, an opportunity arose that allowed her to spend time in the country entertaining friends, writing her book, and enjoying much needed and greatly appreciated respites from the distraction and noise of Manhattan. Through Virginia Hutchings, Wendy met and became great friends with Peggy Eagan, a great-granddaughter of William Colgate, founder of the Colgate Company, and the daughter of Sidney Morse Colgate, who continued his family's work in the company that by the 1920s had become known as Colgate-Palmolive-Peet. A woman of considerable wealth and social position, the young Margaret Colgate was frequently associated with the society world of Doris Duke and married Edward "Eddie" Eagan, a Rhodes scholar, a distinguished Olympic athlete (the only Olympian to date to win gold medals in both the summer [boxing] and winter [bobsled] games), and later chair of the New York Athletic Commission. Peggy Eagan was also an accomplished photographer, publishing her work in such prominent magazines as *National Geographic*. A dedicated

[14]Jennifer Dunning, "Wendy Hilton's Elan in Baroque Dances Reflected in Music," *New York Times*, April 2, 1974; Rose Anne Thom, "Reviews," *Dance Magazine* (June 1974), 73–74.

[15]The programs for the concerts on October 20 and November 1, 1974, appear to have been lost.

patron of the arts, she generously supported numerous prominent arts organizations and individual artists.

Wendy, like Virginia, was one such artist whose work attracted Eagan's attention. It's unclear exactly what financial benefits, if any, Wendy may have enjoyed from her friendship with Eagan.[16] Money aside, however, Eagan's estate, "Happy Harbor," in Rye, New York, played an important role in Wendy's life and work for about fifteen years. Located on the edge of Long Island Sound with beautiful grounds and stunning views of the water, Happy Harbor became a wonderful escape from Manhattan for Wendy, engaged to house-sit when Eagan was traveling or spending time at one of her other residences. Wendy wrote a large part of her book *Dance of Court and Theater* at Happy Harbor, as it was a perfect retreat for such a project. There Wendy could work easily with Eagan's daughter, Caroline Gaynor, who was a professional editor. Caroline assisted Wendy on the "teaching" portion of the book, working out the basics of baroque dance technique as Wendy described it, and became the book's first "performing" student. The house's living room, with a few pieces of furniture moved to the side, became a dance studio where the two frequently worked.

For those who were lucky enough to be invited there for a day or a weekend, Happy Harbor—or "Rye" as her visitors generally referred to it—was a favorite place to visit Wendy and taste a finer way of living than most were accustomed to. When Eileen Cropley was not touring, she joined Wendy there. Frequent guests were Wendy's close friends Dino (Constantine) Cassolas, Claire Melley, and Miriam Cooper. Claire described the four on their shore weekends as "an outrageous quartet, determined to have a high old time. We had fierce Scrabble matches, we swam in the summer, and we enjoyed Mary's [the cook] 'Mile-High Pie.'"[17] Dino recalled delightful evenings of Viennese waltzes, with everyone dancing and taking turns at the piano. Rainy afternoons brought out Scrabble and another of Wendy's favorites, Trivial Pursuit. Wendy was a master of both and an aggressive and unsympathetic competitor.

I always looked forward to an invitation to Rye. Although the large black entrance gates that announced the Eagan estate and the short drive through the woods to the home were, on my first visit, intimidating, the house itself was not only grand, but also comfortable, and Wendy made everyone feel at home. My favorite memories are of Caroline's bedroom—the room I always hoped I'd be assigned for the night—with its many windows and glorious view of the Sound, and of Mary delivering my breakfast, complete with silver tray, to my door. I had never before, and haven't since, been treated to such luxury. Like other students willing to travel there, I had a couple of private dance lessons in the living room and met a few times with Wendy and dance colleagues on professional matters. But mostly I just visited, spending much time wandering through the grounds, picking vegetables for dinner from the gardens with Wendy, wading in the Sound, and perusing

[16]Wendy also secured financial assistance for others. Through her efforts, Eagan contributed to Philippa Waite's study of baroque dance with Wendy in New York and California. Waite, interview by Susan Bindig, September 3, 2005.

[17]"Remembering Wendy Hilton, 1931–2002: A Program of Dance and Music Celebrating Her Life and Work," The Juilliard School, May 30, 2003.

the wonderful library for a book to read in the evening. At times, I also had to work with Wendy in her role as house-sitter. During one visit, Wendy, Miriam Cooper, and I had a hilarious time rounding up the chickens that had escaped from the coop; I can't think of three less-qualified people for that task. I also have a vague memory of another visit when I watched Wendy uncharacteristically toiling at the kitchen sink scrubbing pot after pot and trying to get them as shiny as Mary could. But Wendy's favorite memory of my helping around the house—one that she enjoyed recounting to friends on numerous occasions—was of my supervision of a delivery of new kitchen appliances. Wendy had left the house for a few hours to run an errand and had forgotten to warn me of the pending delivery. She returned to find me standing wide-eyed in the middle of the kitchen surrounded by two of each appliance—one old, one new—with Mary and Eddie, the caretaker, arguing at fever pitch with the delivery men about how the old appliances should be disposed of. I remember Wendy walking into the kitchen and laughing hysterically at the chaos, although I was not amused.

Anne Witherell shared a story of observing firsthand Wendy's limited domestic skills during a visit to Rye.

> Wendy certainly tried her best to avoid this room [the kitchen]. She told me, "There are a lot of English people who have no appreciation of food. They just eat because it is functional. I have learned to appreciate food, but not so much to cook it."[18] When pressed, she was a fair hand at boiling water for coffee, tea, and the odd egg. She could operate a toaster. One unusual evening the two of us were at Happy Harbor in Rye. All of the help was gone, and we were miles from the nearest rotisserie chicken. Wendy said lightly, "Let's have spaghetti!" and entered that enormous kitchen. I stood in disbelief in the doorway. She boiled water. She emptied an entire box of pasta into the pot. She pulled out a block of frozen ground beef and a bottle of catsup. Finally, she turned to me and said, "If there is anything you can imagine doing to prevent disaster, do not hesitate to step in."

It would be impossible to overstate the importance of Happy Harbor and of Wendy's friendship with Peggy Eagan to this story. Happy Harbor was truly a haven for Wendy, a favorite site for a little work, a lot of play, and a chance to enjoy the outdoors, which she loved so much. She found it to be a place for "a good rest and a period of spiritual recovery for the surroundings are glorious."[19] Many years after Eagan's death and the sale of the estate, it would also be Wendy's final resting place.

Amid her travels and many engagements, Wendy continued to teach at Douglass College and SUNY Purchase. Her position at Douglass would last through the spring of 1975 through the music department and the efforts of its chair, Professor Kunrad Kvam.

[18] Anne Witherell, letter to John Witherell, November 27, 1974.

[19] Wendy Hilton, letter to Meredith Ellis Little, January 17, 1975.

> I was overjoyed at the opportunity. My teaching schedule was reduced to one day per week, but I began to develop a small group of seriously interested students from both the music and dance departments.

Douglass also provided Wendy with another significant choreographic opportunity. In 1974–75, the college celebrated the opening of its new Philip J. Levin Theater with a production called *Masque of a Midsummer Night.* Directed by theater department chair John Bettenbender, it combined the text of Shakespeare's *A Midsummer Night's Dream* with music from Henry Purcell's *The Fairy Queen.* Wendy was invited to choreograph the masques that interspersed the text—the Masque of the Four Seasons and the Masque of Night—and general movement for a concluding apotheosis.

Wendy needed eight dancers, six women and two men. The latter were next to impossible to find at a women's college like Douglass, despite its affiliation with Rutgers College, so she imported two dancers from New York, Charles Garth and Haynes Owens, who had performed in her company. The women were Donna Waks, Fern Schwartzbard, and I, all from the dance department, and three others from the music department whose faces I can remember but whose names I cannot. I also do not have a program to consult.[20] Apologies to my unnamed but highly valued classmates and fellow dancers.

Dancing in *Masque of a Midsummer Night* was a revelation for me, and it literally changed my life. First, it brought me back to baroque dance. The promise of performing in such an elaborate production lured me into signing up for Wendy's class again. As I had made no effort to remember anything about the style from my one-semester introduction, I lurked at the back of the class relearning old steps and trying to keep up with the rest of the class on new ones. I loved it. Once we began to work on *Masque*, everything we had been studying in the studio, now placed in the context of a fully realized production, suddenly made sense to me. We worked on full choreographies in class, but our primary purpose was to become more facile with Beauchamps-Feuillet notation and the steps. I don't recall working on performance quality at that point in our studies; we were thrilled just to make it to the end of a dance successfully. For the production, however, we focused on performance quality, and that work brought so much life to what heretofore had been mostly an academic study.

I can still remember bits of the choreography for the gavotte that Donna and I danced as Spring as well as for the passepied that we danced with Charles and Haynes as Summer in the Masque of the Four Seasons. Donna and I struggled with the cross-rhythms in the gavotte, still a relatively new dance form for us then, and dreaded that we would begin incorrectly and be out of sync with the music throughout. We began each performance with an exchange of anxious looks and relaxed only after completing the opening contretemps de gavottes successfully with the music.

After the passepied, Charles and Haynes danced a difficult entrée grave as Autumn. This was the first time we had seen the more virtuosic men's

[20]Neither the libraries of Rutgers University nor the archives of its Mason Gross School of the Arts have programs for this production.

theatrical style of dancing and were amazed by its complexity and by Charles' and Haynes' wonderful performances. For Winter, the dancers (Fern and my unnamed colleagues) walked elegant, weaving patterns that were meant to imitate the movement of the sun, moon, and stars in the winter sky. The eight of us as quiet specters of the night in the Masque of Night performed a similar "walking" choreography; the meandering patterns we traced were meant to reflect the ceaseless wandering that was our fate. I remember little about the apotheosis that closed the entire production other than that we had to kneel painfully on one knee for a long time and complained about it bitterly under our breaths.

Wendy did not seem to enjoy working on this production. She disagreed with many of Bettenbender's directorial decisions and, hence, generally did not get along with him. None of the costumes, except for those of Night (which she would use later at Juilliard), met her standards. During the final rehearsals, we would find Wendy curled up on a bench under one of the staircases in the theater lobby, as she couldn't bear to watch anything but the dancing. At one rehearsal, she told us that she had gone home after the previous evening's stressful run-through to a nightcap of valium and scotch. In addition to everything else, we were being introduced to a new side of Wendy.

We dancers, however, enjoyed every minute of *Masque*, from mastering the dances, to the late rehearsals, to learning to breathe in our tightly laced costumes. For me, I never expected to become so fully engaged in the form. I realized that after I graduated a month or so later, I would have to continue to study and perform baroque dance. I didn't know that Wendy would provide that opportunity surprisingly quickly.

While *Masque* was in its final rehearsals, Wendy was already engrossed in her next project with Albert Fuller, a production of Jean-Philippe Rameau's tragédie lyrique *Dardanus* at the Juilliard Theater. Their highly successful collaborations at Alice Tully Hall in 1973 and 1974 persuaded Juilliard President Peter Mennin to allow Fuller to take on this far more ambitious project. Mennin's agreement unfortunately did not guarantee financial support for such an elaborate and expensive production. So Fuller took costumes and sets from the existing Juilliard stock and, through Wendy, borrowed additional costumes from the Douglass production of *Masque of a Midsummer Night*. But costs were still high, and Fuller, in his tenacious efforts to establish early music at Juilliard, spent a considerable amount of his own money to bring this production to fruition. Although Wendy was still not officially on the faculty of the Dance Division, Martha Hill supported *Dardanus* as a special dance project in order to get a fee for Wendy through Mennin.

Fuller engaged Wendy to choreograph the many entrées in this five-act opera, providing her with her first opportunity to present baroque dance on such a large scale and with a large cast of twenty-six dancers. Wendy invited me and my fellow Douglass dancers Donna and Fern to join the cast. In her notes, Wendy wrote that she brought us on board because she needed dancers trained in the style to supplement the core of dancers she had developed at Juilliard. That may have been true to some extent, but I also know that, as with all her serious students over the years, she wanted to give us as many opportunities to study and perform as she could. Whatever the reason,

Donna, Fern, and I were thrilled to be asked and to be dancing in New York, particularly at Lincoln Center.

Despite the significance of the production, the amount of time devoted to preparation and rehearsal, and the cost, *Dardanus* had only one performance, on October 28, 1975. The single, Tuesday-night performance nonetheless drew important critical reviews. Andrew Porter reviewed *Dardanus* for the *New Yorker.* His support for Wendy's choreography and for her work with Fuller, which he voiced in reviews of their earlier collaborations, continued with *Dardanus.* He wrote:

> At the Juilliard School last week, a production of *Dardanus* by Rameau, Handel's contemporary, filled the Juilliard Theatre. A devoted *ramoneur*, I delighted in this opportunity of seeing and hearing the score, or at least large parts of it, take shape in sight and sound. It was done not complete but in substantial excerpt, with a linking narration. . . . It was a simple but attractive production. A special feature, which set it aside from the few other Rameau stagings that have come my way, was Wendy Hilton's choreography, built from eighteenth-century steps. Rameau has been called the greatest ballet composer of all time, and dance is an essential element of his lyric dramas. His dance music vividly suggests physical movement, and, conversely, Albert Fuller, who directed *Dardanus*, has said that his instrumentalists have been inspired to stylish articulation and phrasing by watching Miss Hilton's dancers in authentic action. . . . Enjoyable in itself, it [*Dardanus*] could be a pilot to the full presentation of a Rameau opera for which the [*sic*] Juilliard is well equipped.[21]

Donal Henahan, reviewing for the *New York Times*, was at odds with Porter about Wendy's choreography. He found it "constricted" (although less so than in previous productions) yet recognized that the "stiffness . . . could be "attributed to a narrow 18th-century dance idiom." The production as a whole, however, was, he felt, "a step in the right direction" for introducing audiences to such rarely presented and important works.[22]

Dardanus also brought a change to Wendy's affiliation at Juilliard. That fall, she was scheduled to teach in both the Drama and Dance Divisions. At the last moment, the Drama Division had to make some changes in its teaching schedule that were incompatible with Wendy's teaching and rehearsals for *Dardanus.* She was forced to choose between the two and not surprisingly decided to continue with *Dardanus* and move to the Dance Division. Fortunately, Martha Hill was able to hire her permanently, and thus began what would be a significant and very fruitful appointment for Wendy.

[21]Andrew Porter, review of *Dardanus, New Yorker* (November 10, 1975), 157–8.

[22]Donal Henahan, "Opera: A Staging for 1739 'Dardanus,'" *New York Times*, October 30, 1975.

Fourteen: 1975–1981

The End of Wendy's Performing Career ~ Joining the Juilliard School's Dance Division ~ Working with Jerome Robbins ~ Thea Musgrave and Mary, Queen of Scots

Change and challenge dominated Wendy's life over the next few years. Although she finally secured a plum job in Juilliard's Dance Division, her positions at Douglass College and SUNY Purchase ended. The success of *Masque of a Midsummer Night* brought an ironic close to her appointment at Douglass, where her classes in three departments—dance, music, and theater—had dwindled to just one late Friday-afternoon class offered by the music department and attended by only a half-dozen students. A continuing appointment could no longer be justified. A similar situation may have existed at Purchase, where her contract was not renewed. While disappointing, the trimming of her schedule allowed Wendy to concentrate fully on the productions she was engaged to stage at Juilliard and on a parallel position she was developing at Stanford University. These appointments would soon have her dividing her time between the two coasts, an arrangement she would love for the varied work both offered and, in Stanford's case, for the warm, sunny weather.

The most significant change in Wendy's life at this time, however, was the end of her performing career, which was at its peak. The severity of her torticollis became sadly clear at an engagement at the Carmel (California) Bach Festival in the summer of 1975. Even with resting before a performance, she could no longer quiet the head tremors, which at this point were the predominant feature of her condition, or control the increasing rotation of her head to the left. Her performance at the Carmel festival was her last.[1]

That fall, however, shortly after *Dardanus*, Wendy was scheduled to dance with the Ensemble for Early Music at Alice Tully Hall. At the November 25 performance, she was to present the New York premiere of a suite of dances to songs from Michel L'Affilard's *Principes très faciles* (1705), which she had been developing with harpsichordist Erich Schwandt and soprano Julianne Baird.[2] The program had already been performed at the Eastman School of Music in upstate New York, where Schwandt was a music professor and Baird a student, and at Stanford. In New York, Wendy was to perform the suite with harpsichordist Frederick Renz and countertenor Daniel Collins. Wendy, however, changed the New York program at the last minute to feature instead a suite of her dances from *Dardanus* performed by her Juilliard dance students.[3] In her notes, Wendy's simple and plausible explanation for the

[1]Anne Witherell tells the full story of Wendy's engagement at the Carmel Bach Festival in chapter 16.

[2]For a discussion of L'Affilard's *Principes très faciles* and the work of Schwandt, Baird, and Hilton, see chapter 16.

[3]Two different programs for this concert are included in Wendy's papers, one that lists her performance of the L'Affilard dances and a second that features the suite from *Dardanus*.

substitution was that Collins could not get to New York in sufficient time to rehearse with her. My fellow Douglass baroque dancers and I, however, planned to attend the performance, and Wendy sadly explained to us that she had to cancel her performance because of the growing problems with her torticollis. Perhaps, though, both reasons contributed to her decision—Collins's crowded schedule may have provided Wendy with a graceful exit from a performance that had long been advertised but, owing to her deteriorating condition, she could not possibly go through with.

I did not know Wendy well enough then to discuss her decision to stop dancing. It seems, though, that she confided in only a few close friends about her condition. She was very private and, in my experience of her, dealt with such things alone and in her own way.

Wendy's new and growing work at Juilliard and Stanford, however, marked the beginning of a fresh chapter in her career. She now would focus on teaching and choreography, and in both areas, would make a lasting mark.

At Juilliard, Wendy was hired at first only to choreograph for the school's productions. Even though she was now firmly in the Dance Division, a formal class in which she could teach the baroque style was not offered. Her dancers had to learn the style as they learned her choreography—not an ideal arrangement, even with dancers of such high caliber. It also showed how little was known about the demands and nuances of the style. As her dance faculty colleague Elizabeth Keen noted, Wendy engaged in a yearly "physical/cultural re-indoctrination with class after class of new students imbued with twentieth-century rambunctiousness. She had to tame jazz bunnies and hyperactive super dancers and then attune them to her own exacting mentality, one that was particular to the extreme."[4] Wendy, however, made the arrangement work. She wrote of her first days with the Dance Division:

> My arrangement with Miss Hill was that I would work at Juilliard from school reopening each January and prepare a twenty-minute piece for the spring dance concert, usually held each March. She would not let me teach classes; technique and style, therefore, had to be learned at rehearsal. (And yet somewhere in there I did have a class because Kenneth Merrill played for it, then Kenneth Mallon—on Saturday mornings, I think.) Students auditioned, and I usually had a cast of about twenty-four. I don't believe that any students who did baroque dance ever dropped out during their four years at Juilliard. Considering the pressure they were under, this was a great compliment to the work.

Although Wendy began her appointment in January 1976, she would not present her first major work until the spring of 1978. Through her collaborations with Albert Fuller and her teaching in the Drama Division, she had already established an excellent reputation at the school and was able to draw students into her projects easily. Still, she needed the full two years not only to teach and polish the choreography but also to pull together the costumes, scenery, and music.

[4]Elizabeth Keen, "Remembering Wendy Hilton, 1931–2002: A Program of Dance and Music Celebrating Her Life and Work," The Juilliard School, May 30, 2003.

> The first piece I did for the Dance Division (for which I have a program) was "Divertissement from *Les Festes vénitiennes*" with original dances by Louis Pécour and music by Campra. I had three priorities at Juilliard: to teach and show original eighteenth-century pieces, choreograph pieces in the style for larger groups since almost all the extant dances are for one or two dancers, and provide a varied and theatrically effective piece. Here I was helped enormously by the stage department, who always provided me with a beautiful backdrop hired at great expense (thank you, Miss Hill!) from the Banff Opera House. The costume people loved doing the baroque pieces, and many costumes would be borrowed from the Drama Division period productions.
>
> One of the serious matters was getting a good musical performance from the student orchestra. Playing for the dance concert was regarded as a punishment and was indeed hung over their heads as a threat by the gentleman in charge of the student orchestras. The student conductor, Ronald Braunstein, was determined to overcome the attitude of his players. He had come to many of my rehearsals with the dancers and felt that if the students could see what they were playing for, it would help. He, therefore, had a tape made at one of the orchestra rehearsals and made the players watch while the dancers went through the piece. This helped enormously, and the playing greatly improved.
>
> With a small number of male students in school, this year two men were imported from the Stanford group: Ronald Harris-Warrick and Richard Semmens.[5]

Wendy introduced four of the six dances from *Les Festes vénitiennes* in studio performances at the school on March 23 and November 3, 1977,[6] and then formally premiered the full work in the annual dance concert on March 11–12, 1978. The program featured an entrée for a Harlequin, a solo loure for a man, three danses à deux, and a concluding minuet and passepied for twelve women.

In her very brief notes on *Les Festes vénitiennes* for this book, Wendy added a reminder to herself to "confess about Harlequin." In the end, she never had a chance to admit to her long hidden transgression. She had, however, confessed what I believe was the offense to me one day at a rehearsal of the work that I attended. It was an example of her sometimes overzealous attention to historical detail resulting in an insensitive decision that deeply affected her dancers and colleagues. When choosing the cast for the work, Wendy did not want to include a particular student because he was African American. She pointed out to me that there never would have been any persons of color at the eighteenth-century French court, so why should she

[5]By this time, Wendy had cultivated a group of devoted students at Stanford University, who performed on campus and in the local community. The group had been working on the dances from *Les Festes vénitiennes*, so importing Ron and Rick was a logical move. Although she no doubt needed additional men dancers (only two others were part of the cast of twenty dancers), this is another example of Wendy's ongoing efforts to provide her interested students with as many opportunities as possible.

[6]March 23, 1977, "An Open Class and Rehearsal of Baroque Dance," and November 3, 1977, Event I: "An Open Class and Rehearsal of Baroque Dance (Work in Progress)."

include them in her works? She was adamant and believed her position was wholly reasonable. I do not recall who disabused her of the idea, but Wendy was forced to cast the student, Bruce Davis. To meet what she saw as an aesthetic necessity, however—and probably to get her own way, if only in part—Wendy chose to cast Davis as Harlequin because she could mask him. No one would have to know the color of his skin.

In an ironic twist, Wendy's delightful choreography for Harlequin and Davis's performance of it were the highlights of the work, if not of the entire concert. Wendy based her choreography on the three extant notations of dances for an eighteenth-century harlequin, which (as far as she knew) had not been reconstructed since the eighteenth century, and added her own clever and humorous touches. Davis brought both high technical skill and a gift for comedy to the dance that captivated everyone, including Wendy. It was an overwhelming success for all. Jack Anderson, dance reviewer for the *New York Times*, confirmed in his review of the full Juilliard concert that Wendy's piece was the highlight of the evening:

> One of the admirable things about the Juilliard Dance Ensemble is that it enables its members to perform works representing many choreographic styles. Thus Saturday afternoon's program at the Juilliard Theater included a premiere, a noted work from the modern dance repertory and a historical period piece.
>
> It was the period piece that proved most attractive. In 1710, André Campra composed "Les Festes Venitiennes," which had choreography by Louis Pécour of the Paris Opéra. For Juilliard, the Baroque dance scholar Wendy Hilton attempted a reconstruction of a divertissement from that work. Conceived as an outdoor entertainment in a palace garden, the suite was not only pleasant in itself but also served as a sampler of how 18th-century dance could be variously noble, whimsical and grotesque.
>
> Bruce Davis portrayed a hopping Harlequin. Russell Lome appeared in a stately solo that contained 18th-century versions of beaten steps that remain part of today's classical vocabulary. Yael Baresh and Nan Friedman offered a pas de deux in which each woman moved as mirror image to the other, Teresa Coker and Ronald Harris-Warrick were sweet shepherds, and in the appropriately named "Air Comique" Tzipora Levenbolm portrayed a nagging wife who kept jostling her husband (Richard Semmens).[7]

While preparing this first major work for the Dance Division, Wendy maintained a busy career outside Juilliard. Her company remained active a while longer, although two concerts in the spring of 1976 seem to have been its last. The first at the Newark (New Jersey) Museum on March 14 featured Elizabeth Haberer in solo dances with the New York Consort of Viols. On April 3–4, the company performed with the Smithsonian Chamber Players and the American Country Dance Ensemble in "Music and Dance from the

[7]Jack Anderson, "Juilliard Ensemble Offers Varied Dance," *New York Times*, March 13, 1978.

Age of Jefferson" at the Smithsonian Institution. Why Wendy did not pursue further work with her company is unclear. Perhaps with her growing reputation, she opted to forgo the many demands and high expense of maintaining a company in favor of pursuing the new and at times potentially more highly visible opportunities that now came her way.

In late November 1976, the first of such opportunities came, surprisingly, from Rosalyn Tureck.

> November 20, 1976
>
> Dear Wendy,
>
> Recently I gave your name to the Jerome Robbins Office via Columbia Artists Management. They were interested in knowing with whom I had worked on the dance. I trust that this will prove beneficial to you and good things come of it.
>
> Sincerely yours,
> Rosalyn Tureck[8]

Soon after, Robbins contacted Wendy to consult on his ballet *The Goldberg Variations*. Robbins had been inspired to create the 1971 ballet by Tureck's playing of the Bach work, and it seems that he may have consulted with her on the music and perhaps on his choreographic treatment of it.[9] Tureck also wrote the program notes for the New York City Ballet production. The ballet, however, had had a somewhat troubled history, which resulted in numerous revisions, and suffered from largely unenthusiastic reviews.[10] Was Robbins, five years later, hoping to revise the ballet further and looking for new choreographic ideas from Wendy? Wendy wrote of their meetings:

> Jerome Robbins was deeply involved with *The Goldberg Variations* and anxious to consult with me. He had seen everything available at the New York Public Library and had masses of photographs of plates, costumes from the eighteenth century, from eighteenth-century sources. He had really done his homework there.[11]
>
> What he needed from me was some baroque dance technique. It seemed a little after the fact to me as the ballet had premiered a few years earlier, but we had two sessions at his home.
>
> When we said good-bye, he remarked, "I wouldn't come and see it; you'll probably hate it." I had not really intended to go anyway

[8]This letter was the final communication between Wendy and Tureck.

[9]"Robbins was inspired to his choreography by a concert of Pianist Rosalyn Tureck. 'I felt when I first heard her play the Variations,' he says, 'that it was a journey, a trip, that it took you in a tremendous arc through a whole cycle of life and then, as it were, back to the beginning.'" John T. Elson, "Classic Achieved," *Time*, June 21, 1971, http://www.time.com/time/magazine/article/0,9171,905207,00.html. Deborah Jowitt in her biography of Robbins cites a letter from Tureck to Robbins about the ballet. Jowitt, *Jerome Robbins, His Life, His Theater, His Dance* (New York: Simon & Schuster, 2004), 395.

[10]Jowitt, 392–95.

[11]Jowitt notes Robbins's interest in the eighteenth century and in Wendy in her discussion of his preparations for the ballet *The Arts of the Gentleman*, which he was preparing in the late 1970s but never completed. "[H]e was inspired in part by the eighteenth-century manual *L'Ecole des armes* and its wonderful plates; by Pierre Rameau's 1725 manual, *The Dancing Master*; and by the work of Baroque dance scholar Wendy Hilton." Ibid., 438.

> and didn't until a year or so later when publicity for the Stanford workshop listed that "Miss Hilton has been consulted by choreographers such as Jerome Robbins." "Lord," I thought, "now the students will ask me about the *Goldbergs*." So I caught the last performance of the season at the New York City Ballet. I was terribly surprised because, apart from one or two moments in the opening aria, the theme, there is absolutely nothing in the whole piece to suggest baroque dance technique, or style. In addition, I found it quite lacking in invention and the great musicality that I found in *Dances at a Gathering* to selected pieces by Chopin.

While Wendy's brief work with Robbins had, in the end, little obvious effect on his work—or on her own—Wendy was gratified that the highly influential Tureck, through this contact and "from the copious program notes she wrote for the ballet, was still spreading the word about baroque dance."

Offers to work on two operas came her way next. George Houle invited Wendy to restage her choreography for *La Dafne* for a new production at Stanford, and a Juilliard connection opened the door for Wendy to choreograph the American premiere of *Mary, Queen of Scots*, an important new opera by the contemporary Scottish composer Thea Musgrave.

With George again part of the music faculty at Stanford and Wendy a member of its summer faculty, the conditions were ripe for restaging *La Dafne*. I was thrilled to be asked to join the dance ensemble, as I was then a graduate student in dance at UCLA and could easily commute to Palo Alto for rehearsals. I joined Stanford dancers Ron and Rebecca Harris-Warrick, Peter Nye, Elisabeth Rebman, and Rick Semmens. Wendy was able to rehearse with us after the annual workshop on baroque music and dance in July, which we all attended, at least in part, and then again in November, just prior to the opening of the opera on December 1, 1977.

Wendy also taught stage movement to the chorus, made up of Professor of Music William Mahrt's Early Music Singers. Mahrt recalled his relief at the clarity of Wendy's explanations to the singers, who, while highly talented musically, were less adept with movement. He noted about Wendy's work, "The mark of a master is the ability to teach amateurs to do something well."[12]

It was enormously exciting to perform in such a unique undertaking. From my point of view, however, the Stanford production of *La Dafne* may have been somewhat lacking as a theatrical experience. A shoestring budget did not permit an opulent set like that created by Santo Loquasto for the Pro Musica productions. Instead, a simple raised platform for the chorus was constructed by a local handyman. Palm branches gathered from George's neighbor's yard decorated the stage of Stanford's Dinkelspiel Auditorium to "make it more sylvan."[13] Loquasto's costumes were retrieved for the Stanford production, but they were in unfortunate condition. After the 1974 Hunter College performance, they had been leased to the Costume Collection of the

[12]William Mahrt, interview by Anne Witherell, September 6, 2004.

[13]George Houle, interview by Anne Witherell, August 30, 2004.

Figure 46. *La Dafne*, Stanford University, 1977. Photo by David Crawford Houle, courtesy of George Houle. Dancers, *left to right*: Elisabeth Rebman, Richard Semmens, Rebecca Harris-Warrick, Ronald Harris-Warrick, Susan Bindig, and Peter Nye.

Figure 47. *La Dafne,* poster, Stanford University, 1977.

LA DAFNE

by

Marco da Gagliano

Directed by George Houle

Choreography by Wendy Hilton

Cast

Venus Sally Sanford
Cupid Julianne Baird
Apollo Anthony Antolini
Ovid Louis Botto
Dafne Julianne Baird
Tirsis Louis Botto

Shepherdesses

Wendy Bennett
Joan Ferguson
Marion Rubinstein

Sarah Mead
Deborah Teplow
Lynne Toribara

Constance Keffer
Judith Maleon

Shepherds

Christopher Sheeline
Theodore Libbey
Paul Wieneke

Richard Lee
William Mahrt (director)

Neil Willits
Douglas Wyatt

Dancers

Susan Bindig
Rebecca Harris-Warrick
Elisabeth Rebman

Ronald Harris-Warrick
Richard Semmens
Peter Nye

Python Holly Antolini

Instrumentalists

Margaret Fabrizio, *harpsichord*
Elizabeth Keefe, *harpsichord and virginals*
Kent Underwood, *theorbo*
Mark Wardenburg, *theorbo*
Jason Paras, *viola da gamba*
Herb Myers, *violin and recorder*
Stephanie Sirgo, *violin*
Robert Flexer, *viola*
David Smith, *dulcian and rackett*

Production Staff

Set designed and constructed by Tom Richardson
Costumes supervised by Joanne Fanizzo, assisted by Marion Logan
Lighting by John Hughes
Makeup supervised by Ann Houle
Hair styles by Pamela Rose
Stage manager: Gerardo Huseby
Assistants to the director: Richard Semmens and Theodore Libbey
Publicity: Marcia Tanner
Photography: Margaret Fabrizio, Jose Mercado and David Houle
Italian diction: Emily Olmstead

Figure 48. *La Dafne* Stanford program.

Theatre Development Fund for general use[14] and even had survived a fire (so we were told).[15]

The cast, however, more than made up for any lack in the stage decoration or costumes. The singers featured in the solo roles would soon afterward forge major performing careers in early music. Sopranos Julianne Baird (Dafne/Cupid) and Sally Sanford (Venus), students in the Stanford doctoral program, would go on to perform with many of the major early music groups and have distinguished careers as solo performers and early music scholars. Tenor Louis Botto (Tirsus/Ovid), who was engaged for these performances from San Francisco, would found the internationally celebrated men's vocal group Chanticleer.

The three performances, on December 1, 2, and 3, received warm reviews. The *San Francisco Examiner* cited "a couple of excellent vocal performances, enthusiastic playing by a Renaissance ensemble, and elegant dancing," while the *San Francisco Chronicle* noted the high quality of the music ensemble and the "charming tone" of the dancing. The *Palo Alto Times* bestowed the highest praise, calling the production "an elegant, delectable and touching spectacle" and underscoring the "high style and grace which ruled the evening." The *Times* also provided the dancers' favorite review, describing us as "comely" and "supple."[16]

While rehearsing the Stanford *La Dafne*, Wendy must have also been deep into preparations for *Mary, Queen of Scots,* which would open just a few months later. *Mary* had its world premiere at the Edinburgh International Festival in September 1977 by the Scottish Opera, with Peter Darrell, a former colleague of Wendy's in the West Country Ballet and the cofounder director of the Scottish Ballet, as the choreographer.[17] Wendy was engaged to choreograph the American productions: the premiere by the Virginia Opera Association (March 29 and 31, April 2, 3, and 5, 1978) and the later productions by the San Francisco Opera's Spring Opera Theater (April 12, 14, 20, and 22, 1979) and the New York City Opera (1981 spring season). Why a ballet choreographer rather than a historical dance choreographer was selected for the Scottish Opera production is not clear. Perhaps Darrell's recent, well-received ballet, *Mary, Queen of Scots* (1976), made him a natural choice. Wendy was selected through John Aler, who had sung the title role in Juilliard's production of *Dardanus*. Aler recommended Wendy to

[14]James Grolin, *Pied Piper: The Many Lives of Noah Greenberg* (Hillsdale, NY: Pendragon Press, 2001), 389.

[15]Happily, there was one sensational, if controversial, costume to brighten the performances. Harpsichordist and music-faculty member Margaret Fabrizio, who was playing in the orchestra, asked if she could make her own costume. On the night of the performance, she changed in the men's dressing room and emerged looking exactly like a famous portrait of Monteverdi, complete with a beard. Some of the cast were outraged. Wendy, however, felt it was the perfect joke, particularly since the costume was of high quality.

[16]Michael Walsh, "Stanford's Lively *Dafne*," *San Francisco Examiner*, December 2, 1977; Robert Commanday, "Gagliano's *La Dafne*: 17th Century Opera Staged at Stanford," *San Francisco Chronicle*, December 5, 1977; and Michael Andrews, "An Elegant Spectacle from Operatic History," *Palo Alto Times*, December 2, 1977.

[17]*Mary, Queen of Scots* premiered at the Edinburgh International Festival on September 6, 1977, with an additional performance on September 8. The Scottish Opera gave further performances of *Mary* in Newcastle, Wolverhampton, and Glasgow.

the American productions' director, David Farrar, who, in consultation with Musgrave, decided to hire her. Farrar felt that historical dance would serve well both the character development and the musical and dramatic demands of the ballroom scene at the close of Act I, where all of the dancing in the opera is found.[18]

While dancing is called for in only this one scene, it comes at a pivotal moment in the opera and helps move the dramatic action forward significantly. The opera covers the eight-year period in Mary's life from her return to Scotland as the widowed Queen of France, through her struggles to retain the Scottish throne, to her demise at the hands of her cousin Elizabeth. At the ball through the dancing, Mary makes an unfortunate choice that speeds her decline as queen. Musgrave wrote of the dramatic challenges the ballroom scene presented to the choreographer and performers:

> One of the most exciting and challenging scenes to control was the ballroom scene which ends Act I. Challenging, because I wanted to show different levels of thought and feeling simultaneously; it had to be simple and clear, but dramatically tense and gripping. On the surface all is well: there is a group of court dances (a pavan, a saltarello, several branles and so on) led by Riccio, but alongside these we see the growing attraction of Mary and Darnley, with Bothwell and James becoming uneasy allies in their distrust and fear. Later in the scene, when Riccio sings his Orpheus song, there is another more tense level of feeling underlying the surface: here the true thoughts of Mary, James and Bothwell are expressed in a series of asides. Then the action becomes more explicit, with the juxtaposition of the court dances and the bawdy Scottish reel tune of the soldiers. The scene ends with an explosion as Bothwell insults Darnley and Mary banishes Bothwell. Mary refuses James's offer of help and makes the disastrous decision to marry Darnley.[19]

Wendy left few notes on any of her choreography. For *Mary*, though, in an interview just prior to the opening of the San Francisco production in 1979, she outlined the dramatic and choreographic challenges she faced in the ballroom scene and some of the decisions she made. She also gave a clear idea of just how carefully and thoughtfully she approached all of her work:

> It's been very rewarding working with Thea Musgrave. She wrote the libretto, you know, and worked out all the dramatic action very carefully. The dancing serves a real dramatic function, it's not merely decorative.
>
> The dancing occurs in the ballroom scene at the end of Act I. The scene is complex. It begins with the singers—Mary and her suitor Darnley—joining the courtiers in a dance. I used real historical court dances for the most part: the pavane, branle double, and branle gai, which are basic and simple. In one short section, the singers are dancing to the stage band playing Elizabethan music while singing different music with the pit orchestra. This creates interesting juxtapositions. It wasn't easy to do, but it's amazing how well it works.

[18]David Farrar, e-mail messages to Susan Bindig, October 9–12, 2007.

[19]Thea Musgrave, "Mary Queen of Scots," *Musical Times* 118, no. 1614 (August 1977), 625–27.

> When Mary and Darnley sing their love duet, four courtiers dance behind them. Here I tried to choreograph an impression of a dance rather than a real dance, that would look farther away than it is and not intrude on the main action. It has a dreamlike quality; the figures blend into each other in continuous circular patterns with no obvious beginning or end. This dance is more atmospheric than the others.
>
> Historically, Mary was known as a skillful dancer. So the dance I composed for her to perform with two court ladies is quite a tricky one.
>
> The climax of Act I is a sort of duel between rival dance styles. The Scots General Bothwell resents the English Darnley's influence over Mary and her importation of these refined dances from the French court. He and his soldiers swagger over, interrupting a group of dancing courtiers with a rowdy Scots reel. Mary saves what might have been a tense situation by joining in with them, and the act ends with everyone on stage joined in the dance.
>
> The challenge for the choreographer in the Musgrave work goes beyond a mere knowledge of the dances of the period. You need to blend the dances in the scene dramatically, to make them effective but not obtrusive. In this opera, there's no corps de ballet; the dancers are all dramatis personae.[20]

Wendy's choreography and the ballroom scene were well received by critics. After the Virginia premiere, Andrew Porter wrote in the *New Yorker* that Wendy's choreography "combined authenticity and dramatic aptness." *Time* magazine referred to the ballroom scene as one of the "masterly touches" of the opera. Donal Henahan, reviewing the New York production for the *New York Times* wrote:

> Perhaps the opera's richest such episode comes at the end of the first act, in a ballroom interlude that does not stop the action to permit the ballet to come on, as in most opera dance scenes, but propels the drama forward. Wendy Hilton's choreography and the nimbleness of the City Opera cast, headed by Ashley Putnam as Mary, helps Miss Musgrave's score mightily at this point.[21]

Thanks to Wendy, I had the opportunity to see a dress rehearsal of the New York City Opera's production of *Mary*. By now I had embarked on my own historical dance career, and Wendy felt it was important for me to see the work. In her typical style, she had bent someone to her will and gotten permission for me to attend this otherwise closed rehearsal. She met me at the stage door of the New York State Theater and ushered me quickly through the stage and the orchestra to a seat in the first ring, the orchestra being reserved for personnel associated with the production or with Lincoln Center. I recall peering over the railing and seeing Beverly Sills in one of the front rows.

[20]Wendy Hilton, interview by Marcia Tanner, press release for Stanford University News Service, April 1979.

[21]Andrew Porter, "Mary in Virginia," *New Yorker* (May 1, 1978), 136–41; Annalyn Swan, "Queen Mary in Virginia," *Time*, April 17, 1978, http://www.time.com/time/magazine/article/0,9171,916078,00.html; and Donal Henahan, "Opera: 'Mary, Queen of Scots' by City Troupe," *New York Times*, March 2, 1981.

I'm quite sure that Wendy and I stayed only through the end of Act I and the ballroom scene, which is, of course, all she really wanted me to see. My most vivid memory is of a branle—maybe a simple or a double—performed by all women with Mary, I think, in the center. This was the first time I had seen Renaissance dances in the French style from Arbeau's *Orchesography* used in a dramatic setting, having until then observed or danced them only in a classroom. I had always had more trouble imaging the Renaissance style on a stage than the baroque style and was surprised how apt it felt.

The other thing I remember about this day was Wendy nervously trying to select an outfit to wear on opening night, as she was to take a bow on stage with the conductor, director, and principal singers. After the rehearsal we went back to her apartment (a third-floor walkup in the East 30s), where she asked my opinion on a long black skirt with various combinations of black tops and shawls. I think this otherwise insignificant scene has stayed with me because Wendy always had the sparest of wardrobes and I never before had seen her fuss about clothing—or, I think—ever again. While she appreciated fashionable clothing, it seemed to hold little importance for her. Costumes for a performance, about which she was highly particular, were another matter entirely.

Between the Virginia and California productions of *Mary*, Wendy was back in New York for an unusual assignment: to work with her Juilliard students on a suite of Renaissance dances for a birthday celebration, on November 13, 1978, for the Chamber Music Society of Lincoln Center. The "Wendy Hilton Renaissance Dancers," who would only have this one engagement, performed with the Suzanne Bloch Ensemble,[22] joining such varied acts as the "Easy on the Tuba" jug band, the Greenwich Morris Men, the Bucky Pizzarelli Trio, and the magician Jeff Sheridan. The dancers and the Bloch Ensemble gave two performances on the promenade level of the New York State Theater, with three or four other acts going on at the same time. The audience was free to roam and watch what they preferred, making for a fun but noisy engagement. The dancers performed sixteenth-century dances from both Arbeau (a pavane, a suite of branles, and a galliard) and Caroso ("Allegrezza d'Amore"), which were interspersed with singing and instrumental music by the Bloch ensemble. Wendy wrote of the engagement:

> While it is true that there were no early music studies at Juilliard, there was Suzanne Bloch. Her presence was a favor of Peter Mennin, who had been a close friend of her father, the composer Ernest Bloch. Suzanne had her own little room at Juilliard where she taught recorder to interested students, perhaps about six, at the most, at one time.
>
> Suzanne and I were asked by Norman Singer if we would provide some Renaissance music and dance for a birthday celebration for the Chamber Music Society of Lincoln Center, for which he was the executive director. Martha Hill gave the project her blessing, and we duly gave a performance on the promenade level of the theater between the marble statues. We danced and played for twenty minutes,

[22]The program was also performed a few days earlier, on November 10, at the Juilliard Dance Division's Dance Event IV in the Juilliard Theater.

twice. Although a bit haphazard, it was great fun. A note on the program says, 'This is a party! Program subject to many changes!' It was!

Wendy's academic life also flourished. Despite her limited formal education—a fact that few recognized—she continued to carve out a distinguished career as a dance historian and scholar. By now, plans for her book, if not the writing itself, were well under way. In the summer and fall of 1976, she wrote her first major scholarly article, "A Dance for Kings: The 17th-Century French Courante," which would prove to be an important addition to the baroque music and dance canon and to her scholarly career.[23] Published the following spring in the highly regarded journal *Early Music*, the article discussed the relationship of the dance to its accompanying music and emphasized its elegance, gracefulness, and sophistication, and, as she believed, its place as the greatest of the French dances. The courante, she felt, was not a "throwaway," as some thought, but a cornerstone of the style; it was to be played with commitment and a deep understanding of the musical decorations and of the structure of the beat. Most important, as she would repeat many times over the years to skeptical musicians, "courantes should not be played fast."[24] Wendy felt that this article was one of the most important she wrote and considered using it as the basis of a book, an idea that never came to fruition.

While Wendy's work at Juilliard focused almost exclusively on performance, her work elsewhere included both the scholarly and the performance aspects of baroque dance. In the spring of 1977, a month-long teaching engagement took her to Victoria, British Columbia, where she also presented a paper at the eighth annual meeting of the American Society for Eighteenth-Century Studies on May 5, assisted by her students from Stanford University. I was again invited to join the Stanford dancers in this venture. I recall demonstrating steps for Wendy's talk and the rest of the group performing some of the repertoire they had developed by then. We also collaborated with students from the University of Victoria, where Erich Schwandt was now a professor of music. Otherwise, I remember little else of our work there. My most vivid memories are of the fun we had—indulging in afternoon tea at the Empress Hotel, Wendy insisting on introducing some of us to retsina at dinner one evening, and being completely bowled over by the gardens with masses of tulips in full bloom. I have a wonderful photo of Wendy, looking very stylish in a black-and-white striped coat, standing in front of a Victoria city bus whose route sign, she said, mirrored the London bus route she used to travel as a child.

[23]Wendy Hilton, "A Dance for Kings: The 17th-Century French Courante," *Early Music* (April 1977), 160–72. Wendy reprinted the article in a revised edition of her 1981 book. See *Dance and Music of Court and Theater: Selected Dance Writings of Wendy Hilton* (Stuyvesant, N.Y.: Pendragon Press, 1997).

[24]Kenneth Cooper provided insights into Wendy's musical ideas about the courante. Cooper, interview by Susan Bindig, August 9, 2005.

Figure 49. Wendy in Victoria, British Columbia, for the 8th Annual Meeting of the American Society for Eighteenth-Century Studies, May 1977. Photo by Susan Bindig.

Wendy's next major teaching appointment came from the Department of Dance at the University of California, Irvine (UCI) in the summer of 1978. The dean of fine arts, Clayton Garrison, was highly interested in introducing early dance at UCI and in luring Wendy to teach there beginning in the fall. An opera director with a particular interest in early Italian opera, Garrison was eager to have Wendy's expertise as well as dancers skilled in the styles for his productions.

Wendy's duties at Juilliard that semester limited her time on the West Coast, and UCI turned to me to fill in. I, too, had been hired at Irvine as a lecturer in the dance department, having just completed my master's degree in dance at UCLA. My initial appointment for the 1978–79 academic year was to teach only lecture classes in dance history. But with Wendy's absence, my position grew quickly to include studio classes in Renaissance and baroque dance until she was able to take over in the late spring. The following fall, UCI offered Wendy a more official and very lucrative position as a visiting lecturer for one quarter per academic year, a post that would continue through the 1980–81 academic year.[25] As with SUNY Purchase and Douglass, Wendy would juggle this appointment with her work at Juilliard and at Stanford.

Until Wendy joined me in Irvine in April 1979, I knew her primarily as a teacher, not as a colleague or close friend. Our relationship changed that spring. Not only did I find myself working in a professional partnership with her at school, but I also came to know her personally outside the campus. I

[25]Sincere thanks to Margaret Murata, professor of music, for much information on Wendy's time at the University of California, Irvine. Murata and her ensemble collaborated with Wendy on numerous performances.

became acutely aware of the severity of her torticollis and the many limitations it brought. Driving was out of the question. This did not affect her in Manhattan, but in the sprawl of southern California, it was an enormous liability. I believe she took the bus to campus, as she did when she was at Stanford. While the route from her studio hotel room in Laguna Beach to campus was about twenty minutes to a half hour by car, the bus route was much longer and indirect. Getting basic necessities—groceries and the like—was impossible without assistance. I had a car and helped her often. Wendy would phone me in Irvine, where I lived, as she was leaving her room for the grocery store on foot. I would then drive to Laguna Beach and meet her outside the store to take her home and unload her packages. Although I don't recall specific occasions, I'm sure I drove her to campus at times too. An equal frustration for Wendy was reading, which she loved. With her head fully rotating to the left, she could not find a way to hold a book comfortably and so, for the most part, had to abandon one of her favorite pastimes. Remarkably, she remained cheerful through it all, at least on the surface. The day she told me about her trouble with reading was one of the only times I saw her truly discouraged and sad about her condition, which at this time was slowly deteriorating.

Irvine and Laguna Beach also lacked the variety of cultural activities that Wendy was so accustomed to having at her fingertips in New York, and she found that there was little for her to do outside her work on campus. Her hotel room, despite its proximity to the beach where she could walk, was dreary. Unable to escape easily, she was frequently bored. But the work was rewarding and the financial benefits high, so Wendy returned to Irvine for as long as she was able.

That first spring in Irvine, in 1979, Wendy and I also shared a position at the University of California, Riverside (UCR). The course, Music and Dance at the French Court 1650–1750, was offered through both the dance and music departments, with Christena Schlundt and music colleague M. I. Emerson lecturing and Wendy and I teaching technique and notation. As with the classes at Irvine, I taught for the first five weeks, and Wendy took over for the remaining half of the quarter.

Although her appointment at UCI ended in 1981, a new intercampus graduate dance-history program at the University of California allowed Wendy to continue teaching in southern California beginning the next academic year. Initially, the Dance History Consortium comprised the UC campuses of Riverside, Los Angeles, Irvine, Santa Cruz, Santa Barbara, and Davis, making for a very rich program both academically and artistically. Wendy was pleased to be invited to participate, with a teaching arrangement similar to that at UCI of one quarter per year. Her course in baroque dance was part of the core curriculum.[26]

Wendy still offered most of her classes at UCI, where baroque dance was popular and where she had cultivated a strong following among the dance students. Students from UCR and UCLA were bussed to her classes. However, since faculty members as well as students in the program were expected to travel between the campuses, she was eventually invited to offer

[26]Emma Lewis Thomas, letter to Paige Whitley-Bauguess, n.d.

classes at UCLA.[27] The program's specialization in early dance developed particularly through efforts of Emma Lewis Thomas, a professor of dance history and Renaissance dance at UCLA and offered the promise of developing specialists in the area. Besides teaching, Wendy would be asked to advise master's degree candidates working on their theses. Her tenure with the program, however, lasted only four years, until 1985, and she advised only one thesis during that time, that of Paige Whitley-Bauguess, who was then studying at the Riverside campus and later developed a distinguished career of her own in baroque dance.[28]

The intercampus program also increased the visibility of Wendy's work, enabling her to develop an active touring group, which presented lecture-performances on baroque dance, its notation system, and the relationship between the dance and its music. The group, based at UCI, consisted at various times of James Blaine, Peggy Stephens, Elizabeth Terzian, Linda Tomko, and Philippa Waite. They performed at venues throughout southern California, including the University of Southern California, Sherman Gardens in Huntington Beach, the Getty Museum (now the Getty Villa), Scripps College, the William Andrews Clark Memorial Library, and the California Institute of the Arts, as well as at the program campuses.[29]

Wendy also began to teach at an annual summer workshop that would run through the mid-1990s at various locations in the East: first in Ipswich, Massachusetts, at Castle Hill, as the International Early Dance and Music Institute (1973–83); then in Amherst, Massachusetts, at Amherst College, as the International Early Dance Institute (IEDI) (1984–86); and in Towson, Maryland, first at Goucher College (1987–92) and then at Towson State University (1993), both also as the IEDI.[30] These workshops were akin to those in Ely, Vermont, and at Mount Holyoke College in that their faculty comprised prominent early dancers and musicians and their curricula spanned the fifteenth through the eighteenth and eventually the nineteenth centuries. At the IEDI, however, a second week of intensive dance seminars allowed students to continue, if they wished, and concentrate on only one dance style. Wendy again taught with Ingrid Brainard, Julia Sutton, and Charles Garth; other faculty over the years included Elizabeth Aldrich and Sandra Hammond, who taught nineteenth-century ballroom dance and early nineteenth-century ballet, respectively. From 1989 to 1992, when interest in baroque dance at the IEDI had grown considerably, I joined Wendy to teach intermediate-level baroque technique during the first week and an intensive intermediate seminar during the second. Baroque dancer and teacher Thomas Baird assumed this role for the 1993 workshop, which would be the last.

Wendy's approach to her classes was the same as for other workshops, with a focus on both technique and notation and the reconstruction of

[27]The classes at UCLA began after the program base moved to UCR. Ibid.

[28]Patricia Paige Whitley (Whitley-Bauguess), "An Eighteenth Century Dance Reconstruction: Two Dances Performed by Mlle. Guyot," master's thesis, University of California, Riverside, 1986.

[29]Linda Tomko, interview by Anne Witherell, September 2005.

[30]An attempt to revive the workshop and move it to Colorado College in 1995, with Wendy and Linda Tomko teaching baroque dance, proved unsuccessful.

original baroque choreographies. She would teach similar workshops over the years. Beginning in 1977 and continuing through the late 1980s, she taught workshops in Renaissance and baroque dance at Sam Houston State University in Houston, Texas, at the invitation of dance-department chair Mary Ella Montague. From 1988 to 1994, she led an annual weekend workshop, at Montclair State University, Montclair, New Jersey, organized by Professor of Theatre and Dance Linda Roberts Alexanderson.[31] The summers of 1990 and 1992 would find Wendy in New Zealand, teaching two-week sessions in baroque dance through the efforts of baroque dancer and scholar Jennifer Shennan and the Centre for Continuing Education of Victoria University, Wellington.[32] In 1992 a spring-semester course at Agnes Scott College in Atlanta, Georgia, culminated in a concert organized by dance scholar and writer Peggy Lamberson and featuring Thomas Baird and Lamberson in dances from Pablo Minquet y Yrol's *El Noble Arte de Danzas à la Francesa* (c. 1758).

Back in New York in early 1978, Wendy had begun to work on her next baroque piece for Juilliard, "An Entertainment for His Majesty George II," a suite of English dances by Anthony L'Abbé and of new choreography in the baroque style by Wendy. As with *Les Festes Venitiennes*, individual dances from the suite were first presented at a studio concert on December 13, 1979, and at an afternoon concert at the Juilliard Theater on January 16, 1980.[33] The work premiered at the Dance Division's formal concert, also at the Juilliard Theater, on March 14–15, 1980, earning high praise from critics. Jennifer Dunning wrote in the *New York Times*:

> . . . the Juilliard Dance Ensemble's annual concert Friday at the Juilliard Theater was more than an inspired recital. It was an evening of very good theater crisply performed, and a high point in any dance season.
>
> Most impressive was "An Entertainment for His Majesty George II," a suite of eight dances set to music by Handel choreographed by Anthony L'Abbé, an 18th-century court dancing master, with additional choreography by Wendy Hilton, who directed the reconstruction. This was Baroque music and manners brought to vivid life, from the cheerful first measures of the opening bourée [*sic*] to the intricate paths of the "Country Dance," on which the curtain fell as if the four couples might go on dancing for two and a half more centuries, so believably gracious and of another time were the dancers.
>
> The dancers glided through a minuet with rigid torsos and formally curved arms, heads inclining very slightly in glances at fellow

[31]Wendy's first workshop at Montclair in 1988 was sponsored by a New Jersey Governor's Challenge for Excellence grant. It also funded, in part, Linda's own initial study of baroque dance with Wendy. They collaborated on a performance in November 1990 at Columbia University, "Singers, Instrumentalists, and Dancers in Performance," cosponsored by the Department of Music, Collegium Musicum, and the Department of Dance at Barnard College.

[32]For a further discussion of the New Zealand workshops, see chapter 17.

[33]Dance Event VI, December 13, 1979, and Dance Event IX, January 16, 1980.

> dancers. But for those glances they might have been dolls winding along precisely laid-out mechanical tracks. The small, hopping jumps in the somewhat faster "The Prince of Wales" bourée [*sic*] and the buoyant traveling steps in relevé and tantalizing models for familiar ballet steps in the faster rigaudon were all, too, peculiarly of the period. A lyrical but complex sarabande for Nan Friedman and Francine Landes as well as Tatsuo Mochizuki's elegant hornpipe with demanding beaten steps were of an expressiveness more of our time.[34]

Clive Barnes wrote in the *New York Post*:

> One of the most valuable aspects of the Juilliard School is, of course its Dance Department, and one of the most valuable aspects of that Dance Department is the ecumenical nature of its teaching, which embraces classic ballet, modern dance, classic Spanish dance and baroque dance. It is just about as rounded a choreographic training as you could hope for.
>
> This season, which opened last night, is clearly calculated to show off the versatility of the dancers, although there was not a pure classic work on the program. We did, however, have the first New York performance of *An Entertainment for His Majesty George II*, a series of early 18th-century dances by a French dancing master to the Courts of George I and II, Anthony L'Abbé. The dances, set to Handel, had been reconstructed by the baroque specialist Wendy Hilton. Of considerable historic interest, they were stylishly danced by the young ensemble.[35]

Reading such reviews and looking at the films of Wendy's works, I'm struck by the insistence of reviewers to relate baroque dance to the ballet that grew out of it. *Dance Magazine* reviewer Michael Robertson wrote of "George II," "We could see here the infancy of ballet; turnout was already employed, and the basic transition steps were in use. And a small vocabulary of virtuoso steps was being accumulated."[36] It's a temptation impossible to resist and a worthy discussion, but much is missed by following that tack. The ingenuity of the floor patterns, the intricacy of the footwork with some of its idiosyncrasies (e.g., the flexed foot at the ankle), and the particular character of each of the dances with their smaller dynamic range than the baroque style's later progeny were frequently lost in a search for the familiar.

"An Entertainment for His Majesty George II" opened on a minuet for ten women already in progress. Wendy's choreography wove the dancers into groupings of 3-3-4, 4-4-2, 3-3-2-2, 5-5, and finally of all ten dancers together. The patterns melted into each other and were punctuated by pirouettes that arrested the motion, briefly bringing the dancers into unison or distinguishing one pattern from the next. I always found these large group minuets to be especially powerful and moving; they were the epitome of elegance and simplicity and of the baroque style, and I never tired of them.

[34]Jennifer Dunning, "Dance: Juilliard Group in L'Abbé's 'George II,'" *New York Times*, March 16, 1980.

[35]Clive Barnes, "Varied program by Juilliard dancers," *New York Post*, March 15, 1980.

[36]Michael Robertson, review of the Juilliard Dance Ensemble, *Dance Magazine*, (August 1980), 73–76.

Other dances choreographed by Wendy on the program were a rigaudon for two couples, a sarabande for two ladies, and a closing country dance for four couples. The dances by Anthony L'Abbé were "The Prince of Wales" (L'Abbé/Handel, 1727), an unidentified "Gigue" (most likely, "Jigg" [L'Abbé/de Lacoste, c.1725]), and the "Pastoral performed by a Gentleman" (L'Abbé/Paisible, c.1725).[37]

One of the Juilliard student dancers in this production was Mark Haim, who later would become a well-known dancer and choreographer, receiving accolades for his own 1997 choreography for *The Goldberg Variations*. But at this time, he was a young student dancer, with whom Wendy particularly enjoyed working and to whom Wendy may have given, as he states below, his first performing "break." Haim also provides a look at how Juilliard students worked with Wendy and briefly alludes to the rigaudon for four from "George II," in which he danced. (He also danced in "The Prince of Wales" and in the concluding country dance.)

> I worked with Wendy while a student at the Dance Division of Juilliard from 1979 to 1983. Having had an extensive classical music background in piano studies at the Manhattan School of Music's Preparatory Division, music had always been a big love of mine. Wendy saw that the minute she saw me, and I immediately got reined in to baroque dancing. I had had very little classical dance training at the time and was far behind most of my fellow students. So working with Wendy was my way into not only learning about baroque dance but about performance in general. In some respects, she gave me my "first break."
>
> In addition to my musical background, I think Wendy was in admiration of my "baroque look." Without ever saying it, I knew she liked my big nose.
>
> Wendy had the reputation at school of being the "Queen of Baroque Dance"; everything about baroque dance in the U.S. had come from her. Whether this was true, I don't know, but you can imagine there was a certain degree of awe and respect for her with that kind of reputation. No one at school ever had the intention of graduating and pursuing court dancing; however, we were all happy to study it and learn about it.
>
> Working with Wendy was a perpetual challenge in accuracy, detail, and patience. Oh! And memory. I can remember spending hours shaping the curves of our arms and hands with Wendy "sculpting" them until the shape and, more importantly, the feeling became natural. You could always tell a Juilliard dancer who was working on a baroque production; his/her calves were twice their normal size! And it was a constant battle with Wendy to lower our relevés when we were spending so much time in our classes trying to relevé higher and higher.
>
> Wendy would generally rehearse us on Saturdays, an hour or two for each dance that was being reconstructed. After a week of classes and rehearsals from 9 a.m. to 9 p.m., Saturday was always a real stretch for us. I can remember how loopy we would get during

[37]The gigue and the hornpipe were set to music by Handel for this piece.

> our rigaudon rehearsal. The pattern for the four of us went on and on and on—with repetitions, variations, A,B,A,C,C,A, etc. Wendy demanded a lot but also had tremendous compassion and patience. My awe and slight fear of her quickly melted away as I found out that she could have a wicked sense of humor and actually loved to laugh. In some respects, I think that is also why the two of us got on so well. It was the perfect combination of work, detail, with an underlying boisterous, earthy, and slightly subversive attitude.
>
> One thing we could never understand but loved to imitate: Wendy always came to rehearsals dressed in a knee-length skirt so that we would be able to see the footwork in detail. Quite often, as she demonstrated, she would pull up the hem of her skirt to provocative heights bordering on the obscene! It was our favorite part of rehearsal.[38]

Wendy repeated "An Entertainment for His Majesty George II" in the April 3–4 performances of the 1981 spring concert at Juilliard.[39] Again the piece received rave reviews, and it was praised in the Sunday *New York Times* column "Critics' Choices" as "a luminous depiction of Baroque manners, music, and court dance."[40] Anna Kisselgoff wrote that the dances were "exquisitely staged."[41]

[38]Mark Haim, e-mail message to Susan Bindig, January 23, 2008.

[39]The Juilliard dance concerts were usually presented over four days, in this case April 3–6, with each work performed on only two.

[40]Jennifer Dunning, "Critics' Choices," *New York Times*, April 5, 1981.

[41]Anna Kisselgoff, "A New Sokolow Opens Juilliard Annual," *New York Times*, April 6, 1981.

Fifteen: 1981–1994

Scholar and Writer ~ Southern California ~ Juilliard Dance Ensemble ~ Leaving the Juilliard School

Given her contract with Juilliard, it's surprising that Wendy was not obliged to present a new work for the 1981 student concert. Perhaps she persuaded Hill that she needed to focus all her attention on her book, which was published just prior to the concert. It would not have been a frivolous request, given the unfortunate roadblocks the book encountered en route to publication. For Wendy, another delay would have been unthinkable.

The publication of Wendy's book, *Dance of Court and Theater: The French Noble Style, 1690–1720*, was a monumental event both for her and for the field of early dance. David Leonard of Dance Books in London joined publisher Charles Woodford in the project and took one thousand copies upon publication for distribution abroad. Critics from dance, music, and theater praised the book in promotional reviews for its art and scholarship. Dance historian Selma Jeanne Cohen found that "the introductory chapters set the social scene [of the baroque period] in a manner at once informative and entertaining, while the detailed analyses of the steps and eighteenth-century dance notation illuminate the often murky directions in the original manuals." Musicologist Robert Donington wrote, "This is a most unusual and fascinating book, on what I should call a break-through [*sic*] in modern

Figure 50. Wendy with her newly published *Dance of Court and Theater: The French Noble Style, 1690–1725,* 1981.

music-theatre . . . altogether our generation of baroque fans are going to find her book as valuable as it is original." The most enthusiastic review may have come from Andrew Porter, an admirer of Wendy's work at Juilliard: "This lucid and richly illustrated study, written by a scholar and historian who has turned research into living movement, should do much to increase understanding—and enjoyment—of one of civilization's high achievements."[1]

For Wendy, *Dance of Court and Theater* firmly established her reputation as a leading scholar as well as an artist. For baroque dance, it was, and still is, the only publication that lays out in a systematic way a full theory of performance practice based on the thorough analysis of original sources. A landmark study, the book remains a staple of any dance scholar's library.

Wendy swore that she would never write another article or book. The emotional toll had been too great, and she attributed her increasingly debilitating torticollis to long days hunched over her writing. Nonetheless, she seriously contemplated, if only briefly, writing a second book and producing a supplementary video and even considered applying to the Guggenheim Foundation for financial support. And no sooner was *Dance of Court and Theater* in the final stages of publication when another tantalizing writing project came her way.

> Donald Waxman, the composer and pianist, had attended my lecture-demonstrations with the International Bach Society and persuaded me to join him in a *small* volume to continue his Pageant Series for the Galaxy Music Corporation, for which he also worked. The Pageant Series was aimed at piano teachers with young pupils, and it had become famous. Our volume, *A Dance Pageant: Renaissance and Baroque Keyboard Dances*, was intended as an intermediate-level guide to playing stylized dance music with an eye to the dances themselves and what they could say about rhythm, tempo, phrasing, and articulation. Donald selected the approximately fifty examples, and I provided the notes on the dancing. It was to be handsomely illustrated as a publication to celebrate the golden anniversary of Galaxy Music. My contract with Galaxy is dated December 30, 1980, but the eighty-page volume did not see the light of day until 1992!
>
> What happened to so seriously delay its appearance was a series of disasters: Galaxy Music had to move; the staff went on strike; Donald's mother, who lived some distance away, developed cancer and needed his help; Donald fell off a ladder and was injured; and Galaxy Music went broke and was taken over by E. C. Schirmer, Boston. Because of the delays, staff who had worked on the volume

[1]Over the years, Wendy's pioneering work would receive harsh criticism as research in the field increased and conflicting theories emerged about step performance and, in particular, about the tempi of the various dance forms. Many dance scholars today believe that the tempi she advocated were far too slow. When *Dance of Court and Theater* was reprinted in 1997, some lamented that Wendy did not address these issues or offer revisions to some of her early theories. [See Sarah McCleave, review of *Dance of Court and Theater: Selected Writings of Wendy Hilton*, by Wendy Hilton, *Music and Letters* 82 (2001), 100–103.] I cannot address these criticisms specifically but can say that, from personal experience, Wendy was willing to change—and did change—some of her ideas, given sufficient persuasive evidence. She, was not, however, easily persuaded. Wendy does note one such change in the introduction to the 1997 reprint: "A final thank you to then-Stanford student Ronald Harris-Warrick whose noble and gentlemanly execution of the *temps de courante* with his strong, yet gentle continuous bending and rising action on the supporting foot, caused me to retract my idea expressed in Author's Teaching Notes, p. 205 [in the 1981 edition], and wonder how I ever dared to disagree with Rameau!"

> for Galaxy had been replaced, and some of the work we had already completed had to be repeated for the new crew. Much time passed with no news on the book's progress, and I had long ago given up in despair, when Donald called and said, "I need your corrected copy by tomorrow." I cursed. After all the years of waiting, I now had to sit up all night! While I was basically pleased with the final result, the illustrations were not so handsome as some of the photographs had deteriorated in the long wait and came out too dark.

A positive review in the Music Library Association's *Notes* cited the relevance of *A Dance Pageant* not just for the musicologist but also for the performing musician seeking to better understand dance music and to play it with clarity and conviction. The following excerpt from the review highlights Wendy's prime intent in all her scholarship. She was dedicated to bringing baroque dance and its music alive as a performing art, as far more than a museum curiosity. In *Dance of Court and Theater*, she provided dancers with the necessary preliminary tools for such work; in *A Dance Pageant*, she and Waxman did the same for musicians.

> The uniqueness in this volume lies in its union of dance scholarship with keyboard performance, bringing out the relationships between the practical dance and the stylized dance. Even the more advanced specialist or student can benefit from this point of view, as it is indeed rare to see a consideration of practiced dance in conjunction with purely instrumental performance. Not nearly enough has been done in either musical performance or analysis that relates stylized dance music to the actual dance itself, much of which is due to the unfamiliarity and inconvenience of accessing, and then interpreting, information on Renaissance and Baroque dance. Here, Hilton and Waxman have done the job for us, making this information easily accessible and explaining complex material in a clear, simple, and concise manner. The more advanced scholar or performer could find these dance discussions helpful as a starting point for further study. Also of value and convenience is the fine collection of illustrations depicting dancers, costumes, and choreographies assembled under one cover.
>
> Hilton and Waxman have brought the music out of its vacuum, making it less abstract by examining its very real operation in society. Their descriptions of the visual and rhythmic aspects of these dances help make them more immediate and accessible for the average student. Their discussions also demonstrate the value of scholarship to performance, giving us a fine mix of historical research and practical application.[2]

In the fall of 1981, with *Dance of Court and Theater* published and *Dance Pageant* under way, Wendy refocused on Juilliard and began to work on a new piece for the 1982 spring concert. She followed her 1980–81 tribute

[2]Margot Martin, review of *A Dance Pageant: Renaissance and Baroque Keyboard Dances* by Donald Waxman, *Notes* (December 1995), 644–46.

to English dance and the music of Handel with "A Celebration of Lully," which featured dances to the music of the highly influential late seventeenth-century composer and violinist Jean-Baptiste Lully. Like her previous works, it was a suite of dances that provided a generous sampling of the various baroque dance types and of the extant choreographies of the time. "Lully," though, was particularly significant because of three dances: the woman's solo "Chaconne pour une femme" (Pécour/Lully, 1704), the men's "Ballet à huit," from "Ballet de neuf Danseurs" (Feuillet/Lully, 1700), and the solo "Jeux" by Wendy, a harlequinesque piece with juggling. The very long and beautiful chaconne, a virtuosic dance for a professional dancer, would become for Wendy one of her most memorable reconstructions because of its exquisite performance by Juilliard dancer Maria Alvarez. Wendy spoke of Alvarez's dancing many times over the years, citing it as an example of the high level of performance that could be achieved in the baroque style. The "Ballet de neuf danseurs," which is the only fully notated group dance from the baroque period, had never before been reconstructed for a formal performance. A hugely complex work, even in this truncated form, its premiere at Juilliard was a landmark event for the baroque dance world.[3] In

Figure 51. The Juilliard Dance Ensemble in "Celebration of Lully," Juilliard School, 1982. Photo © Peter Schaaf.

[3]Philippa Waite served as Wendy's assistant for "A Celebration of Lully" and learned all the parts from the "Ballet à huit" to teach to the dancers. In a 2005 interview, she noted that during the rehearsal period at least three substitutions were made in the cast, complicating an already difficult task. Waite, interview by Susan Bindig, September 3, 2005.

CELEBRATION OF LULLY

JEAN-BAPTISTE LULLY (1632-1687) was the most influential composer of his day, a violinist, and a gifted comic dancer and mime. He was an all-round man of the theatre, and his influence upon every aspect of 17th-century dance development was crucial. Dance notation came into use thirteen years after his death. The hundred or so extant theatre dances to his music were choreographed for revivals of his works. The *Ballet de neuf danseurs* is the only extant fully choreographed group dance from the Baroque period.*

Choreography	Masters of the Baroque Era
Additional Choreography and Direction	WENDY HILTON
Costumes	JOHN LEE
Lighting	CHENAULT SPENCE

Overture

Chaconne d'Arlequin — **de la Montaigne**

THOMAS HALSTEAD

Gavotte and Menuet — **Wendy Hilton**

LISA GREEN, TINA MANTEL, PHILIPPA WAITE

and

GINA BONATI, ROBIN EVERS, ANDREA FEIER, SUSAN FRITTS
NADINE MOSE, MARGHERITE JOHNSON
CHRISTOPHER BATENHORST, EDWARD DAVIS, PETER DICKEY
JAMES JEON, TED MCKNIGHT, DOUGLAS VLASKAMP

"Aimons, tout nous y convie" (1704)** — **Louis Pécour (1653-1729)**

TINA MANTEL, JONATHAN LEINBACH
JAMES KASS, *Guitar;* LISA BRADEN, *Soprano;* RUBEN BROITMAN, *Tenor*

L'Allemande (1702) — **Pécour**

PHILIPPA WAITE, PETER DICKEY

Chaconne pour une femme (1704) — **Pécour**

MARIA ALVAREZ

Jeux — **Hilton**

DAVID MULLER

Ballet à huit (1700)*** — **Raoul Auger Feuillet (c1650-1709)**

JONATHAN LEINBACH
and
CHRISTOPHER BATENHORST, PETER DICKEY, THOMAS HALSTEAD
TED MCKNIGHT, ROBERTO PACE, DOUGLAS VLASKAMP, GEORGE WAINWRIGHT
LISA BRADEN, *Soprano;* RONDINE HOBSON, *Alto;* RUBEN BROITMAN, *Tenor;* GEORGE FRIDLENDER, *Bass*

Juilliard Chamber Ensemble
JOANN FALLETTA, *Conductor*

Music Collaborator, BAIRD HASTINGS — *Rehearsal pianist,* KEVIN HARVEY

Assistant to Miss Hilton, PHILIPPA WAITE — *Student Assistants,* MARIA ALVAREZ, TINA MANTEL

*Music from: *Armide et Renaud, Le Bourgeois Gentilhomme, Le Temple de la Paix, Thesée, Fragments de Mr. de Lully, Phaeton, Le Ballet du Temps; Bellérophon* (realized by Kenneth Cooper).

**Date of publication, *The Chaconne d'Arlequin* is from an undated MS.

***From *Ballet de neuf danseurs.*

Figure 52. "Celebration of Lully," program, 1982. Reprinted with permission of the Juilliard School.

"Jeux," Wendy drew on dancer David Muller's refined juggling skills to create a memorable piece in which Muller juggled three balls while dancing a complicated solo in the baroque style.

As with her previous works, parts of "Celebration of Lully" were first presented at the division's "Dance Events" on October 15 and 19, 1981. The premiere of the full "Lully," however, was delayed for a year because of an unfortunate accident. Wendy took a serious fall, sustaining debilitating injuries, and, as she wrote, "was in bed for six weeks just before performance time. Pain aside, this was a good thing because it gave the Chaconne [pour une femme] and Ballet [à huit] dancers a better chance." When it was finally performed on March 17–18, 1983, Jennifer Dunning reviewed it favorably:

> The program opened with "Celebration of Lully," a suite of dances choreographed by such noted baroque dance makers as Louis Pécour and Raoul Auger Feuillet set to the music of Jean-Baptiste Lully. Wendy Hilton, who reconstructed and directed the dances, contributed additional period choreography.
>
> This was the handsome-looking, instructive dance, typical of Miss Hilton's work, though a little less lively than previous pieces. The looping tracks along which these dances were set looked like ornate square-dance patterns, but the stiffly upright torsos and ornamented footwork and gestures of the forearms, like the dancers' courtly manners, are of another age. A standout in the good cast was Thomas Halstead, whose Harlequin was a vivid character portrayal in pure movement.[4]

Through her annual works at Juilliard, Wendy developed an important partnership with Baird Hastings, a conductor, Mozart specialist, and the founder and director of the Mozart Festival Orchestra of New York City. He was also the librarian for Juilliard's orchestras and the music adviser to the Dance and Drama Divisions. Hastings first collaborated with Wendy on "An Entertainment for His Majesty George II," and he quickly became an indispensable colleague in her subsequent works. Hastings's primary role was to arrange the music for the orchestra, working closely with the library to make sure all the parts were in order and to identify additional music Wendy might use.[5] He also occasionally rehearsed the orchestra or the conductor, who frequently was a graduate student in conducting.

JoAnn Falletta, now music director of the Buffalo Philharmonic Orchestra and the Virginia Symphony Orchestra, was one such student. Falletta, then a doctoral candidate, conducted the student orchestra for "A Celebration of Lully" and for "Celebration of the French Baroque II" in 1985.[6]

[4]Jennifer Dunning, "Dance: Juilliard Ensemble Concert," *New York Times*, March 20, 1983.

[5]JoAnn Falletta, interview by Susan Bindig, March 4, 2008; Baird Hastings, interview by Susan Bindig, August 29, 2005.

[6]Falletta noted that she conducted one of Wendy's works for "Juilliard at 80," a celebration of the school's eightieth anniversary on October 5, 1985. Although Falletta did conduct for the dance segment of "Juilliard at 80" (for Paul Taylor's *Cloven Kingdom*, which was also featured in the Juilliard Dance Ensemble's 1985 spring concert), I have not been able to document Wendy's participation in the televised event. Falletta, interview.

While Wendy believed that playing for dance was an arduous and unwelcome task for the school's music students, Falletta noted in an interview that for conducting students like her, it was a "plum assignment." "A Celebration of Lully" was her first experience of working with dancers, and she found it both surprising and enjoyable. Falletta noted that Wendy's work with the dancers helped the musicians better understand their role and the music they played. Wendy explained to both the dancers and musicians the musical stresses, the weight of the musical line, and how the phrases were structured. She would demonstrate dance steps and phrases for the musicians to show "the weight and proportion of the musical phrases" and how both the dance and the music "moved." Falletta described Wendy's way of working as "beautifully gentle" and marveled at the way she was able to incorporate that gentleness into the dancing of her young, highly energetic dancers while allowing them to interpret the dancing in their own youthful and fresh way.[7]

Wendy's and Hastings' collaboration on "Celebration of Lully" seems to have extended beyond the Juilliard Theater to a book project of the same name that unfortunately never found a publisher.[8] Like Wendy, Hastings was a writer. He served for a year, at the request of Lincoln Kirstein, as the founding editor of *Dance Index*, upon which he modeled his own journal *Chrysalis: The Pocket Review of the Arts*. When he and Wendy began to collaborate on "Lully," his *Choreographer and Composer: Theatrical Dance and Music in Western Culture* (1983), one of the ten books he would write or edit in his lifetime, was most likely entering the final stages of publication. Wendy and Hastings discussed the book on Lully in a series of letters throughout 1985. Their plan was to publish, hopefully through Galaxy Music, five-part music scores for a suite of eleven dances and songs from Lully's theatrical works for which there were dance scores in *chorégraphie*. As in *A Dance Pageant*, Wendy was to supply notes on the dances. Additionally, they planned a companion volume of the dance notations, which Wendy hoped Princeton Book Company might publish. With the two books and Wendy's *Dance of Court and Theater*, dancers would have the essential materials for reconstructing and performing a significant number of baroque dances. The selection of dances, many of which had been featured in the 1983 Juilliard production, went through numerous iterations to get a representative selection of solos, duets, and groups in the dances and the right balance between meter and tempi in the accompanying music.

It seems likely that Wendy and Hastings hoped for the publication of *A Celebration of Lully* to coincide with the three-hundredth anniversary of Lully's birth in 1987, although their letters did not indicate such a goal. They proposed a fall 1986 publication date, which would have made the materials available for performances or other commemorative celebrations in the anniversary year. Their plans were disappointed, however, when the editorial committee at Galaxy Music turned down their proposal because the music selection was uneven and a two-volume publication with a second publisher

[7]Ibid.

[8]Sincere thanks to George Dorris for giving me a box of music files and letters that detail this project, and was given to him by Baird Hastings.

Figure 53. Wendy onstage with the Juilliard Dance Ensemble at a dress rehearsal of "Celebration of the French Baroque," Juilliard School, 1984. Photo © Peter Schaaf.

Figure 54. The Juilliard Dance Ensemble in "Celebration of the French Baroque," Juilliard School, 1984. Photo © Peter Schaaf.

Figure 55. The Juilliard Dance Ensemble in "Celebration of the French Baroque," Juilliard School, 1984. Photo © Peter Schaaf.

Figure 56. The Juilliard Dance Ensemble in "Celebration of the French Baroque," Juilliard School, 1984. Photo © Peter Schaaf.

THURSDAY, MARCH 15 AND SATURDAY, MARCH 17 AT 8:00 P.M.

CELEBRATION OF THE FRENCH BAROQUE

Choreography	Masters of the Baroque Era
Additional Choreography and Direction	Wendy Hilton
Music	Jean-Baptiste Lully (1632-1687) Andre Campra (1660-1744) Jean Philippe Rameau (1683-1764)
Costumes	John Lee
Decor	Laszlo L. Funtek
Lighting	Chenault Spence
Overture	**Lully**
Gavotte for the Courtiers	**Hilton/Lully**

Gina Bonati, Andrea Feier, Lisa Green, Nadine Mose
Christopher Batenhorst, Peter Dickey
Torbjorn Stenberg, Douglas Vlaskamp
with
Clara Maxwell, Leslie Nelson, Catherine Novak
Solveig Olsen, Kaisha Thomas, Ani Udovicki
Edward Davis, George Wainwright

L'Allemande (1702) — **Louis Pécour/Lully**

Gina Bonati, Christopher Batenhorst

Chaconne d'Arlequin* — **Montaigne/Lully**

Peter Smith

Jeux — **Hilton/Lully**

David Muller

Aimable Vainqueur (1701) — **Pécour/Campra**

Lisa Green, Douglas Vlaskamp
Rachel Rosales, *Soprano*

Menuet — **Hilton/Rameau**

Ladies of the Court

Rigaudon* — **Hilton/Rameau**

Suzanne Harris, Rachel Rapp
Peter Dickey, George Wainwright

Tambourin* — **Hilton/Rameau**

Sara Bragdon, Rachel Rapp
Suzanne Harris, Birgitte Skands
Christopher Battenhorst, Peter Dickey
Torbjorn Stenberg, George Wainwright

Juilliard Chamber Ensemble
Fabio Mechetti, *Conductor*
Baird Hastings, *Music Collaborator*

Maria Rojas, *Harpsichordist* — John Schuker, Brian Zeger, *Rehearsal Pianists*

*The Chaconne d'Arlequin and the steps used in the Rigaudon and the Tambourin are from an undated MS.

The music is taken from Lully's *Thesée, Le Bourgeois Gentilhomme, Fragments de Mr. de Lully* and *Le Ballet du Temps;* Campra's *Hesionne* and Rameau's *Dardanus.*

Figure 57. Celebration of the French Baroque," program, 1984. Reprinted with permission of the Juilliard School.

would most likely be cumbersome. It appears that Wendy and Hastings did not seek another publisher and unfortunately abandoned the project.[9]

Wendy and Hastings again collaborated on the 1984 and 1985 Dance Division concerts,[10] in which they presented "Celebration of the French Baroque," a two-part work that reconfigured dances from her previous works, including "Jeux" and "Chaconne d'arlequin" from "Celebration of Lully"; a minuet, rigaudon, and tamborin from *Dardanus*; and a selection of danses à deux. Both were again very favorably received by the critics. Jack Anderson, in his review of the 1985 "Celebration of the French Baroque II," also noted that Wendy's pieces in general had been some of the more memorable in the Juilliard repertoire.

> Since it was organized by Martha Hill in 1951, the dance division of the Juilliard School has provided young dancers with experience in many styles and idioms. Therefore the performances of the Juilliard Dance Theater are always interesting for revealing what kinds of lessons the dance students have been learning.
>
> In recent years, some of the most interesting offerings at Juilliard have been the suites of Baroque dances staged by Wendy Hilton. One of them, "Celebration of the French Baroque II," was on the program Thursday night at the Juilliard Theater and it included a soprano aria by Campra sung by Rebecca Rosales, instrumental music by Lully and Rameau and dances for aristocrats and peasants arranged by Miss Hilton.
>
> The dancers carefully distinguished between aristocratic elegance and rustic abandon. Moments when their aristocratic steps looked slightly finicky suggested that they were still learning their lessons and that Baroque style was not yet second nature to them. Nevertheless, this was a creditable attempt to enter into the spirit of another age.[11]

The spring of 1985 brought a significant change to the Dance Division at Juilliard and to Wendy's position there. Muriel Topaz, a performer, choreographer, and important figure in the area of dance preservation and notation, replaced Martha Hill as the division's director. Wendy was pleased with Topaz's appointment, as the two had come to know each other through the Dance Notation Bureau, where Topaz had served as executive director beginning in 1978. Wendy looked forward to working with Topaz at Juilliard and to the innovations she would surely introduce. What Wendy had not anticipated, though, was that her own work might be compromised.

[9]Despite her protests, more writing projects came Wendy's way. In the mid-1980s, she was invited to contribute to the *International Encyclopedia of Dance* and wrote important articles on the loure, the minuet, the courante, the entrée grave, the eighteenth-century reverence, and French court dance and its part in the history of ballet technique. See Selma Jeanne Cohen and Dance Perspectives Foundation, *The International Encyclopedia of Dance, 6 vols.* (New York: Oxford University Press, *1998).*

[10]March 15–18, 1984, and March 13–17, 1985.

[11]Jack Anderson, "Dance: Juilliard Group in Varied Bill," *New York Times*, March 17, 1985.

> When Muriel Topaz took over as head of the Dance Division, she naturally made some changes. She wanted me only to teach baroque dance classes and not do any more pieces for the dance concerts. The reason for this decision I perceived only later. She intended to bring in choreographers who had companies and would therefore employ Juilliard dancers after having worked with them at the school.
>
> I met with Muriel and pointed out that the students would only elect to take baroque dance if a fully staged piece were the carrot. We finally agreed that I would teach classes and do a piece every other year for the now annual dance concert. (Under Miss Hill, there had been two a year).

Letters in Wendy's faculty file at Juilliard show that her idea and negotiations with Topaz for a baroque dance class for musicians, beginning in the 1985–86 school year, were also unsuccessful.

With her many commitments in California and increasing offers for workshops and other projects,[12] Wendy might have welcomed a reduction in her work at Juilliard and in New York in general. Instead, she strove to keep baroque dance alive and on New York stages as much as she possibly could. Her first assignment under Topaz's direction, however, was to work not with the dance students and on the annual concert but with the Opera Division and a production of *Don Giovanni*.

> The Opera Division [American Opera Center] was to present Mozart's *Don Giovanni* in the spring of 1986,[13] and so my project that year was to choreograph the two scenes that called for dancing, Act I, Scene 6, and Act II, Scene 10. I was truly looking forward to this until I heard that the director, Dino Yannopoulos, had added to the dinner scene in Act II a group of prostitutes not called for in the libretto. I was appalled! Don Giovanni would never have agreed to paying prostitutes for sex; it was the challenge of the conquest that mattered. I wrote to Yannopoulos expressing my feelings but got no reply.
>
> This was Muriel's first year at Juilliard, and I was anxious not to cause problems. I should have withdrawn from the project early on because, in the end, I did cause an enormous amount of trouble. I refused to have anything to do with the scene with the prostitutes, and so another choreographer, Larry Hayden, was brought in. We shared the choreographic duties—me, Scene 6 ["Inside the Don's Villa," which opens with a masked ball], and Larry, Scene 10—and the $250 fee. Another bone of contention was the tiny set used for the ballroom scene. For the largest scene in the opera—everyone except the Commendatore is on stage—the ample stage of the Juilliard Theater was reduced to about 11 feet by 25 feet. At the production meeting, I protested about fitting in three simultaneous bands, three dances, and everyone else. Mr. Yannopoulos said in exasperation, "This is not a ballet." Would that I could reproduce his tone.

[12]A memo in Wendy's biographical file at Juilliard, dated January 20, 1988, indicates that plans were also under way for a "Baroque Dance Video Project," featuring Wendy and baroque dance specialists Catherine Turocy and Francine Lancelot; the video was to be directed by Wendy and Turocy. The project, it seems, never advanced beyond preliminary discussions.

[13]*Don Giovanni* was performed on April 16, 18, and 20, 1986, at the Juilliard Theater.

> It all took hours and hours and was awful to look at. I bless the [*New York*] *Times* critic who ignored the dancing.[14] So much for *Don Giovanni*. Alas!

Despite the arrangement with Topaz to produce a concert work every other year, Wendy restaged "An Entertainment for His Majesty George II" for the 1986 fall concert (November 14–17), with a preliminary performance of parts of the work at Dance Event X the previous May. Why they deviated from their original arrangement and chose to repeat a piece that Wendy had already presented twice within the previous six years is not clear.

Back on schedule in the fall of 1988, Wendy presented a "Baroque Dance Suite" to the music of François Couperin in the November 11–14 concert. For the first time in her early dance career, she created a work featuring only her own original choreography in the early eighteenth-century style. The six segments of the piece showcased some of the less commonly seen dance types of the style (e.g., a loure, a chaconne, and an allemande)

Figure 58. The Juilliard Dance Ensemble in "Baroque Dance Suite," Juilliard School, 1988. © Martha Swope: Photo by Rebecca Lesher.

[14]Will Crutchfield, "Opera: *Don Giovanni*," *New York Times*, April 20, 1986. Crutchfield, although generous in his remarks, generally agreed with Wendy's assessment of the student production. He wrote, "But although the performance as a whole was creditable, it must be noted that the school's description of its purpose (providing 'performance experience between the final stages of training and the beginning of full-time careers in opera') implies something closer to high professional standards than was achieved here."

BAROQUE DANCE SUITE

Choreography in early 18th century style (1988)	Wendy Hilton
Music from Concerts Royaux Nos. 1, 4 and 8	François Couperin
Costumes	Thomas Augustine
Lighting	Chenault Spence

"DAY": SARABANDE
Karen Richards

TWO PEASANTS: [RIGAUDON]

(Friday & Saturday)	*(Sunday & Monday)*
Laura Doughty, Paul Dennis	Kelley Ward, Paul Dennis

ENTRANCE OF THE COURT: ALLEMANDE

(Friday & Saturday)	*(Sunday & Monday)*
Kristianna Bertelsen, Rachel Durham Seth Hampton, Luis Peral	Laura Doughty, Christine Kessler, Seth Hampton, Luis Peral

LOURE
Seth Hampton, Jeffrey Schmidt

CHACONNE
Paul Dennis

[PASSEPIED]

Amy Alt	Christine Kessler
Kristianna Bertelsen	Karen Kroninger
Laura Doughty	Elizabeth McPherson
Rachel Durham	Christine Morrissey
Sarah Hedrick	Seth Hampton
Nanci Holden	Jeffrey Schmidt

Robert Chen, *Violin*	Adria Sternstein, *Flute*
Eileen Moon, *Violoncello*	James Richman, *Harpsichord*

Figure 59. "Baroque Dance Suite," program, 1988. Reprinted with permission of the Juilliard School.

and alternated between the more expected solos and duets and larger group works (the allemande and a passepied). Jennifer Dunning, who reviewed the concert for the *New York Times*, called the work "the jewel of the program" and noted that it "was a good deal more than a requisite exercise in baroque dance forms, taking on a vivid life of its own in the hands of Miss Hilton and her young performers." Dunning captured the essence of some of the dances saying, "A good many degrees of formality and abandon were represented in the suite of six dances, which opened with a sarabande danced by Karen Richards, a figure of winning graciousness as she glided under a waning moon. At the opposite pole was a chaconne, danced splendidly by Paul Dennis. A boldly extroverted solo with complex footwork and breezy little jumps, it served as eccentric entertainment for the gathered courtiers."[15]

It is ironic that Wendy's works continued to be hailed by the critics as the highlights of the Juilliard dance concerts even as they were cut back in both frequency and scope. Another unfortunate downgrade was in the musical accompaniment, from the Juilliard orchestra or chamber ensemble to a quartet of violin, cello, flute, and harpsichord. While the smaller group may have been as musically and artistically correct for the piece as a larger orchestra, this change too signaled the gradual diminution of baroque dance at Juilliard and was a harbinger of its eventual elimination. Wendy's next work was not even performed on the main stage at the Juilliard Theater or as part of the regular program but in the lobby during intermission. Even though the removal of the piece from the main stage gave the dancing an intimacy and immediacy that was appropriate, it further showed a growing question of baroque dance's place in the Juilliard dance curriculum.

The fall 1991 concert was part of the Mozart Bicentennial at Lincoln Center and featured works all to Mozart's music. Wendy described a tangled lead-up to the concert:

> Perhaps only Neal Zaslaw [a Mozart scholar and the musicological adviser for the bicentennial] could believe that every measure of Mozart should be played in the 1991 bicentennial celebration in New York. It was not possible, and so the period became 1991–91½.
>
> I very nearly destroyed Neal's objective, which I simply could not take seriously. In the spring of 1991, Muriel [Topaz] asked me to prepare the ballet from *Idomeneo* for the fall dance concert, in which all the choreography would be to Mozart. That idea was nipped in the bud when the estimate for the costume budget came to $35,000. As Muriel was committed to using this music, the ballet was choreographed instead by a modern/ballet choreographer, Diane Coburn Bruning, whose work required a smaller cast and less costly costumes.
>
> It is pertinent to my story to point out that there was an individual on the bicentennial committee whose job it was to make sure that all of Mozart's music, every note of it, was played— what, where, when, and by whom. This person had an eagle eye and seemed relentless.

[15]Jennifer Dunning, "Young Artists at Juilliard Confront the Baroque," *New York Times*, November 20, 1988.

> With *Idomeneo* out of the picture for me, Muriel suggested that I prepare authentic dances to Mozart's music to be shown in the foyer of the Juilliard Theater during the intermissions of the concerts, which were scheduled from November 8 to 11. The problem here was that we do not have any authentic dances to music by Mozart. The ballroom minuet ordinaire would have been danced to various of his minuets, and so I chose to set it to Mozart's Minuet No. 1 from Seven Minuets, K65a. Mozart wrote many contradanses, and many examples of this type of dance have survived. I also agreed to adapt one of those to Mozart's music. Another possibility, although it stretched things a bit, was to feature a waltz that had been recently found in a dance manuscript in New Zealand, dated 1826, which was danced to three of Mozart's *Sechs Ländlerische Tänze*, K606. I asked the nineteenth-century dance specialist Elizabeth Aldrich to reconstruct this dance for the Juilliard performances. Things were quickly falling into place, and all was going well. The problem came when Muriel insisted that I select the Mozart contradanse I would use immediately. I protested because I hadn't yet given much thought to the choreography I might use. I nonetheless made my selection knowing full well that I would probably have to change it when I began to work with the students. Imagine my horror, then, when I returned to school in September and saw the title of the contradanse I had selected in large print on a poster outside Alice Tully Hall advertising the dance concert.
>
> My fears about having to select the music so early and quickly, however, were well founded for various reasons. I was able to use only three of the male student dancers, which meant that I had to find a rare bird—a contradanse for six dancers. After much searching in the NYPL Dance Collection, I found a few examples, but the Mozart piece I had selected was too long for it. So I chose another piece of music but said nothing about it, except to Albert Fuller, whose students were to play for me. We agreed to keep quiet about the change. Well, alas, the person keeping track of the music found out, and all hell broke loose. Now someone else would have to be found to play the initial contradanse I had chosen. Who, I wondered, had been scheduled to play the one I was now going to use, Contradanse in G Major, K 269b?
>
> When Elizabeth Aldrich reconstructed the waltz, she too had a problem matching the dance to the music and, in the end, left out eight measures of one of the landlers. Once again, the music police appeared. Eight measures simply could not be omitted. This problem was resolved by having the entire piece played as the audience filed out of the theater.
>
> I really doubt that every measure of Mozart was played in 1991, but that person with the notebook was certainly alert. It seems quite likely that a lot of measures not by Mozart became included just in case they were by him.
>
> In the spring, I also took part in a panel discussion at a conference at Juilliard on "Performing Mozart's Music." I collaborated in this project with the musicologist Wendy Allanbrook, and our papers were published under the title "Dance Rhythms in Mozart's Arias" in *Early Music* in February 1992.

Again, Wendy's work attracted the critics' attention and won their highest praise. *Dance Magazine* published two articles on the concert: a preview article that featured an interview with Wendy, and a review in which dance critic Camille Hardy stressed that the dances presented at intermission were one of the evening's highlights. Jack Anderson in his *New York Times* review agreed that "some of the best dancing occurred during the intermission" and that "this quirk of programming" was inspired and brought a vanished era alive. [16]

Given Wendy's ongoing success at Juilliard and her continuing significant work elsewhere in both dance and music, why would baroque dance be eliminated from the Juilliard dance curriculum in 1994? Wendy left us her side of the story.

> In 1992, Muriel Topaz invited Benjamin Harkarvy to join the Dance Division to strengthen its ballet program, an action that proved a disaster for her (he unexpectedly replaced her as director that same year) and several faculty members. I never liked or trusted Ben. To me there was a strange, quiet arrogance and a certain furtiveness about him, which made me, without realizing it, concoct to avoid him as much as possible. My immediate reaction to his appointment was, "That will be the end of baroque dance at Juilliard," as Ben had no knowledge or experience of baroque dance. Professing himself to be an appreciator of music, he nevertheless failed to see the enormous potential baroque dance has to develop many essential dance skills, particularly phrasing and a sense of rhythm. Perhaps if he had tried it himself, the light would have dawned.
>
> As director, Ben was quite genuinely at a loss as to what to do with baroque dance, and it quickly became clear to me that it would be relegated to less formal workshops and never again be part of a Juilliard dance concert. Ben's eyes were squarely fixed on modern choreography.
>
> My first piece for Ben was presented at three workshops in January 1993.[17] The Kellom Tomlinson manuscript had just been published,[18] and so I suggested that the six dances it contained by Tomlinson himself, as yet unreconstructed outside New Zealand, should be given at the workshop in November. This would be a relatively simple operation since only costumes, not scenery, would be sufficient, and I would need only four dancers, two men and two women. I was only allowed to use first-year students. Two of the Tomlinson dances are very difficult solos for a man, a sarabande and a rigaudon, and in other years I might not have had a first-year student who could attempt them. By the greatest good fortune, I discovered that among the first-year students was a graduate of the Bolshoi School, Andrei Dokukin, who had the necessary technical

[16]Heather Stein, "Mozart Graces Juilliard Program," *Dance Magazine* (November 1991), 12–13; Camille Hardy, "Juilliard Dance Ensemble, Juilliard Theater, November 8–11, 1991," *Dance Magazine* (March 1992), 90, 92; and Jack Anderson, "Dancing Never Stops in Celebrating Mozart, Even for Intermission," *New York Times*, November 11, 1991.

[17]The Juilliard School Dance Division, Workshop #7 (January 21, 1993) and Workshops #8 and #9 (January 22, 1993).

[18]Jennifer Shennan, ed., *A Work Book by Kellom Tomlinson: Commonplace Book of an Eighteenth-Century English Dancing Master, A Facsimile Edition* (Stuyvesant, NY: Pendragon Press, 1990).

skills. The perennial problem of music was once more solved by Albert Fuller, whose student Paul Festa, a violinist, accompanied the dancing.

Ben, who loved to speak at workshops, introduced the Tomlinson event. To give him his due, he asked me to prepare a couple of paragraphs, which he would read since he was ignorant of the subject. All the dancers performed very well with only one or two of the lapses one can expect from first-year students struggling with the intricacies and subtleties of baroque steps as opposed to the different difficulties of nineteenth-century ballet.

For the second year, Ben made one semester of baroque dance a required class for first-year students. It met in the fall semester, as usual. This group of students proved to be wonderful. They loved me and baroque dance, and I loved them. One told me that as a new group, they had bonded in my class.

Baroque dance was once again relegated to a workshop, on December 7, 1993, so I decided to repeat B-D-S/Couperin [Baroque Dance Suite], which Ben could first approve by watching the videotape [of the 1988 concert]. His comment was a dubious "charming." Almost all of the first-year class were in the piece, renamed "A Baroque Entertainment," and everyone was doing very well, until one day about a month before the performance, Ben came to watch rehearsal. Well, "watch" is scarcely the word; he simply took it over. I might as well have melted away through the floor; he would not have noticed. He simply ignored me. But he began to correct the dancers in a style and technique about which he was totally ignorant, ignoring my protests. Of course, any professional eye can see where weak places are, but surely you discuss those with the choreographer. I found myself making a comparison between my dilemma and the feudal rights of a ruler to take the virginity of a newly named servant.

Some of Ben's corrections so confused the dancers at that point, midway between 18th- and 19th-century rhythms in, for instance, the pas de bourrée emboîté, that they never got it right. In fact, he made matters much worse. I decided to keep quiet—actually, I had little choice since when I spoke Ben simply talked over me—and go to see him the following week and discuss the situation. I never had the opportunity, however, because shortly thereafter Ben fell in the street and was injured badly enough to have to stay home until the workshop arrived.

Dress rehearsal proved an even greater debacle. The guest choreographer at the workshop was Jiři Killián, and his work consumed an enormous amount of time at the evening dress rehearsal. By 10 p.m., three of my four musicians had been forced to leave, and there was no time for a proper lighting rehearsal. The trees that I had been so faithfully promised for the stage set (my condition for doing the piece) were two, thin diagonal green stripes on a blue skycloth. For only the second time, the stage department had let me down. The baroque students were tired and dejected by the long wait, and under the circumstances, the run-through was terrible. I expected that Ben would apologize to them and say something encouraging. Instead, he ignored them—until the next morning.

I arrived at Juilliard about 11 a.m. and met one of my students who was in tears. It seemed Ben had called them into his office after morning class and gave the whole cast a thorough dressing-down for their appalling performance the evening before. According to this student, he had talked for some fifteen minutes.

I sought out the wonderful Maria Grandy, a faculty colleague who was in charge of the workshop, and together we rounded up the most deflated and hurt bunch of students I have even seen. Remember, it was the first semester of their first year and their first performance on the Juilliard stage. Maria was wonderful. The two of us worked all day lifting spirits and getting smiles on faces. In the end, they gave an excellent performance.

I saw Ben shortly before the performance and told him, in front of everyone who happened to be on stage, that he had no right to talk to my cast in such a manner, especially over my head. Ben hates confrontations, especially public ones. He waved his arms about and said something to the effect that a person of his international reputation had every right. "Did you think it was a good rehearsal?" he asked. "Of course not," I said. "How could it possibly have been?"

I wonder if Ben congratulated the dancers after their excellent performance, which Maria and I felt equaled that of the original, generally more experienced cast in 1988. I doubt it, but if he did I'm sure it was because he felt that by his talking so severely to the students, he had saved the day.[19]

The workshop was Wendy's last at Juilliard. A month later, on January 18, 1994, Harkarvy wrote to Wendy telling her of his decision to remove baroque dance from the curriculum, noting that his priorities precluded any further development of baroque dance offerings and that he wished to introduce dance studies that were more relevant to Juilliard dance students and their future careers. Wendy responded far more graciously than might have been expected from someone in such a position. In a letter to Harkarvy on January 25, 1994, she did not address his assessment of the value of baroque dance to the Juilliard curriculum but wrote that she, in fact, could not have continued if circumstances had not improved. "A workshop situation without lighting facilities, a backdrop, and the possibility of an orchestra is no place for an effective theatrical presentation of a baroque piece." She did, however, take the opportunity to point out the high quality of the dancers' performances that he, in her view, had so unfairly demeaned.

The great satisfaction for me this year has been in working with such a wonderful group of students. They are all so talented and such warm human beings. Every student worked hard and improved beyond my expectations. No teacher could ask for more than I have received from them. A great happiness indeed.

I look forward to seeing their progress until graduation.

The dance community rallied, and Harkarvy received letters protesting his decision.[20] He was unmoved, however, and Wendy's tenure at Juilliard ended.

[19]Wendy Hilton Personal Papers.

[20]Two such letters were from Linda Tomko of UCR, dated May 27, 1994, and from Nancy G. Heller of the University of the Arts (Philadelphia), dated July 8, 1994. Heller also addressed the concurrent discontinuation of Spanish dance in the curriculum.

Sixteen: 1968–1975

Historical Dance at Stanford University ~ Wendy's First Classes at Stanford ~ Anne Witherell and Louis Pécour's 1700 Recueil de Dances

> Of all my annual engagements, the summer workshop at Stanford University was the one I loved the most. I looked forward all winter to the day when the plane would reach the Sierras and the San Francisco Bay with its wondrous colors and shapes. Someone would meet me at the airport, and the trip down El Camino Real would bring us ever closer to our goal—the drive up Palm Drive with the Stanford Memorial Chapel in full view. On sight of the chapel, I knew I had arrived.

In 1968 Wendy's first trip to the United States included a visit to Stanford University; in 2001 she taught her last historical dance workshop there. For almost thirty years, she led a summer workshop in baroque dance and music at Stanford that, while modest in size, was unparalleled in quality and attracted students from the United States and abroad. For Wendy, "Each and every one of those years was wonderful in the sense of serious endeavor, high levels of achievement, and enormous fun." For participants, the workshop provided an opportunity for full immersion in a unique course of study; it was a two-week oasis of physical and mental challenge set to exquisite music in relaxed, beautiful surroundings. We, like Wendy, loved it.

Long before Wendy's arrival at Stanford, historical dance had become a significant component of the music department's curriculum. Teaching in the early 1950s, harpsichordist and Professor of Music Putnam Aldrich "was a key person in inspiring quite a number of very eager students to think about and perform the musical repertory of earlier centuries, some of which has become quite familiar to us now but was then little known" according to George Houle, who was Aldrich's student at that time.[1]

> There were then few opportunities to make a scholarly study of the performance of early music, although performance practice was considered to be a branch of the study of musicology. The music department believed that performance studies should be integrated with an excellent music history sequence of courses. . . . The faculty were united in placing great value on scholarship in the service of performance.[2]

[1]George Houle, letter to Susan Bindig, April 28, 2000.

[2]Houle, "Stanford's Early Music Program," unpublished ms., n.d., George Houle Personal Papers.

That study extended to dance since a considerable portion of the early music canon is dance music. Aldrich believed that, to fully understand this music, it was essential to experience the dances of the time, not just by seeing them but by dancing them. According to George, "The meters of dance music could only be thoroughly understood and expressed when the dances themselves became familiar, and so we began to learn to dance from original sources."[3] Those sources, most researched and acquired by Aldrich for the department, included Arbeau and eventually Caroso and Negri, as well as secondary sources by Dolmetsch and Écorcheville.[4] Renaissance dance was thus the core of dance study at the start. Aldrich later added to the literary mix Feuillet's *Chorégraphie*, which he purchased during a trip to France, and baroque dance entered the syllabus.[5] Typically, the sources were read, translated, and interpreted by Stanford musicians or scholars who had little or no dance training; the primary purpose was not to recreate historical dances but rather to learn something from them about the music. As George noted, "It wasn't apparent to him [Aldrich] or to us at that point that he was proposing something on the order of a lifetime task, so we blithely started to read and shuffle, step, jump, and sway according to whatever treatise we could find."[6] Aldrich also worked at times with dancers to interpret the more complex baroque dances from the Pécour and Feuillet dance collections bound with *Chorégraphie*.[7] The dancers demonstrated the results of those collaborations for the music students to incorporate into their own explorations.

Marilyn Somville, a graduate student in the 1950s, noted that curiosity about dance music grew out of Aldrich's graduate seminars. For one term, probably sometime between the fall of 1954 and the spring of 1956, as she and fellow graduate student John Planting remember, Patrick Wymark, a Shakespearian actor from London's Old Vic, taught them historical dance. A visiting professor in the Stanford theater department, Wymark joined Aldrich's seminar to teach reverences, bransles, the pavan, and la volta—the last of which Somville recalls dancing with Aldrich on one occasion. Wymark's sessions mark the first time Planting remembers dancing in a music class.[8] Wendy, it seems, was not Stanford's only British dancing master.

[3]Ibid. He continued, "The resources of historical performance study such as original documents, historical notation, instruments, dance, ceremony, and esthetics were major concerns in the curriculum."

[4]Thoinot Arbeau, *Orchesographie* (Langres: Jehan des Preyz, 1589); Fabritio Caroso, *Nobiltá di dame* (Venice: il Muschio, 1600); Cesare Negri, *Le gratie d'amore* (Milan: Pacifico Ponti & Gio. Battista Piccaglia, 1602); Mabel Dolmetsch, *Dances of Spain and Italy,1400–1600* (London: Routledge and Paul, 1954); Jules Écorcheville, *Vingt suites d'orchestre du XVIIe siècle francais* (Paris: L. Marcel Fortin; Berlin: L. Liepmannssohn, 1906; reprint, New York: Broude Bros., 1970); and Raoul-Auger Feuillet, *Chorégraphie ou L'Art de décrire la dance* (1700; reprint, New York: Broude Brothers, 1968). Erich Schwandt, letter to Anne Witherell, February 26, 2005.

[5]Meredith Ellis Little, interview by Anne Witherell, September 17–18, 2004.

[6]Houle, letter, April 28, 2000.

[7]M. [Raoul A.] Feuillet, *Recueil de dances* (1700; reprint, New York: Broude Brothers, 1968); M. [Louis] Pécour, Recueil de dances (1700; reprint, New York: Broude Brothers, 1968). Both are bound with *Chorégraphie* in the Broude Brothers edition.

[8]Marilyn Somville, interview by Anne Witherell, November 22, 2004; John Planting, interview by Anne Witherell, September 3, 2004. Somville became a professor of musicology at the University of Iowa and at Rutgers University, where she also served as dean of the Mason Gross School of the Arts. Planting was the music department administrator at Stanford from 1957 to 1988.

From then on, dancing influenced musical interpretation throughout the music department's home, the "Knoll," whether on the hardwood floors inside or in the grassy courtyard. George, who joined the music faculty in 1962, taught some of the dance classes offered by the department. Meredith Ellis Little, a doctoral student in the 1960s, recalls that by 1962 she, too, was teaching some of those classes. Between the formal classes, professors and students alike engaged in enthusiastic practice sessions that, while polishing their technique, also left a rich trove of humorous memories of earnest dancing, including George dancing the galliard in the courtyard with keys jingling in his pockets and Aldrich dressing up as the Présence in homemade pantaloons.[9]

These efforts resulted in scholarly work that, owing to its innovation, saw much success. At a national meeting of the American Musicological Society in New Orleans in the mid-1960s, a scholarly paper with dance demonstrations given by Meredith and Palo Alto dancer Luba Blumberg generated such excitement that an encore of the full presentation was demanded by their very enthusiastic audience.[10] Most importantly, out of these endeavors came two scholarly works that capture the essence of historical dance at Stanford just before Wendy's influence was felt: Aldrich's *Rhythm in Seventeenth-Century Italian Monody* and Meredith's doctoral dissertation "The Dances of J. B. Lully (1632–1687)."[11]

Wendy's arrival in 1968 would herald a sea change in this work. She would build on the great enthusiasm and dedicated scholarship of these practitioners and develop dancer/musicians with refined dance technique and a more nuanced approach to the music they played. And she would inspire even greater excitement for historical dance at Stanford and make it one of the major centers for the study of baroque dance.

Between 1968 and 1974, Wendy visited Stanford twice; she taught informal classes and began to lay the groundwork for her future work there, including the annual workshop in baroque dance and music. Elsewhere, she collaborated with graduates of the Stanford music department of the 1950s and 1960s, many of whom had gone on to pursue academic careers.

Wendy's first trip to Stanford with Régine Astier in 1968 introduced her to the music department and to George Houle.[12] News of that visit spread, and, soon after, those graduates who were most interested in early music and historical dance began to hear about her. "Somebody or several somebodys told me I should get in touch with Wendy Hilton," Meredith remembers.

[9]Joan Benson, letter to Anne Witherell, March 1, 2005. Benson, a Grammy-winning clavichordist, was a member of the music faculty at this time.

[10]Meredith Ellis Little, interview by Anne Witherell, September 17–18, 2004.

[11]Putnam Aldrich, *Rhythm in Seventeenth-Century Italian Monody* (New York: W. W. Norton, 1966); and Helen Meredith Ellis, "The Dances of J. B. Lully (1632–1687)" (PhD diss., Stanford University, 1968).

[12]See chapter 10 for Wendy's account of that first trip to Stanford.

By that time, Meredith had joined the music faculty of Oakland University in Rochester, Michigan, where she taught Renaissance dance as one of her academic assignments and directed a group that toured six states. When marriage took her to the East Coast, she caught up with Wendy in Connecticut, and the two began to discuss possible future collaborations.[13]

Harpsichordist, musicologist, and Stanford PhD Erich Schwandt also knew of Wendy, and they, too, would eventually collaborate professionally. Essential to Wendy's story at this point, however, is his encouragement of Anne Witherell in the study of historical dance through his faculty position at the Eastman School of Music in Rochester, New York. Anne, who would become Wendy's principal assistant in the Stanford workshop's first years, enrolled at Eastman in 1967 to study the trombone but also embarked on a study of historical dance there under Schwandt's guidance. While Eastman offered no formal studies in this area, its Sibley Music Library, full of original dance sources, provided the materials for her studies and for her senior thesis on the minuet. Anne noted about her early research, "Although this seems incredible today, I pored over and danced around those sources without a dance teacher or class, without seeing a film, and with almost no secondary sources. My approach was certainly very pure. My dancing can only have been peculiar."[14]

After eighteen months of her solitary study, Anne, at Schwandt's encouragement, attended the 1970 meeting of the American Musicological Society in Toronto to hear—and see—Meredith's paper on the sarabande. Meredith, she was told, was working with a new dancer for the demonstrations. Schwandt invited Anne and Eastman graduate students Deanna Bush and Jan Irvine to join him at the dress rehearsal for the event. Anne recalled that the performance was a revelation.

> Meredith talked and later played harpsichord to accompany George Houle on baroque oboe, while the "new dancer," Wendy Hilton, took the stage. What I saw made a very deep impression. Here was an artist performing those early dances in a way I had not imagined possible. I wrote home describing Wendy's "dreamy, introspective, elegant, floating sarabande." It was clear to me that if I was to make much sense of historical dance, I had to find a way to work with Wendy.[15]

Anne's determination to study with Wendy took her to the Dance Notation Bureau's weekend workshop in Manhattan in April 1971 and to the two-week Institute of Court Dances of the Renaissance and Baroque Periods at Mount Holyoke College in the late summer.[16] That fall she entered Stanford University's graduate program in musicology, which was "astounding, delightful, and definitely the right place for me. With respect to historical dance, the atmosphere was a mixture of enthusiasm and curiosity. I was encouraged to do all I could in the field."[17] That included teaching the required

[13]Little, interview by Anne Witherell, September 17–18, 2004.

[14]Anne Witherell, letter to Susan Bindig, April 26, 2009.

[15]Ibid.

[16]See chapter 12 for descriptions of the two workshops.

[17]Witherell, letter, April 26, 2009.

"dance labs," Friday afternoon dance classes to accompany the performance-practice seminars. Even with her limited studies in the area, Anne was still the most qualified to teach these classes. Faced with the responsibility of weekly classes, however, Anne was even more eager to continue her own training with Wendy. The opportunity came sooner than expected.

Wendy returned to Stanford in the spring of 1972 following engagements in southern California. Anne remembers her visit and classes in some detail.

> Wendy gave a series of classes. These were held in an old school building that the music department used for applied music studios. The studios (former classrooms) circled a beautiful hardwood floor, suitable for assemblies in schooldays of yore and dance labs later. The class was challenging for me, as usual. Others who took these classes included George and Glenna; Joan; graduate students Peter and Victoria Hurd, and Susan Willoughby; and Stanford music librarian Elisabeth (Beth) Rebman and her husband Ken. One of the sessions offered the opportunity for many of the music students to accompany the dancing. A harpsichord was available. Soloists on recorder and gamba took turns, as well. My trombone was in the corner, as I was on my way to an orchestra rehearsal. Wendy suggested that I accompany her solo loure from Gatti's *Scylla* on trombone. It seems that was an audition of sorts, and it went quite well.
>
> As is often the case with freelance artists, Wendy was multitasking on this trip. George had just landed his dream job: a two-year sabbatical from Stanford to direct the New York Pro Musica. When I told Wendy this news, which cannot possibly have been news to her, she smiled and said, "How nice for me!" We all imagined that if George was in a position to hire a choreographer, he would hire Wendy. He was and he did.[18]

In the following two years, Wendy would have little contact with Anne and the music department. During George's absence, his departmental responsibilities were assumed by William Mahrt, whose principal interests were medieval and Renaissance sacred vocal music. Mahrt was assisted by Meredith, back in California from her work at Oakland University and in the East and now a recognized specialist in baroque instrumental music and historical dance.

Under Meredith's direction, historical dance at Stanford changed appreciably. She introduced elaborate early music and dance productions, the first of which was "The Masque of the Flowers," performed on May 29, 1973. A doctoral project of John Robison, a student of Meredith's at Oakland University, the masque was far more complex than anything attempted to date at Stanford.[19] Additionally, it was to be performed for the public at the university's Dinkelspiel Auditorium, another new challenge for the department.

Robison produced a critical edition of the masque, which served as the basis of the production. Casting singers was not a problem, given the crop of talented musicians at Stanford at the time. Judith Malafronte, a master's student who later would have a distinguished performing and teaching

[18]Ibid.

[19]Little, interview, September 17–18, 2004.

career, recalls singing a lead role[20]; Doug Wyatt, a bass who would later join the men's vocal group Chanticleer, took one of the other leads. Recruiting and training dancers, a job that fell to Anne, was another issue entirely. Particularly difficult was finding dancing men, and the masque called for ten of them. Anne recalls that her first dance directing job was far more challenging than she would have preferred:

> Dancing in the masque was a stretch for all of us. In the labs, the dancing musicians focused primarily on matching their steps to music. We danced in place (the galliard) or in endless circles (nearly every other step). The notion of the floor pattern was completely foreign to us, as was more than one couple dancing as part of a larger choreography. We did our best.[21]

A year later, on April 3, 1974, Meredith produced a second such production, *Ballo di Donne Turche* by Marco da Gagliano. She took a more active role in the choreography this time, discussing her interpretations with Judith Kennedy, director of dance for the Oregon Shakespeare Festival and an occasional consultant to Meredith. Anne again recruited and trained the dancers. She noted that this production

> was far more elaborate than the masque, including a boat with a gangplank, down which dozens of dancing choristers sashayed in a pavane. Eight dancing couples were joined by fourteen singers and instrumentalists, all in costumes designed for the occasion. About the ballo, Meredith recalled, "Nobody gave me a budget, so I just kept spending." Those were the days![22]

Working side by side with the dramatic productions was a group of dancer-musicians dedicated to the study of baroque dance technique. By January 1974, the group had completed all the dance labs and wished to study baroque dance beyond the basics. The group included Beth Rebman; librarian Marlene Wong; music graduate students Ross Duffin, Lynne Toribara, and Rebecca (Becky) Harris-Warrick; and Ronald (Ron) Harris-Warrick, Becky's husband. To accommodate the demand, Meredith and Anne organized some new classes and taught more advanced ballroom choreographies. The classes also led to the establishment of an informal performing group. They premiered their new dances to much acclaim on June 2, 1974, at the home of graduate student and violinist Dixie Zenger, with former music department chair William Loran Crosten as the Présence. Beginning with this modest performance, early dance quickly became a thriving cottage industry at Stanford. Whether for a madrigal dinner, a class to cap a unit in Renaissance studies, or an official paper at a scholarly conference, people knew they could call Stanford's music department where eager students welcomed invitations to perform.

Guidance from Wendy soon became essential. The group advanced quickly, and Meredith and Anne, despite their best efforts, were straining

[20]Judith Malafronte, interview by Anne Witherell, August 2006.

[21]Witherell, letter, April 26, 2009.

[22]Ibid; Little, interview, September 17–18, 2004.

their resources. For Anne particularly, the responsibilities of teaching dance at Stanford without input from Wendy had become draining. Anne corresponded with Wendy during her two-year absence from Stanford, from 1972 to 1974, and tried doggedly to study with her but with little success. Anne decided, therefore, "to pull up stakes and move to New York."[23] With a scholarship from Wellesley College, Anne was able to take a year's leave of absence from Stanford to study dance with Wendy (even though Wendy had not agreed to teach her at this point) as well as harpsichord with Schwandt beginning in autumn of 1974. Greater opportunities than Anne imagined—for herself and for others—would emerge from this bold move.

The summer of 1974 brought Wendy to Stanford to teach at a Workshop in Early Music and Dance. During the 1973–74 academic year, Meredith wrote a proposal for the two-week workshop, which Mahrt then presented to a faculty

music
at stanford

Summer Session, 1974

workshop in early music and dance

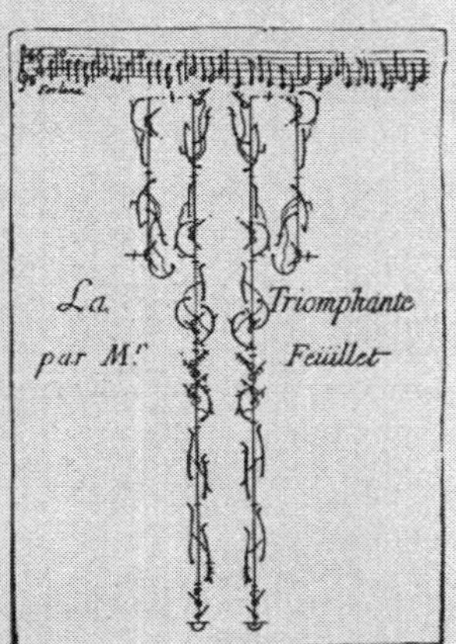

June 24-July 5, MTWThF 9-12, 2-5. 2 units.
WENDY HILTON and MEREDITH LITTLE, directors
assisted by Virginia Hutchings

Two classes daily in technique and style of European court dance from late 16th-century Italy and early 18th-century France. Lectures in history and characterization of dance types, relation of dance and music, Feuillet notation; discussions and experiments in application of dance information to performance of music. Activities will be geared both to musicians and to dancers, and several students will be chosen to accompany Miss Hilton in a concert.

WENDY HILTON has performed dances from the French Baroque court throughout the U.S., in Canada, and in England. She teaches at the Juilliard School, Douglass College, and SUNY at Purchase, and is writing a book on French court dance. Last summer in Italy, she choreographed dances for the New York Pro Musica's production of Marco de Gagliano's opera, *La Dafne*.

MEREDITH LITTLE, musicologist, dance historian, and harpsichordist, is the author of 22 articles on dance and music for the forthcoming 6th edition of *Grove's Dictionary of Music and Musicians*.

Application deadline: June 1. Fee: participants $140; observers (participation with no credit) $100

Figure 60. Workshop in Early Music and Dance, flier, 1974.

[23]Witherell, letter, April 26, 2009.

A LECTURE-DEMONSTRATION: DANCE AND MUSIC OF THE EARLY EIGHTEENTH CENTURY

Stanford University
Dept. of Music

WENDY HILTON
with
VIRGINIA HUTCHINGS, Keyboard

Dinkelspiel Aud.
July 1, 1974

Other instruments played by students in the Stanford Baroque Dance Workshop:
Dixie Zenger, violin — Alice Olson, viola da gamba
Lynne McFarland, violin — Anne Witherell, trombone

(Recorded music will be used for the movements from the Dieupart suite and the Bach orchestral suite.)

PROGRAM

I. L'Allemande
First published in dance notation in 1702
Music by Jean-Baptiste Lully (1632-1687) or André Campra (1660-1744)
Dance by Louis Pécour

II. Dances adapted from original sources and performed to instrumental music.

Movements from Suite in G minor — Charles Dieupart (1700-1740)

Courante
Gavotte
Gigue

Minuet in A major — G. F. Handel (1685-1759)

Movements from Suite in C major for Orchestra — J. S. Bach (1685-1750)

Gavotte
Bourée

Movements from Suites for Klavier

Courante: English Suite in A major
Allemande: French Suite in E major
Loure: French Suite in G major

III. Gigue de Roland
First published in 1700
Music by Lully
Dance by Feuillet

Loure from Scylla
First published in 1712
Music by Teobaldo de Gatti (c. 1650-1727)
Dance by Pécour

Canarie from Alcide
First published in 1712
Music by Louis de Lully (1664-1713) and Marin Marais (1656-1728)
Dance by Pécour

Figure 61. "Wendy Hilton with Virginia Hutchings," workshop concert program, 1974.

committee for approval. George, due to return to Stanford from New York, had given the workshop his blessing. It was to be part of the regular series of summer electives that the Stanford music department offered for its own students and for interested scholars and musicians from outside the university. It would include instruction in dance by Wendy and in musicology and theory by Meredith. Meredith felt that the course would have broader appeal if Wendy taught both baroque and Renaissance dance, and so, for this first workshop, classes in Italian dance from the early seventeenth century were proposed.[24] The proposal also included an accompanist for the dance classes, and Wendy recommended that her now regular performing and teaching colleague, Virginia Hutchings, join her. Virginia not only would play for Wendy's classes but would also teach a music class and coach workshop musicians on aspects of dance accompaniment. The proposed workshop received the full endorsement of the committee and was scheduled for June 24 to July 5.

The two-dozen participants who signed on for this experiment included a core of Stanford music graduate students; local early music enthusiasts; harpsichordists and harpsichord builders; recorder players and gambists; a few of Meredith's former pupils from Michigan; scholars, including some Stanford alumni; and Stanford's harpsichord teacher Margaret Fabrizio. As most musicians at that time felt more confident about Renaissance dance than baroque dance, the idea of including some early seventeenth-century dance did attract a number of participants. Trained dancers, however, were underrepresented in the group.

On Monday, July 1, Wendy presented a lecture-demonstration, "Dance and Music of the Early Eighteenth Century." To augment her lecture with slides, Wendy danced the women's parts of "L'Allemande" and the "Gigue de Roland"; the loure from *Scylla* and the canary from *Alcide*; and a selection of her own choreography to movements from Charles Dieupart's Suite in G Minor and from J. S. Bach's Orchestral Suite in C Major, BWV 1066. For the Dieupart and the Bach, she danced to recorded orchestral accompaniment; for the rest, to Virginia on piano and to a small student ensemble (Dixie Zenger and Lynne Toribara, violins; Alice Olson, viola da gamba; and Anne on trombone) that Virginia had coached. The opportunity for musicians to accompany dancing was an essential element of this and future workshops. The local and campus press covered the performance. The *Palo Alto Times* found it "enchanting" and noted that the audience received Wendy's dancing enthusiastically. The review pointed out the subtlety and complexity of the baroque style as well as the elegant line required for its correct performance, as ideally demonstrated by Wendy.[25]

The workshop participants, particularly the Stanford students, greeted Wendy's classes with enthusiasm. The dancing was far more difficult than many had imagined, but all met the challenge. Anne, who served as Wendy's student assistant, wrote a detailed review of the 1974 workshop for *Current Musicology*, which gave a full picture of the classes, lectures, and other activities.

[24]Little, interview, September 17–18, 2004.

[25]Gay Weaver, "Baroque dance teacher presents enchanting lecture-demonstration," *Palo Alto Times*, n.d.

> Wendy Hilton, who has been active as a choreographer, dancer, and dance historian in both England and New York, where she teaches at the Juilliard School, taught the dance classes. She stressed the style and formidable technique of early 18th-century French court dance. The steps, which may be puzzled out by a determined amateur armed with the works of Feuillet and Pierre Rameau, were presented as part of a logical and exhilarating technique of dance movement. The students practiced patterns preserved in dance notation in the 18th-century choreographies. The daily introductory classes found musicians learning to move, and dancers adopting a new technique and adjusting their style to that of the early 18th century. Miss Hilton also coached couples who had reconstructed 18th-century choreographies and [she] devoted certain classes to Italian dances of the early 17th century, which were of particular interest to some of the workshop students.
>
> Virginia Hutchings, who currently pursues an active concert career in Europe and has worked with Miss Hilton for several years, taught the music classes, whose subject was rhythm in the performance of early 18th-century dance music. Miss Hutchings explained and demonstrated musical means of mirroring and enhancing the sense of motion and direction of the dances. Open rehearsals of the instrumental ensemble for Miss Hilton's concert, coached by Miss Hutchings, were an invaluable lesson in dance accompaniment.
>
> Dr. Meredith Little of the Stanford faculty, who is known for her dissertation on the dances of Lully (Stanford, 1967) and for her subsequent research on early dance music, taught the musicology class. She provided background material in choreographic notation and surveyed the choreography and dance technique sources from early 17th-century Italy and 18th-century France. Dr. Little also presented the results of recent research in her field and offered a preview of her articles on 18th-century dance forms which will appear in the sixth edition of *Grove's Dictionary of Music and Musicians*.[26]

In addition to serving as the workshop student assistant and occasional historian, Anne, along with her roommates, was a frequent host for workshop-length stays by faculty and participants at her home in Palo Alto. Anne noted that in 1974, both Wendy and Virginia stayed with her, the first of many such pleasant sojourns.

> My roommates Dr. Paul Pentel and Dr. John Kobayashi, both medical students, were enjoying the relative leisure of a nurses' strike and so had more time than usual to get to know our house guests. John was learning to make chicken teriyaki, a hobby we all encouraged. He remembers that, before their visit, he had never met a dancer or any professional performer for that matter. Wendy and Virginia's concert left him spellbound. Paul left an indelible impression with his mixed drinks, (margaritas?) and backrubs. He remembers a summer of food and fun and that, despite the neck spasms that had begun to plague her, Wendy remained charming and upbeat. "She was the least demanding house guest."[27]

[26]Anne Witherell, "Report from Stanford University: Summer Workshops—1974," *Current Musicology* 19 (Spring 1975): 11.

[27]John Kobayashi, interview by Anne Witherell, July 2004; Paul Pentel, interview by Anne Witherell, July 2004; and Witherell, letter, May 2009.

Wendy loved staying at Anne's home. It was a lively house with lots of character, and its proximity to downtown Palo Alto was a plus. Wendy wrote briefly of her time there:

> The sun shone, there was no humidity, and I was completely happy in Anne Witherell's house on Channing Street, shared with several other students, mostly in the medical school. There was a beautiful yard and a sun deck. Virginia stayed there too and it was always great fun. Palo Alto offered many excellent restaurants, and the cool evenings were perfect for walking about. [28]

Although the first workshop was an unqualified success, it had not met all of Wendy's criteria, and a second workshop was hardly a foregone conclusion. Wendy spent an extra week in California that July working out the details for a workshop the following summer. The proposal that she and George developed outlined parallel workshops in baroque dance and music that would extend over four weeks. The proposal noted that, during the first week, Wendy was to "instruct and rehearse Stanford dancers, who have been working all year on their own, preparing for a special recital to take place at the end of the workshop." The formal two-week workshop would follow with daily instruction in baroque dance only (even though it was still advertised as a Workshop in Early Music and Dance) and classes in baroque music especially designed for dancers. Complementing those classes were lectures on dance notation, accompaniment of dance, musical ornamentation, and analysis of rhythm; a solo piano recital by Virginia; and a dance recital by Wendy. The music institute taught by George would focus on the performance of baroque music with special attention to ensembles playing for dance. Following the two-week workshop, an additional week of concentrated instruction would be offered for more advanced dancers and musicians, selected from the workshop participants by Wendy and George, respectively. Anne would again participate as Wendy's assistant.

Wendy hoped to expand Virginia's role in the workshop with the solo piano recital. This part of the proposal proved contentious, however, because the piano was not considered by all to be a legitimate instrument for playing Bach's music. A piano recital at an early music and dance workshop seemed particularly inappropriate. With Wendy's strong encouragement, the music department offered Virginia a recital for 1975 but with a rather significant caveat: she had to agree not to play Bach. Wendy, it seems, agreed to the concession, and it's not clear whether she shared this part of the arrangement with Virginia. Once the recital was approved, however, Wendy hurried

[28]Over the years, Wendy enjoyed the hospitality of a number of Palo Alto residents, who were happy to open their homes to her. Wendy wrote: "When Anne graduated and left that area I stayed with a good friend Lois Nisbet, who had taken the workshop several times. Betty Kaplan was another generous Stanford hostess, and the old Cardinal Hotel sometimes filled the gap."

to Carmel and its annual Bach festival to secure engagements for Virginia and herself. Virginia would not be curbed from playing Bach on piano in Carmel and, Wendy hoped, might find the restriction on the Stanford concert more palatable.

Wendy's support of the use of modern instruments to accompany baroque dance was ironically in direct contradiction—which she did not seem to recognize, or just chose to ignore—to her own belief that *only* baroque dance should be performed to the music of Bach. She was so firm in this conviction that she refused to watch ballet or modern works choreographed to this music; hence, her initial snub of Jerome Robbins's *Goldberg Variations* despite her consultation on the work. Nicholas Gunn recalled that when Paul Taylor's *Esplanade*, choreographed to two works by Bach, premiered in 1975, Wendy refused to see it even though he and Eileen Cropley, both members of her New York company, danced key roles.[29] Taylor had even caught her sneaking out of one of his company's concerts early to avoid seeing the work. Finally, however, she relented and saw *Esplanade* on television and loved it.[30] "Of course," she noted with clear amusement, "I had the sound turned off."

Wendy's point was that a musician's ability to support dancing effectively in rhythm, tempo, and affect, regardless of the instrument played, was paramount.[31] She felt—and many disagreed—that few musicians possessed that talent. For Wendy, Virginia, like Tureck, was one of those rare musicians. Workshop participants who had the pleasure of dancing to Virginia's playing recognized its truly special qualities. Our musical experience in the dance studio was exceptional and memorable. We floated to Virginia's music, were buoyed by it. It actually had the capacity to make the dancing seem easier than it was. Anne noted that workshop participants "developed a deep appreciation for Virginia's musical helping hand as we fought first to remain vertical and later to add some art to our steps."[32] Workshop regulars Lois Nisbet and Richard (Dick) Lee felt that Virginia "made us levitate"; her playing "carried us along."[33]

Wendy left California with confidence that plans, if not finalized, were well under way for the 1975 workshop. She returned to New York to finish her appointments at Douglass College and SUNY Purchase and for her last year with Juilliard's Drama Division. Another Stanford project—to advise

[29]Nicholas Gunn, interview by Susan Bindig, October 30, 2007. *Esplanade* is choreographed to J. S. Bach's Violin Concerto in E Major, BWV 1042, and to the largo and allegro movements of the Double Concerto for Two Violins in D Minor, BWV 1043.

[30]Wendy saw *Esplanade*, with Nicholas (Eileen had left the company before the filming) through the *Dance in America* series by WNET. The film is now available as *Paul Taylor Dance Company: WNET/Dance in America: Esplanade and Runes* (New York, WNET, 1998).

[31]Meredith Little felt that Wendy didn't care what instrument accompanied her classes, but it had to be played with elegance. Little, interview, September 17–18, 2004.

[32]Witherell, letter, April 26, 2009.

[33]Lois Nisbet, interview by Anne Witherell, September 7, 2004; Richard Lee, interview by Anne Witherell, August 28, 2004.

Anne's doctoral dissertation—had come her way, however, before she boarded the plane. Anne noted,

> At some point during the week of workshop negotiations, Wendy said to me, "I understand you have plans for me." We discussed my ideas for the upcoming academic year and Louis Pécour's 1700 *Recueil de Dances*, a PhD topic which had been the "perfect!" brainchild of George Houle. She agreed to be my adviser and remarked that she felt it was good for a student to work independently for a period of time. For better or worse, I had been forced to work independently for a period that would now end.[34]

Having already secured the funding and arranged for a year's academic leave, Anne returned that fall to Rochester, New York, which would serve as her base for the year. She looked forward to pleasurable hours in Eastman's Sibley Library exploring further its rich collection of dance sources and to practicing harpsichord, dance, and trombone.

Wendy agreed to work with Anne once a month in Manhattan. Sometimes they would meet at Wendy's apartment, where they would exchange manuscripts—a chapter of Anne's dissertation for a section of the new book Wendy was writing—before finding space for a dance lesson. Other times, they would meet at Happy Harbor for dance lessons in the living room. For Anne, the 1974–75 academic year was sheer bliss.

In January of 1975, Erich Schwandt invited Wendy to collaborate with him on a project focusing on seventeenth-century dance songs by Michel L'Affilard, which he and Eastman student Julianne Baird had been working on for some time.[35] The score featured a set of pendulum markings for each of the dance-songs, which held great fascination for the scholarly community engaged in debates over the proper tempi for dance-inspired baroque music. Schwandt hoped Wendy might choreograph some dances to the songs and sent her a tape of Julianne and himself performing the L'Affilard pieces.

Wendy liked the songs and the idea of dancing to singing. Not all of the metronome markings suited her, but enough of them did, and she and Schwandt were able to construct a suite of eight dances: gavotte, bourrée, two minuets, passepied, sarabande, gigue, and canary. Wendy took as her model original choreographies from the period, which she modified with her own choreography to complement the songs. The first performance of the L'Affilard work with Wendy, Julianne, and Schwandt was in Kilbourn Hall at the Eastman School of Music on May 16, 1975, in a program dedicated to Putnam Aldrich, who had recently passed away. Wendy and Schwandt shared the narration duties. Anne, who was present for the performance, recalled that she was awestruck by the beauty of the performance on all levels—dancing, singing, and accompaniment. Plans for encore performances were made.

Wendy and Anne, however, quickly turned their attention to the fast-approaching Stanford workshop as there was little over a month to prepare. Wendy was the first to arrive in California and unhappily discovered that very few arrangements had been made. Anne, had she been at Stanford, would

[34]Witherell, letter, April 26, 2009.

[35]Michael L'Affilard, *Principes très façiles* (Paris, 1705).

have already been engrossed in preparations, and no one had been assigned to those duties in her absence. When Anne's plane landed a few days later, she was greeted at the gate by Wendy, Beth Rebman, and all of Anne's former students dancing the minuet. Anne remembers Wendy saying to her, "I'll be your assistant if you'll be mine." The happy scene at the airport belied the chaos Anne would soon face.

Despite the odds and Wendy's high demands, Anne did a remarkable job in record time. When she arrived, Virginia's recital, scheduled for the first evening of the workshop was not on the summer concert calendar, had no publicity, no program, no piano, no piano tuner, or rehearsal times planned; all were in place by the time Virginia appeared shortly thereafter. Class schedules were finalized, rooms reserved, and study materials printed and copied. The students were met with an organized, smooth-running workshop and were completely unaware of the mayhem that had preceded their arrival. In the end, the workshop was, if anything, even better than the first in 1974.

Wendy's and Virginia's concerts were well-received by the audience and an inspiration to the workshop students. Virginia's recital on July 7 featured Beethoven's Sonata in E Major, op. 109, and Schumann's Fantasy, op. 17. Wendy, in her concert on July 11, performed the L'Affilard pieces with Julianne singing and Anne playing the harpsichord. Schwandt, teaching at Brigham Young University for the summer, was unable to participate but had taught Anne his continuo realizations. Additional coaching by Virginia and Margaret Fabrizio prepared Anne well for the concert.

At the close of the workshop, Wendy was scheduled to dance in a program at the Carmel Bach Festival, tape the L'Affilard songs at Stanford, and return to Carmel for a second performance. Virginia also was to give at least one all-Bach recital at Carmel. It was to be a hectic month at best, followed by a period free from performing and teaching when Wendy could edit the L'Affilard videotape, set up the 1976 workshop schedule, and begin to work with the Stanford group on the dances from Pécour 1700 (as they now referred to the 1700 *Recueil de Dances*) for Anne's doctoral recital scheduled for the spring of 1976.

The bright promise of Wendy's career was almost entirely shattered at Carmel. Her performance there would be her last. Anne was both part of the lead-up to the concert and present for the performance itself. She remembers the episode vividly.

> In the mid-1970s, the Carmel Bach Festival and the Stanford early music program represented two distinct approaches to baroque performance practice. Stanford promoted performances on replicas of early instruments and careful study of period sources. Carmel was an enormously popular commercial venture, a three-week summer concert series featuring only the music of Bach and his contemporaries played on modern instruments. Its tickets always sold out. What they had in common for many years was the festival's conductor, Sandor Salgo, who was also on the Stanford music faculty. When Sandor didn't have enough professionals to fill out his Carmel ensemble, he would hire promising Stanford students: James DeCorsey, horn; David Sullivan, bassoon; Mark Volkert, violin. In 1974, he even hired me to play trombone.

The tale of Wendy and Carmel began in the summer of 1974. It is worth telling in some detail because it reveals a great deal about Wendy, in particular the lengths to which she would go to help someone else's career. It would also bring the end to her performing career, and it is important to clear the forest of myth that sprang up around her departure from the stage.

Sandor contacted Wendy for the first time during the 1974 workshop. An immediate conversation was impossible due to the combination of their schedules. It was my understanding that Sandor hoped Wendy might choreograph a ballet or opera by a baroque composer for the 1975 festival.

Rather than return a call, Wendy decided that she and I should go to Carmel to see a concert. Since I did not own a car, this involved the afternoon Greyhound, then finding a place to stay, finding tickets to the sold-out concert, and scoring an invitation to the after-concert party. Probably it was necessary for Wendy to size up the situation before anyone in Carmel knew who she was. Wendy was not interested in choreographing for the festival once she saw its tiny stage. Even if Sandor's promise to provide her with "the finest dancers" (memory fails me here: from Los Angeles? Las Vegas?) intrigued her, there was no place to put them. Wendy's real goal was to arrange some concerts for Virginia, which would allow her to perform Bach on the piano, bring in a better fee, and make her 1975 trip to California worthwhile.

Amazingly, we made it to Carmel, found two free beds, booked two seats for the concert, and strolled to the party. My instructions there were to introduce Wendy and Sandor and discreetly step aside. Sandor was the last to arrive. When it seemed appropriate, I introduced my teachers. Wendy said something in Hungarian, startling Sandor, as I drifted out of earshot. A bit later, Wendy returned along with the order to find a ride to Palo Alto that night. This was not easy as it was nearly midnight, but we caught the last VW bug north with one of Sandor's conducting students, Jason Klein, and his wife, Carole. This was my first full day as Wendy's private student, and I did wonder how I would survive my education.

The road to hell in Carmel was certainly paved with the best intentions on everyone's part. Sandor seemed very gracious about Virginia's recital, even agreeing to pay for her airfare. Virginia was happy to play Bach and, indeed, her recitals were very enthusiastically received. Her popularity reached such a pitch that dinner at a restaurant one evening was interrupted by phone calls from gentlemen asking her out. She was the toast of Carmel.

Wendy elected to perform her lecture-demonstration with Virginia. They were scheduled to appear on evening concerts on July 18 and 25 [1975] with the Bach cantata "Lobe den Herren" [BWV 137] and the Mozart Clarinet Concerto [K. 622] on the first half, an intermission to clear the stage, and the lecture-demonstration to close the evening. For the July 18 concert, Ken and Beth Rebman, workshop student Lois Nisbet, Stanford faculty member and clavichordist Joan Benson, Ron and Becky Harris-Warrick, and I were in the audience, as well as many members of the Carmel Orchestra. I recall writing to my mother describing the incredible beauty of the loures.[36]

Then the unthinkable had happened. Wendy was asked not to perform her second concert at the festival. The Carmel musicians learned of the episode first because of the adjustments to the concert schedule. "A shutter of silence seemed to fall over the incident," said David Sullivan who played in the orchestra that summer and had also seen Wendy perform.[37] None of the musicians seemed to know the cause of the cancellation.

Ken and Beth Rebman had spent the night in Carmel and had planned a day of feasting and celebration with Virginia and Wendy the next day. Instead, Wendy felt she could not be seen in public; the remaining trio had a rather somber brunch.

Virginia stayed in Carmel to practice for her solo recital, and the Rebmans returned Wendy to Palo Alto to prepare for the L'Affilard taping on July 22. No one yet had told me anything about the Carmel incident, and it did not occur to me to ask. After the taping and a celebratory dinner at Channing Street, Wendy told me what happened. She said, "I didn't want to tell you this before because I knew how upset you'd be." I was completely nonplussed that Sandor would cancel such a beautiful performance. I thought that, even if he had considered it to be mediocre, there would have been much less fuss if he had just let the show go on.

Naturally, I told Wendy her performance had been stunning. What possible excuse could Sandor have given her? Wendy and Virginia said that Sandor objected to Wendy's tremor and furthermore, that her performance did not meet the standards of the festival. That was the first explanation I had. Wendy never danced again in public.

Meanwhile, the rest of the Stanford crew had to be warned not to return to Carmel for a second concert. A bevy of theories about the cancellation emerged. One was that, in dismissing Wendy, Sandor had reacted to a negative review. This was not at all the case. Wendy's performance received two reviews, in the *Sacramento Bee* and the *Carmel Pinecone*. Both were extremely positive, embarrassingly so in view of the fact that they appeared after Wendy had been dismissed.

Sandor never mentioned Wendy's health to me when I spoke with him after her death. He felt terrible, that the event had been "a minor disaster." What Sandor did say was: "The Carmel audience did not come to be educated, they came to be entertained."[38] Perhaps a lecture-recital, particularly as the second half of an evening concert which had begun with Bach and Mozart performed by a chorus and a full orchestra of modern instruments, was doomed from the start. Where was the grand finale, the major work? The audience had not paid top dollar for tickets and dressed to the nines to hear a British lady talk, show slides, and dance a handful of five-minute dances that didn't look very difficult. I can only wonder what the planners had been thinking.

Had it not been for Carmel, would Wendy have gone on dancing? I really don't think so. For most of the 1974–75 New York

[36]Anne Witherell, letter to Louise Witherell, July 29, 1975.

[37]David Sullivan, interview by Anne Witherell, September 4, 2004.

[38]Sandor Salgo, interview by Anne Witherell, August 28, 2004.

> season, she had not danced with her company. She arranged their concerts and taught the dances. Her L'Affilard performances were the exception that season, and all of that dancing was out of town. Wendy did not know what to do about her health, especially when it seemed she might have Parkinson's disease. She still held British citizenship and considered returning to England to take advantage of their nationalized health plan if things deteriorated. Fortunately, it never came to that. At the end of that summer, she began telling people that she would dance no more. She would write, teach, and choreograph.[39]

Despite her desolation and before walking away from performing entirely, Wendy managed to summon the energy and resolve to tape the L'Affilard dances as planned. On August 22, Schwandt, having completed his work in Utah, Wendy, and Julianne gathered on the stage of Dinkelspiel Auditorium, along with stage manager John Hughes, a cameraman, and Anne, who was on hand to assist as needed. The resulting film, while dark and grainy, shows Wendy at perhaps her finest. Sadly, this film remains one of the few records of Wendy dancing.[40]

Wendy's increasing presence at Stanford fostered an amount of historical dance activity found at few universities in the mid-1970s. By the fall of 1976, her appointments and courses in baroque dance at Douglass College and at SUNY Purchase had ended. Stanford, therefore, joined the Juilliard School; the New England Conservatory of Music, where Julia Sutton taught; and a handful of others as one of the rare schools to offer historical dance studies throughout the academic year. Wendy had also developed a group of skilled musician-dancers at Stanford who could teach for her when she was in New York or elsewhere. In her absence, the Stanford classes were taught by Anne, Beth Rebman, Becky Harris-Warrick, and Richard (Rick) Semmens, a new PhD student in musicology in 1975–76.

The rapid approach of Anne's dissertation recital added rehearsals to an already busy class and work schedule for all involved. The dedicated company who devoted long hours to the spring performance included Becky Harris-Warrick, Beth Rebman, Marlene Wong, Lynne Toribara (McFarland), Beverly Simmons, Carole Terry, Ross Duffin, and Ron Harris-Warrick. Those who were accomplished musicians—Becky on flute, Lynne on violin, Beverly and Carole at the harpsichord—took turns accompanying the dancing. Anne directed, narrated, and danced. The program comprised the following dances from Pécour 1700:

[39]Witherell, letter, April 26, 2009.

[40]A copy of the unedited tape can be found in the DD-NYPLPA: Wendy Hilton, Erich Schwandt, and Julianne Baird, *Music and dance from the court of Louis XIV: 14 dances and airs from Michel L'Affilard's* Principes très-faciles *(Paris 1705)*, 1975, videocassette.

"La Bourrée d'Achille" (Colasse), Ron and Anne

"La Mariée" (Lully), Becky and Ron

"Le Passepied" (Anon.), Lynne and Marlene

"La Contredance" (Lully), Beth and Ross

"Le Riguadon des Vaisseaux" (Anon.), Becky and Lynne

"La Bourgogne" (Anon.), Marlene and Ron

"La Savoye" (Anon.), Beverly and Carole

"La Forlana" (Campra), Beth and Ron

"La Conty" (Campra), Ron and Anne

Fortunately, Wendy was able to visit Stanford often during that academic year to lend her discriminating eye to rehearsals. The group also arranged supplemental classes to take full advantage of Wendy's presence. The fees from those classes along with free room and board (usually at Channing Street), inexpensive airfares, and a small honorarium from Stanford for advising Anne's dissertation made the deal financially viable. That Wendy loved to be in California only added to the appeal of the arrangement.

Before the debut of the full Pécour 1700 in June, however, another doctoral recital provided a preview of some of the dances. Keyboard player Jack Ashworth, a candidate for the Doctor of Musical Arts (DMA) degree, decided that there should be dancing on one of his recitals required for the degree and invited Anne to join him. He, too, had participated in dance classes during his studies and had, at one point, been Anne's dance partner. His program on March 6, 1976, featured well-known baroque flutist David Hart, visiting from the Oregon Shakespeare Festival, and Stanford gambist Laura Carroll playing both instrumental and dance music. Anne was joined by Ron Harris-Warrick for the concert; she noted that it "was a very pleasant warm-up for my own doctoral recital and for the video Ron and I would make of all the dances."[41]

Wendy returned to Stanford for Anne's dissertation defense on May 6, 1976, and remained for the rest of the month to help the group prepare for the recital on June 2.[42] The dances improved rapidly, and other preparations flowed smoothly, even the costumes, which the group had confronted with dread. The theater department loaned gentlemen's costumes that were suitable for Ross and Ron. The ladies were not so fortunate and made their own over the year with Wendy's guidance. They were also not at all of the period, consisting of a leotard and long skirts that were dyed to match, but worked well. Beth Rebman oversaw much of the work because of her experience

[41]Witherell, letter, April 26, 2009.

[42]Besides Wendy, the committee members for Anne's defense were George Houle, Professor of Music Leonard Ratner, Professor of Religion Edwin Good (an active musician), Renaissance music specialist Imogene Horsley, and Professor of Music Education Wolfgang Kuhn. Wendy prevailed since the bulk of the dissertation concerned the reconstruction of the dances. She asked Anne about her sources, but then asked, "What is there in the dance technique which affects the performance of the musical accompaniment?" Anne recalls that she answered well. Witherell, letter, April 26, 2009. Anne's dissertation was published in 1983 (Witherell, *Louis Pécour's 1700* Recueil de Dances [Ann Arbor, Mich, UMI Research Press, 1983]).

with making ballet costumes. Wendy even pitched in to dye a few waistbands in the final hours.

The program went well, and the crowd was large and enthusiastic. The music department was out in force and extremely supportive. Rick Semmens, who would dance with the group the next year, remembers a beaming George Houle going up to Anne after the program saying, "Oh *Anne*!"[43] To Anne's surprise, she even received a few fan letters in the following weeks.

The recital was a turning point for baroque dance at Stanford. What may have been viewed as an avocation and merely an adjunct to music was now recognized as an artistic and academic study of equal status. The lecture-demonstration would also become a standard format for presentations of baroque dance for years to come and copied by many.

Through Wendy's teaching, the members of the Stanford dance group were now acknowledged as skilled performers. The 1976 summer workshop was significant for the introduction of trained dancers to those ranks—Fern Schwartzbard and Donna Waks, my colleagues from Douglass College, and me. After our performance in *Dardanus* at Juilliard, Wendy had encouraged us to attend the Stanford workshop. We were surprised to discover that we already had a reputation at Stanford as the "Douglass Dodgers" (we were the East Coast team!), and we were thrilled to meet our West Coast counterparts. Until this point, the experienced class (it hadn't yet achieved the status of an advanced class) comprised primarily hardworking Stanford musicians.  With the addition of dancers, the class changed. The step sequences became longer and more complex, giving, as Anne remembers, "some of us panic attacks. . . . Wendy refused to slow down the class, and it was a good challenge for us. It was good for the workshop as well. Dancers would be with us forever."[44]

Virginia Hutchings returned to the workshop in 1976 to accompany Wendy's classes, teach a course on baroque dance and music, and give a recital. She would continue in these roles through 1983. Although forbidden in 1975, Virginia's 1976 recital, and all her recitals thereafter, included Bach. On this concert, she played the Partita No. 6 in E Minor, BWV 830, along with Mozart's Sonata in C Major, K 330, and Beethoven's Sonata in A-flat Major, op. 110. The reason for this happy development is unclear, but no one questioned it.

Wendy, now retired from performing, decided that the dance concert would be presented by the workshop students. The performance included an encore of the full Pécour 1700 concert and two dances from the Douglass College production of Purcell's *The Fairy Queen*: a gavotte choreographed by Wendy and danced by Donna and me and a minuet for eight ladies choreographed by Donna. Donna's minuet, from a Douglass class assignment to

[43]Richard Semmens, interview by Anne Witherell, September 2, 2004.

[44]Witherell, letter, April 26, 2009.

choreograph a group minuet incorporating some of the principles we had learned about the form, was the only student-choreographed work ever featured in a workshop concert.[45]

Over the years, the structure of the workshop evolved to meet the needs of both new and repeating students. In 1974 Wendy taught all the dance technique and dance notation classes, Virginia a daily music class, and Meredith a daily musicology class. By 1976 a class in advanced dance notation was needed as well. As a result, Anne was promoted to Wendy's teaching assistant and, in addition to her administrative duties, taught the beginners' technique and notation classes, freeing Wendy to coach the advanced notation projects. A second pianist to play for Anne's classes was also needed. The first of these was Artis Wodehouse, a Stanford graduate music student, who years later would win awards for her reconstructions of Gershwin piano rolls.

In the early days of the workshop, a typical morning would include a dance technique class at the beginning or experienced level, dance notation, and scheduled coaching or practice time for a notation project. Virginia's music class and Wendy's technique class for all levels were the core afternoon offerings. The combined-level class, always the last class of the day, benefited the beginners in particular, who gained much from dancing among the experienced dancers and learning from their example. It also gave the beginners the chance to work with Wendy and Virginia every day, as their morning technique class was now taught by the assistant with the second accompanist. Over the years, the daily class times would vary, but the principal offerings of the workshop remained the same.

Special classes and lectures were scheduled throughout the two weeks. A bibliography class, generally offered on day two and taught initially by Anne or Beth, introduced the workshop participants to the music library's substantial holdings in early music and dance. These included copies of dance materials, particularly of dance notations, that Wendy had gathered from her research in Europe. The Lully Archive, inaugurated around 1977 and completed and catalogued in the mid-1980s, gave students access to more than one thousand items on microfilm on the music of Lully. Students were free to study and copy these materials, if they could find the time. Another source was the exceptional personal dance library of Leslie Getz, an independent dance scholar living in the area in the workshop's earlier days. Leslie generously opened her library to participants if she owned material that was vital to their work and not available on campus. Visiting scholars, treated to such a rich collection of resources, were often torn between spending time in these libraries and attending class. The temptation for some was to work day and night and risk complete collapse.[46]

On the last day of the workshop, participants presented their dance reconstructions for Wendy's feedback. The beginners struggled through "La Bourrée d'Achille," and the more experienced students tackled dances that

[45]When asked about the process of choreographing the minuet, Donna could only recall that Wendy had given the class quite a bit of freedom. Donna Waks, interview by Anne Witherell, September 6, 2005.

[46]Julie Andrijeski, interview by Anne Witherell, October 2005.

suited their skill level. For many years, returning students were assigned "La Bourgogne" as their second notation project because it provided, in one choreography, the opportunity to explore four of the central dance forms: courante, bourrée, sarabande, and passepied.

A surprising adjustment to the workshop schedule came in 1976. The daily musicology class was omitted and a position for an annual visiting scholar was inaugurated. In 1976 Erich Schwandt was offered the position; he gave a lecture on his L'Affilard research and collaboration with Wendy, shared a recital with another Putnam Aldrich pupil, Natalie Jenne, and played continuo for the student dance concert. This arrangement became the template for the workshop for years to come. Visiting scholars over the years included Stanford art historian Dwight Miller explaining the artistic and cultural ambiance of Versailles; Albert Cohen speaking on the development of the Lully Archive; and Cohen, George Houle, and Becky Harris-Warrick discussing editions of Lully ballets and operas that came out of their research at the archive.

The workshop was not all work. Many evenings found the group at someone's home for a potluck or an impromptu party. Anne's house on Channing Street seemed to be the party hub, and she and her roommates were happy to host workshop gatherings. I recall many fun nights there after long days in class. Dinners at the Good Earth and many jaunts to Swenson's for Swiss orange chip ice cream filled other evenings. Beth and Ken Rebman were also gracious hosts of memorable gatherings for either the entire group

Figure 62. Wendy and Anne Witherell relaxing at a workshop brunch, July 1976. Photo by Susan Bindig.

or a smaller subset at their home in Redwood City. Beth, a terrific cook, always provided sophisticated fare. I particularly remember an evening party where she and Ken treated us to superb paella made from scratch on the grill and a Sunday brunch with a bounteous menu (the particulars of which have long been forgotten) to celebrate, I believe, the close of a workshop.

The Fourth of July, which often fell within the two weeks of the workshop, always provided an excuse for a party or picnic. Usually a group would take a picnic to the Stanford Dish, the parkland in the Stanford Foothills, which, after an arduous climb, offered a breathtaking view of the entire San Francisco Bay. Everyone would lie about on blankets and watch the fireworks from San Jose to Candlestick Park. It was a favorite workshop evening for years. Wendy even enjoyed it, when we could convince her to join us.

Just relaxing after classes in the early evenings in or around Stanford's coffee house or student union provides some of my best memories of leisure at the workshop. In the sunny but cool late afternoons, many of us would gather for an hour or so before dinner in an attempt to soothe tired feet and brains. Successes and frustrations with class and with baroque dance in general were discussed over many pitchers of Anchor Steam beer. More importantly, friendships, professional collaborations, and even love developed and flourished. Many of those relationships continue today—or are, for the most part, warm memories.

Seventeen: 1976–2001

New Directions for Historical Dance at Stanford University ~ Development of the Workshop on Baroque Dance and Its Music

The 1976–77 academic year brought further opportunities for the resident Stanford group. Graduations and new jobs relocated Ross, Beverly, and Marlene, and their replacements had to be found. Rick Semmens and I were the new recruits. I was now pursuing a master's degree in dance at UCLA and could drive or fly to Palo Alto when needed. The group's repertoire expanded and included both ballroom and theater dances carefully chosen by Wendy to match our abilities.

The next hurdle was costumes. The lone review of the Pécour 1700 concert had been very positive about the dancing, music, and narration, but found the costumes, particularly the women's, lacking.[1] More authentic costumes, therefore, became essential. Beth and Lynne, the more skilled costumers of the group, bore the brunt of the design and construction, working with the complex instructions in Norah Waugh's *The Cut of Women's Clothes, 1690–1930*. They did a wonderful job, but both vividly recall sitting at sewing machines in tears over the challenges of constructing boned corsets.[2]

By the spring of 1977, baroque dance had emerged as the face of the music department. Ron and Anne auditioned for a local television program. Some of the group entertained at university President Richard Lyman's home on May 23. Earlier that month, others traveled to Victoria, British Columbia, to perform for Wendy at the Eighth Annual Meeting of the American Society for Eighteenth-Century Studies. This engagement necessitated a month of frequent rehearsals with Wendy, which, combined with the high demands of graduate school and jobs, exhausted everyone.

Just a few weeks after the Canadian performances, on May 31, the full group presented another public concert at Stanford. This performance featured two of the Pécour 1700 favorites, "La Savoye" and "La Mariée," along with ballroom dances newer to the group's repertoire, "Aimable Vainqueur," "L'Allemande," and "La Venitienne" (Pécour/Mouret, 1715). The theater segment of the program included the "Entrée à deux Dancée par Mr. Dumirail and Mlle. Victoire à l'Opéra *Hésionne*" (Pécour/Campra, 1704) and a suite of dances from Campra's *Les Fêtes Vénitiennes*. A chamber ensemble of baroque instruments accompanied the ballroom dances, and a small orchestra of modern instruments conducted by graduate student Theodore Libbey (who later became known for his work with National Public Radio) accompanied the theater dances. Anne, as in the past, narrated the program, this time in a lime-green evening dress given to her by Wendy. As Anne noted, the dress almost made up for the fact that she was sidelined as a dancer that evening because of an injury. The group repeated much of the same

[1]Dorothy Nichols, "Charming courtly Baroque dances," *Palo Alto Times*, June 3, 1976.

[2]Lynne Toribara, interview by Anne Witherell, September 5, 2004.

Figure 63. Stanford dancer-musicians before a concert, Dinkelspiel Auditorium, May 31, 1977. *Left to right*: Carol Terry, Rebecca Harris-Warrick, Kent Underwood, Lynne Toribara, Mary Eliot, and Sally Sanford.

program on June 30, as part of the summer workshop, with three new dancers (Daniel Herr, Peter Nye, and Sally Sanford) and three new dances ("La Royalle" [Pécour/Lully, c. 1713], "La Saltarelle Nouvelle" [Pécour/Campra, 1722], and the "Gigue de Roland").

In 1978 a significant addition to the workshop's core offerings was a daily extra-help class for the beginners, taught by Rick. The workshop attracted a broad spectrum of students from music and theater, and, for many, the workshop was their first attempt at dancing. Given the difficulty of the style, the volume of material to learn, and the workshop's rapid pace, some of the participants were overwhelmed by day two. Rick's thorough teaching, patience, and sense of humor calmed nerves and brought them quickly up to speed.

Joining the workshop that year as a dance-class musician was Nicholas Isaacs, new to the music department's DMA program. Nick referred to his position as the workshop's "on-call pianist," a title that does not capture the extent of Nick's contributions. Nick played for lecture-demonstrations as well as for all of Anne's classes and for some of Wendy's. He also eventually worked with Wendy and Virginia on dance notation projects, each of which had unique musical needs. When asked what he learned from working with

Wendy, Nick said that he found her teaching at once "mercilessly critical yet never unkind." Her classes provided "a lasting sense of how to play dance music, something I didn't know that I didn't know at the time."[3]

One of the many unexpected pleasures of the workshop in the late seventies and early eighties was what Anne calls impromptu musicales. With so many talented musicians in one place, it was only a matter of time before they gathered to make music for the workshop participants. The daily schedules for the 1978 and 1980 workshops even reserved times on the closing Fridays for an "informal music session" and "exams and impromptu performances," respectively. The inspiration behind these gatherings was one of Wendy's close friends, Dino Cassolas, who attended his first workshop in 1977. Dino, a tenor with the Waverly Consort and chair of the voice department at the City College of New York, was also a well-known recitalist and performed with many fine pianists including Virginia. His presence seemed to encourage such music-making. The 1978 workshop was full of special musical moments. The first featured Dino and Harlan Hokin, a Channing Street resident and tenor who would soon head to New York to further his already international career. They sang Monteverdi's "Zefiro torna" to a rapt workshop audience draped around the Dinkelspiel Auditorium stage. On another day, Dino worked with Anne on some vocalises she was playing on trombone. And on yet another day, Dino and Virginia performed Robert Schumann's *Dichterliebe*, op. 48, one of their favorite collaborations.[4] *Dichterliebe* was so wonderful that day that Wendy was inspired to dance with Virginia accompanying her, something she had not done since Carmel. The musicales continued for as long as Dino attended the workshop. Over the next few years, he and Virginia delighted the group with a performance of Franz Schubert's *Die Winterreise*, D 911/op. 89, and introduced us to Wendy's favorite and often-requested aria, "Where'er You Walk" from Handel's *Semele*, which, as it always did, brought Wendy to tears.

With the 1979 workshop came another change in personnel. Anne, who had served as Wendy's assistant since 1976, decided to step down from that role. Wendy, then, offered the position to me. At the previous summer's workshop, Wendy had invited me to give the lecture-demonstration that I had developed for my master's concert at UCLA.[5] Based on my research and the concert, Wendy felt that I was the natural successor to Anne's pivotal work. The job would be formidable, but as I was just embarking on my own academic career, I was thrilled by the offer and accepted immediately.

[3]Nicholas Isaacs, interview by Anne Witherell, September 7, 2004. Nick remained part of the workshop through 1990. He joined the music faculty of Santa Clara University and directs and teaches piano at the Community School of Music and Arts in Mountain View, California.

[4]Dino recalls that, when Wendy first introduced him to Virginia in the early 1970s, Virginia asked, "Do you know *Dichterliebe*?" When Dino answered that he did, Virginia suggested she accompany him on the spot. "But I don't have my music along," he protested. Virginia said, "No problem. In what key do you sing it?" *Dichterliebe* quickly became one of their great favorites. Constantine Cassolas, interview by Anne Witherell, November 2005.

[5]Susan Bindig, "Early Eighteenth Century English Court Dance: An Interpretation of Three Choreographies by Mr. Isaac for Queen Anne," master's thesis, University of California, Los Angeles, 1978.

Wendy was a master teacher, and the chance to teach by her side at this significant workshop was a privilege and an unparalleled opportunity. The assistant's position had grown over the three years of Anne's tenure and had become more of a coteaching position by the time I stepped in. Thankfully, I was assigned few organizational duties. I was very much Wendy's colleague, and she treated me as such, which, at this point in my career, took a little getting used to.

Wendy, though, did not permit me to bask in my newfound status. She was, after all, still my teacher, and I, her student. One of my annual tasks was to present a lecture-demonstration. After one of my first presentations, Wendy, in a tone that clearly indicated there was a problem, asked where I had obtained a certain piece of information about the minuet. Today I cannot at all remember what the problem was, but Wendy was clearly unhappy with my gaffe and graciously but firmly suggested that henceforth she should read my lectures before I gave them. Her message was clear, and I was appropriately put in my place. The happy result of this infraction, though, was that Wendy not only served as my fact-checker but also taught me how to write a proper lecture. I recall one session in Anne's room at the Channing Street house, with Wendy stretched out on a bed and me on the floor surrounded by notation and other papers. We had a lively and lengthy discussion of the essential qualities of the hornpipe. If only I had taped it and other similar discussions we had. The clarity of her thinking, the precision of her writing, and her careful way of organizing and presenting material were expert. I now turned to Wendy for advice not only on my dancing but also on my scholarship and would do so throughout my career. The immediate result of these collaborations, though, was that the facts I presented to the workshop participants in my lectures were correct and up to date, much to everyone's benefit.

For the workshops from 1979 to 1982, Wendy and I taught all the dance-technique and most of the notation classes. An increasing number of dancers began to attend the workshop, raising the level of technical ability and the need for additional classes and coaching. Beginning in 1980, in addition to the extra-help class, Rick led the beginners' notation class, freeing me to work with the participants who had progressed beyond the basics. Effectively scheduling classes, lectures, and practice times became increasingly tricky.

In 1981, perhaps owing to the publication of Wendy's book, the workshop had its highest enrollment—thirty five. Wendy was surprised and delighted but also concerned because she was now confronted with about a dozen students for whom an intermediate dance technique class was essential. As the final enrollment was confirmed only a week or so before the start of the workshop, Wendy made a last-minute decision to add the class, which she and I would share teaching. The intermediate class also added at least a half-dozen new dances to be reconstructed and coached by me. Wendy and I taught nine-to-ten hours daily that summer with hardly a break. It was so hectic that Wendy frantically stopped me one day on campus and asked, "Is it your turn or mine to teach the intermediate class?" When I assured her that it was my day, she said, almost collapsing, "Thank god!" and quickly ran off in search of quiet and probably a cup of tea.

The 1981 workshop was memorable for many reasons and provides a good example of the workshop at its best. By then many of the core Stanford dancers had graduated and secured academic jobs around the country—unfortunate for the workshop but certainly wonderful for them. A new group of participants, however, including more dancers, became workshop regulars. Linda Tomko, who would later succeed me and become the workshop's codirector, had been attending annually since 1978, when she joined me for a few days to dance in my lecture-demonstration. We had been graduate students together at UCLA and met in Professor Emma Lewis Thomas's Renaissance dance class. It took only that one visit to Stanford to hook Linda firmly on baroque dance and to the workshop for its remaining years. Philippa Waite, who would also join the faculty, first came to the workshop in 1981 from Cardiff, Wales, at the suggestion of Molly Kenny Galvin of the Domenico Dance Ensemble and Philippa's teacher in Great Britain. Philippa had begun dancing and teaching on her own in Wales and took a break to study with Wendy in the United States, first in New York and then at Stanford. She was an accomplished dancer looking to polish her skills.

Eileen Cropley also attended in 1981. Although she had worked with Wendy in England in the Domenico Dance Ensemble and in the U.S.-based Wendy Hilton Baroque Dance Company, she had never actually studied the technique or the dance notation systematically. She came to Stanford to fill that gap in preparation for a new career in teaching, which would eventually include some classes in baroque dance with, as she noted "Wendy's book as my Bible."[6] Eileen's refined and nuanced baroque dancing, even in sneakers owing to her ailing knees, became a model for all of us. Her final-exam performance of the ballroom minuet in cutoffs and sneakers is burned in my memory as one of the most exceptional and beautiful baroque dance performances ever. Her unaffected ease and regality and the clarity of her gesture and steps finally revealed for me why the minuet, on its surface such a simple dance, was considered the queen of dances in its day. The spirit that Eileen and her partner, Dick Lee, brought to the minuet that day was an inspiration; their performance confirmed the minuet as my favorite dance.

The technique classes that year were vibrant and fun both to teach and to take. The technical proficiency or sheer determination of the participants allowed for more challenging movement sequences at all levels and for the exploration of a wider range of dance forms. The advanced class, for example, now began to struggle with the more musically difficult forms such as the courante, a dance that Wendy loved to teach but that frustrated us enormously. The intermediate class proved to be an important addition to the curriculum and increased appreciably the quality and quantity of significant dance projects. All participants—beginning, intermediate, and advanced alike, even the most frazzled—were committed to meeting the challenges Wendy set, which made for energetic and purposeful classes and some truly beautiful dancing.

Virginia's music class continued to inspire. By 1981 it met only four or five times during the two weeks to accommodate the demands placed on

[6]Eileen Cropley, letter to Anne Witherell, October 31, 1981.

Figure 64. A light moment at the Stanford workshop: the advanced dance class in a *minuet du soleil,* complete with sunglasses, Roble Dance Studio, mid-1980s. Photo by Susan Bindig.

Figure 65. The opening circle of the *minuet du soleil*, Roble Dance Studio, mid-1980s. Photo by Susan Bindig.

Virginia's time by the increasing number of dance projects she accompanied with Wendy. Even in its reduced format, Virginia's class was meaningful to participants. Dick Lee recalled that in her classes, which combined lecture-demonstration, recorded examples, and analysis, "I began to hear so much in music I had never heard before!"[7] Linda Tomko, Anne, and I, our schedules permitting, attended her classes year after year. For Anne, "the chance to hear an artist of her caliber talk about music and her thought process when preparing a performance was priceless."[8] For me, Virginia provided information I sought about communication with musicians, which for dancers with little formal musical training can be tricky terrain.

While Virginia continued to give her annual piano concerts, yearly formal dance concerts were no longer possible. Wendy had neither a core group of dancers with a sufficiently extensive repertoire nor a musical group to play for the dancing. The Friday informal showings, therefore, began to take on greater importance than mere final exams. The proceedings became more structured, and the dance offerings more varied owing to the number of reconstruction projects in any given year. Costumes for the performing faculty were added to show participants the clothing required for a full performance in the style.

Within all the work, there was always time for fun, lots of it. That year, Wendy, Dino, Eileen, and a few other close friends of theirs rented an entire bed and breakfast, complete with pool and hot tub, for the full two weeks. It was the site of some memorable evenings. On arrival at the end of the day, hors d'oeuvres and drinks—mainly scotch, in abundance—appeared. Some of us would sit on the edge of the hot tub with our legs in the water allowing the jets to massage our tight, overworked calves while enjoying the food and libations. Others just relaxed around the pool in lounge chairs. There was always lots of laughter. Linda and I were happy to take advantage of the pool on the nights we were invited. Some minor internal strife apparently built up among the tenants, but for those of us who just stopped by for a few hours in the evenings and were unaware of any tension, an invitation to the B&B was never refused.

Wendy was always concerned with keeping the workshop fresh for both new and returning students, leading her to make what she saw as necessary changes in the syllabus and to the personnel over the years. The now hectic daily pace of the workshop, while exciting, wore on her, as her battle with the torticollis sapped her energy. She needed breaks for complete rest each day and visits to a chiropractor a few times a week. In the face of her growing disability, she decided that another dance instructor was essential. The position had to be unofficial and unpaid as the workshop did not have sufficient funds to support it. Wendy hoped, however, that it would be seen as an opportunity to gain more experience in the baroque dance field and

[7]Richard Lee, interview by Anne Witherell, August 28, 2004.

[8]Witherell, letter, April 26, 2009.

that a significant reduction in the course fee would be adequate compensation. Linda Tomko, now a baroque dance specialist and a visiting lecturer in dance at UCR, was a natural choice for this role, as was Philippa Waite. In 1983 Linda and Philippa joined Rick to fill various teaching needs, including covering the beginning or intermediate technique classes and coaching notation projects.

For the 1984 workshop, Wendy also decided to make a more radical and controversial personnel change, one that, I believe, brought her deep personal unhappiness: she replaced Virginia. The details of how Wendy handled the change remained a private matter between the two of them. Suffice it to say that it was prompted by a fortuitous meeting between Wendy and the Dutch recorder virtuoso Marion Verbruggen at the International Early Dance Institute in Amherst, Massachusetts. Wendy was on the dance faculty and invited me, as I was now teaching at Mount Holyoke College and living just a few miles away, to repeat my lecture-demonstration from the Stanford workshop a few weeks earlier. When Wendy was looking for musicians to accompany my dancing, Marion volunteered. Her playing and that of harpsichordist Mitzi Meyerson, who also volunteered for the performance, so impressed Wendy that she invited them to Stanford for the following summer. Not only did Wendy appreciate their superb musicianship, she also saw it as the opportunity to bring baroque music played on instruments of the period to the workshop.

Marion and Mitzi introduced a new structure to the workshop and attracted a significant number of new musicians to it. Now a participant could sign up for a dance emphasis, as always, or for a music emphasis to study recorder or harpsichord with Marion or Mitzi, respectively. Crossover between the two segments of the workshop was encouraged. Wendy and Marion felt strongly that the musicians should dance as well as play their instruments. So a one-hour dance class, squeezed in at the noon hour and taught by me, was introduced that year. The dancers, in turn, enjoyed Marion and Mitzi's playing for classes, concerts, and for the exams and studio performance that closed the workshop.

With Marion and Mitzi fully occupied with their own ensemble classes and private lessons, Wendy invited Rick to teach the music class. A scholar of French baroque music and dance, not to mention a veteran of Virginia's classes and the Stanford baroque dancers, Rick brought firsthand knowledge of dance to the class that was valuable and appreciated by all who attended. He, Linda, and Philippa also continued to assist with the technique and notation projects when needed.

Accompanying the advanced dance technique class proved to be a more challenging and eye-opening experience than either Marion or Mitzi expected. Marion recalls that they truly learned to accompany dancing through Wendy's very concise directions: "We learned a lot in our little corner [of the stage or studio], more than one would guess."[9] Mitzi found Wendy to be "a systematic and rather severe teacher, very thorough, watching carefully every second." Playing for her classes proved both frustrating and rewarding for Mitzi:

[9]Marion Verbruggen, interview by Anne Witherell, July 2007.

> It was very tiring to play for the [advanced] class, because the musical impulses I would normally have done for expressive reasons were not permitted. One could not make a ritardando at the end of a cadence because it would interrupt a dance movement. This made me so confused—what was the right way to play a piece with a dance title? Must we always be so strict with the rhythm, even if there are no dancers? Wendy and I talked about that, but I don't think we got very far.
>
> The time I spent with the baroque dance class at Stanford helped me so much as a musician. It was not an easy apprenticeship, but it gave me things I could not have learned in some other way. I would say that the sense of pulse and timing is my strongest feature (including then, the ability to break this underlying beat with rubato). When I teach my harpsichord students now, I get up and dance with them, and then everything becomes clear.[10]

Marion and Mitzi's presence also brought dance concerts back to the workshop. The first was in 1985, with dancing by Linda, Philippa, me, and a newcomer that year, James Blaine. James had danced with Philippa in Wendy's classes at UCI. A gifted dancer, he provided an excellent model of men's dance technique. The instrumental part of the concert featured works by Handel, Boismortier, Hotteterre, Balbastre, and Philibert. The danced program comprised a number of familiar works ("La Bourgogne," "Aimable Vainqueur," and "L'Allemande"), some newer repertoire ("Gigue a Deux" from *Philomele* [Pécour/de la Coste 1712], "Entrée de deux dancée par Mlle. prouost et Mlle Guiot a l'opéra d'yssée" [Pécour/Destouches, 1712], "Canarÿe dancée par Mlle. prouost et Mlle Guiot au triomphe de la mour" [Pécour/Lully, 1712]), and a closing "Chaconne for Arlequin" (Le Rousseau/Anon., c.1728) danced with energy and humor by James.

Marion and Mitzi, like Virginia, also gave their own concert each year. It was an especially important event for their music workshop students and was always well received. The Peninsula *Times-Tribune* wrote of one of their concerts that:

> Verbruggen and Meyerson performed a charming concert at Stanford University, with recorder tones softly blossoming and virtuoso playing of the brightest animation. Verbruggen does not seem to breathe. The art of lavishly embellished music is to render the most difficult ornamentation fully, to be free in expression, yet to come out within the rhythmic frame with impeccable nicety. Verbruggen is a master of style.[11]

[10]Mitzi Meyerson, e-mail message to Susan Bindig, June 25, 2009.

[11]I was unable to locate the date of this review, but it had to be for one of Marion and Mitzi's concerts in 1984 or 1985, when they were the only musicians on the workshop faculty. Mitzi recalled another concert where things, initially, did not go as smoothly as planned in an otherwise brilliant concert.

"In one concert I gave with Marion, I was to play the first piece (an Italian piece—Castello, Di Selma, or Fontana) on the organ. We sat on the organ bench together, me with my back to the audience, and Marion next to me and facing them. We had practiced this way in the afternoon, and all had been fine. We took the upbeat breath together and began to play, but the only sound that came out was a forlorn little "poot" from Marion's recorder. Someone had unplugged the organ, and there was no sound from me at all. Marion gave me a furious (cont.)

That a modest-sized workshop on such a specialized topic might confront financial problems should surprise no one. Wendy always managed the lean times shrewdly, but the problems became more pressing and harder to resolve in the mid-1980s. Funding was becoming an issue for the Stanford music department and by extension for the workshop. University regulations for scholarships changed, resulting in a dramatic cut in support for the department's graduate programs.[12] The workshop's feeder program quickly began to dry up.[13] As fewer Stanford music graduate students joined the workshop, Wendy contacted the dance department to recruit a few of their students.[14] The overall enrollment decreased nonetheless.

The 1986 workshop, my last, revealed some of the stresses that had begun to creep into the workshop owing both to the decline in the number of students (from thirty-five in 1981 to the high teens only five years later), particularly at the beginning level, and to dwindling funding from the music department. Enrollment for the workshop that year remained below par until the last minute. Wendy, as a result, cancelled my participation with a plan to cover all the teaching herself—or to work out some other arrangement. Just days before the workshop was to start, however, she called me to say that enough new enrollments had arrived that week to support my participation. I was to get on a plane and be in Palo Alto and ready to teach by opening day. Eleventh-hour changes to teaching schedules, rehearsal arrangements and other responsibilities put unusual pressure on the workshop staff. Tensions ran high, and everyone ended up overworked and exhausted.

The underlying stress did not diminish the overall quality of the workshop and seemed to go unnoticed by the participants. In fact, the workshop was, as usual, highly successful in terms of quality dancing and musicianship. The students, though fewer in number, were hard-working and eager. Nonetheless, the financial problems showed no promise of diminishing, and Wendy decided that another change to the workshop dance personnel was necessary. For the 1987 workshop, she invited Linda to replace me as the second dance instructor. My cross-country airfare and the salaries for all the faculty were becoming increasingly difficult to cover, and Linda was an established West Coast resident. Wendy did not expect me to pay for my travel to the workshop or to take a lesser salary, so we decided that my tenure at the workshop should end. To say that money was the sole reason for this decision, however, would diminish the importance of appointing Linda to the faculty. Linda and I, at that point in our careers, could easily substitute for each other as we were both accomplished as baroque dancers and as

---

glance, as if to say, "What? Did you forget to play?" Then, an amazing thing happened. I was attacked by the biggest belly laugh of my life, great waves of "HO! HO! HO!" There was a stunned silence in the hall, but then the audience began to laugh uncontrollably too. We all simply howled together for about a minute. I will never forget that event." Meyerson, e-mail message, June 28, 2009.

[12]John Planting, interview by Anne Witherell, September 3, 2004.

[13]William Mahrt, interview by Anne Witherell, August 31, 2004.

[14]Albert Cohen, interview by Anne Witherell, September 10, 2004.

teachers. Linda would bring another fresh approach to the workshop and its organization, and she would be a key player in helping the workshop to thrive for another sixteen years.

The balance of workshop students began to tip from musicians to dancers. Over their years of collaboration, Wendy and Linda introduced complementary offerings to the workshop to meet the needs of the changing student population, such as an early morning general warmup, country dancing, and men's theatrical dance technique. Linda, in her new role, though, quickly recognized the effectiveness, importance, and uniqueness of the basic syllabus Wendy had devised and used for years—something that had been difficult to appreciate as a student immersed in it. She found that the "daily instruction in notation, movement technique, and musical matters that coalesced in the reconstruction projects was consistently confirmed" by the rapid progress of the new students each year. Further, she felt that "it gave students a kind of agency that commercial studio dance instruction classes in the modern dance or ballet vein typically did not." Rather than learn the dancing strictly by imitation, the workshop students "deciphered choreographies themselves, received input from their teachers, and came up with a unique interpretation of the choreography."[15] The process gave them greater insight into the dancing, and, for Linda, opened a window onto a more integrated way of teaching.

First-rate musicians continued to be essential to the workshop's syllabus and to its success. Marion and Mitzi would continue as the core music faculty through 1989. Additional musicians joined them, beginning in 1986 with Stanford music faculty member and viol player Martha McGaughey. Baroque violinist Monica Huggett and viol player Sarah Cunningham (who with Mitzi made up the internationally lauded Trio Sonnerie) followed in 1987; viol player and artistic director of the Newberry Consort, Mary Springfels, joined Marion and Mitzi for the 1988 and 1989 workshops. The music offerings (and hence the workshop's overall student population) expanded to include intensive workshops in violin and viol.

The music workshops, like the dance workshop, followed a basic format. Each consisted of three-hour master classes in the mornings, ensemble coaching in the afternoons, and as much practice time as possible. The daily dance class designed for the music students and taught usually by Linda or Philippa was an essential part of the day. Linda noted that this ongoing collaboration between the workshops made for especially interesting and invaluable interchanges among the students.

> The music students were supposed to provide the live music, and when I taught them they decided that each of them would serve one day as the accompanist for the class, so as to maximize their own "dance learning" opportunities on the remaining days of the

[15]Linda Tomko, e-mail message to Susan Bindig, August 2, 2009.

> class. And they freely gave each other feedback while they were in the throes of dancing. It made me smile one day when a dancing music student called out mid-sequence to that day's instrumentalist, "Don't speed up!" And sometimes the music-student accompanist joked with her or his fellow students about their dancing.[16]

The music faculty played for only the advanced dance class, and an accompanist for the other technique classes was still needed. Nick Isaacs continued in this role until 1990. A wonderful addition to the accompanist faculty, who probably did not realize just how much his exuberant personality lifted everyone's spirits, was James Goldsworthy. Jim was completing his DMA and had taken the workshop in the mid-1980s. He had joined the faculty as an accompanist in 1986, when he played primarily for my technique classes and for a number of the notation projects. He worked with Wendy and Linda in this role through 1993.[17]

In 1987 Marion, Trio Sonnerie, the dance faculty, and a few advanced dancers combined to present what was probably the last formal dance concert that the workshop offered. The program included instrumental works by Hotteterre, Forqueray, Leclair, Philibert, Parcham, Purcell, and Dowland. Linda and Philippa, with Nena Couch, James Blaine, Jody McGeen, and Karl Baumann performed a wide range of dances, from the simplest of the ballroom dances, "La Bourrée d'Achille," to complex theater dances, including "Passacaille of Armide" (L'Abbé/Lully, c.1725), "Entrée pour une femme," from *Atys* (Pécour/Lully, 1712), and "Pastoral performed by a Gentleman" (L'Abbé/Paisible, c.1725). The concert exemplified the range of the repertoire available to dancers highly skilled in the baroque dance style.

At the close of the 1989 workshop, Wendy recognized that the always shaky budget could no longer support Marion and Mitzi, let alone other musicians they might like to have join them. Their fees plus the international airfares could no longer be justified despite the unquestioned enthusiasm for their work and the significant contributions they made to the entire venture. Wendy, again, would have to hire new musicians and reorganize that segment of the workshop for the summer of 1990.

The workshops of the early to mid-1990s were remarkable for Wendy's tenacity in the face of declining support from the university and of her own ill health. The financial and administrative pressures only increased, requiring a "human WD-40" (as longtime workshop participant Jody McGeen termed the solution) to keep things running smoothly.[18] That oil was provided by Melinda McGee, administrative director of the Stanford music department.

[16]Ibid.

[17]Jim, upon completing his doctorate, developed an international performing and teaching career and is a professor of music at Westminster Choir College of Rider University in Princeton, New Jersey.

[18]Jody McGeen, interview by Anne Witherell, September 3, 2004.

Figure 66. Heather Mackler, Wendy, and Louise Pescetta, Roble Dance Studio, 1995. Photo courtesy of Heather Mackler.

Figure 67. Workshop participants in a closing photo, outside Roble Dance Studio, 1994. *Top, left to right*: Susan McFadden, Billbob Brown, Arthur Hornig, Peggy Lamberson, Mary Putterman, Marilyn Browne, Marsha Knight, and Hugh Murphy. *Bottom, left to right*: Linda Tomko, Yasuko Hamanaka, Bronwen Pugh, Caroline Small, Heather Mackler, Yvonne Abner, Melinda McGee, Louise Pescetta, Chrystelle Bond, Pat O'Brien, Paige Whitley-Bauguess, and Tom Baird.

Melinda kept the workshop gears turning from 1988 to 1999, and her importance to the workshop and to Wendy cannot be overstated. She worked with Wendy and Linda to create a realistic budget and also helped with registration, housing, transportation, injuries, and countless other issues as they arose.

Melinda's assistance went beyond efficient management. A dancer herself, Melinda was one of the workshop's most enthusiastic champions. Despite looming budget deadlines for the music department, she took a daily class with Wendy during many workshops, recognizing the value of the high level of instruction offered. For Melinda, Wendy was an artist who could teach, who could vigorously challenge an advanced dancer and patiently encourage a beginner's first steps. She felt that "what Wendy did and taught *belonged* at Stanford. It was of that caliber." She also echoed Putnam Aldrich's convictions about dance and music, noting, "It is critical for musicians to learn to move."[19]

One administrative change that deeply affected the workshop was the music department's 1992 decision to discontinue its DMA program, effectively bringing an end to early music at Stanford. The workshop, as a result, would no longer enjoy the many benefits of a university department affiliation. It would function independently and have low priority for access to some teaching space and securing other instructional necessities. Additionally, university credit could no longer be offered for the workshop, which deterred some much-needed students from enrolling.[20] The future of the workshop looked grim. Wendy wrote to Anne Witherell at the close of the workshop that year, "The Stanford W. S. [workshop] survived once again. We live from year to year. It is amazing that, with all the performance [studies in the music department] going out-of-the-window [*sic*], we are still there."[21] Melinda, however, resolved to overcome the administrative hurdles that threatened the workshop's integrity and, at times, its place at Stanford. With her unwavering support, guidance, and hard work, the workshop not only survived the threats but flourished in spite of them.

With the departure of Marion and Mitzi, finding new music faculty became a central task for Wendy. Through the unwitting assistance of one of the Stanford workshop's participants, Wendy's search ended in New Zealand, probably the last place she would have expected to find a musician that met her high requirements. Dance critic, historian, and baroque dancer Jennifer Shennan and her partner Christopher Francis came to the United States from Wellington, New Zealand, in 1988 to study with Wendy in New York, at Stanford, and at the International Early Dance Institute. Until then, their studies had consisted of deciphering baroque dance notations with the aid of Wendy's and Anne Witherell's books and with little professional input on the results. Jennifer taught classes in baroque dance in Wellington and directed a highly respected performing ensemble, Sonnerie. Her work with Wendy in the States was eye-opening, and Jennifer resolved to introduce Wendy

[19]Melinda McGee, interview by Anne Witherell, August 31, 2004.

[20]Louise Pescetta, interview by Anne Witherell, September 8, 2004.

[21]Wendy Hilton, letter to Anne Witherell, August 27, 1992.

to New Zealand. By 1990 she had raised the necessary funds, and Wendy traveled to Wellington to lead a two-week workshop, similar in structure to that at Stanford and complemented by a lecture series that featured historians, musicologists, theater designers, and art historians. Even New Zealand's fencing champion participated and spoke on overlaps in fencing and baroque dance technique and terminology.

Not only was the workshop so successful that it was repeated in 1993, but it also introduced Wendy to Jennifer's colleague from Sonnerie, baroque violinist Bronwen Pugh. Bronwen had studied at the Royal Conservatory in The Hague with Sigiswald Kuijken, toured Europe with several baroque orchestras and ensembles, and was a founding member of the New Zealand–based baroque music ensemble Restoration as well as Sonnerie. Her playing was so impressive that Wendy engaged her for the Stanford workshop. Bronwen recalled a "cautious" Wendy asking her, "Do you come to America?"[22] The two worked out a mutually acceptable economic arrangement, and Bronwen joined the workshop faculty as its lead music instructor for the summer of 1990 and returned for 1992 through 2001. (Patrick Lindley, a Los Angeles–based harpsichordist and frequent workshop musician, replaced her for the 1991 workshop.) Rick Semmens or Anne teaching the music class and Jim Goldsworthy serving as a second accompanist rounded out the music faculty of the early 1990s.

At Stanford, Bronwen, like the workshop musicians who preceded her, accompanied the advanced and, in some years, the intermediate dance technique classes and worked closely with Wendy and the students on notation projects. Additionally, she accompanied Wendy to the coaching sessions and played for them. Linda, who as a workshop student relied solely on tape recordings provided by the workshop musicians for notation sessions, observed the significance of Bronwen's "steady 'playing' presence" at those sessions.

> I discovered as I helped Wendy work out the workshop's daily schedule of classes and rooms that Bronwen went along with Wendy during week two to the intermediate and advanced notation classes and played live—sometimes passages, sometimes the whole choreography—as part of that class. So students could practice at other tempi, talk about musical matters with both Wendy and Bronwen, and get that rare and rich experience of working with live music for the second week.[23]

Formal dance and music concerts were no longer possible as Bronwen worked alone. With the early music program dismantled, the music department could not provide collaborators; students who could both play music and dance, as in the early days of the workshop, were few. "Wendy was passionate about a workshop with MUSIC," Bronwen noted, and devised new ways to keep music as an essential workshop component.[24] In 1994, for example, Wendy announced that the workshop would focus on the music of

[22]Bronwen Pugh, interview by Anne Witherell, July 15, 2006.

[23]Tomko, e-mail message.

[24]Pugh, interview.

Marin Marais and on eight notated dances choreographed to music from his operas *Alcide* (1693), *Alcione* (1706), and *Sémélé* (1709). In other years, the music of Purcell, Telemann, and François Couperin as well as music selections from Wendy's publication with Donald Waxman, *A Dance Pageant*, provided the focus for reconstruction projects and for the dance sequences for the advanced class.[25] This new focus also raised the level of the dance projects, allowing more students, particularly the advanced dancers, to attempt some of the more difficult choreographies in the baroque repertoire rather than just watch them in concert. Bronwen's playing was essential to the success of this new workshop component.

The lack of a formal dance concert was more than compensated for by the new music focus and by the addition to the faculty of Paige Whitley-Bauguess (1992) and Thomas Baird (1993), former members of Catherine Turocy's New York Baroque Dance Ensemble turned independent baroque dance performers and scholars.[26] Tom and Paige, with workshop participant Yasuko Hamanaka, the director of a baroque dance and music group in Tokyo, offered superb informal demonstrations in full costume.[27] Their studies of the more theatrical side of baroque dance added another dimension to the dance syllabus. Tom's work on men's theatrical technique, in particular, was a welcome challenge for both the men and women in the advanced dance technique class. Paige and Yasuko, along with Linda, provided elegant, polished models of the women's technique for the ballroom and the stage.

The students were inspired to perform as well. The Friday afternoon dance demonstration, therefore, took on greater importance, evolving from a private informal showing of the dances reconstructed over the two weeks to a public performance of both student and faculty work. The performance was given in the dance studio, and so it retained an informal air. Its complexity grew over the years, however, and formal rehearsals were added to an already packed daily schedule. Linda recalled the careful planning required and the positive benefits for the students.

> For some years, as I remember it, the Friday demonstrations primarily featured notation projects danced by students. Then some sequences from the advanced technique class were added. In both cases, rehearsals took place in the notation or technique classes; the program order was posted on Thursday; and a quick run-through with Bronwen was held sometime on Friday morning. But as other advanced class sequences (and in some years, an intermediate class

[25]Waxman and Hilton, *A Dance Pageant: Renaissance and Baroque Keyboard Dances* (Boston: Galaxy Music, 1992). Wendy's dance sequences to selections from the book were also featured in collaborative performances by Linda and Waxman in California, New York, and Florida. Tomko, e-mail message.

[26]In their long dance partnership, Tom and Paige performed and taught baroque dance internationally and collaborated on numerous baroque reconstruction and choreographic projects, including productions of André Danican Philidor's *Le Mariage de la Grosse Cathos*, Henry Purcell's *Dido and Aeneas* and *The Fairy Queen*, and John Blow's *Venus and Adonis*.

[27]Yasuko Hamanaka attended the workshop from 1987 to 2000, having first encountered Wendy in 1983 through her book. She imported Wendy's work to Japan through her own research and teaching and through inviting Tom, Paige, and Linda to Tokyo to perform with her company. Yasuko considers her work with Wendy "a treasure." Yasuko Hamanaka, e-mail message to Anne Witherell, June 2, 2005.

> sequence), country dances, and costumed dances by the faculty were added, entrances and exits, cues, and other stage movement required attention. A Thursday afternoon rehearsal was introduced, therefore, to acclimate everyone to the particular demands of a studio performance, which for some of our students was a new experience. What began as a purely functional addition to the schedule quickly became an invaluable part of the workshop offerings in which performing skills were honed.[28]

Few printed programs for the Friday demonstrations remain. Sometimes a narrator would guide the proceedings and provide commentary, precluding the need for a formal program. Notes that do remain on some of the demonstrations show how Wendy carefully shaped these programs. In many ways, the designs of the Stanford programs were not unlike those she devised for concerts at Juilliard and other venues. Wendy paid close attention to the distinguishing characteristics of various dance types, capturing the baroque instrumental suite's spirit in the alternation of dances with livelier tempi with those of a more somber mood. She carefully chose dances for the intermediate and advanced dancers that showed them to their best advantage. Her fully costumed faculty was showcased in ballroom and theatrical dances that required refined technique and nuanced performing skills, providing an impressive close to the afternoon.

Unique offerings of these demonstrations were the class sequences, which were far more than the mechanical exercises one might expect.

Figure 68. Tom Baird, Wendy, and Paige Whitley-Bauguess at the workshop registration, Braun Music Center, 1997. Photo by Heather Mackler.

[28]Tomko, e-mail message.

Figure 69. Meredith Little and Wendy, Braun Music Center, 1997. Photo by Heather Mackler.

Figure 70. Paige Whitley-Bauguess teaching intermediate dance notation, Roble Dance Studio, 1998. Photo by Heather Mackler.

Particularly at the advanced level, these could be intricate choreographies for ten to twelve dancers. Minuets were the most commonly presented dances, but Wendy's group choreographies over the years also included a gigue, rigaudon, courante, hornpipe, and sarabande. These dances were unique not just because they were Wendy's original creations or because notated group dances from the eighteenth century are scarce and rarely performed; the study of group dances was a distinctive feature of the Stanford workshop curriculum, introduced because of Wendy's own deep interest in them and in choreography in general. Other baroque dance workshops limited their explorations to the extant notated repertoire, but Wendy provided Stanford students with the opportunity to explore the choreographic possibilities of the style beyond those three-hundred-plus notated dances, almost all of which are solos and duets. These lessons were invaluable for those who pursued baroque dance professionally and who inevitably would be asked to choreograph in the baroque style.

The Friday demonstration comprised only completed reconstruction projects performed at an intermediate or higher skill level, leaving some less-proficient students without a performance opportunity. Recognizing the gap and the students' need to perform, Linda introduced "Sharing the Dance," an informal gathering scheduled for the second Friday morning in which all intermediate notation projects, regardless of the reconstructers' technical proficiency, were shown. It provided everyone with the opportunity to learn from the invaluable feedback offered by their fellow students, whether they were planning to perform the dances elsewhere or use the dance analysis in published works. As Linda noted, "They knew the movement technique, knew the notation challenges, knew the music types, knew what their classmates had been wrestling with, and were able to discuss the results in detail."[29]

With so much talent in both the faculty and students, the workshop thrived in the early 1990s. To manage the new faculty and expanded offerings, Wendy decided that the workshop needed a codirector and promoted Linda to that position in 1993. Together, they would develop the workshop offerings even further. In 1994, however, the workshop was dealt a blow from which it would never entirely recover. Wendy was diagnosed with cancer. With surgery scheduled for early August and uncertainty surrounding the treatment, she was unable to attend the workshop that summer. Linda gathered the participants on the workshop's first morning and told them of Wendy's illness and of her necessary absence that year. As Wendy intended, the workshop continued without her with few modifications or complications, but she was sorely missed. Melinda McGee felt the 1994 workshop was an outstanding example of the workshop pulling together to support Wendy's work. It confirmed for her that, compared to other dance workshops, Wendy's was cooperative rather than competitive.[30]

[29]Ibid.

[30]Melinda McGee, interview.

Wendy returned to the workshop in 1995, but the cancer and the extensive treatment required had taken its toll. One of the many sad results of her illness in the workshop's later years was her inability to teach all workshop students personally. She tired quickly and arrangements had to be made for rests during the day. By the late 1990s and early 2000s, she had only enough energy to teach the advanced dance technique class and coach some of the advanced notation projects.

Although she no longer was the imposing physical presence of earlier workshops, Wendy continued to inspire all of the participants. For Chrystelle Bond, a dance professor at Goucher College and a workshop student beginning in the mid-1980s, Stanford and Wendy provided "a serious but fun atmosphere" and "a supportive but critical audience" that built confidence. Chrystelle recalled Wendy's highly encouraging attitude ("Try it; you can do it.") when her students needed a boost as well as her look of dismay when things did not go well.[31] For some students, that disappointed look coupled with Wendy's larger-than-life reputation terrified them. Heather Mackler, a country dancer who began to attend the workshop in 1993, was surprised when some of her fellow students admitted their fear of Wendy, whom she found approachable and supportive. But Heather, too, found that "her stomach dropped" when Wendy appeared without notice at the door of the intermediate class to check on their progress. Heather also recalled a particularly memorable and intimidating moment in class when Wendy, clearly displeased, said to the group, "I don't suppose I could get you to look like you're enjoying this."[32] Others, like New Zealander Chris Francis, were not at all anxious and just delighted in the music and the dancing and the chance to study with Wendy: "For me, her characteristic facial expression was a wonderful wide-eyed laugh, full of delight. She could be fierce, but I never felt intimidated—only goaded on. I had the impression that her physical ailments took a great toll on her, but that never seemed to compromise her teaching. She was 100 percent there in the classroom."[33]

Maintaining that strong presence for the advanced technique class required more energy than Wendy could always muster, so, little by little, she turned over some of her other duties to her faculty. The freed time allowed her to rest and fully prepare for the class and for the notation projects she coached. The faculty became busier than ever, but as Linda noted, it became part of their job to "respond to the moment and do what was needed to help the workshop go forward."

The new arrangement, while challenging, allowed the faculty to identify opportunities and implement changes that, under other circumstances, might not have been possible. In 1995 one such change was the addition of country dancing to the combined-level class, now taught by Paige and occasionally Linda. Jody McGeen, an enthusiastic country dancer, suggested the addition, and Wendy and Linda immediately recognized its value—for the class itself, for attracting new students to the workshop, and for returning students

[31]Chrystelle Bond, letter to Anne Witherell, June 18, 2006.

[32]Heather Mackler, interview by Susan Bindig, October 28, 2009.

[33]Chris Francis, letter to Anne Witherell, September 10, 2005.

who, Linda emphasized, "*loved* country dance."[34] Taught by Paige and Tom, country dancing quickly became a popular attraction of the workshop. It fit perfectly in the combined-level class and was scheduled for the last thirty minutes or so of the hour-and-a-half class, providing an energizing close to a long and rigorous day of dancing.[35] By the last years of the workshop, one or two country dances were featured in the closing studio demonstration.

In 1998 the workshop celebrated its twenty-fifth anniversary with former faculty, past students, and other workshop friends gathering with Wendy at Stanford to mark the occasion. Wendy's health was particularly fragile that summer from a recent round of chemotherapy; it limited her participation to only one week. In public, however, Wendy appeared as vital as ever. As in the past, she swept into the dance studio and taught a vigorous class, making light of the turban she wore to cover her hair loss.

Wendy's vigor, however, belied her struggle with the weakness and fatigue that resulted from her treatment. Those of us who helped behind the scenes knew just how taxing that one week was for her. As a former faculty member, I was invited to the celebration. At Wendy's request, I was happy to attend for just the second week of the workshop so that I could travel with her and help her settle into her room. Others assisted her throughout the week with various arrangements for food and for rests throughout the day. Most of the responsibility for Wendy's many needs fell to Linda, as the workshop's co-director, who managed to meet these additional demands with skill and grace.

The silver-anniversary workshop was a true celebration. Wendy was thrilled to be marking this landmark in her career, and we were delighted that she was well enough to attend. I don't think that the more recent students had given much thought to the workshop's long and inspiring history. They were delighted, therefore, to hear Meredith Little's lecture on its early days. Wendy's publications and those of her students and colleagues were on display in the dance studio and demonstrated the impressive scholarly reach of the workshop. I was invited to speak on my recently completed doctoral dissertation, which features a substantial section on the eighteenth-century dance notations for a harlequin and was heavily influenced by my studies and teaching at Stanford.[36] Anne returned too but was sidelined from most of the festivities by a broken ankle she had suffered on her first day in California. On the workshop's closing day, when Anne rolled into the dance studio in her wheelchair, she was quickly surrounded by many of the workshop students eager to meet the author of *Louis Pécour's 1700 Receuil de dances*, a book they consulted almost as much as Wendy's.

[34]Jody McGeen, interview, September 3, 2004; Tomko, e-mail message.

[35]Country dancing was taught initially by Tom, with Paige taking over the class after a few sessions. Linda and Rick shared the teaching duties one year, and in 1999 guest lecturer Carol Marsh taught the class emphasizing the country dances in André Lorin's *Livre de contredance* (c. 1685).

[36]Susan Bindig, "Dancing in Harlequin's World" (PhD diss., New York University, 1998).

Anne recalled that the performance on the final Friday "was splendid. The audience included Albert Cohen, William Mahrt, and Leonard Ratner [of the Stanford music faculty], as well as many of the hosts and hostesses [who provided housing for Wendy, the faculty, and, at times, needy students]." The program was particularly rich, with individual sections devoted to ballroom, country, and theater dances from England, Germany, and France. Meredith narrated, providing details on the dances, their creators, and the cultural milieu in which the dances flourished. As with many of these closing demonstrations, no printed program remains for this particularly significant performance. Notes taken and carefully preserved by workshop participant Louise Pescetta, provide a list of all the dances and dancers featured that afternoon:

I Commentary, Meredith Little

"Passacaille of Venus and Adonis" ("Passagalia of Venüs and Adonis" [L'Abbé/Desmarets, 1725]), Julie Andrijeski

II England

"The Maid Peeped Out at the Window, or the Friar in the Well," country dance for 16

Advanced Class Sequences: minuet for 8; rigaudon for 10

"The Prince of Wales," Linda Tomko and Susan Bindig

"The Marlborough" (Isaac/Paisible, c.1710), Chrystelle Bond and Louise Pescetta

"The Pastorall" (Isaac/Paisible, 1713), Linda Tomko and Marie-Nathalie Lacoursière

III Germany

"La Milanoise," country dance for 12

IV France

"La Canarie" ("Canarye dancée par Mlle. prouost et Mlle Guiot au triomphe de la mour" [Pécour/Lully, 1712]), Linda Tomko and Yasuko Hamanaka

Entrées seules of Mlle. Guiot, Paige Whitley-Bauguess

Gavotte from *Atys*

Loure from *Scylla*

Gigue from *Tancrède* ("Gigue pour une femme, Seul dancee par Mlle. Guiot a lopera de tancrede" [Pecour/Campra, c.1713])

Chaconne, danced as a Harlequina (based on "Chaconne for Arlequin" [Le Rousseau/Anon., c.1728]), Yasuko Hamanaka and Gina Bonati

"La Bacchante," country dance for 10

Figure 71. Rehearsing a country dance, Roble Dance Studio, 1999. *Left to right*: Jill Chadroff, Linda Tomko, Pat O'Brien, Marie-Nathalie Lacoursière, Yasuko Hamanaka, and Veerle Fack. Photo by Heather Mackler.

Baroque Dance and Its Music

27th Annual Workshop at Stanford University

July 24 - August 4, 2000

For Dancers, Dance Scholars, Choreographers, Musicians, Musicologists, and Theater Movement Specialists

Wendy Hilton, Director

Linda Tomko, Co-Director	**Baroque Violins:**
Susan Bindig	**Bronwen Pugh**
Richard Semmens	**Julie Andrijeski**

Lectures during Week II by Drs. Bindig, Semmens and Tomko

The Baroque Dance Summer Workshop at Stanford University offers intensive study in the style, technique and notation of French court and theater dance at the beginning, intermediate, and advanced levels; the individual dance types and their music; performance technique, etiquette, and bows and courtesies.

Daily activities include two technique classes, the second concluding with contradances; a dance notation class; a music class or lecture-demonstration; and time to use the music library with its extensive dance collection and the Lully Archives. Beginning and intermediate couples are allocated a one-hour daily practice slot. Evening practice space is also available. Advanced students are allocated practice space and have four private, or semi-private, notation sessions with Wendy Hilton. Admission to the advanced group is at the discretion of the faculty, and students should discuss with Ms. Hilton *well in advance* the dance they wish to study. The Workshop concludes on August 4th with a farewell party at 5:00 p.m. for faculty, students and guests.

Beginning Workshop students will study one of the first dances to be published in Beauchamp/Feuillet notation in Paris, 1700: Louis Pécour's famous danse à deux *la Bourée d'Achille* (bourée, menuet, bourée) to music by Lully's pupil Pascal Colasse. Intermediate students move forward in time to 1709 and to England for P. Siris' *The Brawl of Audenarde* (courente, menuet, gigue), music anon. Advanced students will have an additional notation project this year, the dancing of which will occupy the last half-hour of the advanced technique class. The project material dates from 1734, when in Metz, Germany, a shepherd play *Ludus Pastoralis* was given. Dedicated to Claude de Saint Simon, formerly Bishop of Metz, the dances were by D. Dalizon, the music by D. Maillard. The last dance, a *Ballet general*, consists of a 13-page gigue for eight men. Copies of the dance with a part assigned will be sent to advanced students as they apply for the Workshop so that they can come with the work prepared except where they have questions. These will be answered in the private notation sessions or at the conclusion of the dance class if they are general.

The country dances or contradances which conclude the day will be from France, England and Germany.

Susan Bindig will give a lecture, accompanied by videotape illustration, on Harlequin and the Baroque style. Richard Semmens will lecture on circumstances of the development and early history of public balls in Regency France. Linda Tomko's lecture will consider the shepherd play *Ludus Pastoralis* in context with two other group choreographies from 1700 and 1711.

Workshop Administrator: Louise M. Pescetta, phone/fax (415) 337-7779; e-mail: Dolascetta@earthlink.net

72. Workshop on Baroque Dance and Its Music, flier, 2000.

Figure 73. After the final dance demonstration, Roble Dance Studio, 2000. *Left to right*: Jody McGeen, Jill Chadroff, Veerle Fack, and Susan Bindig.

Figure 74. Wendy and Yvonne Abner at a workshop closing picnic, 1990s. Photo by Heather Mackler.

Following the performance, Linda hosted an outdoor reception and dinner, where we toasted the many individuals who helped the workshop prosper over the years. For Wendy, this wonderful afternoon was capped by university organist and former workshop student Robert Bates spiriting her away for what had become for them an annual rite—a private performance of Bach on the Fisk-Nanney organ in Stanford's Memorial Chapel.

The workshop continued for three more years. Wendy no longer handled any of the administration. "Linda will handle it," was her usual answer to my occasional questions about plans for the following summer's workshop. Melinda's departure from the music department in 1999 could have proved disastrous for the workshop. Linda, however, engaged Louise Pescetta to assist her with the administration. Louise was a vital addition to the workshop team, working with Linda on almost all details, from publicity to housing arrangements to the workshop's closing party. She continued in this role through the final workshop in 2001.

Other significant changes were in the workshop's personnel. Paige left after the 1998 workshop because of scheduling conflicts between the workshop and her own baroque dance projects and performances[37]; she was replaced in 1999 and 2001 by Marie-Nathalie Lacoursière, a student in Quebec of Jocelyne Lépine and a longtime workshop participant. Baroque violinist and baroque dancer Julie Andrijeski had joined Bronwen as a class accompanist in 1998 and continued in that role through 2001. Musicologists Carol Marsh and Meredith Little returned to the 1999 workshop to lecture on dance notations, their creators, and the notated repertoire. For the 2000 workshop, Wendy invited me to fill the second dance-assistant position and Rick Semmens to lecture on his recent research on *les bals publics*.[38]

Surprisingly, Wendy's health was only a minor contributor to the demise of the workshop at Stanford. It would have been impossible for her to continue eventually, but at the close of the 2001 workshop, she wrote to Anne that the many administrative hurdles had finally become insurmountable.

> Stanford finally made it impossible for us to continue. Roble [dance studio] is now shared by Drama (on top) & Dance. Mem. Aud. [Memorial Auditorium] charges for every chair and for a person to see we do no harm. Dink [Dinkelspiel Auditorium] is booked all next summer and also undergoing two weeks of repairs. Well, it's been coming for years. Now it's happened. I'm back on the chemo & so next year seems very remote.[39]

[37]One of Paige's ongoing summer projects was the East Coast Baroque Dance Workshop that she and Tom Baird with pianist Hugh Murphy developed and ran from 1999 to 2008. The one-week workshop held at Rutgers University was purposely scheduled not to conflict with the Stanford workshop and gave particularly enthusiastic baroque dance students the opportunity to attend a second workshop each summer.

[38]Rick's work resulted in the book *The Bals Publics at the Paris Opéra in the Eighteenth Century* (Hillsdale, NY: Pendragon Press, 2004).

[39]Wendy Hilton, letter to Anne Witherell, August 18, 2001.

Wendy, a dancer and scholar with a passion for music, was first attracted to the Stanford University music department because it exhibited a solid commitment to historical dance through a thriving program in early music. The workshop she developed, as Stanford Professor of Music Albert Cohen noted, "proved to be a superb adjunct to that program."[40] It also became one of the best workshops (some would argue, *the* best workshop[41]) in baroque dance and music, attracting a diverse group of students from beginners to professionals and representing many nations. Wendy herself observed that "students have come from many parts of the world as far as New Zealand, England, Japan, and Nova Scotia. Baroque dance and its music have spread far and wide from Stanford." Unquestionably, that community of international scholars and practitioners, fostered and nurtured at the workshop, is, as Rick Semmens wrote to me, one of her greatest legacies.[42] Through them and their students, Wendy's work lives today.

[40]Albert Cohen, "Remembering Wendy Hilton, 1931–2002: A Program of Dance and Music Celebrating Her Life and Work," The Juilliard School, May 30, 2003.

[41]Heather Mackler observed that the Stanford workshop was the benchmark against which other early dance workshops were frequently measured. Mackler, interview.

[42]Richard Semmens, e-mail message to Susan Bindig, August 12, 2009.

Eighteen: 1994–2002

A Cancer Diagnosis ~ Working with the Juilliard School's Music Division ~ Editing a New Dance and Music Book Series ~ Beginning her Memoirs ~ Death and Commemoration

In the summer of 1994, shortly after she left the Juilliard Dance Division, Wendy was diagnosed with cancer. Earlier that year, her masseuse had alerted her to an "abnormality," as Wendy referred to it, in her right side and urged her to have it evaluated. From the outset, Wendy sensed that the condition was serious. Her doctors, however, took several months to reach a diagnosis, and it was not until early August when she underwent surgery for ovarian cancer that had metastasized to her colon.

Thus began eight years of medical treatment—no more surgery, but numerous rounds of chemo and other therapies, all of which Wendy faced head-on with a nerve that many admired. Some even observed that she seemed to have choreographed her illness (and eventually her death). She pursued the finest medical care and got it; her surgeon, she claimed, was one of the top in his field. She also came to know every health and social service available to Manhattan's senior population—free transportation around the city, a low-priced plan providing greatly reduced prescription costs—and used them to ease her way through the ordeal. That she beat the small odds of surviving such an advanced cancer beyond five years is then perhaps not so surprising. Wendy was determined to live as long and as well as she could.

In her usual, extremely private way, as with the torticollis, Wendy would talk only occasionally about her cancer and had a way of making it clear that questions about it were not welcome. She preferred to focus on other things. Today I can say with confidence that Wendy had ovarian cancer—metastatic ovarian cancer stage III-C—because of the medical notes she left in her papers, including a transcript of the operation itself. But at the time of the initial diagnosis and for years after, I was never sure exactly what type of cancer she had. I was not alone in this. For many of us, even though we saw or spoke with her frequently, the details of her illness remained vague.

That first summer of her illness, after the surgery, Wendy recruited a group of friends to help her through her convalescence. Living alone, she was concerned about needing help in the night and so asked someone to stay with her each weeknight. Since I was traveling from Pennsylvania, my night was Friday to take advantage of the weekend. Others who lived and worked in Manhattan—Tom Baird, Becca Menon, Barbara Barr, Pat Rader—stayed the other nights. Wendy and I listened to music, watched television, talked. I made meals, which initially she hardly could eat. I remained on Saturday morning until a visiting nurse or her next companion arrived or was en route.

I recall two particular things Wendy asked me to do for her during my visits—to read the manual that explained her upcoming chemotherapy and to purchase the wig she would need as a result of the treatment. I understood fully why she could not bring herself to handle either task. The manual contained a long, exhaustive list, with detailed descriptions, of frightening side-effects. I decided to tell her about only some of them and, fortunately, those were all she needed to know as she was spared from most. For the wig, she had only $100 to spend—not enough for something nonsynthetic and of reasonable quality. (At the time, neither of us was aware of the many services available for providing cancer patients with good wigs and other head coverings.) Nevertheless, I had little difficulty getting financial assistance from her friends and students, and we put together enough money to purchase an attractive human-hair wig. I gave it to her with a card listing all the contributors. Although appreciative, Wendy understandably found it hard to be truly happy about such a gift.

The cancer at times cut through Wendy's steeliness and exposed a vulnerability that, in other circumstances, we were rarely permitted to see. She was delighted by a stuffed animal given to her by Becca Menon for company during the long weeks of recovery. It claimed a proud place on her bed. I also recall the day when she began to lose her hair. She telephoned me in tears saying that it had begun to come out in small clumps. Her hair loss, though, ultimately had a happy consequence. At the end of her treatment, when her hair began to grow back, she discovered that she looked fabulous with gray, crew cut–like hair. Add sunglasses and a black turtleneck sweater, and Wendy looked very hip. To her amazement, strangers stopped her—on the street, in the grocery store, in the elevator—to tell her how wonderfully stylish her hair was and how well it looked on her. For someone who never gave much thought to her appearance, Wendy was tickled by the attention. She never colored her hair or let it grow longer again.

Wendy was able to work during the eight years of cancer treatment that would follow. Her schedule, however, was greatly reduced. Her main academic appointment was now at Stanford at the summer workshop, but with Linda handling all of the workshop administration, she was able to devote her waning energy only to teaching. She also continued to offer private classes periodically in Manhattan, as she had since her days with Rosalyn Tureck.

The early 1990s brought Wendy into contact with harpsichordist Kenneth Cooper and flutist Paula Robison. They met through Becca Menon, a frequent concert-going companion of Wendy's, at one of Cooper and Robison's concerts at the Metropolitan Museum of Art's Temple of Dendur. Both subsequently worked with Wendy in the next few years and were affected by the musical integrity she brought to dancing and the insights she provided for their own musicianship. In a 2005 interview, Cooper spoke of Wendy's devotion to "truth" in her scholarship and to rigorous research coupled with lively performance. He noted that she did not see any incompatibility between the two and always looked for impassioned performance *and* stylistic integrity. At his invitation, Wendy taught a number of workshops over the next few years at the Manhattan School of Music, where Cooper is a member of the faculty.[1]

[1]Kenneth Cooper, interview by Susan Bindig, August 9, 2005.

Paula Robison decided, at Wendy's recommendation, to explore the dancing itself. After one of the concerts with Cooper and a performance of Handel's *Water Music*, Wendy suggested that Robison would probably play even better if she knew the dance steps that were performed to the music. For Robison, "It was an epiphany when Wendy demonstrated [some dance steps] on stage," and so she accepted Wendy's offer of lessons. Robison had only two, perhaps three, lessons, but they had a deep and lasting effect on her. She found Wendy to be "a marvelous teacher: kind but firm, rigorous, and perceptive." She also appreciated Wendy's warm sense of humor even while insisting on meticulous movement at all times. The classes demonstrated the complexity of the dance steps but the simplicity of the overall style, pointing up how too much ornamentation, whether in music or dance, can potentially spoil a desired effect.[2]

Despite her dismissal from the Dance Division, Wendy's ties with Juilliard had not been completely severed, and she now worked occasionally with the Music Division's Department of Vocal Arts. Most significantly, in September 1995, she in collaboration with Edward Berkeley and Kenneth Merrill of the vocal arts faculty produced "A Purcell Workshop" in celebration of Henry Purcell's Tricentennial.[3] In the program notes, music director Merrill wrote that the production took "music from *The Fairy Queen* and other dramatic works to create a 'fantasy' around two pairs of star-crossed lovers. As in the French opera models which Purcell admired and imitated, we have interwoven song and dance throughout." Assisted by Tom Baird, with whom she now frequently collaborated, Wendy reconstructed five country dances from various editions of John Playford's *The Dancing Master*—"Man Was for Woman Made," "Buskin," "Wa Is Me," "What Mun I Do," and "St. Martin's Lane"—danced by the full cast, and the danse à deux "Les Contrefaiseurs" (Pécour/Purcell, 1702) danced by two students from the Dance Division who continued to work with her.

Much of Wendy's attention turned to writing and editing. Although her zeal for writing never increased—she continued to find it an onerous task—Wendy was as committed as ever to preserving and making available important material in the history of dance and music. Around 1987 she had been engaged as the general editor of a new book series, "Dance and Music: Studies in the Alliance of Two Arts," by Pendragon Press, a music publishing company based in upstate New York and owned by Robert Kessler. Throughout the 1990s, she and Kessler published more than a dozen outstanding works, including facsimile editions of three rare manuscripts housed in the Alexander Turnbull Library of the National Library of New Zealand: *A Work Book by Kellom Tomlinson: Commonplace Book of an Eighteenth Century English Dancing Master* (1992); *A New Most Excellent Dancing Master:*

[2]Paula Robison, interview by Susan Bindig, December 31, 2005.

[3]"A Purcell Workshop," September 29–30, 1995, Chamber Opera Theater, Juilliard School. Musical Direction: Kenneth Merrill; Stage Direction: Edward Berkeley; Dance Direction: Wendy Hilton; English Diction: Kathryn LaBouff.

Figure 75. Wendy, outside Braun Music Center, Stanford University, late 1990s. Photo by Heather Mackler.

The Journal of Joseph Lowe's Visits to Balmoral and Windsor (1852–1860) to Teach Dance to the Family of Queen Victoria (1992); and *The Extraordinary Dance Book T.B. 1826* (2000). Although many of the series' titles focused on early dance, Wendy also solicited books on Jacques-Émile Dalcroze and Vaslav Nijinsky, as well as a unique study of dance of the central Pacific. In 1993 the Dance and Music series was honored with a special citation for excellence from the Dance Perspectives Foundation through its annual competition for the De La Torre Bueno Prize, awarded to a book of scholarly distinction in dance. A year later, the foundation gave the competition's top prize to the second publication in the series, Maurice Esses' three-volume *Dance and Instrumental Diferencias in 17th and Early 18th Century Spain*. The series republished Wendy's own *Dance of Court and Theater* under the new title *Dance and Music of Court and Theater: Selected Writings of Wendy Hilton* (1997), which supplemented the full text of the original work with reprints of her two articles published in *Early Music*[4] and with a new article, "*Aimable Vainqueur* or *The Louvre*." Over the next few years, Wendy would solicit three more manuscripts for the series, although she would see only one through publication. Linda Tomko, whom Wendy handpicked as her successor at Pendragon Press, would handle the details of future titles for the renamed "Wendy Hilton Dance and Music Series."[5]

[4]"A Dance for Kings: The 17th-Century French Courante, Its Character, Step-Patterns, Metric and Proportional Foundations," *Early Music* (April 1977), 160–72; and "Dances to Music by Jean-Baptiste Lully," *Early Music* (February 1986), 50–63.

[5]A complete list of the books published in the Wendy Hilton Dance and Music Series can be found at the front of this book.

On the heels of the reissue of her book and on the recommendation of colleagues, Wendy decided to record her life story. Initially, the project was to be an oral history, as suggested and coordinated by Pat Rader of the Dance Division of the New York Public Library for the Performing Arts. After a few sessions, however, Wendy opted for a more formal approach and decided instead to convert those initial conversations into the beginnings of a book. She asked me to lend a hand since I had, by then, been working as a professional editor for a number of years. I hesitated at first, knowing that this supposedly small project could easily grow into a large commitment that demanded far more time than I could give. I finally agreed and outlined the firm terms of my participation. Little by little, though, Wendy, as she had done so many times before, managed to pull me deeper into the project despite my best efforts to resist. Over the next few years, Wendy and I would spend many hours over many weekends going over the manuscript, discussing supplementary information, and poring over photographs. The book became one of the major projects of her last years.

Apart from her ongoing work with Pendragon Press and at Stanford, Wendy's last noteworthy professional engagement may have been her first and only radio interview, given for WKCR, the radio station of Columbia University. Each December, WKCR celebrates the winter holidays with "BachFest," a popular, ten-day, around-the-clock celebration of the music of J. S. Bach. The station intersperses recordings of the entire Bach repertoire with commentaries by its announcers and interviews with artists—largely musicians—on the important role Bach's music plays in their work. In the late 1990s, the "BachFest" organizers invited Wendy to discuss dance and Bach's music. In a humorous twist to what should have been a fairly straightforward engagement, Wendy's pending interview created an unexpected and inexplicable stir around the station.

As Phil Schaap, WKCR's jazz specialist and longtime radio host, tells the story, some of his colleagues at the station assumed that Wendy was a superstar and, as a result, her interview became one of the most hotly anticipated events of the festival. Her pending visit took on a life of its own, creating, as Schapp noted, "its own level of energy. Everyone was falling all over themselves to see her." Perhaps Wendy's most surprising fan was WKCR's hip-hop/reggae host, Al Boogie (Alan Gordon). He would breathlessly announce her upcoming visit on his show: "She's coming!" "She's going to be here!" "On New Year's Eve, she's actually coming here!" Schaap, too, found himself caught up in the excitement and making similar eager announcements on his own show. Ironically, the interview was scheduled for one of the least popular days of the festival, when the station staff, regardless of their excitement about the interview, preferred to be elsewhere ringing in the new year. But Al Boogie remained loyal and made a special visit to the station to get Wendy's autograph.[6]

A companion story comes from Becca Menon about one of their many concert outings. Like the WKCR story, it shows that although Wendy's

[6]Phil Schaap, interview by Susan Bindig, June 30, 2006. The WKCR archives do not have a recording or written transcript of Wendy's interview, which, Schaap believes, was in 1999.

opportunities had declined by this time, her reputation had not. Indeed, it seemed to have taken on an almost mythic quality in the New York ether—which perhaps surprised Wendy most of all. When Becca and Wendy arrived at a concert at Alice Tully Hall, the ushers, for reasons neither could fathom, began to fawn all over Wendy. The flattery went to such lengths that Wendy decided that Becca should pretend not to know her and ask the ushers who she was. They set the scene so the ushers could easily see Wendy standing by a pole when Becca pointed her out. Becca approached the ushers with her question and was taken aback when the ushers gushed, "We don't know, but she's a legend!" An equally stunned Wendy could only assume that they had seen her around Lincoln Center or knew she was from Juilliard.

In Wendy's last years, attending music concerts, which had always been a favorite pastime, now took an even more central place in her life. Music had always been a passion—on numerous occasions she said she wanted to be a singer in her next life. Now she attended as many concerts as possible and knew every angle for securing discount or free tickets. In the spring of 2001 Diane Winkleby, a friend and former Stanford student visiting from England, accompanied Wendy on a particularly memorable musical outing to Carnegie Hall to "Meet the Composer" Peter Lieberson. In the Green Room afterward, Wendy met Lieberson's wife, the mezzo-soprano Lorraine Hunt Lieberson, whose singing Wendy found thrilling and deeply moving and who was perhaps her favorite singer since Kathleen Ferrier. Wendy relished their meeting.[7] That same spring, dance scholar George Dorris recalled a conversation with Wendy about a concert by the Berlin Philharmonic she was looking forward to and determined to attend despite a recent, marked decline in her health:

> Perhaps my favorite memory of Wendy comes from the spring of 2001, when we had lunch one day. The doctor had given her only a short time to live. "But I can't die now," she announced. "I have tickets in September for Abbado and the Berlin Philharmonic!" She was there, of course.[8]

Tom Baird tells how he and his partner, Hugh Murphy, made extensive arrangements to take Wendy to a concert by pianist Lang Lang in Central Park that same summer, including renting a wheelchair and arranging transportation to the park. When the concert was cancelled, Wendy sank into such misery for several days that Tom and Hugh worried she might die right then of utter disappointment.[9]

Wendy also enjoyed traveling to visit her friends—Morag Cattanach Veljkovic in Florida, Eileen Cropley in Michigan, and Mary Ella Montague in

[7]Diane Winkleby, interview by Susan Bindig, August 15, 2005.

[8]George Dorris, "Remembering Wendy Hilton, 1931–2002: A Program of Dance and Music Celebrating Her Life and Work," The Juilliard School, May 30, 2003.

[9]Thomas Baird, interview by Anne Witherell, n.d.

Texas; they were Wendy's most frequent hosts. Eileen recalled Wendy's visits warmly:

> We would take almost daily walks at the Grand Mere dunes conservation park—up and down, up and down, till we gained the peak and came upon the most magnificent view of Lake Michigan, and then we would run, roll, fall down the steep descent and into the water laughing as we went. As the years passed by, this became more and more of a challenge for Wendy—but each year she came here, she "made it." For her it was an annual victory which made her feel she was still "living."[10]

Morag's memories of Wendy's visits were also fond but humorous and describe the sometimes imperious Wendy whom I and others knew well:

> She stayed with me many times over the past thirty years, and over the last ten of her life, she came here each winter, usually for two or three months. Boy, did we argue. Wendy at my home:
>
> —I have always had beagles. She doesn't care for dogs. I told her the dog stays.
>
> —I put on classical music. She turns it off if it is not an approved orchestra of her choice—the Berlin Philharmonic.
>
> —I want to watch the news; she wants to watch—*Cagney and Lacey*.[11]

In early 2002 Wendy was told by her doctors that her cancer had spread. Over the next few months, she faced a number of predictions of her death. Diane Winkleby recalled visiting Wendy in February 2002 at her apartment. Wendy was not looking forward to another round of chemotherapy three weeks later, which she called "a bore" and knew would have little effect. She also voiced concern to Diane about the books in the Pendragon series not being completed after her death.

Hospice finally became necessary. With the assistance of Caroline Gaynor, Wendy was able to remain in her apartment with around-the-clock care. Her small studio apartment quickly filled with the medical paraphernalia required to treat her condition and keep her comfortable. Many of Wendy's friends in Manhattan—Tom Baird, Liz Keen, Becca Menon, Pat Rader—continued to help Wendy in these last months. Dino Cassolas and Francis Polizio, a frequent music-concert companion, visited regularly. Others who did not live nearby buoyed Wendy's spirits with frequent phone calls and care packages. I visited as much as I could to work on the book.

In the summer before her death, knowing that she had only a few months to live, Wendy turned the book over to me. We were far from finished; in fact, we had completed only through her coming to America with

[10]Cropley, "Remembering Wendy Hilton, 1931–2002."

[11]Veljkovic, "Remembering Wendy Hilton, 1931–2002."

Rosalyn Tureck in the late 1960s. I was to write the rest. I do not recall actually agreeing to this plan, but one afternoon at the end of a work session, she sent me home with as much of her memorabilia as I could carry to the train station; the rest went with me on subsequent visits. I will never forget the sad look on Wendy's face as I left her apartment that day. I realized that I was leaving with her life wrapped up in boxes and paper bags. I made it only to the elevator before I started weeping, and I cried as I walked the four blocks up Eighth Avenue to the Pennsylvania Station and through much of the train ride home. I was grateful for my sunglasses. For me, even though I saw Wendy numerous other times, that day was our goodbye.

Wendy died in her apartment on Saturday, September 21, 2002, with a hospice aide present. She must have sensed that she was failing earlier in the day, as she called Dino Cassolas and asked him to visit. He went to see her as quickly as possible. Dino recalled sadly how the hospice aide, at Wendy's request, lifted her easily from her bed to show him how light and frail she had become. Caroline Gaynor and Francis Polizio also visited Wendy that day. In the evening, Liz Keen, to whom Wendy had assigned medical power of attorney, received the call that Wendy had died. The word spread quickly.

Wendy's passing was noted in dance publications and leading newspapers internationally. The significance of her work was confirmed and celebrated. In the *New York Times*, Jennifer Dunning highlighted Wendy's artistry and skill as a teacher:

> Many of her most vivid and revealing reconstructions and choreographing of Baroque dance were created for Juilliard students. . . . The dances were performed for the most part with a luminous purity, ease, and respect that were surprising from young dancers training in the comparatively boisterous dance arts of the 20th century.[12]

Later in the year, Anna Kisselgoff mourned Wendy's death in her 2002 review of dance for the *Times*. With Beverly Brown, Rod Rogers, David Wood, Pauline Tish, and others, Wendy joined the "too many dancers, teachers, choreographers, and visionaries" lost in 2002 and remembered by Kisselgoff.[13]

A few weeks after Wendy's death, on October 18, Caroline Gaynor hosted a memorial dinner in Manhattan at Krour Thai, Wendy's favorite local restaurant. (A visit to Wendy frequently included dinner there or takeout warmed on her tiny stove.) About a dozen were able to attend, including Tom Baird, Hugh Murphy, Becca Menon, Robert Gutman, Miriam Cooper, Wendy Kassel, Judith Davidoff, Francis Polizio, and me. We spent a cheery evening reminiscing about good times with Wendy. It was a quiet, simple

[12]Jennifer Dunning, "Wendy Hilton, 71, Specialist in Recreating Baroque Dance," *New York Times*, October 1, 2002.

[13]Anna Kisselgoff, "The Critics/10 Moments: Elegiac Splendor and Wild Invention," *New York Times*, December 29, 2002.

celebration of her life that I think Wendy would have liked. That Sunday, Caroline, along with Francis, Tom, and Hugh, carried Wendy's ashes in a silver pitcher to the waters off Happy Harbor, a place of so much happiness and peace for Wendy, and spread them close to where she had learned to swim.

The idea of organizing a larger, more formal commemoration came, I believe, from Tom. Linda Tomko, Anne Witherell, and I were happy to join him in the planning. Wendy had made it very clear that if there were to be a commemoration, it should not be religious in any way, although I doubt any of us would have argued for a religious service, even without her dictum. We decided that the perfect tribute to Wendy would be an evening of dance, music, and spoken tributes and began looking for a dance studio to rent for the event. We were quickly dismayed, however, at the difficulty of finding a suitable space and at the high cost of mounting our production and providing a simple reception. Tom had more brilliant ideas: to ask if we might use a studio at Juilliard and to solicit donations through the invitations we would send.[14] We were sure that gaining the use of a Juilliard studio was a long shot, but we were desperate. Tom made the contact, and we were amazed and thrilled to find that not only did Juilliard permit such events for their faculty, but also there was no fee. Moreover, Juilliard would contribute a production manager and wine for the reception. Only one date was available in the small theater that was appropriate: Friday, May 30, 2003. We reserved it immediately.

Preparations took much of the winter and spring. The program, which we called "Remembering Wendy Hilton, 1931–2002," interspersed short tributes to Wendy's life and career with performances of dance and music, all by friends, colleagues, and students. Jennifer Shennan and Yasuko Hamanaka, who traveled from New Zealand and Japan, respectively, joined Paige Whitley-Bauguess, Linda Tomko, and Tom Baird in danced elegies. Kenneth Cooper, Judith Davidoff, Hugh Murphy, and Julie Andrijeski honored Wendy with performances of Bach, Marais, Matteis, and of some of the dance music that was central to Wendy's career. As expected, a recording of retired Dino Cassolas singing Handel's "Where'er You Walk" brought everyone to tears. Liz Keen, Anne Witherell, and I gave spoken tributes. Rick Semmens delivered a tribute by Bob Kessler, who was unable to attend. More than one hundred of Wendy's colleagues and friends attended the early evening event, which was poignant, joyful, and loving.

That Wendy's life touched the lives of so many was clear from the tributes included in the commemoration booklet that accompanied that May performance. Although, as her New Zealand colleagues noted, Wendy hated hyperbole, it seems appropriate that her story should close with a sampling of those testimonials.[15]

[14]To our surprise, donations poured in. They not only paid for the program but also allowed us to contribute over $3,000 to the Dance Division of the New York Public Library for the Performing Arts for the future cataloguing of Wendy's papers.

[15]"Remembering Wendy Hilton, 1931–2002."

Colin Russell on her career:
"She was a pioneer, who opened the door for so many to know of, learn from, and execute the intricacies of this noble art, of baroque dance. So few had taken that route, but she kept on as a dancer, choreographer, teacher, researcher, and author."

John Broome on her dancing:
"This is perhaps my most endearing memory of her—moving at speed but with such relaxed dignity. She was an exquisite dancer and moved with what I can only describe as a beautifully fluent precision. I think the past flowed in her veins more vividly than the present. Supreme in mind and body, she towered above us all."

Jennifer Shennan on her teaching:
"The example of Wendy's impeccable combination of teaching and scholarship set the highest standard."

Geraldine Stephenson on her collegiality:
"She was a delight to work with, dedicated and with great charm and efficiency and generosity to her colleagues."

Leah Kreutzer on the privilege of working with her:
"Wendy's world was one of grace and coherence and form, symmetry and containment, humanity and imagination the likes of which I had never known. And joy! Like Wendy herself. Wendy and her work centered me, made me happy."

Amen.

Selected Bibliography

Much of the material for this book came from Wendy Hilton's personal papers, which include programs, fliers and other promotional items, clippings, and photos that document her career in both England and America. These were supplemented by interviews and correspondence with more than one hundred of her colleagues and friends, who also donated materials from their own private collections. Archival and printed sources and media provided further documentation of her career and include Wendy's own writings, prominent articles and reviews about Wendy and her work, selected works from the early dance literature, and other helpful material.

Archives

Baird Hastings Personal Papers, Private Collection

Wendy Hilton Personal Papers, Private Collection

Wendy Hilton Biographical File, Juilliard School
Juilliard Dance Division Production Photographs

Rosalyn Tureck Collection, Music Division, New York Public Library for the Performing Arts

V&A Images, Victoria and Albert Museum

John Vickers Archive, University of Bristol Theatre Collection

G. B. L. Wilson Photographic Archive, Royal Academy of Dance

Printed Sources and Media

Anderson, Jack. "Dance: Juilliard Group in Varied Bill." *New York Times*, March 17, 1985.

———. "Dancing Never Stops in Celebrating Mozart, Even for Intermission." *New York Times*, November 11, 1991.

———. "Juilliard Ensemble Offers Varied Dance." *New York Times*, March 13, 1978.

Armstrong, Jocklyn. "The Interpretation of Bach: The Role of Dance, The Metropolitan Museum of Art, October 23, 1969." *Dance Magazine* (December 1969): 78.

Barnes, Clive. "New Ballets by Walter Gore," *Dance and Dancers* (November 1953): 15.

———. "Varied program by Juilliard dancers." *New York Post*, March 15, 1980.

———. "West Country Ballet: The First Season." *Dance and Dancers* (July 1956): 29–30.

Belt, Byron. "Bach Study with Tureck." *Newhouse Newspapers*, July 10, 1969.

———. "A Brilliant 'Happening.'" *Newhouse Newspapers*, April 19, 1974.

Cardus, Neville. *Kathleen Ferrier: A Memoir.* London: Hamish Hamilton, 1954.

Coton, A. V. "Ballet with a Difference: Folklore Tales." *Daily Telegraph* (London), n.d.

———. "Perfect Stage for Ballet." *Daily Telegraph* (London), June 24, 19

Coton, A. V., and Susan Lester. "Theatre Arts Ballet." *Ballet Today* (January 1954).

Coton, A. V., and Piers Pollitzer. "Two Tributes to Audrey de Vos: The Critic; the Student." *Dancing Times* (October 1965): 20–21.

Crisp, Clement. "Walter Gore's Choreographies." *Dance Research* 6, no. 1 (Spring 1988): 23–29.

Dale, Margaret. "Ballet and BBC TV." *Dancing Times* (March 1963): 332–34.

Dahms, Sibylle. "Derra de Moroda's Collection of Baroque Dance Sources." *Dance Research* (Winter 1997): 142–49.

Davis, Janet Rowson. "Ballet on British Television, 1933–1939." *Dance Chronicle* 5, no. 3 (1982–83): 245–304.

de Laban, Juana, ed. *Institute of Court Dances of the Renaissance and Baroque.* New York: Congress on Research in Dance, 1972.

de Mille, Agnes. *Dance to the Piper.* Boston: Little, Brown, 1952.

Dunning, Jennifer. "Critics' Choices." *New York Times*, April 5, 1981.

———. "Dance: Juilliard Ensemble Concert." *New York Times*, March 20, 1983.

———. "Dance: Juilliard Group in L'Abbé's 'George II.'" *New York Times*, March 16, 1980.

———. "Wendy Hilton, 71, Specialist in Recreating Baroque Dance." *New York Times*, October 1, 2002.

———. "Wendy Hilton's Elan in Baroque Dances Reflected in Music." *New York Times*, April 2, 1974.

———. "Young Artists at Juilliard Confront the Baroque." *New York Times*, November 20, 1988.

Ellis, Helen Meredith. "The Dances of J. B. Lully (1632–1687)." PhD diss., Stanford University, 1968.

Fawkes, Richard. *Welsh National Opera.* London: Julia MacRae Books, 1986.

Ferrier, Winifred. *The Life of Kathleen Ferrier.* London: Hamilton, 1969.

Grolin, James. *Pied Piper: The Many Lives of Noah Greenberg.* Hillsdale, NY: Pendragon Press, 2001.

Hardy, Camille. "Juilliard Dance Ensemble, Juilliard Theater, November 8–11, 1991." *Dance Magazine* (March 1992): 90, 92.

Harriton, Maria. "Margaret Dale: TV Ambassador." *Dance Magazine* (November 1969): 24–27.

Henahan, Donal. "Music: Delightful *Dafne*." *New York Times*, March 14, 1974.

———. "Opera: 'Mary, Queen of Scots' by City Troupe." *New York Times*, March 2, 1981.

———. "Opera: A Staging for 1739 'Dardanus.'" *New York Times*, October 30, 1975.

Hilton, Wendy. *The Art of Dancing: French Dances of the 17th and 18th Centuries*, 1972. Videocassette.

———. Clippings. Jerome Robbins Dance Division, New York Public Library for the Performing Arts.

———. *Celebration of Lully*. New York: Juilliard School, 1983. Film.

———. *Celebration of the French Baroque*. New York: Juilliard School, 1984. Film.

———. *Dance and Music of Court and Theater: Selected Writings of Wendy Hilton*. Stuyvesant, NY: Pendragon Press, 1997.

———. "A Dance for Kings: The 17th-Century French Courante." *Early Music* 5, no. 2 (April 1977): 160–72.

———. *Dance of Court and Theater: The French Noble Style, 1690–1725*. Princeton, NJ: Princeton Book Company, 1981.

———. "Dances to Music by Jean-Baptiste Lully." *Early Music* 14, no. 1 (February 1986): 50–63.

———. "A Discordant Note." *Los Angeles Times*, April 2, 1972.

———. *An Entertainment for His Majesty George II*. New York: Juilliard School, 1981. Videocassette.

———. "French Baroque Dances in the Serious or Noble Style: Their Notation and Performance." In *Themes in Drama 3: Drama, Dance and Music*, edited by James Redmond, 71–84. Cambridge: Cambridge University Press, 1981.

———. "History of Ballet Technique: French Court Dance," "Courante," "Entrée Grave," "Loure," "Minuet," and "Révérence: Early Eighteenth-Century Modes." In Selma Jeanne Cohen and Dance Perspectives Foundation, *The International Encyclopedia of Dance*. 6 vols. New York: Oxford University Press, 1998.

Hilton, Wendy, and Wye J. Allanbrook. "Dance Rhythms in Mozart's Arias." *Early Music* 20, no. 1 (February 1992): 142–49.

Hilton, Wendy, and Susan Bindig. "Getting Started in Dance." *Dance Chronicle* 30, no. 2 (May 2007): 291–329.

Hilton, Wendy, and Clement Crisp, Mo Dodson, Winnie Fuller, Nicola Gaines, Beryl Grey, Ivor Guest, et al. "Belinda Quirey MBE: A Tribute from her Friends." *Dance Research* 16 (Winter 1998): 44–66.

Hilton, Wendy, Erich Schwandt, and Julianne Baird. *Music and dance from the court of Louis XIV: 14 dances and airs from Michel L'Affilard's* Principes très-faciles *(Paris 1705)*, 1975. Videocassette.

Hilton, Wendy, and Rosalyn Tureck. "Dance Forms Employed by Bach in His Music," July 11, 1968. Audiocassette. Rosalyn Tureck Collection, New York Public Library for the Performing Arts.

Hilton, Wendy, and Rosalyn Tureck. "Dance Forms Performed by Bach in His Music," July 18, 1968. Audiocassette. Rosalyn Tureck Collection, New York Public Library for the Performing Arts.

Hilton, Wendy, and Rosalyn Tureck. "The Dancing Bach: A Celebrated Pianist and a Dancer-Scholar Discuss the Interrelationships of Baroque Music and Dance Terms." *Dance Magazine* (October 1969): 47–50, 82.

Hilton, Wendy, and Donald Waxman. *A Dance Pageant: Renaissance and Baroque Keyboard Dances*. New York: E. C. Schirmer, 1992.

Johnson, Harriett. "Words and Music: Pro Musica Closes with *Dafne*." *New York Post*, March 13, 1974.

Jones, Sterling. "The Story of an Early Music Quartet." Unpublished ms., n.d.

Jowitt, Deborah. *Jerome Robbins, His Life, His Theater, His Dance*. New York: Simon & Schuster, 2004.

Kealiinohomoku, Joann W., ed. *Dance History Research: Perspectives from Related Arts and Disciplines*. New York: Congress on Research in Dance, 1970.

Kisselgoff, Anna. "Baroque Dances Stir Interest Anew." *New York Times*, April 5, 1971.

———. "The Critics/10 Moments: Elegiac Splendor and Wild Invention." *New York Times*, December 29, 2002.

———. "Miss Hilton Excels in 8 Baroque Dances." *New York Times*, May 18, 1972.

———. "A New Sokolow Opens Juilliard Annual," *New York Times*, April 6, 1981.

Little, Meredith Ellis, and Carol G. Marsh. *La Danse Noble: An Inventory of Dances and Sources*. New York: Broude Brothers, 1992.

Loney, Glenn. "May I Have This Minuet, Mrs. Millament? Wendy Hilton Teaches Baroque Dance." Dance Magazine (July 1972): 64–68.

McDonagh, Don. "Wendy Hilton Gives Bach Court Dances." *New York Times*, July 19, 1968.

———. "Aristocratic Life in 17th Century Is Evoked by Hilton Dance Group." *New York Times*, October 22, 1974.

Musgrave, Thea. "Mary Queen of Scots." *Musical Times* 118, no. 1614 (August 1977): 625–27.

Porter, Andrew. "Mary in Virginia." *New Yorker* (May 1, 1978): 136–41.

———. "Musical Events: Branching Out." *New Yorker* (March 24, 1973): 137.

———. Review of *Dardanus. New Yorker* (November 10, 1975): 157–58.

Quirey, Belinda. *May I Have the Pleasure? The Story of Popular Dancing.* London: BBC, 1976.

"Remembering Wendy Hilton, 1931–2002: A Program of Dance and Music Celebrating Her Life and Work." The Juilliard School, May 30, 2003. Memorial program.

Sherman, Robert. "Music: 'Dafne' Premiere: After 365 Years, the Work Arrives at Caramoor a Day Late." *New York Times*, July 24, 1973.

Stein, Heather. "Mozart Graces Juilliard Program." *Dance Magazine* (November 1991): 12–13

Swan, Annalyn. "Queen Mary in Virginia," *Time*, April 17, 1978. http://www.time.com/time/magazine/article/0,9171,916078,00.html.

Trowell, Brian. "Some Memories of Belinda Quirey." In *Belinda Quirey and Historical Dance*, edited by David Wilson, 45–48. London: Early Dance Circle, 1997.

Tureck, Rosalyn. "Bach and the Dance: A New Dance School of the Institute for Bach Studies." *Music Clubs Magazine* (April 1969): 28–29.

Walker, Katherine Sorley. "Walter Gore." In *International Dictionary of Ballet*, edited by Martha Bremser, 1:590–93. Detroit, MI: St. James Press, 1993.

Weaver, William. "A Vintage Year for the Spoleto Festival." *International Herald Tribune*, July 3, 1973.

Witherell, Anne. *Louis Pécour's 1700* Recueil de dances. Anne Arbor, MI: UMI Research Press, 1981.

———. "Report from Stanford University: Summer Workshops—1974." *Current Musicology* 19 (Spring 1975): 11.

Woodwards, Chris. *London Palladium: The Story of the Theatre and Its Stars.* Lindley, Huddersfield, UK: Jeremy Mills Publishing, 2009.

Interviews and Correspondence

Linda Roberts Alexanderson, Julie Andrijeski, John Ashworth, Régine Astier, Julianne Baird, Thomas Baird, Geoffrey Bayfield, Joan Benson, Chrystelle Bond, William Burdick, Suzanne Burdon, Deanna Bush, Laura Carroll, Constantine Cassolas, Jill Chadroff, Albert and Betty Cohen, Kenneth Cooper, Eileen Cropley, Mary P. Crosten, Jeni Dahmus, Mark Dalrymple, Judith Davidoff, Janet Rawson Davis, Patricia DeCorsey, George Dorris, Ross Duffin, Dione Ewin, Margaret Fabrizio, Veerle Fack, Maria Fay, JoAnn Faletta, David Farrar, Ann Lydekker Fellows, Chris Francis, Molly Kenny Galvin, Charles Garth, Caroline Gaynor, Nina Gilbert, James Goldsworthy,

Nicholas Gunn, Robert Gutman, Mark Haim, Patricia Halverson, Yasuko Hamanaka, Rebecca and Ronald Harris-Warrick, Baird Hastings, Timothy Hext, Harlan B. Hokin, Michael Holmes, George and Glenna Houle, Jan Irvine, Nicholas Isaacs, Natalie Jenne, Sterling Jones, Mark Kahrs, Elizabeth Keen, Yvonne Kendall, Judith Kennedy, Margaret Kimball, John Kobayashi, Leah Kreutzer, Carol Kutsch, Jennifer Lane, Frederick Lee, Jocelyne Lépine, Theodore Libbey, Judith Linsenberg, Ed Lipinsky, Meredith Little, Heather Mackler, William Mahrt, Judith Malafronte, Melinda McGee, Jody McGeen, Rebecca Menon, Mitzi Meyerson, Sonya Monosoff, Margaret Murata, Thea Musgrave, Herbert Myers, Lois Nisbet, Barbara Palfy, Scott Pauley, Paul Pentel, Louise Pescetta, Janis Pforsich, John Planting, Bronwen Pugh, Patricia Rader, Leonard and Inge Ratner, Elisabeth Rebman, Frederick Renz, Paula Robison, Sandor and Priscilla Salgo, Phil Schaap, Philip Schreur, Brenda Schuman-Post, Erich Schwandt, Judith Schwartz-Karp, Richard Semmens, Jennifer Shennan, Beverly Simmons, Joan Smiles, Marilyn Somville, Mary Springfels, Mark and Isabelle Starr, Geraldine Stephenson, David Sullivan, Yuko Tanaka, Marcia Tanner, Carole Terry, Elizabeth Terzian, Emma Lewis Thomas, Linda J. Tomko, Lynne Toribara, Morag Cattanach Veljkovic, Marion Verbruggen, Philippa Waite, Donna Waks, Ruth Waterman, Janet Albisser Westenberg, Patricia White, Paige Whitley-Bauguess, Diane Winkleby, Anne Witherell, Marlene Wong, and John Zorn.

Index

Wendy Hilton is abbreviated in the index as WH.

Page numbers in italics designate photos.

Titled baroque dances are listed with their choreographer/composer.